CACREP 2009 Standards

1. **PROFESSIONAL ORIENTATION AND ETHCIAL PRACTICE** - studies that provide an understanding of all of the following aspects of professional functioning:
   a. history and philosophy of the counseling profession,
   b. professional roles, functions, and relationships with other human service providers, including strategies for interagency/interorganization collaboration and communication
   c. counselor's role and responsibilities as an interdisciplinary emergency management response team
   d. self care strategies
   e. counseling supervision models, practices and processes
   f. professional organizations including membership benefits, activities, service to members and current issues
   g. professional credentialing, including certification, licensure and accreditation practices and standards
   h. the role and process of the professional counselor advocating on behalf of the profession
   i. advocacy processes needed to address institutional and social barriers that impede access, equity, and success for clients
   j. ethical standards of professional organizations and credentialing bodies and applications of ethical and legal consideration in professional counseling

2. **SOCIAL AND CULTURAL DIVERSITY** - studies that provide an understanding of the cultural context of relationships, issues and trends in a multicultural society related to including all of the following:
   a. multicultural and pluralistic trends, including characteristics and concerns between and within diverse groups nationally and internationally
   b. attitudes, beliefs, understandings, and acculturative experiences, including specific experiential learning activities designed to foster students' understanding of self and culturally diverse clients
   c. theories of multicultural counseling, identity development and social justice
   d. individual, couple, family, group, and community strategies for working with and advocating for diverse populations, including multicultural competencies.
   e. counselors' roles in developing cultural self-awareness, promoting cultural social justice, advocacy and conflict resolution and other culturally supported behaviors that promote optimal wellness and growth of the human spirit, mind, or body.
   f. counselors' roles in eliminating bias, prejudices and processes of intentional and unintentional oppression and discrimination
   g. ethical and legal considerations

3. **HUMAN GROWTH AND DEVELOPMENT** - studies that provide an understanding of the nature and needs of individuals at all developmental levels and in multicultural context, including all of the following:
   a. theories of individual and family development and transitions across the life-span
   b. theories of learning and personality development including current understanding about neurobiological behavior
   c. effects of crises, disasters and other trauma-causing events on persons of all ages
   d. theories and models of individual, cultural, couple, family, community resilience
   f. human behavior, including an understanding of developmental crises, disability, psychopathology and situational and environmental factors that affect both normal and abnormal behavior
   g. theories and etiology of addictions and addictive behaviors including strategies for prevention, intervention and treatment
   h. theories for facilitating optimal development and wellness over the life span

4. **CAREER DEVELOPMENT** - studies that provide an understanding of career development and related life factors, including all of the following:
   a. career development theories and decision-making models
   b. career, avocational, educational, occupational and labor market information resources, visual and career information systems
   c. career development program planning, organization, implementation, administration, and evaluation
   d. interrelationships among and between work, family, and other life roles and factors including the role of multicultural issues in career development
   e. career and educational planning, placement, follow-up, and evaluation
   f. assessment instruments and techniques that are relevant to career decision making
   g. career counseling processes, techniques, and resources, including those applicable to specific populations in a global economy

5. **HELPING RELATIONSHIPS** - studies that provide an understanding of counseling in a multicultural society, including all of the following:
   a. an orientation to wellness and prevention as desired counseling goals
   b. counselor characteristics and behaviors that influence helping processes including
   c. essential interviewing and counseling skills
   d. counseling theories that provide the student with models to conceptualize client presentation and that help the student select appropriate counseling interventions. Students will be exposed to models of counseling that are consistent with current professional research and practice in the field so they begin to develop a personal model of counseling.
   e. a systems perspective that provides an understanding of family & other systems theories and major models of family and related interventions.
   f. a general framework for understanding and practicing. consultation
   g. crisis intervention and suicide prevention models including the use of psychological first aid strategies.
   h. ethical and legal considerations

6. **GROUP WORK** - studies that provide both theoretical and experiential understandings of group purpose, development, dynamics, counseling theories, group method skills, and other group approaches in a multicultural society, including all of the following:
   a. principles of group dynamics, including group process components, developmental stage theories, group members' roles and behaviors, and therapeutic factors of group work
   b. group leadership styles and approaches, including characteristics of various types of group leaders and leadership styles
   c. direct experiences in which students participate as group members in a small group activity , approved by the program, for a minimum of 10 clock hours over the course of one academic term

7. **ASSESSMENT** - studies that provide an understanding of individual and group approaches to assessment and evaluation, in a multicultural society including all of the following:
   a. historical perspectives concerning the nature & meaning of assessment
   b. basic concepts of standardized and non-standardized testing and other assessment techniques including norm-referenced and criterion-referenced assessment, environmental assessment, performance assessment, individual and group test and inventory methods, psychological testing and behavioral observations,
   c. statistical concepts, including scales of measurement, measures of central tendency, indices of variability, shapes and types of distributions, and correlations
   d. reliability (i.e., theory of measurement error, models of reliability, and the use of reliability information)
   e. validity (i.e., evidence of validity, types of validity, and the relationship between reliability and validity)
   f. age, gender, social and cultural factors related to the assessment of individuals, groups and specific populations
   g. ethical strategies for selecting, administering, & interpreting assessment and evaluation instruments and techniques in counseling

8. **RESEARCH AND PROGRAM EVALUATION** - studies that provide   an understanding of research methods, statistical analysis, needs assessment, and program evaluation, including all of the following:
   a. the importance of research in advancing the counseling profession
   b. research methods such as qualitative, quantitative, single-case designs, action research, and outcome-based research
   c. statistical methods in conducting research and program evaluation,
   d. principles, models, and applications of needs assessment, program evaluation, and use of findings to effect program modifications
   e. use of research to improve evidence based practice
   f. ethical and culturally relevant strategies for interpreting and reporting the results of research and program evaluation studies.

To

Michelle, Taylor Grace, and Caroline Scott

Amy, Emma, Sam, and Claire Royal

and to

Elizabeth ("Betsy") Kissinger

Counselor As Consultant

David A. Scott

Clemson University

Chadwick W. Royal

North Carolina Central University

Daniel B. Kissinger

University of Arkansas, Fayetteville

Los Angeles | London | New Delhi
Singapore | Washington DC

Los Angeles | London | New Delhi
Singapore | Washington DC

FOR INFORMATION:

SAGE Publications, Inc.
2455 Teller Road
Thousand Oaks, California 91320
E-mail: order@sagepub.com

SAGE Publications Ltd.
1 Oliver's Yard
55 City Road
London EC1Y 1SP
United Kingdom

SAGE Publications India Pvt. Ltd.
B 1/I 1 Mohan Cooperative Industrial Area
Mathura Road, New Delhi 110 044
India

SAGE Publications Asia-Pacific Pte. Ltd.
3 Church Street
#10-04 Samsung Hub
Singapore 049483

Acquisitions Editor: Kassie Graves
Editorial Assistant: Elizabeth Luizzi
Production Editor: Brittany Bauhaus
Copy Editor: Diane DiMura
Typesetter: C&M Digitals (P) Ltd.
Proofreader: Eleni-Maria Georgiou
Indexer: Jeanne Busemeyer
Cover Designer: Candice Harman
Marketing Manager: Shari Countryman

Printed in the United States of America

A catalog record of this book is available from the Library of Congress.

9781452242187

This book is printed on acid-free paper.

14 15 16 17 18 10 9 8 7 6 5 4 3 2 1

Contents

Introduction to the Series   ix

Preface   xi

Acknowledgments   xiv

Chapter 1: Introduction and Overview of Consultation   1

   Introduction   1

   Learning Objectives   2

   Guided Practice Exercises   2

   Historical Perspectives   3

   Working Definition and Types of Consultation   5

   CACREP Standards   14

   Multicultural Considerations   15

   Chapter Keystones   15

   Web-Based and Literature-Based Resources   15

   References   16

Chapter 2: The Role of Consultant and Consultee   18

   Introduction   18

   Learning Objectives   19

   The Consultation Relationship: A Working Alliance Prespective   19

   The Working Alliance Model   20

   The Consultation Role   27

   Consulting Roles   31

   Chapter Keystones   37

   Web-Based and Literature-Based Resources   38

   References   38

Chapter 3: Necessary Skills of a Consultant   43

   Introduction   43

   Learning Objectives   44

Foundational Skills 44
Multicultural Considerations 45
Cross-Cultural Consultation Competencies 47
Nonprofit versus For-Profit Consultation 49
Fiscal and Organizational Responsibilities 51
Generating Proposals, Contracts, Workshops,
    Marketing, and Fee Structures 53
Use of Technology in Consultation 64
Consultation Report Writing 68
Chapter Keystones 70
Web-Based and Literature-Based Resources 70
References 71

Chapter 4: Consultation Stages **73**

Introduction 73
Learning Objectives 74
Preliminary Stage 75
Exploration and Goal Setting Stage 77
Intervention and Implementation Stage 84
Outcomes Stage 87
Termination Stage 89
Multicultural Considerations 94
Chapter Keystones 95
Web-Based and Literature-Based Resources 95
References 95

Chapter 5: Behavioral and Cognitive-Behavioral Consultation **97**

Introduction 97
Learning Objectives 98
Behavioral Consultation 98
Guiding Principles of Behavioral Consultation 100
Process of Behavioral Consultation 100
Behavioral Consultation Approaches 102
Cognitive-Behavioral Model of Consultation 112
Observation and Assessment 119
Multicultural Considerations 119
Chapter Keystones 121
Web-Based and Literature-Based Resources 121
References 122

Chapter 6: Solution-Focused Consultation **126**

Introduction 126
Learning Objectives 127

Current Perspectives 127
Solution-Focused Consultee Consultation 128
The Solution-Focused Consultee Consultation Process 128
Multicultural Considerations 133
Chapter Keystones 133
Web-Based and Literature-Based Resources 135
References 136

Chapter 7: Ethical and Legal Aspects of Consultation **137**
Introduction 137
Understanding Ethical and Legal Codes in Consultation 137
Ethical Principles 140
Multicultural Considerations 156
Chapter Keystones 156
Web-Based and Literature-Based Resources 158
References 158

Chapter 8: Consultation in Mental Health Settings **160**
Introduction 160
Learning Objectives 161
Historical Background 161
Foundations of Mental Health Consultation: Key Points and Approaches 163
The Consultation Process 166
The Consultation Alliance (Relationship) 166
Types of Mental Health Consultation 168
Current Trends 185
Multicultural Considerations 190
Chapter Keystones 191
Web-Based and Literature-Based Resources 192
References 192

Chapter 9: Consultation in Education (or School System) Settings **197**
Introduction 197
Learning Objectives 199
Historical Background 199
School-Based Consultation and Collaboration 201
Consultation With Teachers 201
Consultation With School Administrators 203
Consultation With Parents 206
School-Based Mental Health Consultation 207
Instruction-Based Consultation 211
Systems-Focused Consultation 213
Group Consultation 213

Multicultural Considerations   214
Chapter Keystones   216
Web-Based and Literature-Based Resources   216
References   216

Chapter 10:   Consultation in Career Counseling Settings   223

Introduction   223
Learning Objectives   224
Direct Services: An Important Distinction in Career Consultation   224
Current Trends   225
Career Consultation Settings   238
Program Evaluation   242
Multicultural Considerations   245
Chapter Keystones   247
Web-Based and Literature-Based Resources   248
References   248

Chapter 11:   Consultation in Organizational Settings   250

Introduction   250
Learning Objectives   251
What Is an Organizational Setting?   251
Trends and Implications for Mental Health Consultants in Organizations   255
Multicultural Considerations   266
Chapter Keystones   268
Web-Based and Literature-Based Resources   269
References   269

Chapter 12:   Epilogue   271

Interview with Richard Parsons PhD and Naijian Zhang PhD   271

Index   277
About the Authors   286

Introduction to the Series

Counseling and Professional Identity in the 21st Century

The role of counselor-as-consultant is not new. However, at this time of increasing demand for services and reduction in service resources, consultation takes on new meaning and value to the professional counselor. Consultation, as you will soon come to discover, provides a paradigm for both expanding a counselor's impact and engaging counselors in those services which not only provide remediation but foster prevention.

Counselor As Consultant is a text that not only introduces the reader to the expanse of theory and research supporting this mode of service delivery but also fosters the ongoing development of the reader's own professional identity and skill set so that the reader can serve as a *Counselor as Consultant.*

As is obvious, one text, one learning experience, will not be sufficient for the successful formation of your professional identity and practice. Becoming and being a counselor will be a lifelong process—a process that we hope to facilitate through the presentation of this text and the creation of our series: *Counseling and Professional Identity in the 21st Century.*

Counseling and Professional Identity in the 21st Century is a new, fresh, pedagogically sound series of texts targeting counselors in training. This series is NOT simply a compilation of isolated books matching that which is already in the market. Rather each book, with its targeted knowledge and skills, will be presented as but a part of a larger whole. The focus and content of each text serves as a single lens through which counselors can view their clients, engage in their practice and articulate their own professional identity.

Counseling and Professional Identity in the 21st Century is unique not just in the fact that it "packaged" a series of traditional text, but that it provides an *integrated* curriculum targeting the formation of the reader's professional identity and efficient, ethical practice. Each book within the series is structured to facilitate the ongoing professional formation of the reader. The materials found within each text are organized in order to move the reader to higher levels of cognitive, affective, and psycho-motor functioning, resulting in the assimilation of the materials presented into both the professional identity and approach to professional practice. While each text targets a specific set of core competencies (cognates and skills), competencies identified by the Council for Accreditation of Counseling & Related Educational Programs (CACREP) as essential to the practice of counseling (see the inside front cover of this book), each book in the series will emphasize each of the following:

- the assimilation of concepts and constructs provided across the text found within the series, thus fostering the reader's ongoing development as a competent professional;
- the blending of contemporary theory with current research and empirical support;
- a focus on the development of procedural knowledge with each text employing case illustrations and guided practice exercises to facilitate the readers' ability to translate the theory and research discussed into professional decision making and application;
- the emphasis on the need for and means of demonstrating accountability; and
- the fostering of the reader's professional identity and with it the assimilation of the ethics and standards of practice guiding the counseling profession.

We are proud to have served as coeditors of this series feeling sure that each book within it will serve as a significant resource to you and your development as a professional counselor. Let your journey begin!

Richard Parsons, PhD

Naijian Zhang, PhD

Acknowledgments

This book would not have been possible without the support and guidance from many special people, both personally and professionally. The opportunity to create a counselor-as-consultant text benefitting current and future mental health professionals requires the foresight and support of a range of talented individuals. In our case, we thank Rick Parsons and Naijian Zhang for coming up with this innovative series of texts and for all of their support and guidance. We also want to thank all the staff at SAGE Publications (specifically, Kassie Graves and Elizabeth Luizzi) who helped in the development of this text and for their tremendous support, encouragement, insights, and talents as we moved from conceptualization to completion of a text specifically designed to optimize knowledge base and future work of the counselor as consultant. Production of this text would not have been possible without the tremendous help of Brittany Bauhaus and Diane DiMura at SAGE Publications.

Much gratitude goes to several of our current students for all of their help and contributions: current Clemson University graduate student, Brooke Simecka, for her contributions of case illustrations and exercises in several chapters; and current doctoral students at the University of Arkansas, Kevin Kirkpatrick and Christopher Carver, for their assistance with research and editing.

We would also like to thank the reviewers for all of their beneficial suggestions and insights for the text: Mona Robinson, Ohio University; Leo R. Sandy, Plymouth State University; Cindy Silitsky, St. Thomas University; and Gaston Weisz, Adelphi University.

We could not have completed this text without the support and understanding of our family members. Our families helped in ways that would be too exhaustive to describe and also supported us as we tried to maintain that elusive work–life balance. We are sure that our family members are the happiest that the book is finished!

fundamental elements of consultation within the counseling professional, this text utilizes the mission and standards set forth by the Council for the Accreditation of Counseling & Related Educational Programs (CACREP). In doing so, the text is designed to ensure that students and counseling practitioners alike remain attuned to the requisite knowledge, skills, and experiences necessary to encourage mastery of the practice of consultation and heighten their identity as a professional consultant. This process also fosters the development of more complex cognitive structures that facilitate the critical analysis and reflectivity necessary to succeed in consulting environments where complex inter- and intrapersonal dynamics and organizational and systemic demands are the norm. Counselors acting as consultants should expect to encounter and be able to adapt to the concerns and needs of an increasingly diverse range of mental health and allied health professionals. Although grounded in the ethical, legal, and CACREP standards of the counseling profession, this text will also work to integrate appropriate consultation models, competencies, and best practices of other mental health, allied health, and even business models. The ultimate goal of this addition is to provide the counselor as consultant with the broadest knowledge base on consulting in order to ensure that they can compete in an increasingly diverse marketplace. Thus, counselors acting in the role of consultant are well equipped to organize information and make meaning of experiences in a more comprehensive, integrated, and differentiated manner, thereby broadening their potential to effect positive change in a variety of settings.

Current textbooks used by counselor training programs consistently provide the content recognized as fundamental to professional practice. These texts consistently present the *fundamentals* of the consultation process. While these texts provide a well-thought-out approach to a specific set of skills, there remains a need to orient counselors-in-training (and current practitioners) to the counselor as consultant in relation to the more contemporary counseling paradigms of wellness and professional identity, along with the more traditional roles and responsibilities counselors have encountered in the consulting role.

To that end, the text *Counselor as Consultant* was conceptualized as a means to order and explore the traditional understanding of counselor as consultant paradigm while advocating the need to remain attuned to the challenges counselors may encounter as they adopt the role of consultant as a member of the counseling profession in the 21st century. To meet this challenge, *Counselor as Consultant* is designed as an evidence-based text that seeks to blend the historical importance and influence of the constructs, models, and theories related to the counselor as consultant with the more contemporary aspects of this role within the context of current CACREP standards and the dynamic landscape of the counseling profession. Inherent within the text will be analysis, activities, case studies, reflective exercises, and author contributions organized around the central goal of enhancing the reader's level of critical thinking, knowledge base, identity as a professional counselor, and self-awareness surrounding the roles and responsibilities of a consultant.

Table AP-1   2009 CACREP Standards Related to Consultation

Chapter(s) in Book	CACREP Standard
PROFESSIONAL ORIENTATION AND ETHICAL PRACTICE:	
1, 2	1.b. professional roles, functions, and relationships with other human service providers, including strategies for interagency/interorganization collaboration and communications
7	1.j. ethical standards of professional organizations and credentialing bodies and applications of ethical and legal consideration in professional counseling
HELPING RELATIONSHIPS:	
3	5.b. counselor characteristics and behaviors that influence helping processes
3, 4	5.c. essential interviewing and counseling skills
All	5.f. a general framework for understanding and practicing consultation
8	5.g. crisis intervention and suicide prevention models, including the use of psychological first aid strategies
SOCIAL AND CULTURAL DIVERSITY	
All	2.d. individual, couple, family, group, and community strategies for working with and advocating for diverse populations, including multicultural considerations
CLINICAL MENTAL HEALTH COUNSELING	
8	C.1 describes the principles of mental health, including prevention, intervention, *consultation*, education, and advocacy, as well as the operation of programs and networks that promote mental health in a multicultural society
SCHOOL COUNSELING	
9	M.4. understands systems theories, models, and processes of consultation in school system settings
CAREER COUNSELING	
10	C.2 career development program planning, organization, implementation, administration, and evaluation

Rationale/The Need

Becoming a mental health professional is a developmental process involving a personal and professional awareness of the simplicity and complexity of counseling's relational and procedural elements. So too is the development of the knowledge base and skill sets implicit to the role of practice of consultation. In order to address these

Preface

Counselor as Consultant

Counselor As Consultant is designed to address specific competencies identified as essential to developing an understanding of the processes of professional consultation and the development of a counselor's identity as a consultant (see Table AP-1). The material presented not only addresses those competencies identified by the Council for the Accreditation of Counseling & Related Educational Programs (CACREP, 2009) as fundamental for counselors as consultants but also provides a framework for *all mental health professionals* who are interested in providing consultation services.

Specifically, the text

- provides the reader with a view of the goals of consultation, including an introduction to the notion of integrating a wellness paradigm into the dual notions of the counselor's identity as a consultant and as a means of facilitating positive and effective consultation outcomes;
- encourages readers to reflect on and address their personal and professional motives for becoming a professional consultant, including their personal state of wellness and/or life adjustments that may be necessary in order to establish and maintain the level of "best practice" as a consultant;
- highlights consultant characteristics and behaviors that influence consultation relationships and processes;
- identifies, defines, and reviews essential consultation skills;
- describes foundational consultation constructs, theories, and models that form the basis for recognizing and addressing typical (and some atypical) consulting issues, conceptualizing consultant and consultee issues and concerns, and fully engaging in the provision of professional consultation;
- reviews and provides a clear description and analysis of the relevant historical and contemporary research supporting the practice of professional consultation by and among professional counselors;
- highlights the need for the employment of measures of accountability; and
- provides a brief discussion of the growing influence of coaching within the business mental health disciplines and briefly discusses coaching and its differences from counseling and consulting.

Introduction and Overview of Consultation

Introduction

Throughout my years as a counselor educator, I have lost track of how many times I have been asked by students in class, "Consultation in mental health, what does that mean?" Imagine taking the skills and techniques learned in your graduate program and applying those to helping individuals and organizations in your community, state, or even on the other side of the world! Mental health consultation brings together the knowledge and skills of traditional counseling with the ability to reach consultees in settings such as schools and small or large organizations that need students in specialized assistance. Did you know that businesses and schools of all sizes regularly use the services of consultants to help with a myriad of issues? Did you also know that consultation is a billion dollar industry (Aron, 2012)? Well, get ready for a journey through this exciting topic! We will explore the unique ways mental health consultation can serve our communities. Mental health consultation has become a vital component of training for all types of mental health professionals. Most graduate school accrediting agencies have incorporated consultation into the standards of training for counseling and other mental health graduate programs. So, whether you want to work with the small bakery downtown or your countries' largest school system (or both), mental health consultation could be a viable career option.

The goal of this book is to provide information to mental health professionals on how they can serve as consultants in some of the most popular settings in the world of work. Through numerous guided practice exercises and discussion points, this book will help you explore the challenges and rewards of being a mental health professional consultant. We support the idea that learning about consultation can best be achieved by blending theory with practice, with the main focus on exploration via case illustrations, exercises, and discussion points. While we have focused the book on the current related standards for consultation as developed by the Council for Accreditation of Counseling & Related Educational Programs (CACREP), readers will quickly realize that this book can be used by other mental health professionals (social workers, psychologists, marriage and family) acting as consultants.

LEARNING OBJECTIVES

After reading this chapter you will

- Memorize and be able to recall the historical background of mental health consultation
- Define and be able to demonstrate the types of consultation used by consultants
- Define and be able to explain the term *consultation*
- Be familiar with the current CACREP standards for consultation

Before continuing on in this text, please take a few minutes to complete the self-assessment located in Guided Practice Exercise 1.1. No need to worry about answering "don't know" during the pretest, the answers to the questions can be found throughout this text. Also, don't forget to complete this self-assessment again at the end of the semester to evaluate how much your knowledge of mental health consultation has changed!

Exercise 1.1: Self-Assessment Pretest and Posttest

Part of the process in learning about consultation is evaluation of your knowledge pertaining to consultation. Below is a pretest and posttest that will help evaluate the development in knowledge about consultation. The test is designed to take place during the first meeting and then at the end of the training.

1. *Is there one definition of consultation that can be used in every setting? Explain your answer.*

2. *Explain why consultation is now a part of established standards for most mental health professionals.*

3. *Explain the difference between consultation and supervision.*

4. *Explain the difference between consultation and traditional mental health counseling.*

5. *Explain the role of the consultant.*

6. *Explain the role of the consultee.*

7. *Describe the skills needed to be an effective consultant.*

8. *Describe some of the settings in which a consultant could provide services.*

9. *Do you need to keep records and be skilled in report writing to be a consultant? Please explain your answer.*

10. *Describe the role of ethics in consultation.*

11. *Is there a code of ethics for consultants?*

12. *Describe a few of the models of consultation.*

13. *What are the stages in the consultation process?*

14. *Explain the need for consultants to have knowledge and training in issues related to diversity and multiculturalism.*

15. *Can consultants play an important role in school settings? How?*

16. *Can consultants play an important role in mental health settings? How?*

17. *Can consultants play an important role in career counseling settings? How?*

18. *Can consultant play an important role in organizational settings? How?*

19. *Describe what the term* consultation *in mental health means to you.*

Historical Perspectives

Consultation is a common practice and has been used since early in the 13th century (Gallessich, 1982) when physicians would request a *consult* by another physician with typically more training or experience in a certain area. The consulting physician would examine the treating physician's patient and work collaboratively to reach a diagnosis and treatment plan for the patient. The term *consultant* is used in many fields, such as finance consultant, travel consultant, wedding consultant, to name a few (Gibson & Mitchell, 2008).

Mental health consultation caught the attention of the National Institute of Mental Health (NIMH) back in the 1950s (MacLennan, 1986) and was considered to be a piece of the overall system of care in the mental health field. The area of mental health consulting picked up speed when the government passed the Mental Retardation Facilities and Community Mental Health Centers Construction Act Amendments of 1965 (Pub. L. 89–105), which provided funding to hire service providers to serve as consultants in mental health agencies. Although funding was now being provided, many professionals lacked the proper training to serve as mental health consultants (MacLennan, 1986).

In 1970, Gerald Caplan published the beginning standards of mental health consultation with his book, *The Theory and Practice of Mental Health Consultation*. In his book, Caplan created the mental health consultation model which established many of the guidelines that are used today to describe the practice of mental health consultation. Caplan began his exploration and development of mental health consultation when he worked with emotionally disturbed immigrant children in Israel. The program in Israel worked with thousands of children located in hundreds of individual residential centers throughout the country. Caplan's team was assigned to work with the residential center's *instructors* on how to deal with the difficult children at each of the centers. Caplan (1970) discovered that by shifting the focus from a specific child to the actual relationships between the children and instructor, he could change the entire approach the instructors were using with *all* of the children in the program and not just one child. So instead of traveling between programs, exhausting resources, he could work with the instructor to reach all of the children in a specific residential center. Thus, modern day mental health consultation was created.

Exercise 1.2: Consultation for Many

As described earlier, Gerald Caplan began using consultation to work with residential program staff and *indirectly*, the adolescent clients. Take a few moments and think about a situation where this type of consultation could be used in an organization. Create a scenario where the consultant goes into an organization and works with the consultee (manager/administrator) and *indirectly* affects how the consultee will work with the employees within the organization.

_____

_____

_____

_____

_____

_____

Caplan went on to work with Erich Lindemann at Harvard University who was working on the foundations of mental health consulting. At the time, Lindemann (1944) was also working on the creation of a crisis theory to help the survivors of the 1942 Coconut Grove Fire. Lindemann and his team helped Caplan move his philosophy and thinking away from traditional mental health counseling to more of a focus on mental health consultation and the delineation of the two schools of thought. While mental health consultation retains many aspects of traditional mental health counseling, consultation has its specific roles, definitions, and procedures that differentiate it from mental health counseling. Researchers Douglas Fuchs, Lynn Fuchs, Jeannette

Dulan, Holley Roberts and Pamela Fernstrom (1992), even stated that one of the most used and highly regarded services in schools and mental health agencies are consultation services.

Working Definition and Types of Consultation

There have been many attempts to define consultation and a definition of consultation continues to be a question generated by countless students in our programs. Chapter 2 will provide a more in-depth description of the roles and definitions of the counselor as consultant. Caplan (1970) suggested that the term of *consultation* is viewed very differently by different professionals and could be used to describe any activity performed by a specialist. DeWayne J. Kurpius and Dale R. Fuqua (1993) concluded that the definitions of consultation by professionals are very similar in nature and can be different based on consultation settings, goals of consultation, and even theoretical orientation.

Over the past 40 years, numerous professionals have created very useful definitions of consultation. As you will see below, there are similarities found within the definitions that serve as a guide when working as a consultant. Several definitions have been proposed, including the following:

- It is a process of interaction between two professional persons—the consultant, who is a specialist, and the consultee, who invokes the consultant's help in regard to a current work problem with which he is having some difficulty and which he has decided is within the other's area of specialized competence (Caplan, 1970, p.19).
- The term *consultant* is usually understood to mean someone who gives professional advice or services regarding matters in the field of that person's special knowledge when asked to do so by an agency (Cook & Buccino, 1979, p. 105).
- It means tripartite interactions in human services agencies. The consultant (a specialized professional) assists consultees (agency employees who are also professionals) with work-related concerns as the third component (Gallessich, 1982, p. 6).
- Basically, consultation is a type of service performed by counselors, psychologists, and human resource workers in which they assist another person who has responsibility for a case or program (Dougherty, 2009, p. 10).

In an effort to continue the process of defining consultation and begin the conversation for ourselves, we pose this question: Is there one definition of consultation that will work in all settings and with all populations? The answer is *not really*. We view consultation in the same scope as the authors above. Consultation can be viewed as a mental health professional (consultant) helping facilitate change in a person or organization (consultee) of an identified issue that would benefit the person, organization, or both.

While only having one definition of consultation would limit the diverse settings and diverse issues (multicultural and diversity issues will be specifically discussed and expanded on in several chapters within this text) that consultants deal with in the field,

Exercise 1.3: Definition of Consultation

Directions: Some of the most popular and widely used definitions have been provided in this chapter. Now it's your turn.

1. *Either individually or in groups, create your own definition of consulting.*

_____

_____

_____

2. *Was your definition different from the ones in this chapter? How?*

_____

_____

_____

3. *Was your definition different or similar to those in your class? Explain.*

_____

_____

_____

there is some common ground in consultation. Below are a few of the common beginning steps in consultation with a case illustration, with Case Illustration 1.1 and Figure 1.1 as tools to help understand the process. Expanded discussion of the stages of consultation is found in Chapter 4.

Figure 1.1   Beginning Steps in the Consultation Process

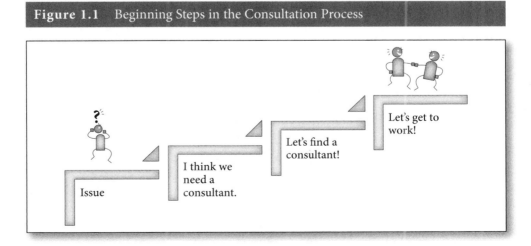

Issue

I think we need a consultant.

Let's find a consultant!

Let's get to work!

1. *The consultee sees an issue that needs to be addressed.* We don't like to use the term *problem*, due to the inherent nature of the term and the "issue" may be one of increasing the effectiveness or reach of an already successful program.

2. *The consultee decides that a professional with expertise in examining and assisting in resolution of issues related to specific settings is needed.* The consultee decides that change needs to happen and that having a "fresh and knowledgeable perspective" may enable this change to occur. This fresh perspective will require the assistance of someone with specific training in consultation.

3. *The consultee seeks out an individual to serve as consultant.* There continues to be discussion on whether the consultant should be internal or external of the setting. Our recommendation—get the best person for the job. A professional consultant will be able to maintain objectivity throughout the process or will recuse herself or himself if needed.

4. *The consultee and consultant enter into a professional working relationship in order to address an issue.* Issues such as length of consultation, payment of consultation services, termination of services, and limitations and boundaries of consultation will be discussed and confirmed at this point. Also, remember that the consultee does NOT have to accept or incorporate the recommendations of the consultant. The consultant is only there to provide the consultee with recommendations and assist the consultee as requested. As you can see, first and foremost, issues in the consultation relationship are consultee specific and focused. As in traditional counseling, the focus has shifted to client-driven services and away from the old pathological view of services.

Case 1.1: Beginning Steps

Step 1: *The consultee sees an issue that needs to be addressed.*

Denver works as a licensed social worker in a community mental health center. Over the past several months, he has noticed a marked increase in the amount of requests for couples counseling. Currently, the center does not offer couples counseling but wants to be proactive in meeting the needs of their clients. Denver has been assigned the task of determining if establishing an ongoing couple's counseling group would be beneficial to their clients but also fit into the financial structure.

Step 2: *The consultee decides that a professional with expertise in examining and assisting in resolution of issues related to specific settings is needed.*

Denver quickly realizes that stretching the center's budget and adding more responsibilities on to the current staff needs to be a well-thought-out decision. Denver wants to make this decision based on more than anecdotal data and have a well-developed plan to present to the center's board members.

(Continued)

(Continued)

Step 3: *The consultee seeks out an individual to serve as consultant.*

Denver remembers talking to a professional mental health consultant at the state counseling association's annual conference and had actually kept her contact information, *just in case* a situation like the current one presents itself at his agency. Denver knew that she had expertise in analyzing current trends in community agency programs and also some grant writing experience. Denver requests permission from his board to contact the consultant to inquire about services.

Step 4: *The consultee and consultant enter into a professional working relationship in order to address issue.*

Denver contacts the professional consultant, Jean, who is very interested in helping and states that she has helped other agencies with the same dilemma of growing their programs. Jean provides Denver with all of the specifics about the role of consultation and establishes the fees for service. Denver takes this information to the board members who agree to the fees and also the consultation services. Denver and Jean enter into a professional consultant–consultee relationship that will include the agency and the possible programs needing to address the issues of the clients in the community.

Types of Consultation

Mental health consultation is not just a one-size-fits-all theory that can be applied to all settings and situations. Within consultation, there are different types of consultation that the consultants may find themselves in when providing consultation. The classic discussion surrounding types of consultation is provided by Caplan's 1970 categorization of consultation types (see Chapter 8 for a more detailed description of Caplan's types). Other types of consultation are described in several other chapters in this text. Caplan described the types of consultation in the following ways:

- *Client-Centered Case Consultation*

As the name implies, the goal of consultation services is to provide services to a specific client. Caplan (1970) stated, "the primary goal of the consultation is for the consultant to communicate to the consultee how this client can be helped" (p. 32). An example could be when a group-home staff member requests help from the agency counselor in dealing with a client's anger outbursts at the group home.

- *Consultee-Centered Case Consultation*

In this type, the consultant actually facilitates growth in the consultee to learn and use new skills so that the consultee can improve personal work with a specific group of clients. Caplan (1970) states "the aim of this type of consultation is frankly

to educate the consultee" (p. 33). For example, a manager at a local company wants to learn to improve personal communication skills to be a more effective manager when dealing with employee's needs during the work day.

- *Program-Centered Administrative Consultation*

In program-centered consultation, the consultant helps a program's administration in program development. The consultant could also assist in making changes to an already existing program to enhance the effectiveness of the program. Caplan (1970) suggested that the consultant could provide long- and short-term options that the administration could use to address the needs of the program.

- *Consultee-Centered Administrative Consultation*

In this final type, the consultant works directly with the consultees to help them with their issues of working together to make the organization successful. Many times, organizations will have leaders that struggle to come together for the good of the organization, resulting in lowered organization effectiveness (i.e., lower earnings, loss of positive public perception, inability to meet the demands of the consumer). The consultant will work with the consultees on their communication with others, improving leadership characteristics, and overall group dynamics.

Figure 1.2 provides a useful decision tree based on Caplan's (1970) types of consultation. A consultant could follow the *consultation triage* in selecting what type of consultation may be needed in working with a consultee (person or group). As with any consultation process, recycling through the decision-making process may be needed as changes arise in the providing of consultation services. The case exercises (see Exercise 1.1) will help you in your decision-making process on selecting the type of consultation needed for a specific situation.

Advantages of Mental Health Consultation

With the growing need for mental health services and the dwindling amount of resources to provide these services, mental health consultation can serve as one of the options to reach a high number of clients while maintaining costs for the agency or school. Mental health consultants can train professionals in ways to handle crisis situations, provide professionals with information about local resources, and help consultees develop effective programs in their communities. Elizabeth L. Teed and John A. Scileppi (2007) remind us that consultants can work with teachers, police officers, nurses, organization managers, and other "front-line" individuals who then go and work with an even larger number of clients on a daily basis. Consultation services can be a short-term, flexible, and very strong option to meeting the needs of clients in the schools and local communities (Reddy, Barboza-Whitehead, Files, & Rubel, 2000). There is also the growing field of *coaching* or *executive coaching* that has its roots in consultation. Chapters 8, 10, and 11 will provide more information about this growing field. Carolyn F. Swift and Saul Cooper (1986) contend that consultation can take place

Figure 1.2 Consultation Triage. Based on Caplan's (1970) types of consultation.

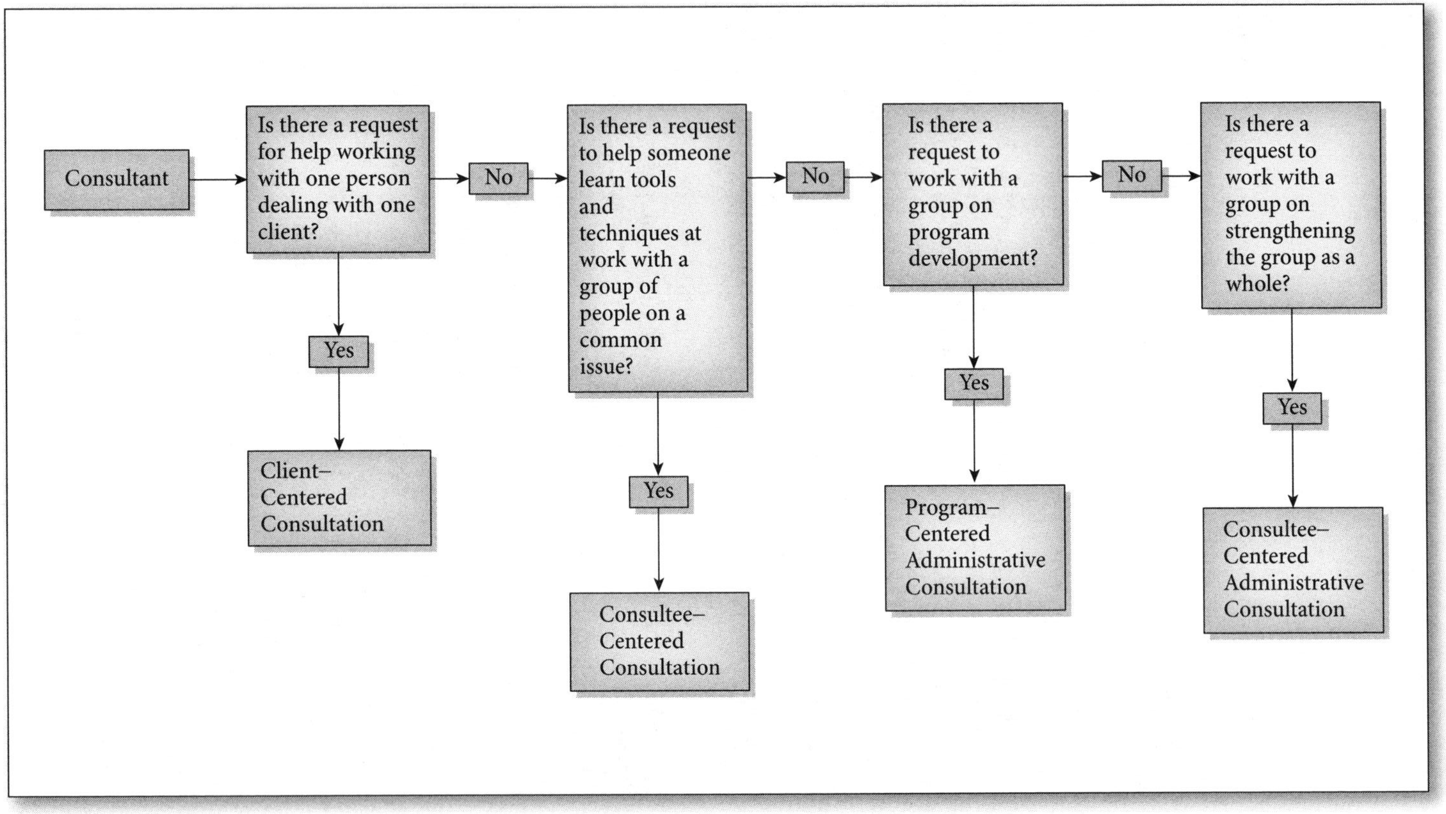

Exercise 1.4: Consultation Types

Directions: Provided are five examples of the need for consultation. Using Caplan's 1970 Types of Consultation, determine which type is described for each scenario. List the type below each scenario and your reasons for selecting the specific type.

Scenario 1

The staff at East Middle School started an antidrug afterschool program for kids with behavioral issues who may be experimenting with drugs. At first, they had a great turn-out because the most popular teacher was leading it, but with the start of a new year and the departure of this teacher, the attendance numbers have dwindled. So the staff administration seeks the help of a consultant who can offer ideas as to how to build the numbers again. The consultant suggests that the program be offered during a study hall period, a time when kids are anxious to do anything but study.

Which type of consultation does this describe and why?

_____

_____

Answer: Program-centered administrative consultation

Scenario 2

Jenny, a group addictions counseling facilitator, is struggling to get her client, Bob, to speak in the group counseling sessions. Participation is required, and if Bob continues to be silent in the group, his therapy will have to be terminated and he will be put back on parole. So, Jenny seeks the help of a consultant who is knowledgeable about addictions counseling for advice on how to reach this client before he is banned from the group.

Which type of consultation does this describe and why?

_____

_____

Answer: Client-centered case consultation

Scenario 3

The employees at a local news station are struggling to meet the daily quota of current stories to be reported by deadline, a demand that's been routine for years. So the news station's people contact a consultant to come into the office and figure out what is affecting the group production. The consultant learns that there has been a change in staffing. The new leadership has led to micromanaging of every position to the point that workers are asked to triple check their work, ultimately leading to less efficiency

(Continued)

(Continued)

overall. The employees are given the chance to express their frustration with the leadership and a new strategy is developed with the input of the workers and the manager that leads to positive motivation, efficient self-monitoring and cross-checking, and quicker results.

Which type of consultation does this describe and why?

_____

_____

Answer: Consultee-centered administrative consultation

Scenario 4

Nick is the director of an insurance company. He has the opportunity to earn a major bonus if the company can increase their clientele numbers by 5%. He is struggling to get his employees to work harder and finds them complaining about him, calling him "nagging" and "a tyrant." A few workers have even threatened to quit. So Nick contacts a consultant to help him learn how to instill positive motivation in his workers. Together, they create a plan that has an appealing incentive for everyone involved if the goal is met, all the while making it easier to encourage everyone to join him in putting in the extra effort.

Which type of consultation does this describe and why?

_____

_____

Answer: Consultee-centered case consultation

Scenario 5

The most frequented movie theatre in town has suffered a major loss in ticket sales over the past four months. Manager Nelson believes many people are opting to save money and rent movies, but he wonders if there is something about the theatre that is repelling people. So manager Nelson contacts a consultant to make an inspection of the theatre and its management to see what positive changes can be made to attract more movie goers. The consultant takes a week to inspect the theatre and talk with the employees and learns that the bathrooms have been neglected for daily cleaning based on an oversight in employee scheduling. Also, after doing some research, the consultant explains that compared to other theaters in the town, this theatre charges a dollar more for night movies and doesn't offer a student discount.

Which type of consultation does this describe and why?

_____

_____

Answer: Consultee-centered administrative consultation

in numerous settings, including businesses, government agencies, schools, mental health agencies, and hospitals. We also know that mental health consultation can now occur in almost any setting.

Exercise 1.5: Where Would You Like to Work?

The text briefly highlighted several settings where consulting can take place. Think about several settings that may interest you and your work as a consultant.

Directions: Write down a couple of settings that you would like to work in as a consultant. Also write down why you think you would like to work in these settings. Finally, write down if you would need any specific training to work in these settings.

1. *Consultation settings:* _____

_____

_____

2. *Why you like these settings:* _____

_____

_____

3. *Any special training for this setting?* _____

_____

_____

Organizations will seek consultation services for anything related to the organization. All consultants (including mental health consultants) need to only practice consultation in areas where they have expertise or special training. Larry Greiner and Ilse Ennsfellner (2011) remind us that, unfortunately, many consultants have had to learn to be consultants by on-the-job training during actual consulting activities. If you are using this text in your graduate training, then your program is cognizant of the necessity for mental health professionals to have training in consultation skills. A quick examination via the World Wide Web reveals that there are very few (if any) professional associations for consultants and even fewer for mental health consultants. As the number of mental health consultants continues to increase, there will need to be professional associations that maintain training and standards for their members to provide a level of protection and comfort for consultees.

Consultation has continued to change and become more setting specific, which we will discuss in the subsequent chapters. Specifically in Chapters 5 and 6, we will discuss some of the newer and relevant models of consultation. Our discussion on the brief solution-focused model of consultation will be relevant in this age of insurance-driven therapy *(consultation can be a billable service)* and insurance companies' desire for a speedy solution. Consultants can work with general practitioners and other primary care providers in educating them on recognizing and referring patients with a mental illness to mental health professionals (Teed & Scileppi, 2007).

Effectiveness of Consultation

As with any treatment modality, the ability to examine the effectiveness of the modality is essential. The growing body of research into the effectiveness of consultation continues to provide promising results indicating the strength and usability of consultation. Reddy et al. (2000) conducted a meta-analysis of child and adolescent consultations from 1986 to 1997. The results indicated positive effects on both the clients and consultees. Gordon Gibson and Kathleen M. Chard (1994) reviewed 1,643 consultation outcomes, which revealed a moderate overall effect. The study also mentioned that, even back in 1994, there was enough empirical support for the use of consultation intervention services. Research by Karol M. Wasylyshyn (2003) and Erik de Haan, Anna Duckworth, David Birch, Philippa Hardman, and Claire Jones (2013) supported executive coaching as an effective treatment modality that falls within the consultation framework. Further research into consultation will continue to provide evidence to mental health professionals about the effectiveness of consultation services in various settings.

CACREP Standards

Counselor education programs across the country are encouraged to establish and maintain a set of standards that provides consistency and accountability in their programs. The Council for Accreditation of Counseling & Related Educational Programs (CACREP) was founded in 1981 to serve as a national accrediting organization for counselor and related education programs. As an independent agency and a member of the Council on Postsecondary Accreditation, CACREP accredits master's level programs in addiction, career, clinical mental health, marriage, couple and family, school and student affairs, and college counseling programs. They also accredit doctoral programs in counselor education and supervision (CACREP, 2012).

CACREP acknowledges the important role counselors can play as consultants in many different areas. Included on the inside of the front cover of this book is a detailed listing of the relevant CACREP standards and where they are located in the text. As you will see, CACREP views learning about and incorporating consultation skills on the same level as learning about basic and advanced counseling techniques. CACREP includes components of learning and using consultation in clinical mental health settings and school settings. Consultation is also identified within these fields and also career, addictions, student affairs, and college counseling.

Not only does CACREP (2009) see the importance of consultation, the majority of other mental health accrediting bodies, including the Council on Rehabilitation

Education (CORE, 2010), the National Association of Social Workers (2008), American Association for Marriage and Family Therapy (2012), and the American Psychological Association (APA, 2009), view consultation as a critical technique and tool for their mental health professional members. Support for mental health professionals working as consultants is now commonplace and widely accepted as a role of many mental health professionals.

Multicultural Considerations

A part of this textbook that you may find beneficial is a focus on multicultural considerations. We have tried to include a discussion of multicultural issues and considerations in each chapter and how diversity is an integral part of the consultation process. Consultants will need to be aware of the continued change in the U.S. workforce and how these shifting demographics will impact the agencies, schools, and organizations they work with as consultants. The U.S. Census Bureau (2012) reports that the next 50 years will be a turning point in racial makeup with no one group holding an overall majority over other groups. Minorities (those not in the non-Hispanic White population) will be over 50% of the population by 2060. Patricia Romney (2008) summarized that organizations are very different that there were 50 to100 years ago with significant changes in diversity and cultural dynamics. Both Romney (2008) and Derald Wing Sue (2008) support the need for consultants to be very cognizant of the issues related around social justice and respecting employees from different backgrounds and cultures. Consultants are no different from mental health professionals in their need and requirement to continue to seek knowledge and understanding of diversity and its effects on people and organizations.

Chapter Keystones

- Mental health consultation is a growing field with various setting options.
- Defining consultation usually involves the consultant assisting the consultee by providing expertise in the area of concern.
- Graduate program accrediting agencies have endorsed consultation as one of the practice standards for training in mental health.

Web-Based and Literature-Based Resources

Websites

Council for Accreditation of Counseling and Related Educational Programs (CACREP): http://www.cacrep
.org
American Counseling Association (ACA): http://www.counseling.org
American Association for Marriage and Family Therapy: http://www.aamft.org

American Psychological Association: http://www.apa.org

National Association of Social Workers: http://www.socialworkers.org

Council on Rehabilitation Education: www.core-rehab.org

Mental Retardation Facilities and Community Mental Health Centers Construction Act Amendments of 1965 (Pub. L. 89-105): http://www.law.cornell.edu/topn/mental_retardation_facilities_and_community_mental_health_centers_construction_act_amendments_of_1965

National Institute of Mental Health: www.nimh.nih.gov

References

American Association for Marriage and Family Therapy. (2012). *Revised AAMFT code of ethics.* Retrieved from http://www.aamft.org/imis15/content/legal_ethics/code_of_ethics.aspx

American Psychological Association. (2009). *Guidelines and principles for accreditation of programs in professional psychology.* Retrieved from http://www.apa.org/ed/accreditation/about/policies/guiding-principles.pdf

Aron, L. (2012). Psychoanalysis in the workplace: An introduction. *Psychoanalytic Dialogues, 22,* 511–516. doi:10.1080/10481885.2012.717041

Caplan, G. (1970). *The theory and practice of mental health consultation.* New York, NY: Basic Books.

Cook, T. D., & Buccino, A. (1979). The social scientist as a provider of consulting services to the federal government. In J. Platt & R. Wicks, *The psychological consultant* (p. 104). New York, NY: Grune & Stratton.

Council for Accreditation of Counseling & Related Educational Programs. (2009). *CACREP 2009 standards.* Retrieved from http://www.cacrep.org/doc/2009%20Standards%20with%20cover.pdf

Council for Accreditation of Counseling & Related Educational Programs. (2012). *About CACREP.* Retrieved from www.cacrep.org

Council on Rehabilitation Education. (2010). *Accreditation manual for masters level rehabilitation counselor education programs.* Retrieved from http://www.core-rehab.org/Files/Doc/PDF/OREStandardsPrograms.pdf

de Haan, E., Duckworth, A., Birch, D., Hardman, P., & Jones, C. (2013). Executive coaching outcome research: The contribution of common factors such as relationship, personality match, and self-efficacy. Consulting Psychology Journal: Practice and Research. Advance online publication. doi:10.1037/a0031635

Dougherty, M. A. (2009). *Psychological consultation and collaboration in school and community settings* (5th ed.). Belmont, CA: Brooks/Cole.

Fuchs, D., Fuchs, L. S., Dulan, J., Roberts, H., & Fernstrom, P. (1992). Where is the research on consultation effectiveness? Journal of Educational & Psychological Consultation, 3(2), pp. 151–174.

Fuchs, D., Fuchs, L. S., Hamlett, C. L., & Ferguson, C. (1992). Effects of expert system consultation within curriculum-based measurement, using a reading maze task. *Exceptional Children, 58,* 436–450.

Gallessich, J. (1982). *The profession and practice of consultation: A handbook for consultants, trainers of consultants, and consumers of consultation services.* San Francisco, CA: Jossey-Bass.

Gibson, G., & Chard, K. M. (1994). Quantifying the effects of community mental health consultation interventions. *Consulting Psychology Journal: Practice and Research, 46*(4), 13–25. doi:10.1037/1061-4087.46.4.13

Gibson, R. L., & Mitchell, M. (2008). *Introduction to counseling and guidance* (7th ed.).Upper Saddle River, NJ: Pearson.

Greiner, L., & Ennsfellner, I. (2011). *Management consultants as professionals, or are they?* (CEO Publication T 08-10 [546]). Los Angeles, CA: Center for Effective Organizations. Retrieved from http://ceo.usc.edu/pdf/t08_10.pdf

Kurpius, D. J., & Fuqua, D. R. (1993). Fundamental issues in defining consultation. *Journal of Counseling & Development, 71,* 598–600.

Lindemann, E. (1944). Symptomatology and management of acute grief. *American Journal of Psychiatry, 101,* 141–148.

MacLennan, B. W. (1986). The organization and delivery of mental health consultation in changing times. In F. Mannino, E. Trickett, M. Shore, M. Kidder, & G. Levin, *Handbook of mental health consultation* (pp. 247–278). Rockville, MD: U.S. Department of Health and Human Services, National Institute of Mental Health.

National Association of Social Workers. (2008). *Code of ethics of the National Association of Social Workers.* Retrieved from http://www.socialworkers.org/pubs/code/code.asp

Reddy, L. A., Barboza-Whitehead, S., Files, T., & Rubel, E. (2000). Clinical focus of consultation outcome research with children and adolescents. *Special Services in the Schools, 16*(1/2), 1–22. doi:10.1300/J008v16n01_01

Romney, P. (2008). Consulting for diversity and social justice: Challenges and rewards. *Consulting Psychology Journal: Practice And Research, 60*(2), 139–156. doi:10.1037/0736-9735.60.2.139

Sue, D. W. (2008). Multicultural organizational consultation: A social justice perspective. *Consulting Psychology Journal: Practice and Research, 60,* 157–169.

Swift, C. F., & Cooper, S. (1986). Settings, consultees, and clients. In F. Mannino, E. Trickett, M. Shore, M. Kidder, & G. Levin, *Handbook of mental health consultation* (pp. 247–278). Rockville, MD: U.S. Department of Health and Human Services, National Institute of Mental Health.

Teed, E. L., & Scileppi, J. A. (2007). *The community mental health system: A navigational guide for providers.* Boston, MA: Allyn & Bacon.

U.S. Census Bureau. (2012). *U.S. Census Bureau projections show a slower growing, older, more diverse nation a half century from now.* (Report No. CB12-243). Washington, DC: U.S. Government Printing Office.

Wasylyshyn, K. M. (2003). Executive coaching: An outcome study. *Consulting Psychology Journal: Practice and Research, 55,* 94–106. doi:10.1037/1061-4087.55.2.94

2

The Role of Consultant and Consultee

Introduction

Consultation as a distinct professional service is practiced in a wide variety of settings and disciplines (e.g., medicine, business, education, mental health). The role of the consultant can be viewed broadly or narrowly given the various methods and contexts in which it is applied. Perhaps the most succinct way to begin a discussion about what is a consultant and what does a consultant do may be to employ a refrain heard often in the training of graduate-level counseling practitioners. That is, "It depends." Prior to looking at the elements that distinguish consultant roles, though, it is critical to discuss an issue that is fundamental to and thus binding of consultation across role variation—the centrality of the consultant–consultee relationship.

Any consultation endeavor should begin (continue and end) with the realization that the consultant–consultee relationship, or alliance, is a multidimensional construct found at the heart of any consultation endeavor. This extends to an understanding of the alliance as a multidimension construct that values both the interpersonal and process (i.e., "working") elements of the consultant–consultee dynamic. Therefore, the information in this chapter is presented with the view that consultants must internalize these dimensions while remaining attuned to the unique ethical and environmental conditions that could influence the alliance and, ultimately, consultation outcomes. Further, we challenge the reader to recognize and retain the alliance as a hallmark of any discussion of consultation roles and their implications for consultation outcomes.

As a result of reading this chapter you will

- Understand Bordin's working alliance model as a framework for conceptualizing the relational and procedural elements of the consultant–consultee dynamic
- Examine specific cases and use guided exercises to explore the relational and procedural aspects of Bordin's working alliance model in relation to critical areas of consultation (i.e., role formation & role selection)
- Understand the ethical and multicultural competencies inherent within the consultant's roles and responsibilities
- Understand role structuring and formation and primary considerations for selecting an appropriate consultation role
- Understand the various consultation roles available to consultants and their challenges, benefits, and implications
- Be knowledgeable of the ethical and multicultural competencies inherent within the consultant's roles and responsibilities

The Consultation Relationship: A Working Alliance Perspective

Counseling and allied mental health professions certainly recognize consultant-consultee dynamic as a critical feature of consultation and one that is bolstered by the use of empathy and genuineness (Brown, Pryzwansky, & Shulte, 2011) and the basic listening and attending skills (Ivey, Ivey, & Zalaquett, 2010). For instance, Ivey et al. write that consultants are viewed more positively by consultees when basic listening and attending skills are present. While the importance of these qualities is undeniable, competencies in basic listening and attending skills alone are insufficient in relation to providing a full accounting of the counseling (and consultation) relationship (Gelso & Carter, 1985). That is, the consultant–consultee dynamic, similar to the counselor–client and supervisor–supervisee dynamic, involves both relational and procedural elements (Chen & Bernstein, 2000).

The current view of the consultation relationship implicitly addresses both the relational and procedural elements. Still, we posit that this description does not fully account for the dynamic, multidimensional, and interrelated nature of the consultation alliance. For instance, viewing the consultation relationship solely in terms of establishing and maintaining a supportive, collegial, and support relationship (Gutkin & Curtis, 1999) could result in a failure to link the interpersonal dynamic with the inherent procedural aspect of the dynamic. In essence, recognizing that the consultant–consultee dynamic involves relational and procedural aspects underscores the notion that each element has the potential to impact the dynamic (Fitzpatrick, Iwakabe, & Stalikas, 2005) and outcomes. For instance, a mutual agreement on the consultation goals could be mitigated by a lack of trust between the consultant and consultee. Conversely, disagreements on consultation tasks and goals may be more easily resolved when a strong affective bond is present. As a result, current and future counselor–consultants must consider the full range of factors associated with the consultant–consultee dynamics and, and their potential impact on consultation outcomes To address such concerns, we frame the consultant–consultee relationship through Bordin's 1979 working alliance model, an empirically supported relationship model that requires active consideration of both relational (i.e., interpersonal) and procedural (i.e., working) dimensions of the consultant–consultee dynamic. Applying the model to consultation does, however, require consultants to be aware of the distinctions in form and function among counseling, supervision, and consultation. Table 2.1 highlights key similarities and distinctions among the consultation, counseling, and supervision alliances.

Key insights can also be gained regarding personal characteristics, skills, and behaviors that may impact specific elements of the alliance or the alliance as a whole. In the supervision literature, for instance, studies suggest that supervisor ethical behavior (Ladany, Lehrman-Waterman, Molinaro, & Wolgast, 1999), interpersonal style (Spelliscy, Chen, & Zusho, 2007), and degree of supervisee self-disclosure (Hill & Knox, 2002) can impact the quality of the alliance. More specifically, weaker supervisory alliances have been linked with an increase in supervisee perceptions of unethical behavior by supervisors (Ramos-Sánchez et al., 2002). Research has also illustrated the model's broad applicability and impact on therapeutic (Norcross & Wampold, 2011) and supervisory (Ladany et al., 1999) outcomes. To that end, we strongly encourage readers to remain current on the working alliance research (see additional resources and references at end of chapter).

The following sections provide a more detailed overview of Bordin's working alliance model. Within this review, we call your attention to changes in key descriptors. For example, "relationship" will be replaced with "alliance" and "process/procedure" will be used to illustrate the "working" element of the consultant–consultee dynamic. Additionally, the consultation literature has described *collaboration* as a specific professional service (Brown, Pryzwansky & Schulte, 2011) and competency (Dougherty, 2013) that is applicable in a variety of school- and community-based programs (Friend & Cook, 2012; Mellin, Anderson-Butcher, & Bronstein, 2011; Brown, Pryzwansky & Schulte, 2011). In Bordin's model, collaboration is framed as a core ingredient of the change process (Bordin, 1979, 1983) and refers to the agreement between the key actors (i.e., counselor–client, supervisor–supervisee, consultant–consultee) on critical goals and tasks as well as a quality affective bond. We again urge current and future counselor–consultants to understand the interplay between the two core elements of the alliance and remain flexible given the various dynamics at play in any consultation endeavor.

The Working Alliance Model

Grounded in the psychodynamic tradition, Bordin's 1979 working alliance model holds wide support among counseling and allied mental health disciplines (Bernard &

Table 2.1 Similarities and Distinctions Between Consultation, Counseling/Therapy, and Supervision Alliances

	Similarities	Distinctions
Consultation	• Collaborative & egalitarian orientation[a,b] • Nonevaluative & nonhierarchical • Generally optional • Core goal is to facilitate a more effective professional[c] • Quality alliance is core consideration; includes relational/interpersonal & procedural (i.e., "working") dimensions	• Primary focus is behavioral change • Can be one time event • Nonevaluative • No administrative authority involved[b]
Counseling/ Therapy	• Collaborative & egalitarian orientation[a,b] • Nonevaluative & nonhierarchical[b] • Generally optional • Quality alliance is core consideration; includes relational/interpersonal & procedural (i.e., "working") dimensions	• Considers affective, cognitive, & behavioral dimensions that could hinder positive client outcomes • Generally framed as including more than one professional interaction • Involves an inherent "therapeutic component"
Supervision	• Considers behavioral dimensions • Core goal is to facilitate a more effective professional[c] • Quality alliance is core consideration; includes relational/interpersonal & procedural (i.e., "working") dimensions	• Considers affective, cognitive, & behavioral dimensions that could hinder professional effectiveness & positive supervisee–client outcomes • Can include a short-term therapeutic focus directed at supervisee's growth & development as a clinician • Requires longitudinal interactions with more experienced professionals • Inherently hierarchical and evaluative • Administrative authority often involved

Notes:

a. Bordin, 1979, 1983.

b. Caplan & Caplan, 1999.

c. Bernard & Goodyear, 2013.

Goodyear, 2013; Strauser, Lustig, & Donnell, 2004). The model operates from the stance that "a collaboration for change" (Bordin, 1983, p. 35) must exist between the consultant and consultee. This collaborative aspect, or shared effort, is also an essential feature of consultation relationships (Caplan & Caplan, 1993). Another key parallel between Bordin's alliance model and the consultation relationship is their agreement on creating positive interpersonal connections during the early stages of the alliance (Erchul, Hughes, Meyers, Hickman, & Braden, 1992; Horvath & Symonds, 1991).

Bordin viewed the alliance as a dynamic and pantheoretical model comprised of three interrelated elements: (1) mutual agreement and understanding of (consulting) goals; (2) mutual agreement regarding the tasks associated with reaching (consulting) goals; and (3) the emotional bond between the (consultant and consultee). In the therapeutic sense, then, Bordin (1979) holds that change occurs within the context of these factors, with threats to the integrity of alliance (i.e., personal or professional conflict) serving as the trigger for therapeutic change. In other words, the tear–repair process is a predictable element of any alliance and should be considered an opportunity for growth and development. For example, a disagreement on a behavior change goal causes a consultee to explicitly note concern about the viability of consultation. Such a response could also impact any or all other elements of the alliance. Bordin, however, views this event as an expected part of the alliance and one that offers a clear opportunity to repair and ultimately strengthen the alliance (i.e., tear–repair process). Overall, while distinctions exist between the therapeutic, supervisory, and consultation alliances, we believe Bordin's working alliance model offers current and future counselor-consultants a more complete schematic for conceptualizing the interplay between the interpersonal and procedural elements inherent within consultant–consultee interactions and their potential impact on consultation outcomes than currently exists.

The Working Alliance: Goals

A central premise of Bordin's 1979 model is that the change process, or "collaboration to change" is grounded in the collaborative efforts of the principle actors. Equally relevant to the consultant–consultee dynamic (and outcome) is Bordin's notion that "no change goals can be reached without some basic level of understanding and agreement between the principals involved" (1983, p. 35). In short, designing clear, realistic tasks and goals that address the cognitive, affective, and behavioral domains of a client or organization should be a shared effort between the consultant and consultee. As noted earlier, the dynamic nature of the alliance requires that consultants remain flexible as variables, such as experience level, developmental level, and culture (i.e., individual, systemic, organizational), could impact the alliance in form and function. For example, shared effort may be counterindicated when consultees expect clear direction from the consultant (Graham, 1998). Overall, though, the shared responsibility of key tasks such as task and goal creation presents opportunities to address the positive and negative aspects of the alliance in order to strengthen the relational and procedural dimensions of the consultant–consultee alliance and, by extension, optimize consulting outcomes.

The Working Alliance: Tasks

In the therapeutic sense, tasks include both behavioral and cognitive dimensions (Bordin, 1979). Of critical importance, however, is a realistic connection between the tasks and overall consulting goals. For example, if a consultee's goal is to increase their documentation skills, tasks must be dedicated primarily to improving this stated goal. In short, consulting outcomes hinge largely on the mutually set goals and tasks and degree to which the tasks facilitate goal accomplishment (Bordin, 1979).

The Working Alliance: Bond

The nucleus of the alliance, the bond, is comprised of the mutual liking, caring, and trust occurring within the alliance *over the course of their work together.* Also described by Bordin in 1994 as "partner compatibility," stronger alliances have been found to reduce the impact of conflict within the supervisory dyad and to facilitate more positive therapeutic outcomes (Norcross, 2002; Patton & Kivlighan, 1997). Conversely, weaker therapeutic alliances have been linked with counseling clients terminating treatment at higher rates (Samstag, Batchelder, Muran, Safran, & Winston, 1998). While consideration of the consultation, counseling, and supervision paradigms is important, these findings are included primarily to illustrate the central importance of a strong consultant–consultee alliance. In short, though, the relational and working elements of counseling and consulting recognize are of the fundamental importance when creating and maintaining a strong consultant–consultee bond. Case Illustration 2.1 helps illustrate the bond's influence in creating and sustaining mutually agreed upon consultation tasks and goals.

Case 2.1: An Example of Early Stage Working Alliance Development

The following dialogue involves an initial face-to-face meeting between a consultant and consultee in a children's advocacy center. Following your review, attend to the discussion questions with a classmate or group from the perspective of the working alliance model described above.

Consultee: Dr. Smith, thank you for agreeing to meet with me. I am the chief medical officer of a nonprofit children's advocacy center. We are charged with providing clinical and school-based mental health and behavioral assessment services for a large rural area. I was referred to you by a colleague with whom you have consulted with in the past.

Consultant: Thank you for contacting me. I appreciate the work that you and your colleagues do here at the center and I hope I can be of some service.

Consultee: Thanks, we appreciate your willingness to work with us. My understanding is that your background will really help us better understand the issues we face and how we can accomplish our goals and mission.

Consultant: Great. For starters, please tell me the type of problem(s) you are encountering.

Consultee: Sure. Well, the downturn in the economy has really impacted some of our main funding sources, including two of our most consistent private donors.

(Continued)

(Continued)

Unfortunately, this has required us to let two of our clinical staff members go, including one of only two that hold a professional license. This has been a terribly difficult scenario because we have all worked together for many years and built up many of our services together. It was so hard having to tell them we didn't have the money to keep them anymore. At the same time, of course, families in our area are really struggling and this has led to an increase in the number of children we are being asked to serve. In short, less staff and increasing case loads.

Consultant: I can see why you would be concerned. It does certainly sound like you are being asked to provide the same level of services with fewer resources. I am encouraged and appreciative of your concern for both your employees and clients. If you were to prioritize your needs, what would they be today?

Consultee: I appreciate you saying that. It has been a difficult situation at times for everyone involved. My financial team is telling me we need to probably double our current level of billable hours. I know that's probably accurate, but my goal would be to increase or at least be more efficient in our service to clients and staff productivity, given our funding sources are not likely to improve greatly for a while because of the economy. I think it would be a good idea to use graduate-level mental health interns as a means to provide more services for our clients. Ultimately, I called because we need help deciding how to proceed.

Consultant: You're right—both the staffing and budget concerns are big issues, particularly with the variety of clinical and school-based services you currently offer. Given what you've told me so far, I agree that a solid goal is to improve the efficiency of your staff. First thing I'd like to do then is to have a full staff meeting so I can hear their perspective on what's going on with their programs and clients and what they perceive their needs to be. Once I have that information, I can provide a series of recommendations that will provide your organization with a more efficient way of managing your human and financial assets and of taking care of your clients until the economy rebounds.

Consultee: Well, I guess that's why we hired you. I was a bit concerned because I wasn't sure if your background was consistent with our agency. I have several ideas I think might work, although I'll wait to hear your recommendations first. Maybe once you talk to our full staff, I could touch base with you to answer any additional questions or clarify what you heard to help you in your assessment and recommendations?

Consultant: That would be helpful, yes. First, let's set up the full staff meeting so I can begin gathering the information I need to make my recommendations. I can then provide you with some feedback and recommendations.

Consultee: That will be a good first step. Thank you.

Exercise 2.1: Examining Alliance Development and Strength

1. *What statements or words suggest the consultant is working to create a collaborative working relationship with the consultee?*

2. *Is there a segment of the consultant–consultee dialogue where you could imagine conflict could arise? If yes, where?*

3. *Assume that the consultant responds defensively to the consultee's stated concerns about his or her background by stating, "Well, I've got more experience in these matters than anyone currently at your agency". What implications could this have on the development of a quality working alliance?*

4. *With a partner, role play how you would address this potential "tear" in the alliance and build toward a stronger alliance.*

5. *Consider the elements of the "bond" (i.e., mutual liking, caring, and trust) individually and in combination. Explore your views in relation to their potential influence on the strength of the overall bond and potential consultation outcomes.*

Case 2.2: An Example of a Consultant Assuming a Directive Role

Consultee: Dr. Smith, thank you for agreeing to work with our agency. As I noted on the phone, I am the chief medical officer of an urban mental health clinic. We are charged with providing outpatient and school-based mental health and behavioral assessment services for a large urban area and our recent

(Continued)

(Continued)

audit by Medicaid/Medicare revealed several HIPAA and documentation deficiencies that need to be addressed immediately. I was referred to you by a colleague who stated your expertise in these areas were instrumental in helping her agency address similar concerns. Have you had a chance to review the materials I sent your before your visit this week?

Consultant: I'm looking forward to working with you. Yes, I've reviewed your concerns and several of your clinical files as well as the final Medicaid/Medicare report.

Consultee: Great. Where would you suggest we begin?

Consultant: Ok, in the day and a half I'm scheduled to be here, I'd like to set up several meetings. I'd like to begin with a 1-hour meeting with a representative from the clinical, medical, and administrative staffs, as well as the full executive leadership team in order to clarify staff concerns and highlight the issues from your official Medicaid/Medicare report that need particular attention. Following this meeting, I will provide two 3-hour training sessions. Based on this meeting and the information in the Medicaid/Medicare report, I will provide targeted 3-hour training sessions on improving documentation for your paraprofessional and clinical staffs, respectively. Of course, synthesis between each group will be discussed. The following morning I'd like to schedule a final 2-hour meeting with the executive team and staff representatives. Here I will summarize the previous day's sessions and provide an overview of the key issues contained in my final written report.

Consultee: That sounds great. I'll work out the logistics. We'll see you tomorrow morning.

Consultant: Thank you. I'm looking forward to getting started. See you soon.

**Exercise 2.2: Examining the "Tasks,"
"Goals," and "Bond" Elements of the Consultation Alliance**

Using the dialogue from Cases 2.1 and 2.2, respectively, examine and discuss the following questions related to the consultation alliance.

1. *Identify statements that reflect dialogue consistent with the "task", "goal", and/or "bond" element of the alliance. How might you add to the dialogue that would enhance each element?*

2. *Describe and explain your impression of the "bond" between the consultant and consultee. Be sure to consider each bond element individual and in combination in your response.*

3. *Cases 2.1 and 2.2 have some distinctions. Do you perceive the "goal" and "task" dimensions of the alliance being addressed differently? If so, describe this difference and your view of how such distinctions could influence this alliance and similar future interactions.*

4. *If you were evaluating the consultant's statements and efforts, what feedback would you provide in order to assist him or her in terms of understanding the quality of the consultation alliance and its potential implications for consultation outcomes?*

5. *If you were the consultee in this scenario, would you have responded in a similar fashion to the consultant's remarks? If no, what changes would you suggest to the consultant?*

6. *What is your perception of the "metacommunication" between the consultant and consultee? Consider your response in relation to the dialogue in Cases 2.1 and 2.2 and the notion of metacommunication on the consultation alliance in general.*

The Consultation Role

Role Formulation and Structuring

Establishing clear role parameters in consultation is a crucial process that requires, among other things, attention to the central elements and dynamics of the working alliance model. Creating effective role parameters includes several core elements, including healthy consultant–consultee communication patterns, mutual goal setting, and the establishment and maintenance of a strong bond. Further, these elements correspond well with the relational side of the working alliance model. Research supports this focus on the relational aspect of creating effective role parameters, including findings that link positive working relationships with stronger consulting outcomes (Erchul et al., 1992) and poor communication as an impediment to progress (Tysinger, Tysinger, & Diamanduros, 2009). While the research they cite is consistent with alliance outcome studies (Horvath & Symonds, 1991; Kivlighan & Shaughnessy, 2000; Patton & Kivlighan, 1997), they refrain from stating outright that relationship dynamics are the key considerations in structuring consulting roles.

Role structuring also involves a working, or action-oriented, dimension consistent with the *procedural* portion of the alliance model and again involves the shared effort and agreement between consultant and consultee on goal and task setting. Some consultants may opt to utilize the expert role during this phase in order to mitigate potential problems such as role ambiguity or role conflict that could reduce active, honest communication (Tysinger et al., 2009). Essentially, consultants and consultees are expected to enter into good-faith deliberations in order to design, implement, and maintain clear and ethical role parameters that are best suited to facilitating positive alliances that will lead to the attainment of the agreed upon consulting goals. Both parties must therefore be knowledgeable of their respective positions, roles, and goals, as well as possess the self-awareness to recognize individual beliefs or biases that could help or hinder the establishment of solid consulting role parameters. For example, in the "direct role" scenario in Case 2.2, limited attention is given to setting mutually agreed upon goals, whereas the dialogue in Case 2.1 suggests that the consultant consistently seeks to establish a shared interest in working together from the beginning. Overall, the following tenets of the working alliance model are present and helpful aspects of creating clear consultation roles:

- Collaboration as a core element in the alliance
- Acknowledgement of potential for conflict and recognition of potential impact on establishing and maintaining clear consulting role parameters
- Recognition of the importance of shared goal and task setting
- Mutual agreement on consultation tasks and goals (Parsons & Meyers, 1984)
- Establishment and maintenance of a strong consultant–consultee bond based on the establishment of an egalitarian, nonhierarchical relationship

While the alliance model is an important consideration in creating effective role parameters, several other visions of consultation roles and their parameters are available. Among the more notable models are the continuum based models of Margulies and Raia (1972) and Lippitt and Lippitt (1986). More specifically, Margulies and Raia describe consulting roles as ranging from those with an expertise focus (i.e., task roles) to roles that are more process oriented. For example, a consultant choosing an expert focus would utilize their professional skill set and capabilities to address a particular consultee concern. Consultants choosing the process role, on the other hand, would center their collaborative efforts on detecting or solving identified client problems. Alternatively, Lippitt and Lippitt (1986) view consulting roles as being on a directive-non-directive continuum. For example, the expertise of a consultant employing a directive approach would be more prominently displayed, while a nondirective approach would feature more collaboration, with the consultant seeking to draw upon the expertise of the consultee.

Counselor–consultants should also consider the potential influence of theoretical orientation, ethical mandates, and culture on role structure. In behavioral theory, for example, the consultant–consultee relationship could range from collaborative to directive (Bergan & Kratochwill, 1990; Myrick, 1977). More specifically, during the initial stages of consultation, the consultant may take a more directive role and act as the point person. In doing so, consultants are placed in control of intervention plans, a position that could cause some distress in cases where a weak bond (low level of consultee trust) exists between the consultant and consultee. Of course, strong bonds may allow for a spirited discussion between the consultant and consultee as role parameters are debated and agreed on.

Exercise 2.3: Distinguishing Directive and Process-Oriented Consultation Approaches

Respond to the following questions based on Cases 2.1 and 2.2.

1. *What statements highlight the distinctions between a counselor–consultant using a directive approach versus a counselor–consultant using a process-oriented approach?*

2. *Which approach do you feel you personally are better suited for at this point in your training or career? Why?*

3. *What strengths do you bring to each type of approach? What challenges might you face with each approach?*

Role Selection

Role selection occurs in the initial phase of consultation and is generally addressed as part of a consultation contract. Here again, professional competency and flexibility are crucial given the cultural (Pedersen, 1991), environmental (Zins & Erchul, 2002) and ethical (American Counseling Association [ACA], 2005) variables that could influence outcomes. Predictably, a culturally encapsulated view of any consultation scenario could also influence role selection have implications when selecting a consultation role. For example, a consultant who lacks cultural sensitivity and awareness could get "lost in their expert role" (Corey, Corey, & Callanan, 2011, p. 401) and not consider how different individuals or systems may interpret and respond to this (or any other) role. In effect, cultural encapsulation or lack of sensitivity to diversity could result in a myopic view of the consultation process and lead a consultant to choose a role that is aligned with their personal preference instead of what may be best suited for the consultation job at hand. Alternatively, consultees who use the same expert over extended periods of time may come to believe that familiarity begets understanding, a perspective also rife with potential problems. Proper role selection thus requires that consultants consider "his or her abilities and frame of reference; the model used; the consultee's characteristics related to expectations, coping style, commitment of change, skills levels; the nature of the problem that consultation is attempting to solve"(Dougherty, 2013, p. 36). To do so requires that consultants regularly engage in critical self-reflection to ensure that cultural and environmental factors have been recognized, discussed, and integrated. Further, consultants must also consider the ethical parameters associated with proper role structuring and selection. For example, standard D.2.a. Consultant Competency of the 2005 ACA ethical code reads

> *Counselors take reasonable steps to ensure that they have the appropriate resources and competencies when providing consultation services. Counselors provide appropriate referral resources when requested or needed.*

In short, intentionality should be a core element of role selection (and function) to ensure that the interrelatedness of relational, procedural, cultural, and ethical variables are considered throughout consultation.

Exercise 2.4: Examining Diversity in Role Selection and Function

1. *First, ask yourself how well you know the multicultural competencies and ethical standards related to consultation. What areas and standards do you need to review? What areas and standards are you more comfortable with at this point?*

2. *Describe how multicultural variables (and your own multicultural competencies) could impact how you select a consultation role.*

3. *If you were asked to provide consultation to a facility in a location that is geographically and culturally different from your own, what steps would you take prepare yourself prior to your arrival? How about as the consultation process unfolds?*

4. *Based on your understanding of your own value system and culture, what consultant roles do you find most intuitive and which do you perceive as potentially most challenging? If possible, compare and contrast your perceptions and reasoning with a classmate.*

Consulting Roles

Advocate Role

The role of advocate is well known to counselors and involves working individually (Tysl, 1997) or in tandem with clients to address their personal and social needs (Linz, McAnally, & Wieck, 1989) through specialized services (Jenkins & Einzig, 1996). Examples may include a broad range of community-based efforts geared toward policy changes that would benefit the social or educational needs and development of clients (McClure & Russo, 1996). In the consulting paradigm, advocacy assumes a directive stance whereby consultants use their influence (Kirst-Ashman & Hull, 2012) to try and effect change. Consultants may utilize this role by advocating for the acquisition of needed resources, increased (or initiation) of preventative health programs, or by aiding others in their attempts to develop more effective decision making (Kurpius & Lewis, 1988). In other words, the advocate role is used by consultants to facilitate individual, organizational/systems changes, such as schools or community-based programs or services (Dahir & Stone, 2009; Lewis, Lewis, Daniels, & D'Andrea, 2011; Lopez-Baez & Paylo, 2009; Speight & Vera, 2009).

The advocacy role in consultation continues to expand, bolstered by the creation and adoption of core advocacy competencies (Lewis, Arnold, House, & Toporek, 2003). The advocate role is also aligned with the social justice belief of advocating on behalf of those who lack the ability to act on their own behalf in both community (Lewis et al., 2011) and school settings (Williams & Greenleaf, 2012). The Individuals with Disabilities Education Act (IDEA), for instance, affords consultants an opportunity to engage diversity issues by choosing a role that promotes a social justice platform, such as a school-based consultant advocating for programs and services that maximize the educational achievement of students with disabilities. As with any consulting action or intervention, consultants should engage in considered self-reflection (Lee, 2007) to ensure their actions are intentional and ethical (ACA, 2005; Remley, 1988) prior to actively pursuing this role. A consultant who is unclear of the parameters of advocacy can turn to standard A.6.a Advocacy of the 2005 ACA ethical code for guidance, which reads

> *When appropriate, counselors advocate at individual, group, institutional, and societal levels to examine potential barriers and obstacles that inhibit access and/or the growth and development of clients.*

Expert Role

If you ever equated the role of a consultant with that of an "expert", you are in good company. The expert role is the most frequently utilized consulting role (Dougherty, 2009), yet like all other role options is indicated only when the consultant has the appropriate training and competencies (see, e.g., ACA standard D.2.a) given the authority (explicit and implicit) that often accompanies the expert role. For example, consultees who seek out experts are assuming that a consultant has the knowledge base and skill set(s) to accurately discern and address their problem or concerns (Stroh &

Johnson, 2006). Other expert role actions could include diagnostic- or solution-based activities (Dougherty, 2009). Case Illustration 2.4 provides an illustration of the expert role in consultation.

Case 2.3: Challenges Encountered When Assuming the Expert Role

Dr. B, a well-respected counseling professional and consultant from a top urban university in the Northeast was hired at great expense by a rural mental health clinic in the South in hopes of streamlining and, if needed, adding specialized services to meet the needs of their clientele. According to all who met with Dr. B, he was professional, knowledgeable, pleasant, and appeared to have a genuine interest in helping the clinic reach their goals. However, as Dr. B outlined his findings and made suggestions, it quickly became clear to all (administrators, practitioners, and support staff) that Dr. B had not fully anticipated or comprehended the true nature of many of the issues the clinic was facing. For example, Dr. B recommended adding more in-home clinical and case management services. In his view and experience, this would bolster the clinic's presence and reputation in their service while addressing the clinic's funding needs by creating services amenable to third-party billing. Yet, despite hearing the client's concerns about geographical isolation, stigmatization of mental health within their rural community, and limited employee resources, Dr. B's suggestions, in the eyes of the client, did not fully address the nature of the problems outlined and, as such, were viewed as interesting but mostly unfeasible given the current financial, geographical, and cultural nuances of the clinic. Ultimately, the clinic chose not to implement any of his suggestions. In short, despite Dr. B's expertise and genuine interest in the well-being of the clinic and its clients, his lack of awareness of the cultural nuances of such a rural area (and, perhaps rural mental health clinics in general and in the South specifically) led to reasonable and well-intentioned suggestions that, ultimately, were unfeasible for this particular clinic given its geographical isolation, cultural stigma against mental health, and the agency's limited employee and financial resources.

This example addresses two distinct dimensions of the expert role. First, the consultant used her expertise to discern the primary systemic and organizational barriers that could be part of the reduction in student engagement in the counseling and psychological services (CAPS). Further, she made several recommendations for resolving the problem of decreased student engagement in CAPS that were based on her accepted clinical and administrative expertise. She also maintained her professional distance in her formal findings and recommendations, a move that allows her to remain clear of direct service provision and require the consultee(s) to develop their own expertise (Lippitt & Lippitt, 1986).

Trainer–Educator Role

The trainer–educator role includes formal and informal dimensions (Dougherty, 2009), although divergent views remain as to whether the prearranged nature of formal training (i.e., seminars) are legitimate consulting roles (Conoley & Conoley, 1992; Lippitt & Lippitt, 1986). What is consistent is that counselors will likely have considerable exposure to consultants using the trainer–educator roles given the need to gain the continuing education credits necessary to retain professional licensure. Like the expert role, the trainer–educator role also assumes the consultant has the specific content knowledge and professional skill set expected of a professional colleague. Case 2.4 illustrates a consultant using the trainer–educator role.

Case 2.4: An Example of a Consultant Assuming the Trainer–Educator Role

Dr. C, a counselor educator, licensed professional counselor, and state-endorsed clinical supervisor, is providing a seminar to the site supervisors who provide supervision to master's level practicum and internship counselors-in-training. The stated goal of the seminar is to provide master's level and licensed counseling professionals with an empirically-based framework for the provision of supervision. To attain this goal, the trainer–educator provides an hour-long lecture on two well-known, evidence-based supervision models along with supporting and outcome data on the models. Following the lecture, the trainer–educator and attendees engage in a more informal dialogue geared toward clarifying the models or other issues identified by the attendees. The final element of the seminar features experiential exercises where attendees are challenged to apply the models to vignettes of real or realistically imagined supervision scenarios. As the attendees are formulating their responses, the trainer–educator made himself available to assist attendees as they grappled with understanding and applying the models. At the conclusion of the seminar, the trainer–educator provided a formal document of participation (i.e., continuing education unit [CEU]) with his professional contact information so attendees could communicate with him about supervision issues in the future.

This scenario highlights several elements of the trainer–educator role. First, the formal setting of a seminar is a common mode of consultant–consultee interaction. Second, the seminar aligns with both the trainer and educator roles (Dougherty, 2009). That is, the seminar is led by a counselor educator who possesses advanced supervision training and skills and created a training format where content (education) and experiential exercises (training) can be utilized for advancing the knowledge base and skill set of attendees. In this narrative, the consultant addresses this concern by challenging attendees to conceptualize the models presented through practice-based clinical vignettes. The consultant's willingness to offer his contact information provides attendees with another potential resource for attendees and highlights the role's focus on making positive longitudinal change for the consultee.

Exercise 2.5: Examining the Trainer–Educator Role

1. *What type of qualifications do you feel would best serve you (or any consultant) who might choose the trainer–educator role?*

2. *Given that a seminar format is often the setting, how would you rate your public speaking skills? How would you improve/continue to improve this key skill set?*

3. *If you were the consultee in this scenario, would it matter if the trainer–educator was a pure academic, had related professional work experiences, or had a blend of academic and related work experience? Elaborate on your response.*

4. *If you chose the role of trainer–educator, what level of contact, and for how long after the consultation ended, would you be willing to engage with the consultee? Explain your reasoning.*

Collaborator Role

Distinguishing collaboration and the role of collaborator in consultation remains elusive (Schulte & Osborne, 2003) and can be confusing at times. Dougherty (2013), for example, reminds us "that the role of collaborator for a consultant is distinct from the service of collaboration" (p. 40). While consultation can involve persuasion (Zins & Erchul, 2002), decision making within consultation is very often thought of as a shared venture between participants (Bordin, 1979; Bryan & Holcome-McCoy, 2007; Caplan, 1970; Macmann et al., 1996). This is seen in the fact that a collaborator role can parallel the expert role (Tysinger et al., 2009), such as when a consultant relies on a consultee to affirm or adapt the expert's suggestions when both have deemed it appropriate. In other words, the collaborator role can fall on a directive or nondirective continuum (Gutkin, 1999), although the degree to which a consultant should use a direct approach in the collaborator role remains unclear (Tysinger et al., 2009). Perhaps unsurprisingly, the collaborator role has also been found to contribute to a healthy working alliance between the consultant and consultee (Meyers, Proctor, Graybill, & Meyers, 2009). What is consistent is that the collaborator role offers consultants an opportunity to share their expertise in a manner that solicits and then honors the consultee's experiences, knowledge, and needs to co-design a means for accomplishing a specific goal.

Fact Finder Role

Fact finding is a common role with the predictable goal of gaining information. Counselor–consultants routinely draw from their counseling knowledge and skills given the need for gathering information, analyzing information, and then providing feedback to the consultee (Lippitt & Lippitt, 1986). For starters, consultants must clarify the reason underlying the choice of fact finder. Dougherty (2013) notes, for example, that appropriate use of this role requires that information gathering be, on balance, a bidirectional effort. If satisfied, attention can turn to the type of information sought (Caplan & Caplan, 1993) and the best collection method(s) available to ensure interventions can be properly evaluated (McLean, 2006). Among the most sought after data by consultants are genetic data, current descriptive data, process data, interpretive data, consultee–client system relationship data, and client system behavior data (Bergan & Kratochwill, 1990; Caplan & Caplan, 1993). Data collection methods include formal consultee or organizational records (McLean, 2006), formal interviews (Busse & Beaver, 2000), consultee observations (Skinner, Dittmer, & Howell, 2000), and surveys and questionnaires (McLean, 2006). For example, a consultant interested in understanding a consultee's clinical caseload may seek current clinical records at the consultee's agency, while consultants interested in how the consultee experiences interactions with clients may choose to conduct interviews. Although interviews may require more time and financial resources (McLean, 2006), advantages include more detailed information (Kratochwill, Sheridan, Carlson, & Lasecki, 1999) and options for adapting interviews to the client or context (Egan, 2005) in order to optimize chances for collecting key data. For a consultant interested in interpretive data, or information with clear subjective and affective features, an unstructured interview may be the best option as they are generally directive and would allow the interviewees (clients/consultees) the freedom to disclose information at their own pace and depth. As always, consideration must be given to personal, cultural, or ethical and legal factors so data collection (White-Kress, Eriksen, Rayle, & Ford, 2005), and the consultation relationship and process as a whole, remain sound.

Process Specialist Role

Consultants opting for the process specialist role will encounter a less directive approach that allows them to address *how* a specific process influences present behavior (Dougherty, 2013). Consider, for example, you are a counseling intern at a school or mental health agency attending your first formal staff or faculty meeting. Prior to the meeting, the clinical supervisor or principal introduced "J. P.," a consultant hired to help individual employees and the organization as a whole function more efficiently. To your surprise, however, you note considerable discord among certain staff members, and on at least two occasions, staff members use "gallows humor" and derogatory terms when describing specific clients or students. If you were the consultant, how would you handle this scenario? We will address it using the process observer and process facilitator roles (Kormanski & Eschbach, 1997).

For example, a consultant using the process observer role may help facilitate the group's discussion on staff discord or the current use of humor at the workplace, provide feedback on the quality of staff communication patterns, or, when appropriate, model or suggest effective problem resolution strategies for resolving staff discord and clarifying acceptable uses of humor with clients and in the workplace. In doing so, consultants should remain responsive to the individual or organizational goals of the consultee and refrain from addressing specific interpersonal issues unless requested (Schein, 1999). Alternatively, the process facilitator would assume a more active role in helping the administrator process the meeting's agenda items, such as asking the staff specific questions about their reactions to the discord between their peers and the use of gallows humor and their perceptions of how it impacted the meeting. By doing so, the focus is not on a longer term goal such as creating appropriate "humor parameters" in the workplace but on highlighting for staff members (and organizations) how the process(es) manifesting within the meeting impact present outcomes—in this case accomplishing the meeting's agenda. Regardless of the role, though, process specialists attend to processes that impact present actions while (unless directed) avoiding interpersonal issues (Schein, 1999). The above scenario illustrates how challenging this could be at times. Case illustration 2.5 provides a short example of how a consultant using the process specialist role engages a consultee.

Case 2.5: An Example of a Consultant Assuming a Process Role

Consultee: Dr. Smith, thank you for agreeing to work with our agency. As I noted on the phone, I am the chief medical officer of an urban mental health clinic. We are charged with providing outpatient and school-based mental health and behavioral assessment services for a large urban area and our recent audit by Medicaid/Medicare revealed several HIPAA and documentation deficiencies that need to be addressed immediately. I was referred to you by a colleague who stated your expertise in these areas were instrumental in helping her agency address similar concerns. Have you had a chance to review the materials I sent you before your visit this week?

Consultant: I'm looking forward to working with you. Yes, I've reviewed your concerns and several of your clinical files as well as the final Medicaid/Medicare report.

Consultee: Great. Where would you suggest we begin?

Consultant: Ok, in the day and a half I'm scheduled to be here, I'd like to set up several meetings. I'd like to start with a 1-hour morning meeting with the executive leadership. I'd like to then have a 1-hour meeting with a representative from the clinical, medical, and administrative staffs, as well as the full executive leadership team in order to gain a better understanding of their concerns and highlight key issues I noted from your official Medicaid/Medicare report. Following this meeting, I will facilitate two 3-hour meetings

> with your paraprofessional and clinical staffs where we will focus on HIPAA and Medicaid/Medicare documentation and discuss the key elements of your agency's formal Medicaid/Medicare report. The following morning before I depart, I will facilitate a final 2-hour meeting with the leadership team and representatives from the clinical, paraprofessional, and administrative staffs. Here I will facilitate a discussion with the intention of clarifying what has been learned and help all sides create appropriate future goals to improve communication between and among all agency levels so specific trainings can be more quickly identified and issues such as poor documentation can be addressed. I will also provide the key insights from my formal written report and answer any questions related to my report.
>
> Consultee: That sounds great. I'll work out the logistics. We'll see you tomorrow morning.
>
> Consultant: Thank you. I'm looking forward to getting started. See you soon.

A final area of consideration when choosing a consulting role involves the paradigm in which the role will be selected and applied. External consultants, for example, may be more objective and less prone to internalizing or being swayed by negative organizational dynamics, yet may experience more constraints on their activities or access to an organization's interpersonal and structural dynamics (Stroh & Johnson, 2006). The world of the internal consultant also has advantages and disadvantages. For one, an internal consultant, or one who is a member of the organization in which they are asked to consult, may possess a deeper and more nuanced understanding of the organization's dynamics and the reasoning behind hiring an internal consultant instead of seeking a more objective perspective. There is no doubt that while an internal consultant may be valuable in clarifying both useful and problematic organizational dynamics, they may also be more susceptible to organizational hierarchies (Caplan & Caplan-Moskovich, 2004) and politics (Block, 2000) that could temper access or impact the extent that their final recommendations would be considered or implemented by organizational leaders.

Chapter Keystones

- Consultation relationships are the core of any consultation interaction. This chapter introduces Bordin's working alliance model as the framework for understanding the relational *and* procedural (i.e., "working/action") dimensions of consultant–consultee interactions.
- The consultant–consultee alliance draws from Bordin's working alliance model and believes that the change process involves a mutual agreement between the consultant and consultee on goals, the tasks necessary to accomplish the goals, and a quality affective bond between them (i.e., mutual liking, caring, and trust).

- Multicultural competence, as well as adherence to appropriate ethical and legal standards, must remain a core element of any decision surrounding the alliance and consulting role.
- Consultants have several roles available to them. Selecting the best "fit" requires attention to cultural, ethical, legal, individual (i.e., consultant and consultee), organizational, and theoretical (see, e.g., working alliance model) dimensions.
- Selecting the most effective consultation role requires thoughtful consideration of role structure and the relational and procedural implications of each type.
- This chapter outlines several widely recognized consultation roles, including: (a) advocate, (b) expert, (c) trainer–educator, (d) collaborator, (e) fact finder, and (f) process specialist. Regardless of choice, the consultants must carefully consider the potential for the role to facilitate goal attainment.

Web-Based and Literature-Based Resources

Websites

American Psychological Association (APA), Division 13: Society of Consulting Psychology: http://www.apa .org/about/division/div13.aspx

Suggested Readings

Bernard, J. M., & Goodyear, R. K. (2013). *Fundamentals of clinical supervision* (5th ed.). Upper Saddle River, NJ: Pearson.

Bordin, E. S. (1979, Fall). The generalizability of the psychoanalytic concept of the working alliance. *Psychotherapy: Theory, Research and Practice, 16*, 252–260.

Bordin, E. S. (1983). A working alliance based model of supervision. *Counseling Psychologist, 11*, 35–42.

References

American Counseling Association. (2005). ACA code of ethics (Rev. ed.). Alexandria, VA: Author.

Arredondo, P., Toporek, R., Brown, S. P. Jones., Locke, D. C., Sanchez, J., & Stadler, H. (1996). Operationalization of the multicultural counseling competencies. *Journal of Multicultural Counseling and Development, 24*(1), 42–78.

Baruth, L. G., & Manning, M. L. (2007). *Multicultural counseling and psychotherapy: A lifespan perspective* (4th ed.). Upper Saddle River, NJ: Pearson.

Bergan, J. R., & Kratochwill, T. R. (1990). *Behavioral consultation and therapy.* New York, NY: Plenum Press.

Bernard, J. M. (1997). The discrimination model. In C. E. Watkins (Ed.), *Handbook of psychotherapy supervision* (pp. 310–327). New York, NY: Wiley.

Bernard, J. M., & Goodyear, R. K. (2009). *Fundamentals of clinical supervision* (4th ed.). Upper Saddle River, NJ: Pearson.

Bernard, J. M., & Goodyear, R. K. (2013). *Fundamentals of clinical supervision* (5th ed.). Upper Saddle River, NJ: Pearson.

Block, P. (2000). *Flawless consulting: A guide to getting your expertise used* (2nd ed.). San Francisco, CA: Jossey-Bass.

Bordin, E. S. (1979, Fall). The generalizability of the psychoanalytic concept of the working alliance. *Psychotherapy: Theory, Research and Practice, 16*, 252–260.

Bordin, E. S. (1983). A working alliance based model of supervision. *Counseling Psychologist, 11*, 35–42.

Bordin, E. S. (1994). Theory and research on the therapeutic working alliance: New directions. In A. Horvath & L. Greenberg (Eds.), *The working alliance: Theory, research, and practice* (pp. 13–37). New York, NY: Wiley.

Brown, D., Pryzwansky, W. B., & Shulte, A. C. (2011). *Psychological consultation and collaboration: Introduction to theory and practice* (7th ed.). Upper Saddle River, NJ: Pearson.

Bryan, J., & Holcomb-McCoy, C. (2007). An examination of school counselor involvement in school-family-community partnerships. *Professional School Counseling, 10*, 441–454.

Busse, R. T., & Beaver, B. R. (2000). Informant report: Parent and teacher interviews. In E. S. Shapiro & T. R. Kratochwill (Eds.), *Conducting school-based assessments of child and adolescent behavior* (pp. 235–251). New York, NY: Guilford Press.

Caplan, G., & Caplan, R. B. (1993). *Mental health consultation and collaboration.* New York: Basic Books.

Caplan, G., & Caplan, R.B. (1999). Mental health consultation and collaboration. Prospect Heights, IL: Waveland Press. (Originally published 1993)

Caplan, G., & Caplan-Moskovich, R. B. (2004). Recent advances in mental health consultation. In N. M. Lambert, I. Hylander, & J. H. Sandoval (Eds.), *Consultee-centered consultation: Improving the quality of professional services in schools and community organizations* (pp. 21–35). Mahwah, NJ: Erlbaum.

Chan, F., Shaw, L. R., McMahon, B. T., Koch, L., & Strauser, D. (1997). A model for enhancing rehabilitation counselor-consumer working relationships. *Rehabilitation Counseling, 41*, 122–137.

Chang, C. Y., & Gnilka, P. B. (2010). Social justice counseling. In D. G. Hays & B. T. Erford, *Developing multicultural counseling competence: A systems approach* (pp. 53–71). Upper Saddle River, NJ: Pearson.

Chen, E. C., & Bernstein, B. L. (2000). Relations of complementarity and supervisory issues to supervisory working alliance: A comparative analysis of two cases. *Journal of Counseling Psychology, 47(4)*, 485–497.

Conoley, J. C., & Conoley, C. W. (1992). *School consultation: Practice and training* (2nd ed.) Boston, MA: Allyn & Bacon.

Corey, G., Corey, M. S., & Callanan, P. (2010). *Issues and ethics in the helping professions* (8th ed.). Belmont, CA: Brooks/Cole.

Dahir, C. A., & Stone, C. B. (2009). School counselor accountability: The path to social justice and systemic change. *Journal of Counseling & Development, 87*, 12–20.

Dougherty, A. M. (2009). *Psychological consultation and collaboration in school and community settings* (5th ed.). Davis, CA: Brooks/Cole.

Dougherty, A.M. (2013). *Psychological consultation and collaboration in school and community settings* (6th ed.). Davis, CA: Brooks/Cole.

Egan, G. (2005) *Essentials of skilled helping: Managing problems, developing opportunities.* Belmont, CA: Wadsworth Thompson.

Erchul, W. P., Hughes, J. N., Meyers, J., Hickman, J. A., & Braden, J. P. (1992). Dyadic agreement concerning the consultation process and its relationship to outcome. *Journal of Educational and Psychological Consultation, 3(2)*, 119–132.

Fitzpatrick, M. R., Iwakabe, S., & Stalikas, A. (2005). Perspective divergence in the working alliance. *Psychotherapy Research, 15(1-2)*, 69–79.

Friend, M., & Cook, L. (2012). *Interactions: collaboration skills for school professionals* (7th ed.). New York, NY: Pearson.

Gelso, C. J., & Carter, J. A. (1985). The relationship in counseling and psychotherapy: Components, consequences, and theoretical antecedents. *The Counseling Psychologist, 13(2)*, 155–194.

Goering, P., Wasylenki, D., Lindsay, S., Lemire, D., & Rhodes, A. (1997). Process and outcome in a hostel outreach program for homeless clients with severe mental illness. *American Journal of Orthopsychiatry, 67*, 607–617.

Graham, D.S. (1998). Consultant effectiveness and treatment acceptability: An examination of consultee requests and consultant responses. *School Psychology Quarterly, 13*, 155-168.

Gutkin, T. B. (1999). Collaborative versus directive/prescriptive/expert school-based consultation: Reviewing and resolving a false dichotomy. *Journal of School Psychology, 37*, 161–190.

Gutkin, T. B., & Curtis, M. J. (1999). School-based consultation theory and practice: The art and science of indirect service delivery. In C. R. Reynolds & T. B. Gutkin (Eds.), *The handbook of school psychology* (3rd ed., pp. 598–637). New York, NY: Wiley.

Horvath, A. O., & Symonds, B. D. (1991). Relation between the working alliance and outcome in psychotherapy: A meta-analysis. *Journal of Counseling Psychology, 38*(2), 139–149.

Ivey, A. E., Ivey, M. B., & Zalaquett, C. (2010). *Intentional interviewing and counseling: Facilitating client development in a multicultural society.* Belmont, CA: Brooks/Cole.

Jenkins, G., & Einzig, H. (1996). Counselling in primary care. In R. Bayne, I. Horton, & J. Bimrose (Eds.), *New directions in counseling* (pp. 97–108). London, UK: Routledge.

Kirst-Ashman, K. K., & Hull, G. H., Jr. (2012). *Generalist practice with organizations and communities* (5th ed.). Belmont, CA: Brooks/Cole.

Kivlighan, D. M., Jr., & Shaughnessy, P. (2000). Patterns of working alliance development. A typology of client's working alliance ratings. *Journal of Counseling Psychology, 47*, 362–371.

Kokotovic, A. M., & Tracey, T. J. (1990). Working alliance in the early phase of counseling. *Journal of Counseling Psychology, 37*, 16–21.

Kormanski, C., & Eschbach, L. (1997). From group leader to process consultant. In H. Forester Miller J. A. Kottler (Eds.), *Issues and Challenges for Group Practitioners* (pp. 133–164). Denver, CO: Love.

Kratochwill, T. R., Elliott, S. N., & Callan-Stoiber, K. (2002). Best practices in school-based problem-solving consultation. In A. Thomas and J. Grimes (Eds.), Best practices in school psychology (4th ed., pp. 583–608). Bethesda, MD: National Association of School Psychologists.

Kratochwill, T. R., & Pittman, P.H. (2002). Expanding problem-solving consultation training: Prospects and frameworks. *Journal of Educational and Psychological Consultation, 13*(1), 69–95.

Kratochwill, T. R., Sheridan, S. M., Carlson, J., & Lasecki, K. L. (1999). Advances in behavioral assessment. In C. R. Reynolds & T. B. Gutkin (Eds.), *The handbook of school psychology* (3rd ed., pp. 350–382). New York, NY: Wiley.

Kurpius, D. J., & Lewis, J. E. (1988). Introduction to consultation: An intevention for advocacacy and outreach. In D. J. Kurpius & D. Brown (Eds.), *Handbook of consultation: An intervention for advocacy and outreach* (pp. 1–4). Alexandria, VA: American Association for Counseling and Development.

Ladany, N., Lehrman-Waterman, D. E., Molinaro, M., & Wolgast, B. (1999). Psychotherapy supervisor ethical practices: Adherence to guidelines, the supervisory working alliance, and supervisee satisfaction. *The Counseling Psychologist, 27*, 443–475.

Ladany, N., & Freidlander, M. L. (1995). The relationship between the supervisory working alliance and trainees' experience of role conflict and role ambiguity. *Counselor Education and Supervision, 34*(3), 220–231.

Ladany, N., Hill, C. E., Corbett, M. M, & Nutt, E. A. (1996). Nature, extent, and importance of what psychotherapy trainees do not disclose to their supervisors. *Journal of Counseling Psychology, 43*, 10–24.

Lee, C. C. (Ed.). (2007). *Counseling for social justice* (2nd ed.). Alexandria, VA: American Counseling Association.

Lewis, J. A., Arnold, M. S., House, R., & Toporek, R. L. (2003). *Advocacy competencies: Task force on advocacy competencies.* Alexandria, VA: American Counseling Association. Retrieved from http://www.counseling .org/Content/NavigationMenu/RESOURCES/ADVOCACYCOMPETENCIES/ advocacy_competen cies1.pdf

Lewis, J. A., Lewis, M. D., Daniels, J. A., & D'Andrea, M. J. (2011). *Community counseling: A multicultural-social justice perspective* (4th ed.). Pacific Grove, CA: Brooks/Cole.

Linz, M. H., McAnnaly, P., & Wieck, C. (Ed.). (1989). *Case management: Historical, current, and future perspectives.* Cambridge, MA: Brookline Books.

Lippitt, G., & Lippitt, R. (1986). *The consulting process in action* (2nd ed.). La Jolla, CA: University Associates.

Lopez-Baez, S. I., & Paylo, M. J. (2009). Social justice advocacy: Community collaboration and systems advocacy. *Journal of Counseling & Development, 87*, 276–283.

Lott, B., & Rogers, M.R. (2005). School consultants working for equity with families, teachers, and administrators. *Journal of Educational and Psychological Consultation, 16*, 1–16.

Macmann, G. M., Barnett, D. W., Allen, S. J., Bramlett, R. K., Hall, J. D., & Ehrhardt, K. E. (1996). Problem solving and intervention design: Guidelines for the evaluation of technical adequacy. *School Psychology Quarterly, 11*, 137–148.

Margulies, N., & Raia, A. P. (1972). Emerging issues in organizational development. In N. Margulies & A. P. Raia (Eds.), *Organizational development: Values, process, and technology* (pp. 475–478). New York, NY: McGraw-Hill.

Martens, B. K., & McIntyre, I. E. (2009).The importance of treatment integrity in school-based behavioral interventions. In A. Akin-Little, S. G. Little, M. A. Bray, & T. J. Kehle (Eds.), *Behavioral interventions in schools: Evidence-based positive strategies* (pp. 59–71). Washington DC: American Psychological Association.

McClure, B. A., & Russo, T. R. (1996). The politics of counseling: Looking back and looking forward. *Counseling and Values, 40*, 162–174.

McLean, G. N. (2006). *Organization development.* San Francisco, CA: Berrett-Koehler.

Mellin, E.A., Anderson-Butcher, D., & Bronstein, L. (2011). Strengthening interprofessional team collaboration: Potential roles for school mental health professionals. Advances in School Mental Health Promotion, 4, 51–61.

Meyers, J., Proctor, S. L. Graybill, E. C., & Meyers, A. B. (2009). Organizational consultation and system intervention. In T. B., Gutkin & C. R. Reynolds (Eds.), *The handbook of school psychology* (4th ed., pp. 921–940). Hoboken, NJ: Wiley.

Myrick, R. D. (1977). *Consultation as a counselor intervention.* Ann Arbor, MI: Eric Counseling and Personnel Services Information Center.

Norcross, J. C., & Wampold, B. E. (2011). What works for whom: Tailoring psychotherapy to the person. *Journal of Clinical Psychology, 67*(2), 127–132.

Parsons, R. D., & Meyers, J. (1984). *Developing consultation skills: A guide to training, development, and assessment for human services professionals.* San Francisco, CA: Jossey-Bass.

Patton, M. J., & Kivlighan, D. M., Jr. (1997). Relevance of the supervisory alliance to the counseling alliance and to treatment adherence in counselor training. *Journal of Counseling Psychology, 44*(1), 108–115.

Pedersen, P. B. (1991). Multiculturalism as a generic approach to counseling. *Journal of Counseling and Development, 70*, 6–12.

Ramos-Sánchez, L., Esnil, E., Riggs, S., Wright, L. K., Goodwin, A., Touster, L. O., . . . & Rodolfa, E. (2002). Negative supervisory events: Effects on supervision satisfaction and supervisory alliance. *Professional Psychology: Research and Practice, 33*(2), 197–202.

Remley, T. P., Jr. (1988). Consultative advocacy differentiated from legal advocacy. In D. J. Kurpius & D. Brown (Eds.), *Handbook of consultation: An intervention for advocacy and outreach* (pp. 18–26). Alexandria, VA: American Association for Counseling and Development.

Samstag, L. W., Batchelder, S. T., Muran, J. C., Safran, J. D., & Winston, A. (1998). Early identification of treatment failures in short-term psychotherapy: An assessment of therapeutic alliance and interpersonal behavior. *Journal of Psychotherapy Practice & Research, 7*, 126–143.

Schein, E. H. (1990). Back to the future: Recapturing the OD vision. In E. Massarick (Ed.), *Advances in Organizational Development* (Vol. 1, pp. 13–26). Norwood, NJ: Ablex.

Schein, E. H. (1999). *Process consultation revisited: Building the helping relationship.* Reading, MA: Addison-Wesley.

Schulte, A. C., & Osborn, S. S. (2003). When assumptive worlds collide: A review of definitions of collaboration in consultation. *Journal of Educational and Psychological Consultation, 14*(2), 109–138.

Skinner, C. H., Dittmer, K. I., & Howell, L. A. (2000). Direct observation in school settings: Theoretical issues. In E. S. Shapiro & T. R. Kratochwill (Eds.), *Behavioral assessment in schools* (2nd ed., pp. 19–77). New York, NY: Guilford Press.

Snyder, E. P., Quirk, K., & Dematteo, F. (2001). Consulting with families, schools, and communities. In T. M. Lionetti, E. P. Snyder, & R. W. Christner (Eds.), *A practical guide to building professional competencies in school psychology* (pp. 69–81). New York, NY: Springer.

Speight, S. L., & Vera, E. M. (2009). The challenge of social justice for school psychologists. *Journal of Educational and Psychological Consultation, 19,* 82–92.

Spelliscy, D., Chen, E. E., & Zusho, A. (2007, August). *Predicting supervisee role conflict and ambiguity: A path analytic model.* Paper presented at the annual meeting of the American Psychological Association, San Francisco, CA.

Strauser, D. R., Lustig, D. C., & Donnell, C. (2004). The relationship between working alliance and therapeutic outcomes for individuals with mild mental retardation. *Rehabilitation Counseling Bulletin, 47*(4), 215–224.

Stroh, L. K., & Johnson, H. H. (2006). *The basic principles of effective consulting.* Mahway, NJ: Erlbaum.

Tysinger, P. D., Tysinger, J. A., & Diamanduros, T. (2009). Teacher expectations on the directiveness continuum of consultation. *Psychology in the Schools, 46*(4), 319–332.

White-Kress, V. E., Eriksen, K. P., Rayle, A. D., & Ford, S. J. W. (2005). The DMM-IV-TR and culture: Considerations for counselors. *Journal of Counseling and Development, 83,* 97–104.

Williams, J. M., & Greenleaf, A. T. (2012). Ecological psychology: Potential contributions to social justice and advocacy in school settings. *Journal of Educational and Psychological Consultation, 22,* 141–157.

Zins, J. E., & Erchul, W. P. (2002). Best practices in school consultation. In A. Thomas & J. Grimes (Eds.), *Best practices in school psychology* (4th ed., pp. 625–643). Bethesda, MD: National Association of School Psychologists.

Necessary Skills of a Consultant

Introduction

What Skills and Tools Are Commonly Used as a Consultant?

Working as a consultant requires knowledge of consultation models, stages, and context. Regardless of what model you use in your consultation activities, what stage you are in the process, or where you find yourself consulting . . . there are some basic skills necessary of the counselor serving as a consultant. This chapter reviews some elements that are considered the foundational skills of consultation. It also covers multicultural or diversity competencies expected of the counselor serving as a consultant.

In this chapter, we define the difference between internal and external consultation activities and address how these activities may differ as nonprofit and for-profit consultations. Fiscal and organizational responsibilities are discussed. Specific attention is paid to the generation of proposals, contracts, workshops or trainings, marketing, and fee structuring.

A particular highlight of this chapter is a discussion of the use of technology in consultation, with the disclosure, acknowledgment, and understanding that this content is constantly changing. We wrap up the chapter with a general review of what content might be included in a written consultation report.

After reading this chapter, you will be able to

- Identify the common foundational skills utilized in all types of consultation activities
- Describe core competencies of consultation with respect to multiculturalism and diversity
- Define internal and external consultation activities
- Differentiate between nonprofit and for-profit consultation activities
- Apply some strategies for generating consultation proposals
- Compose simple and straightforward consultation contracts
- Organize the provision of trainings and workshops as a consultant
- Employ some basic strategies for marketing yourself as a consultant
- Construct a fee structure for yourself as an external consultant
- Discuss some ideas for the different types of technology you might use as a consultant
- Relate an ethical framework for the use of technology as a consultant
- Draft a thorough and comprehensive consultation report

Foundational Skills

What are the counselor characteristics and behaviors that influence the consultation process? This section addresses what are generally regarded as the essential skills in which every consultant should be proficient.

As a consultant, you may learn multiple models for functioning as a professional consultant: You may develop an advanced knowledge of theories and applications within different contexts; you may know all there is to know about what it takes to serve as a consultant in a variety of settings; and you may be the world's biggest expert on a subject and be in constant demand for your knowledge. But there are basic, foundational skills that are common across all models—and common across all contexts and subject areas. These are the skills that drive your work—and are the greatest predictor of your success as a consultant.

Consultation is an interpersonal relationship and it is problem solving in the context of the relationship. It is a basic communication process, utilizing specialized knowledge (Erchul, 2003). Many researchers and practitioners have agreed regarding the core skills used in consultation (Erchul, 2003; Ingraham, 2003; Klein & Harris, 2004; Kurpius, Fuqua, & Rozecki, 1993; J. Meyers, 2002; Moe & Perera-Diltz, 2009).They are

- interpersonal skills,
- communication skills,
- problem-solving skills,

- relationship building skills,
- multicultural counseling skills, and
- group work skills.

Basic counseling skills are the necessary foundational elements that drive the process. Serving as a consultant requires knowledge of interpersonal dynamics and problem-solving skills. The act of consultation includes rapport building, active listening (to consultees and clients), reflection of feelings, using others' vocabulary, clarifying statements, and advanced communication skills. As a consultant, you might model skills for others and make attempts to eliminate resistance. Your consultee may be skeptical or apathetic and a simple reframing of the problem may help to dissolve their negativity. You may need to engage efforts to join a system and identify any potential allies (Moe & Perera-Diltz, 2009).

Good consultants possess basic counseling and process skills. They are good at building and developing relationships and are able to clearly communicate and define a problem while consulting. They have an awareness of when to confront and when to just listen. They understand and can recognize dependency. They have a basic ability to collect and analyze data related to people (Kurpius et al., 1993). They are proficient at advising and collaborating with community groups, parents, other professionals, and organizations. They can identify and solve problems by generating, implementing, and evaluating strategies (J. Meyers, 2002).

In terms of characteristics, a consultant should be professional, adaptable, and possess a good sense of humor (Moe & Perera-Diltz, 2009). Consultants are self-aware of their values and beliefs. They are able to articulate who they are and what they can do (Kurpius et al., 1993). They are sensitive to contextual factors of behavior. It sometimes requires a bit of courage to address and confront a consultee's most difficult issue, so a consultant should be comfortable in difficult interpersonal situations (Lencioni, 2010).

Consultants likely possess content knowledge and skills within a particular specialty area (i.e., an expertise). They may provide direct training related to specialized techniques or transmit specialized knowledge or information. But in the end, they will need to possess essential skills with an ability to select an appropriate process to facilitate collaboration (Klein & Harris, 2004). They will need knowledge regarding behavioral problems and behavioral change. They will have to have an ability to develop positive relationships with their consultees and have an ability to communicate with them. They will need to help people understand problems and help them to identify strategies to solve the problems. In some situations, a consultant will need to work with diverse groups of people and potentially help the groups to make decisions. Consultants will need knowledge and skills in multicultural counseling and consultation (Moe & Perera-Diltz, 2009).

Multicultural Considerations

A consultant is a change agent and an advocate for the consultee and the client. The structure of consultation is nonhierarchical (an open triad), and the process of consultation should therefore be culturally responsive and empowering (Hoffman et al.,

2006). The relationship between culture and consultation is multifaceted and complex. Culture can influence consultation in a variety of ways (Ingraham, 2003). Race, ethnicity, and culture can have an impact on the worldview of the consultant, consultee, and client (Hoffman et al., 2006).

Multicultural consultation is a competency necessary for working with culturally diverse consultees and clients (Holcomb-McCoy, 2004). Culturally competent consultants understand the impact of culture on the consultation process. Without consultant competence in multicultural awareness, knowledge, or skills, consultees and clients might be unintentionally harmed (Li & Vazquez-Nuttal, 2009). Language differences, value differences, and prejudice can all lead to ineffective communication during the consultation process (Holcomb-McCoy, 2004). A problem may be misdiagnosed; interaction between a consultant and consultee or consultee and client could be culturally oppressive. Inappropriate assessments may be used. Consultants need to have a basic understanding of racism, resistance, multicultural assessment, racial identity development, multicultural family counseling, social advocacy, development of partnerships, and cross-cultural interpersonal interactions (Holcomb-McCoy, 2004). They should be aware of social, economic, environmental, political, and cultural contexts of consultation (Li & Vazquez-Nuttal, 2009).

Consultants should also understand their own culture and also be able to attend to their own cultural biases (Ingraham, 2003). They will need to continuously assess their own multicultural competence and be flexible to adjust their style according to the culture and worldview of the consultee (Hoffman et al., 2006; Holcomb-McCoy, 2004).

An effective consultant considers culture as a lens through which one seeks to understand both the content and the process of consultation. The view through the lens includes the work addressed or implemented with the consultee, and also the process involved among the consultant, the consultee, and the client. They will need to be sensitive to the history and needs of the consultee and the client—and be tuned in to the dynamics of this complex triadic relationship (Rogers, 2000). They should be sensitive to their consultees' styles of communication in order to build trust and rapport and reduce perceived resistance (Ingraham, 2003).

A consultant should also know how to address a potential consultee cultural bias and be able to adapt interventions to provide culturally appropriate interventions and adjustments (Ingraham, 2003). Consultees can hold stereotypes and biases that affect the consultation relationship, process, and therefore, the outcome (Holcomb-McCoy, 2004). A consultant will need to be able to recognize and address a consultee's negative racial or cultural attitudes—and then attempt to alter the problematic areas (Holcomb-McCoy, 2004). The prejudices that impact consultation may come from cultural differences—and can be recognized in practice as rejection in the consultation relationship or suggested interventions (Holcomb-McCoy, 2004).

When joining a system or organization, consultants must inform themselves about the culture of the environment (Rogers, 2000). A consultant has the potential influence over systemic factors that perpetuate prejudice, discrimination, and intercultural conflict. A consultant should have the diversity training and skills to recognize and

> ### Case 3.1: Example of Working
> ### With a Consultee With a Diverse Background
>
> Jonathan is an African American counselor who specializes in consulting with organizations that are experiencing race-based problems (e.g., discrimination, recruitment and retention of minorities, diversity awareness, and education). Inherent in the type of work that he does is conflict. Jonathan routinely encounters people within organizations that have different attitudes about race and ethnicity—and are usually culturally different from him. Jonathan is highly in tune with his own background and values and is very skilled in identifying and confronting an individual's potential cultural biases in a positive way. The challenge that he has found is that no person or group of people that he has encountered is the same. The consultee's stereotypes about him or other cultural groups have an impact on the resistance that he encounters. The manifestation of this resistance has been different in each organization he has consulted; each organization has its own culture. The difficulty that he faces is to tailor interventions specific to each consultee and consultee organization. His first steps are usually to identify the problem, confront it, and develop a plan for how to address it in a culturally appropriate way—all this with the assumption that he is able to establish a positive working rapport and alliance.

intervene at different levels within a system or organization. One can have an impact on an individual level but also at a systemic or organizational level (Washburn, Manley, & Holiwski, 2003).

Cross-Cultural Consultation Competencies

Margaret R. Rogers (2000) developed a list of cross-cultural consultation competencies. A consultant should

1. *Understand one's own and others' culture*: A consultant needs to examine his or her own heritage and identity (race, ethnicity, culture) and possess a self-awareness of personal beliefs, prejudices, and assumptions. A consultant should make attempts to learn about the culture and background of consultees and clients in order to better understand (and possible adopt) others' perspectives and values.

2. *Develop cross-cultural communication and interpersonal skills*: A consultant should be able to bridge different perspectives from different groups.

3. *Understand the cultural embeddedness of consultation*: A consultant should be able to view the consultation process through a cultural lens. It is important to consider the culturally embedded organizational forces that may have an impact on the client.

4. *Use qualitative methodologies when gathering data*: The validity of some instruments and procedures may not be able to be projected or generalized to diverse groups. Consultants should be skilled in using naturalistic data-gathering techniques that would account for local cultural and context.

5. _Acquire culture-specific context knowledge_: In order to provide context-relevant services, a consultant should seek to acquire culture-specific information related to the context. This might also include culture-specific issues in assessment, education, and mental health.

Cross-Cultural Consultation Competency Checklist

Cheryl Holcomb-McCoy took a similar approach in 2004 but developed a checklist of behaviors appropriate for culturally competent consultants:

- I am aware of how culture affects traditional models of consultation.
- I can discuss at least one model of multicultural consultation.
- I can recognize when racial and cultural issues are impacting the consultation process.
- I can identify when the race and/or culture of the client is a problem for the consultee.
- I discuss issues related to race/ethnicity/culture during the consultation process, when applicable (Holcomb-McCoy, 2004, p. 182).

Cross-Cultural Consultation Ethical Guidelines

The American Counseling Association's Code of Ethics (2005) contains some elements that may be extrapolated to the consultation relationship with respect to multicultural and diversity competencies in consultation. Below are some modified elements. In most cases, _Consultant_ has been substituted for _Counselor_:

- A.2.c. Consultants _communicate information in ways that are both developmentally and culturally appropriate._
- A.6.a. When appropriate, consultants _advocate at individual, group, institutional, and societal levels to examine potential barriers and obstacles that inhibit access and/or the growth and development of consultees and clients._
- E.6.c. Consultants _are cautious when selecting assessments for culturally diverse populations to avoid the use of instruments that lack appropriate psychometric properties for the consultee and client populations._
- F.2.b. Consultants _are aware of and address the role of multiculturalism/diversity in consulting relationships._

Guided Practice Exercises
Exercise 3.1: Your Consultee Has a Bias

1. _Imagine that you are a consultant working with a consultee who holds a significant cultural bias against people of a specific ethnicity. Where is your responsibility in the relationship?_

2. *Is there anything that you should do?*

3. *Is there anything that you can do?*

4. *How might this impact your relationship with the consultee?*

5. *How might this impact the consulting work that you do with the consultee?*

Nonprofit Versus For-Profit Consultation

The heading of this particular section can be a little misleading. The concept of non-profit versus for-profit consultation is often thought of in terms of the type of consultee organization. Nonprofit organizations are organizations that do not distribute revenues or profits—they reinvest surplus revenues or profits back into the self-preservation of the organization. While consultants can (and do) certainly work within these organizations, it is not the focus of this chapter or section.

Nonprofit Consultation = Internal Consultation

Nonprofit consultation (as opposed to *nonprofit organization* consultation) is generally described as working as a consultant without the expectation of receiving any payment or additional compensation. This may be done with or without some type of formal contract for consultation services. In practical terms, the consultant is likely already employed in another capacity (perhaps as a full-time counselor) and does not expect or need to receive compensation for their consultation activities. Nonprofit consultation is a more common occurrence between two people within the same organization. In other words, the consultant and consultee are both involved in the same organization. We will also refer to this as *internal consultation*. The following are some examples of internal consultation:

- Two counselors are employed by the same organization. One counselor seeks consultation from the other regarding a particular client who is proving to be a difficult client.
- An elementary school counselor consults with a parent regarding the child who is a student at the school. They are discussing strategies related to behavior management at home.

Internal consultation is more likely to be more informal in nature (consulting with a colleague "next door") and might not involve a written contract, goals, or report. It is a more common occurrence than for-profit consultation (counselors are more likely to serve as internal consultants before serving as an external consultant). Professional counselors are often solicited by fellow practitioners to serve as consultants to improve case conceptualization skills. Counselors typically seek consultation as individuals in order to deepen the knowledge and skills necessary to better serve a specific client or student (Moe & Perera-Diltz, 2009).

For-Profit Consultation = External Consultation

For-profit consultation is generally described as working as a consultant with the expectation of receiving payment or other compensation. This arrangement usually involves some type of formal contract for consultation services (but is not required). The consultant may or may not be already employed in another capacity and expects to receive compensation for their consultation efforts.

The consultant and consultee are not likely to be involved in the same organization. We refer to this as external consultation. The consultant is not a regular employee of the consultee organization (they are external) and is likely under contract to provide a specific consultation service. An example might be a counselor who is self-employed and in private practice. An organization in the community contracts with the counselor, who has an expertise in sensitivity training, to provide a series of workshops on the topic.

External consultation is likely to be more formal in nature and involve a written contract, goals, and report. It is less common than internal consultation (counselors are more likely to serve as internal consultants before serving as an external consultant). Professional counselors might solicit to become external consultants and their interventions are typically designed to impact multiple clients and other system members (Moe & Perera-Diltz, 2009).

The framework for external consultation typically focuses on identifying aspects of a system's or organization's functioning that may inhibit the accomplishment of an organization's goals (Moe & Perera-Diltz, 2009). The interventions are provided usually at a systemic or organizational level and the consultee is considered to be the system or organization (yet the consultant may only work with a select number of members of the system or organization). Changes in select individuals or components are seen as being able to have an impact on other components of the system or organization—and therefore change the system or organization as a whole (a domino effect).

Commonalities Between External Versus Internal Consultants

Regardless of what type of consultation your find yourself doing, whether it is internal or external, there are some common traits and behaviors to which consultants should aspire:

- *Professional*: Treat your interactions with all consultees in a professional manner. Use an objective, structured, and methodical approach appropriate to your training. Just because you may be consulting with a colleague next door, it doesn't mean that you act any less professional.

- *Responsive*: An unsuccessful consultant is one who doesn't react, answer, or reply in an effective or timely manner. A good consultant is responsive to the inquiries and needs of the consultees. Be empathic and attempt to be helpful.
- *Collegial*: Consultation is intended to be a relationship between people who operate at the same level (within a hierarchy). Even if employed or contracted as an "expert" related to a consultant's expertise, the relationship should exist as one of equals. Interact with others in a spirit of collaboration regardless of what or who initiated the relationship (Moe & Perera-Diltz, 2009).

You'll need to have a clear understanding of the differences and nuances of functioning as both an internal or external consultant and an awareness of the type of consultation in which you are interested. As mentioned above, the more common type of consultation that most counselors experience is internal (or nonprofit) consultation. But you will need to be prepared to function as an external consultant, when necessary or desired. The next few sections in this chapter address elements of the consultation process that are more common to external consultation. It is important to note that serving as an external consultant can incorporate other complementary helping behaviors—community activism, social justice agent, professional advocacy, coalition building—to further define the professional identity of counselors. By adopting a role of external consultant, a counselor can advocate for the profession as an individual with distinct training and provider of valuable services (Moe & Perera-Diltz, 2009).

Fiscal and Organizational Responsibilities

Consultation, as a business enterprise, experienced a "crash" of sorts in late 2008 that corresponded with the financial meltdown in the United States at the same time. Within one year's time, consulting businesses (e.g., the Center for Nonprofit Management) saw their revenues fall by more than 40% (West, 2010). With the exception of consultants who marketed themselves as helping other organizations secure funding, there was little for-profit consultation business (West, 2010).

Over time, there have been more consultants than there are consultation jobs in the for-profit sector. As a result, more external consultants become "specialists", rather than generalists—and there can be a great disparity in fees paid to consultants (West, 2010). We'll get into fees and fee structuring within the next section of this chapter. For now, it is important to discuss more generalities related to fiscal and organizational responsibilities.

Fiscal Responsibilities

The costs associated with external, for-profit consultation should be provided to the consultee during the initiation of the relationship. A consultant should make an attempt to provide

- an accurate estimate of their fees, and
- a projection of any costs that may be incurred in order to implement any interventions as part of the consultation process.

An agreement related to fees and costs should be reached early as a part of the contract for services. Part of the agreement should also specify how the costs incurred (if any) during intervention implementation will be handled. Will the consultant fund the implementation and expect repayment or will the consultee pay for costs as they are incurred? It should be understood that these costs (regardless of who pays and when) are separate expenses and not part of the consultant's fees.

Organizational Responsibilities

Organizational responsibilities should also be made clear at the beginning of the consultation relationship. A consultant is responsible for assisting the consultee to clarify a problem. The consultant also has a responsibility for providing a rationale that supports the choice of intervention strategies. There should be specification of who implements what during the intervention implementation and what standards there are for implementation. In general, consultees are responsible for implementing interventions based on the standards that are specified.

Standards serve as a guide for the goals for intervention implementation. The standards (or goals) should be concrete, realistic, and achievable by the people directly involved. The quantity of the activities carried out should be specified (who does what, how much they do it, and how many times they do it). In addition to the specifications of the quantity of the implementation, the quality should be specified as well: how strongly the intervention should be implemented (including depth or effort exerted), and the fidelity (accuracy) of the implementation (Gottfredson, 1993).

In an internal consulting example, let's say tutoring services was one of the suggested interventions to a parent (our consultee). The consultant might specify that the client (i.e., a child) receive tutoring from the teacher for one hour each week for six weeks. This specifies who is responsible for providing the intervention, how much they provide the intervention, and for how long. The responsibility is clear. In designating the responsibilities for quality of the intervention, the consultant would specify what subject is presented during the tutoring sessions, maybe what methods or theories are presented related to the subject matter, and possibly that the parent monitors that the tutoring is taking place (Gottfredson, 1993).

The standards (quantity or quality) for implementation of interventions should ideally be guided by past research, prior studies, prior implementations, or other evidence-based methods. Consultants are responsible for researching and being aware of these methods. If such methods are not available, consultants are responsible for making their best, informed estimate as to the standards or level of intervention needed to address the goals of consultation (Gottfredson, 1993).

There should also be some specification for who will monitor the implementation—the consultant, the consultee, a designee of the consultant, or a designee of the consultee. Monitoring implementation provides feedback on the quality, information on obstacles to high-quality implementation, and possibly strategies to overcome obstacles. Methods or tools of monitoring may include logs of services, observations of services being provided, review of rosters, and documents like meeting agendas.

It is the responsibility of the consultant to develop performance standards for intervention implementation with collaboration from the consultee. Should the monitored implementation not go according to plan and performance standards are not met, the consultant is responsible for assessing the obstacles, identifying the problem areas, and providing feedback to all parties involved (Gottfredson, 1993). More of this process is discussed later in the text with respect to the stages of consultation; the important concept presented here is the understanding of alignment of responsibilities during the process.

One point not mentioned above is the consultant's responsibility for behavior that is ethical. In the next chapter, we review specific ethical and legal aspects of consultation. As a professional counselor, you are held accountable to the standards associated with your professional identity. More informally though (as an external consultant), it is recommended that you heartily adopt a professional approach to your consultation activities. If you are under contract with an organization for consultation services, follow through with your designated responsibilities. If you are employed in a capacity outside of your consulting activities, be upfront with your employer regarding your external activities.

Generating Proposals, Contracts, Workshops, Marketing, and Fee Structures

Getting started as an external, for-profit consultant may not be an easy task. For most practitioners, their consultation activities don't serve as their primary source of income. They have a larger, home-base agency or institution that serves as their primary source of support and solace. If you find someone who functions as a full-time external consultant, it has likely taken them some time to reach a point in their career where this became a reality. It didn't happen overnight, and there was likely a great deal of consulting work taken one job at a time in order to achieve a status as a full-time consultant. Part of becoming a successful consultant requires the ability to make connections and generate proposals for consulting work.

Proposals

Writing and communication skills are necessary skills in consulting. You have to be able to communicate during the actual consultation process, but you also need to be able to produce well-written documents to generate potential work. You may need to be on the lookout for Request for Proposals (RFPs), but you may also need to do some research to determine which organizations and settings are willing and able to employ consultants (Moe & Perera-Diltz, 2009). Not every organization will be willing to bring a consultant in to facilitate changes at a system or organizational level. When you do encounter an organization that is willing to hire a consultant, you may find that there is a fairly competitive market and that others have similar expertise. It will be important that your proposal is well written.

When drafting a proposal for an RFP, it is particularly important to address every element, directive, question, or item that is specified within the RFP. Your document should be written with no spelling or grammatical errors and be clear, concise, and to the point. It should cover every element, directive, question, or item requested—and it is recommended that it be presented in the same order in which the information is requested.

Other information that may be included in a written proposal is provided below. This information, in some situations, may be the only content in a proposal if there have not been any specific requests regarding what should be proposed. Incidentally, this information may be the same information you use for marketing purposes. For the most part, this information describes and defines your expertise (West, 2010):

- Your accomplishments within your expertise area or subject
- Your education
- Your previous experiences
- Length of time you have been a consultant
- Other groups you have worked for (disclosed only with their consent)
- Your work on similar projects with similar organizations and the results of those activities
- Projected fees with as many details as you can provide (only tentative until you have a contract in place)
- What you would offer that you believe would be particularly helpful to them

These points should be changed and tailored for each organization to which you send a proposal. It should be specific to their organization and the services that they provide.

Assuming you draft a worthy proposal and it is successfully accepted, you then move on to contract negotiation. The broader context of the contracting phase will be presented within the chapter on stages of consultation. Here, we look at some of the specific content that may be included in a consultation contract.

Contracts: Contract Negotiation

The contract negotiation process can influence the success of the consultation relationship. The term *contract negotiation* refers to the communication about a consultation contract that takes place between the consultant and key stakeholders of the consulting organization (or consultees). Because it occurs at the beginning of the consultation relationship, rapport between the consultant and consultee may just be developing during contract negotiation. A successful negotiation process can potentially facilitate smoother acceptances of later consultation efforts (i.e., a future projection for how things might go between the consultant and consultee). The negotiation involves an agreement not only of fees and costs but also discussion about what might happen during consultation and the focus of the consultation efforts (B. Meyers, 2002).

Contract negotiation is typically viewed as a verbal process, but written documents may be used to confirm certain understandings about the process. The main focus of the negotiation is to discuss and agree on a clear purpose of the process and content of the consultation relationship. If you fail to collaborate and resolve issues during the contract negotiation process, you may be faced with an unsuccessful relationship (B. Meyers, 2002).

During the negotiation process, there may be people who focus on different elements of your work. Some people will focus on time, "How long it will take?", and some people will focus on money, "How much is this going to cost?" (Kurpius et al., 1993). It will be in your best interest to be proactive and address both types of people. Be prepared and ready to discuss such things as fee schedules, resources that may be needed, the purpose, objectives, expectations, and timelines. As your negotiations and discussions progress, and if they progress successfully, you are ready to move on to formalizing your consultation contract. This should only be done after a consultee has agreed to hire you—and that you have thoroughly discussed the project. There should be ample time for questions and issues to be resolved before finalizing a contract.

Contracts: The Formal Contract

Theodore P. Remley (1993) provides a clear definition of the requirements for a consultation contract. He claims there are three elements necessary to form a legal, formal contract:

1. *Offer*: The terms of a consultation arrangement are proposed.

2. *Acceptance*: The person to whom the offer was proposed agrees to the terms.

3. *Consideration*: Something of value (usually money) is proffered in exchange for doing what is specified in the offer.

Without something of value being presented for acceptance (without "consideration"), there is no contract.

It is not required that a contract be in writing for it to exist and be valid. Remley does claim that some federal and state statutes may require that some particular contracts be in writing. For the most part, if a verbal offer is made and there is acceptance (and consideration), then a legal contract exists. You will need to understand that there may be circumstances in which you don't have a written, formal contract (and perhaps haven't yet been paid)—but you still have a legal, contractual obligation to the consultee. As such, you are vulnerable to being sued by a consultee for damages, should something negative happen (Remley, 1993).

It is in your best interest to have a written, formal document. Consultants often use basic letters of agreement signed by the consultant and consultee or simple contracts drafted by one person and then signed by the other. Others may decide to use an attorney to negotiate and draft a formal and lengthy contract. In general, however, the more complete the communication and understanding between the consultant and consultee, the better the chances for a successful consultation relationship. There will be less chances for conflict and unhappiness later in the relationship, should things not go well (Remley, 1993).

When engaging in internal or nonprofit consulting (or perhaps even external consulting with just one person), you will be less likely to have anything written or formal (Kurpius et al., 1993). A legal contract does not exist in internal consultations, when people within the same organization agree to provide consultation services to one another. Because all people are paid by the same employer, "consideration" is not present (and it is a necessary element for a formal contract).

A consultation contract should attempt to match consultee perceptions and expectations with consultant interventions. The contract represents the agreement between the consultant and consultee; the more specific it is, the better both parties will be served. Contracts should do the following:

- clearly specify the consultation work to be done,
- describe in detail any work products expected from the consultant,
- specify a time frame for the completion of the work,
- specify to whom the consultant should report, and
- describe compensation or fees and method of payment.

In addition, contract writers should

- number all pages,
- print the names of all people involved and have each person sign (and date) the document,
- initial any changes (written or typed) to the original document (initialed by everyone), and
- provide at least two copies to be signed so that each person can retain an original.

Remley (1993) recommends that any contract that is considered legal in nature be reviewed and approved by attorneys for both the consultant and consultee before being signed.

Workshops

Training and workshop provision has been and continues to be a multibillion-dollar industry (Cosier & Dalton, 1993). Consultants are frequently contracted to serve in a trainer or workshop-provider role. It might very well be the only activity for which the consultant is contracted to provide. Likewise, there are consultants who only provide trainings and workshops as their consultation business. The line that distinguishes a consultant from a trainer, educator, or workshop provider is hard to draw, and we will therefore not attempt to make a clear distinction. We see the ability to provide trainings and workshops as a function or role within the consultation relationship. As mentioned above, once the consultation relationship is established, the training or workshop may be the only "service" that a consultant provides.

Consultants who are contracted to provide trainings or workshops are usually hired based on their expertise in a specific area for which they are known. They generally have a degree of knowledge, skills, and expertise in the area and likely have a

Case 3.2: Sample Contract

Offer of Consultation

between

David Scott, Chadwick Royal, and Daniel Kissinger (consultants)

and

Jackson County Public School System (consultee)

Scope of Work to be Completed:

The consultants will provide a full-day (7 hours total) training to the school counselors and any other personnel employed within the Student Services Department of the Jackson County Public School System. The training will cover content related to the awareness and assessment of substance abuse concerns of students within the school system. The content will contain elements related to the recognition of substance use, knowledge of different categories of substances, how to assess for substance abuse risk, differentiating abuse versus addiction, a family system's role in substance use, assessment and referral for substance abuse and addiction, and follow-up care protocol.

Products Expected as a Result of Consultation:

The essential product of the consultation service will consist of a full-day training workshop (7 hours maximum, five hours minimum) presented by the consultants. Attendees of the training shall receive a binder of resources and materials related to the topic. It is expected that attendees will be able to:

- Recognize symptoms/indicators of student substance abuse,
- Differentiate different categories of substances,
- Assess students for substance abuse risk,
- Distinguish substance abuse from addiction, and recognize someone who may be addicted to a substance,
- Understand why a student's family should be included when providing assessment/intervention related to a substance problem,
- Assess and refer (intervene) related to a student substance abuse problem,
- Follow-up with students related to substance problems.

Offer of Consultation   Page 1 of 3

(Continued)

(Continued)

The consultee will be permitted to video-record the training activities for future use with Jackson County School System employees. If recorded, the consultee agrees not to copy and redistribute the recording without the consultants' permission. Only one copy of the recording should exist, and it should be maintained by the Office of Student Services of the Jackson County School System. The recording should not be posted on the Internet for public consumption.

The consultant will provide a written evaluation summary of the event.

Expected Timeframe for the Completion of the Consultation:

The training will take place over the course of one day in the spring of 2016. The date for the training will be mutually agreed upon by the consultants and the consultee. The specific date of the training will be decided upon by December 31, 2015. A written evaluation summary of the event will be emailed to the Director of Student Services approximately two weeks after the training event. The consultation is concluded once the training/workshop is completed on the mutually agreed upon day – and the summary evaluation is emailed.

Roles and Responsibilities:

The consultants agree to be present and provide the training on the agreed upon day. The consultant will provide the binders and the material contained within them. The consultants will bring all materials needed to present material, including computers and projectors. The consultants will report directly to the head of Student Services for the Jackson County School System.

The consultee agrees to handle all of the remaining logistics for the training. This shall include (but is not limited to): Securing a location and facilities for the training, food (if appropriate), announcements, marketing, and registration for the event, attendance monitoring, and arrangement of continuing education provisions/certificates (if appropriate).

Compensation/Fees/Consideration:

In return for the provision of the consultation services outlined above, the Jackson County School System agree to pay the consultants a fee in the amount of $ X . This fee includes the time spent presenting the training and any costs that are incurred in the preparation of materials. This amount should be paid within two weeks after the summary evaluation has been emailed to the

Offer of Consultation   Page 2 of 3

Director of Student Services (and no later than four weeks after the training has been provided). This fee does not include travel or lodging expenses. The Jackson County School System agrees to arrange and prepay for the expenses related to airline costs, transportation from and to the airport, three meals, and lodging.

By signing below, the parties acknowledge acceptance of the contract terms.

_____

David Scott, PhD, Consultant   Date

_____

Chadwick Royal, PhD, Consultant   Date

_____

Daniel Kissinger, PhD, Consultant   Date

_____

Jackson County   Date
School System Representative*,
Consultee
*This should be signed by someone with authority to bind/fund contract

_____

Director of Student Services   Date
Jackson County School System, Consultee

- Two original copies of this document will be made (one for the consultants and one for the consultee).

- Any changes made within the original copies should be indicated on all copies and initialed by all parties listed above.

Offer of Consultation   Page 3 of 3 history (or body) of work on the subject matter. The consultee is, in essence, purchasing the consultant's expertise for dissemination. How the expertise is disseminated is the focus in this section regarding the skills necessary for a trainer or workshop provider. An effective consultant demonstrates the following skills:

- *Public speaking*: Speak to a group of people (sometimes large groups of people) in a structured, deliberate, informative, influential, and entertaining way.
- *Pedagogy*: Demonstrate the science and art of education, teaching, and learning. Pedagogical methods might include: (a) maintaining lesson plans, (b) displaying an agenda, (c) emphasizing learning objectives, (d) collaborative learning experiences, (e) observational experiences, (f) reflective experiences, and (g) participatory experiences.
- *Research, assessment, and evaluation*: Apply qualitative and quantitative research methods to determine the needs of a consultee, assess the attainment of learning objectives using rubrics, and evaluate all of the data obtained.

It should be noted that each time you provide a training or workshop, you provide a preview, or dress rehearsal of sorts, of what you can do with respect to other consulting activities. Other consultants have claimed that the provision of trainings and workshops often evolve into other consulting opportunities (Cosier & Dalton, 1993).

Marketing

Networking

External consulting opportunities may often come about as a result of whom one knows, rather than cold calls or proposals submitted to organizations with which you have not previous experience or interaction. Networking is probably the most unrecognized or underrated skill of a successful external consultant. It has been reported that as much as 75% of consulting activities consist of referrals or repeat business from consultees (Cosier & Dalton, 1993). The time that you spend networking (in whatever forms that it might take place) will pay off—and it is in your best interest to build a large network (Jervey, 2004). It may not be your closest colleagues that provide referrals; work opportunities may come from people who know people who are indirectly related—a friend of a friend.

Using technology and social networking is an important method for building a larger network, and we'll cover some of this later. The more old-fashioned, but tried-and-true, method of networking is simply the act of making personal contact with potential consultees or sources of referral:

- Attend gatherings of people that might serve as potential consultees or referral sources. Conferences or workshops that you attend are excellent sources of contact.
- Present sessions and workshops at the same conferences mentioned above. Not only do you provide a dress rehearsal for what you might be able to do for an organization, but you can make direct contact with the people that attend your sessions. These are people who already have expressed an interest in what you have to say by attending your session.

- You might also offer pro-bono workshops within your community, depending on the content of your workshop. Make connections with civic and community leaders.
- Join multiple professional associations related to your area of interest or expertise. This will likely provide you with newsletters and publications—and likely that names of key people involved within the field. They might be people you will want to target in later advertising efforts. You'll also have an instant connection with the group of people who are members.
- Follow up with any leads that you encounter. Engage them in conversation and keep in contact, even if the contact is trivial (Jervey, 2004).

Market Research, Targeting Markets, and Advertising

Without having a preexisting connection to possible consultees, you are left to establish and develop your own business connections. Perhaps the most difficult aspect of developing these connections is knowing who is most likely to contract with you. How do you determine what people or organizations do not currently use a version of what you provide—but could benefit from using it? Making cold calls to random organizations is likely not the best use of your time.

If you decide to advertise, it is recommended that you use a precise or surgical approach. You want to be able to place your promotional materials in the hands of those most likely to do something with it. By joining various professional organizations related to your specialty area, you may have access to a list of members of the organization (with e-mail addresses or mailing addresses). By going to professional conferences and workshops, you may have access to a list of other participants of the conference or workshop (Cosier & Dalton, 1993). You might also target people that you have gone to school with (and older and newer alumni of your programs of study or institutions) who are likely in a similar field or location.

You will want to be aware of the majority industry or trade publications. Write and publish an article for the publication so that you may become more well known. Write and publish journal articles or books on your topic of specialty so that you can establish yourself as an authority on the topic. As you publish articles in journals or books, publish a newsletter or trade publication article that highlights this publication accomplishment. You may also consider publishing a newsletter of your own that summarizes your efforts and accomplishments. This could be sent out to the same lists of people mentioned in the previous paragraph.

The materials sent out should present the following perspective: You are selling your image or *brand*. You should highlight your accomplishments, your experience, and your education so you portray that you are special and unique in some dimension (your expertise). An advantage of working as a consultant is the general low requirement for business capital. The money that is spent in preparing and marketing your work should be directed in a smart and savvy manner. Recognize, maximize, and highlight your strengths. Likewise, you also need to recognize and manage any limitations that you might have.

Fee Structures

Getting started in consultation work may require doing initial work for little or no money in order to cultivate additional work over time. This process is referred to as *consultee mining*. A consultee base must be developed, establishing relationships with those individuals who will pay for your time. In the beginning, you may not be able to ask for as much money or higher fees as you would like. As you develop more consultee relationships, you can ask for more and possibly receive it. *Few external consultants start out making large fees.* The more experience you gain in consultation, the higher fees you are likely to receive for any contract. It is recommended that if you are just beginning to seek contracts, you take any or all contracts you can obtain. A consultee base may be developed by helping new consultees with smaller, low-profit projects. The theory is that these projects may lead into more work with greater fees. Embracing this approach allows the consultee to learn what you can do for them as a consultant and how well you can do it, as Timothy G. Plax (2006) states.

How much to charge for a consultation service seems like a simple enough question, but it is a very complex answer. Most clients would like a detailed estimate of the time spent doing consultation. The problem is that both clients and inexperienced consultants will typically underestimate the amount of time that may be required to complete a consultation service. For example, a one-day workshop will require more hours than are simply spent presenting the content (Plax, 2006). It always takes more time than thought, and it is possible that the consultee will ask for more work than what was originally contracted.

A consultant must consider preparation time, logistical planning, assessing the organizational needs, developing learning objectives, researching the content to present, designing the presentation, and preparing and editing the technology and materials. During the actual delivery of the workshop, a consultant must consider time spent setting up, arranging food and beverages, and cleaning up. There might also be additional debriefing time which includes analyzing feedback, writing a report, and meeting with the consultee to review the report. As a consultant costs out time for a contract, they usually don't consider the time that was spent in client mining, writing a proposal, communicating with the client, and contract negotiation (Plax, 2006).

It is difficult to provide guidelines regarding how much a consultant should charge. Part of costing out services as a consultant is making some type of determination as to what people would actually pay us to do. There are so many factors that enter into the process of estimating fees: prior work history of the consultant, prior work history with a consultee, the size and complexity of a job, the consultee's budget, the size of the consultee's organization, funding available, just to name a few. The more consulting we are able to do, the more our marketability increases, and the more our consultee base grows. As we grow, we are able to be more discriminating in the type and amount of projects that we contract, the clients that we are willing to take, and the amount of money we are willing to accept for our work (Plax, 2006).

Case 3.3: The Art of Negotiation

Kisha submitted a proposal for a two-day external consultation project (presenting a workshop). A fairly large counseling agency in a neighboring region was seeking a consultant to provide specialized training for their employees related to a subject that she knows well. She has five years of experience in the area, has presented on the subject twice at state counseling conferences, and conducted some research (not yet published) while she was in school. She has the knowledge, expertise, and ability to do a good job on the project. The problem is that she has never been paid as an external consultant before—in any area or subject matter. The person at the agency who is responsible for hiring a consultant has communicated with Kisha twice about a possible consultation arrangement, but this person is also considering bringing in a professor from a university across the state to provide the service. The professor is known fairly well for the subject matter but is also known for charging at least $1,000 for a half-day workshop on the subject. The agency is on the fence regarding bringing in a lesser known consultant (Kisha) for less money versus bringing in a well-known consultant (the professor) for more money.

Kisha has a feeling that the agency would rather not spend a great deal of money on a consultant at this time but wants to make sure that the service that they receive is of top quality. She decides to highlight her qualifications and experience but propose a low fee structure (about 50% less than she makes per hour in her full-time job) in an attempt to win the contract and begin to build her consultee–client base. Part of her pitch communicates that she realizes that she could make more money (per hour) by simply continuing to work within her full time counseling job, but she has to start someplace in building a consultation portfolio. The agency staff express their appreciation of her candidness and decide to award her the project.

In any case, Plax (2006) has suggested a specific way to estimate or structure a consultant's fee. Please note that this relates only to a consultant's fees and not any other associated costs related to the consultation.

- Project the amount of time for the service to be completed.
  - A consultant should overestimate their time. As an example, Plax suggests that a consultant estimate, on average, 40 hours preparation time for one actual day of training.
- Estimate an hourly rate.
  - Consider how much you make per hour in a regular full time job and then align your consultation fee-per-hour accordingly.
- Multiply the amount of time projected to complete the service by your estimated hourly rate.

Keep in mind that this amount is pretaxed money and does not include health benefits, vacation time, retirement, or anything else associated with benefits of permanent employment. It is a one-time fee for services, and future work with this consultee is not guaranteed.

Guided Practice Exercises
Exercise 3.2: Simulated Contracting

Partner with a colleague with the intention to conduct a simulated consultation with one of you serving as a consultant and one of you serving as a consultee. Identify the nature and content of the consultation but spend your time developing a sample contract for the consultation efforts. The actual consultation need not ever take place; the contract is the goal of the exercise. Your document should be written and contain the following elements as suggested by Remley (1993):

- Clearly specify the consultation work to be done.
- Describe in detail any work products expected from the consultant.
- Specify a time frame for the completion of the work.
- Specify to whom the consultant should report.
- Describe compensation or fees and method of payment.

Use of Technology in Consultation

Technology hardware and software advancements are made so rapidly that the content written within this section of the chapter is likely outdated by the time you are able to read it. Nevertheless, we will attempt to review what we believe to be the necessary skills needed for the use of technology in consultation. This section will be divided into two parts: (1) the actual technology that can be applied with consultation, and (2) an ethical framework for the use of technology.

Technology Applied in Consultation

Consultants should have a sufficient amount of understanding when it comes to the technology used in consultation. There are multiple categories of technology under which knowledge should exist.

Communication

A consultee's ability to access their consultant, in general, is a critical dimension for most consultees and clients. There are also circumstances in which a consultant may need to be on call during the implementation of an intervention. It could probably go without mention that consultants should be familiar with e-mail and telephone communication, but it is highly recommended for the consultant to be familiar with and embrace mobile technology. Mobile devices, in particular devices known as smart devices, will allow the consultant to receive telephone messages, SMS or text messages, and e-mail communication on the go.

It is also recommended that consultants be familiar with other enhanced abilities to communicate. Videoconferencing over the Internet allows consultants and consultees to have face-to-face, real-time conversations and communication. Some smart devices will enable instant messaging and videoconferencing as well. Some examples of this technology include: Skype, GoToMeeting, Elluminate Live!, and Adobe Connect. A variant in this use of technology is the application of virtual environments (e.g., Second Life). There is a fairly steep learning curve for using virtual environments, and these may not be readily adopted by consultees.

Regardless of the tool or device, the primary concern for consultants is that the technology that they select to communicate (and more importantly, the way in which they use it) be as secure and confidential as possible. This includes telephone, text messaging, e-mail, mobile devices, and webconferencing or webinars.

Networking and Marketing

Social networking has grown exponentially over the last 10 years. Using social networks allow consultants to connect with future consultees and market services that they may provide. A consultant may decide to maintain a personal account or a business account or both. The primary concern for consultants using social networking is that they do not breach confidentiality of their consultees or clients in the content that they post. The posts on social networks should be presented as generic information regarding their field and not any disclosure of work or services that are provided to any specific consultee or client. It should be noted that social networking use is not recommended by the authors for use by counselors. "Liking" or "following" a client or a client "liking" or "following" a counselor is a breach of confidentiality of the counseling relationship. There are other ethical reasons for counselors being very wary of social media, but confidentiality may be the primary concern. Consultants should view their social networking use as a primary way to "market their brand." Some of the more popular social networks used at the time of publishing this text are Facebook, Twitter, LinkedIn, Instagram, and Pinterest.

Content Capturing, Presentation, and Delivery

The primary technologies typically used by consultants when working with the content of their consultation work include software for word processing, spreadsheets, and presentation software. Word processing would be used for drafting documents before, during, and after your consultation activities. Some of the more popular word processors are Microsoft's Word, Apple's Pages, and OpenOffice. Spreadsheets may be used to track expenses or document and analyze data collected during the consultation process. Some of the more popular spreadsheet software includes Microsoft's Excel, Apple's Numbers, and OpenOffice. Presentation software would likely be needed when pitching a proposal for consultation or presenting content to any group of people during the consultation process. Some of the more popular presentation software includes Microsoft's PowerPoint, Apple's Keynote, OpenOffice, and Prezi.

A consultant may also consider using a mobile device to capture and use content on the go. There are mobile versions of some word processors, spreadsheets, and presentation software on smart devices. There are also mobile applications or "apps" (and devices) that allow consultants to capture audio and video of their work in the field. For example, a consultant may want to audiorecord the content from an interview or focus group. Rather than take notes, they can record the meeting and maintain their focus in the here-and-now of what is being related. The recording could be reviewed later.

Document Management, Collaboration, and Sharing

Managing content on multiple computers and devices has created such problems that applications and online resources have been developed to simplify the process. Notes and content on one device can instantly be stored and edited on another device. There are apps, such as Evernote, that allow for notes, pictures, audio clips, attachments, and web clippings to be recorded and organized on something like a smart device (something a consultant would use in the field) and instantly transferred to another device like a laptop computer (provided there is an Internet connection).

Other web resources facilitate simple document storage and access across multiple devices. This is also referred to as *cloud storage*, where the content may be stored on a local device but also stored in a virtual capacity (on a server elsewhere). Some cloud storage is only stored in a virtual capacity. Some of the more popular cloud storage resources are Dropbox, Google Drive, Apple's iCloud, and SkyDrive.

The ability to collaborate on documents and content is another technology skill that is highly recommended. Rather than sending and resending documents for editing and review, there are resources that can be used to instantly share and collaborate on the work. Perhaps the most popular of these resources is Google Docs, which provides access to word processing, spreadsheet, presentation, form creation, and drawing software. One person can create a document using the software, and instantly share a link for another person to access and edit the document. Some webconferencing software (as mentioned above) will allow for instant collaboration as well. Wikis are another tool that may be used to facilitate group interaction and collaboration on a project. A wiki is a web resource that allows multiple participants to add, modify, or delete content of a website document using a web browser. They typically allow for the incorporation of multimedia content.

Assessing, Monitoring, and Evaluating

There may be times in which a consultant needs to collect data: They may need to conduct a needs assessment, conduct a pretest and posttest, survey the client system, or survey the satisfaction of the consultee. As assessments or surveys are used, it takes additional effort to monitor the collection process and even yet more time to collate and analyze the results. There are web resources that can help a consultant conduct assessments, monitor data collection, and evaluate the data received. The web interfaces are fairly easy to use, and a consultant can create simple or complex instruments. Users of the resources can find out fairly easily whether the assessments are being used, who is using them, and how they are being used. Most of the resources will even create an attractive display of the results with graphs and charts (depending on the type of data collected). Some of the more popular resources are SurveyMonkey, SurveyGizmo, and Google Forms.

Ethical Framework for the Use of Technology in Consultation

DeeAnna Merz Nagel and Kate Anthony (2009; see also Suggested Readings) have developed a series of ethical frameworks for various types of mental health professionals. It stands to reason that their series of frameworks can be applied to consultation as well. The primary ethical concepts to keep in mind when using technology as a consultant are listed below:

- *Hardware (when used for communication):* Consultants should understand the basic platform of their own devices and computers and whether or not their consultee's hardware or platforms are compatible with any communication programs being used by the consultant.
- *Software*: Consultants know how to download and upgrade software (and assist clients with it as well) when the software is used for consultation services.
- *Encryption*: A consultant should understand how to access encrypted services, as needed in their communication with a consultee or client. E-mail is not considered a secure form of communication. A consultant should also consider secure storage of records (as needed)—whether it be on secure services of a third-party cloud storage, password-protected mobile devices, encrypted folders on a consultant's hard drive, or password-protected folders on an external drive. When unencrypted methods of communication are used, this should be disclosed and explained (e.g., standard e-mail, mobile telephones, SMS texting, social networking).
- *Backup Storage*: Records and data that are stored on a consultant's device or hard drive should be backed up regularly on an external drive or remotely using secure cloud storage.
- *Password Protection*: Consultants should take steps to ensure the confidentiality of documents and communication using password-protected devices, folders, drives, or computers.
- *Firewalls*: Consultants use firewall protection externally or through web-based programs.
- *Virus Protection*: A consultant does their best to ensure that their work computers and devices are protected against viruses that may be received from others—and that they don't transmit them to others.
- *Methods of Communication*: If a consultant's primary mode of communication is electronic or digital, they still offer contact information that includes a post address, a telephone number, and an e-mail address. A consultant should have an agreed-upon plan for how to communicate and proceed when there are technological problems.
- *Consultee's Technology Skills*: A consultant should screen the consultee's (and possibly the client's) use of technology at the beginning of the consultation relationship and should be screened along the same avenues with the consultant-used technology. Questions may include, but are not limited to, a consultee's experience with e-mail, instant messaging, software and applications used, social networking, SMS texting, webconferencing and VoIP (Voice over Internet Protocol), and telephone access and use (Merz Nagel & Anthony, 2009).

Consultation Report Writing

- It has been noted that consultants are faced with greater accountability within the realm of their services (Brinkman, Segool, Pham, & Carlson, 2007). This view of accountability incorporates the documentation process, specifically related to intervention effectiveness. Consultants must carefully consider how they document their services and their outcomes in accordance with how they are contracted to provide services. If you are contracted to provide a specific service (and draft a report at the end of the process), then your report should be submitted with the expectations addressed in detail. Clearly and accurately documenting the steps taken is essential in providing accountability (Brinkman et al., 2007) and list the following reasons for drafting consultation reports:
- Summarize services
- Convey information that was gathered
- Create a formal document that may assist with future endeavors
- Describe the sequence of events
- Present data gathered during the process that may demonstrate whether or not the consultation was a success

---

Case 3.4: Write the Report

Pat has a consultation agreement with an organization that has its headquarters in another state from where Pat lives—and more importantly—a different state from where the consultation services took place. She had a clear and well-written contract going into the consultation, so she knew exactly what to expect and what to accomplish during her time with the consultee. The problem is that the consultation didn't go exactly according to plan. She did a great job, but there were things that happened that were out of Pat's control. The consultation wasn't as successful as she'd hoped. Now that the bulk of her work is complete, she is faced with submitting a report to the organization regarding the consultation services. This was an expectation that was part of the contract she signed with them.

Pat realizes that the outcome of this relationship can affect how much consulting work she receives in the future. Per her contract, she is going to follow through with submitting a report as requested. She has to keep reminding herself that her report needs to accurately represent the intervention effectiveness—and not attempt to alter the report to reflect a change in the outcome for the better. She realizes that the report may be the only way for the organization to have a clear and accurate understanding of her actions and interventions applied. Because the representatives and decision makers for the organization are in a different state, and were not "looking over her shoulder" during her time on site, the only way that they may be able to interpret her work is to examine the outcome or results. Without the report documenting the process, sequence of events, results, barriers, and successes, the organization representatives may never know how good of a job she did.

A report should be written objectively and concisely, integrating information gathered, and focused on documenting the outcome (Brinkman et al, 2007). It should be written in third-person narrative and be free from a conversational tone. There should be no spelling or grammatical errors, and the paragraphs written in easily digestible lengths.

Strong consideration should be given over how to visually present data, when appropriate. Visual or graphical presentations can organize and relate data about the intervention implementation over time and effectively present an interpretation about the effectiveness of treatment.

A comprehensive report summarizes all of the steps taken during the consultation process and synthesizes the findings with a focus on outcomes. Brinkman et al. (2007) offer a sample detailed ordering of sections for a formal consultation report, which we have modified slightly:

1. *Identifying Information*: Provide the relevant identifying information about the consultant, consultee, and client. Include dates of consultation meetings.

2. *Reason for Referral*: Provide information about the source and concerns that prompted the referral.

3. *Problem-Solving Techniques*: Describe all of the interviews and data-gathering procedures used (including dates). Identify who was responsible for data collection.

4. *Background Information*: Present any information relevant to the consultee's and/or client's functioning (current and past).

5. *Problem Identification*: Summarize the primary concern that was identified.

6. *Methodology for Data Collection*: Describe who collected the data, and how, when, and where it was collected.

7. *Baseline Data*: If possible, provide a visual representation of the baseline data (table or graph).

8. *Problem and Goal Definition*: Provide an interpretation of the possible difference between the expected level of performance and the baseline data. Describe what the goals of consultation were as a result.

9. *Intervention Implementation*: Present a concise summary of the interventions applied. Identify who did what, how it was done, when it was done, and where it was done.

10. *Intervention Data:* If possible, provide a visual representation of the data across baseline and intervention stages of the consultation process.

11. *Intervention Evaluation*: Present a critical evaluation of the consultation process, with respect to baseline and intervention implementation data, the outcome, the problem-solving process, and intervention design.

12. *Summary*: Summarize the information presented in the previous sections.

13. *Recommendations*: Offer specific recommendations that might address ongoing concerns or problems. Describe what components of the process should be continued.

14. *Signature*: Sign and date the document.

Source: Adapted from Brinkman, Segool, Pham, & Carlson, (2007).

Guided Practice Exercises
Exercise 3.3: Office Space Consultation

Watch the movie *Office Space* (Reidel & Judge, 1999) and imagine that you are one of the consultants (one of the Bobs) from the movie (keeping in mind that this movie provides an inaccurate, comical view on consultation that embraces a lot of people's misconceptions about consultation). Draft a consultation report of your work with Initech (Initech is the organizational consultee; Bill Lumbergh is your identified consultee contact).

Chapter Keystones

- There are basic, foundational skills that are common across all models—and common across all contexts and subject areas. These are the skills that drive your work and are the greatest predictor of your success as a consultant: interpersonal skills, communication skills, problem-solving skills, relationship-building skills, multicultural-counseling skills, and group-work skills.
- The relationship between culture and consultation is multifaceted and complex. Culture can influence consultation in a variety of ways.
- Nonprofit consultation is generally described as working as a consultant without the expectation of receiving any payment or additional compensation. For-profit consultation is generally described as working as a consultant with the expectation of receiving payment or other compensation.
- The costs associated with external, for-profit consultation should be provided to the consultee during the initiation of the relationship. Organizational responsibilities should also be made clear at the beginning of the consultation relationship.
- Part of becoming a successful consultant requires the ability to make connections and generate proposals for consulting work.
- How much to charge for consultation services is a complex process. There are numerous factors to consider.
- Consultants should have some knowledge regarding the technology used in consultation: communication, networking and marketing, content capturing, presentation and delivery, document management, collaboration and sharing, and assessing, monitoring, and evaluating.
- Consultants must carefully consider how they document their services and their outcomes in accordance with how they are contracted to provide services.

Web-Based and Literature-Based Resources

Websites

Adobe Connect: http://success.adobe.com/content/en/na/programs/products/connect/1211-web-confer
ences.html?skwcid=TC|22191|adobe%20connect||S|e|21117383062&ef_id=xnFPhkZ9BRwAAIqK:
20130122063441:s

Apple iWork: http://www.apple.com/iwork

Dropbox: https://www.dropbox.com

Elluminate Live!: http://www.elluminate.com/Services/Training/Elluminate_Live!/?id=418

Evernote: http://evernote.com

Facebook: http://www.facebook.com

Google Docs: http://docs.google.com

Google Drive: http://drive.google.com

GoToMeeting: http://www.gotomeeting.com

iCloud: https://www.icloud.com

Instagram: http://www.instagram.com

LinkedIn: http://www.linkedin.com

Microsoft Office: http://office.microsoft.com/en-us

Online Therapy Institute: http://onlinetherapyinstitute.com

Open Office: http://www.openoffice.org

Pinterest: http://www.pinterest.com

Prezi: http://prezi.com

SecondLife: http://secondlife.com

SkyDrive: https://skydrive.live.com

Skype: http://www.skype.com

SurveyGizmo: http://www.surveygizmo.com

SurveyMonkey: http://www.surveymonkey.com

Twitter: http://www.twitter.com

Wiki (What is a wiki, by a wiki): http://en.wikipedia.org/wiki/Wiki

Suggested Readings

Council for Accreditation of Counseling & Related Educational Programs. (2009). *2009 standards* (Section 2d, 5b, 5c). Retrieved from http://www.cacrep.org/doc/2009%20Standards%20with%20cover.pdf

Merz Nagel, D., & Anthony, K. (2009). *Ethical framework for the use of technology in career and school guidance.* Retrieved from http://www.onlinetherapyinstitute.com/id51.html

Merz Nagel, D., & Anthony, K. (2009). *Ethical framework for the use of technology in coaching.* Retrieved from http://www.onlinetherapyinstitute.com/ethical-framework-for-the-use-of-technology-in-coaching

Merz Nagel, D., & Anthony, K. (2009). Ethical framework for the use of technology in mental health. Retrieved from http://onlinetherapyinstitute.com/ethical-training

References

American Counseling Association. (2005). *ACA code of ethics.* Alexandria, VA: Author.

Brinkman, T. M., Segool, N. K., Pham, A. V., & Carlson, J. S. (2007). Writing comprehensive behavioral consultation reports: Critical elements. *International Journal of Behavioral Consultation and Therapy, 3*(3), 372–383.

Cosier, R. A., & Dalton, D. R. (1993). Management consulting: Planning, entry, performance. *Journal of Counseling and Development, 72,* 191–198.

Erchul, W. P. (2003). Communication and interpersonal process in consultation: Guest editor's comments. *Journal of Educational and Psychological Consultation, 14*(2), 105–107.

Gottfredson, D. C. (1993). Strategies for improving treatment integrity in organizational consultation. *Journal of Educational and Psychological Consultation, 4*(3), 275–279.

Hoffman, M. A., Phillips, E. L., Noumair, D. A., Shullman, S., Geisler, C., Gray, J., . . . & Ziegler, D. (2006). Toward a feminist and multicultural model of consultation and advocacy. *Journal of Multicultural Counseling and Development, 34,* 116–128.

Holcomb-McCoy, C. (2004). Assessing the multicultural competence of school counselors: A checklist. *Professional School Counseling, 7*(3), 178–183.

Ingraham, C. L. (2003). Multicultural consultee-centered consultation: When novice consultants explore cultural hypotheses with experienced teacher consultees. *Journal of Educational and Psychological Consultation, 14*(Special issue 3 & 4), 329–362.

Jervey, G. (2004). The brand called Jim. *Money, 33*(11), 55–59.

Klein, M. D., & Harris, K. C. (2004). Considerations in the personnel preparation of itinerant early childhood special education consultants. *Journal of Educational and Psychological Consultation, 15*(2), 151–165.

Kurpius, D. J., Fuqua, D. R., & Rozecki, T. (1993). The consulting process: A multidimensional approach. *Journal of Counseling and Development, 71,* 601–606.

Lencioni, P. (2010). The power of a naked consultant. *Training + Development, 64*(7), 14.

Li, C., & Vazquez-Nuttall, E. (2009). School consultants as agents of social justice for multicultural children and families. *Journal of Educational and Psychological Consultation, 19,* 26–44.

Merz Nagel, D., & Anthony, K. (2009). *Therapy online: A practical guide.* London, UK: Sage. Meyers, A. B. (2002). Developing nonthreatening expertise: Thoughts on consultation training from the perspective of a new faculty member. *Journal of Educational and Psychological Consultation, 13*(1/2), 55–67.

Meyers, B. (2002). The contract negotiation stage of a school-based, cross-cultural organizational consultation: A case study. *Journal of Educational and Psychological Consultation, 13*(3), 151–183.

Meyers, J. (2002). A 30 year perspective on best practices for consultation training. *Journal of Educational and Psychological consultation, 13*(1/2), 35–54.

Moe, J. L., & Perera-Diltz, D. M. (2009). An overview of systemic-organizational consultation for professional counselors. *Journal of Professional Counseling: Practice, Theory, and Research, 37*(1), 27–37.

Plax, T. G. (2006). How much are we worth? Estimating fee for service. *Communication Education, 55*(2), 242–246.

Reidel, G. (Producer), & Judge, M. (Director). (1999). *Office Space* [Motion picture]. United States: 20th-Century Fox.

Remley, T. P. (1993). Consultation contracts. *Journal of Counseling and Development, 72,* 157–158.

Rogers, M. R. (2000). Examining the cultural context of consultation. *School Psychology Review, 29*(3), 414–418.

Washburn, J. J., Manley, T., & Holiwski, F. (2003). Teaching on white racism: Tools for consultant training. *Journal of Educational and Psychological Consultation, 14*(3/4), 387–399.

Weigel, R. G. (1988). Mid-life career change: Taking the plunge. *Journal of Counseling and Development, 67,* 123.

West, M. (2010). Nonprofits face a wealth of options as consulting field expands. *Chronicle of Philanthropy, 23*(1), 9.

4

Consultation Stages

Introduction

Seems like every theory and model has stages, phases, or steps. Consultation is no different. While there is no perfect structure to these stages, they are very useful when entering into a consulting relationship. This chapter presents these as possible stages that you may encounter (and hopefully utilize) when working as a mental health professional consultant. Not every consultation experience will go exactly as planned or by each stage. Two common questions asked by students and beginning consultants are

- "How long will each stage last?"
- "How long does the consultation process last with each consultee?"

Remember that the goal is to help the consultee and not to see how many consultation jobs you can complete in a 6-month time period. Gerald Tindal, Richard I. Parker and Jan Hasbrouck in 1992 said it best, in their research on consultation stages and the concern of time spent in each stage, when they stated "time to be an irrelevant variable" (p. 114) when providing consultation services. June Gallessich (1982) stated that some consultation services could go on for years. Weekly or monthly visits with the consultee may be needed to ensure there is not *program drift* or to help in addressing any new issues. Length of time will be an ongoing discussion between the consultant and consultee.

LEARNING OBJECTIVES

After reading this chapter, you will be able to

- Memorize and apply the general stages of the consultation process
- Discuss how the stages in the consultation process are not a rigid set of rules that must be followed at all times
- Have an opportunity, through case illustrations and exercises, to explore the stages of consultation and how you play a role in these stages
- Appreciate and be able to demonstrate the termination process of consultation

Stages, Steps, Phases

Examining the research on consultation, you will find that there are several different models explaining the various stages of consultation (Caplan & Caplan, 1999; West & Idol, 1990). Most stages, or phases, of consultation include a linear progression through the initial, middle, and final stages. The chapter's description of stages will also follow this flow of progression while at the same time recognizing that the process will not always flow in one direction. There will possibly be times of stagnation, back and forth movement (Allen & Graden, 2002), and the struggle for change.

Figure 4.1 shows the circular nature (with back and forth movement) of consultation, while also acknowledging that there can be linear progress through the stages. The dotted lines indicate possible movement between stages. The consultant and consultee may need to go through the process several times before the consultation services are complete. By allowing for this movement between stages, the consultant and consultee may understand that bumps in the road are all part of the process.

Figure 4.1 The Stages of Consultation

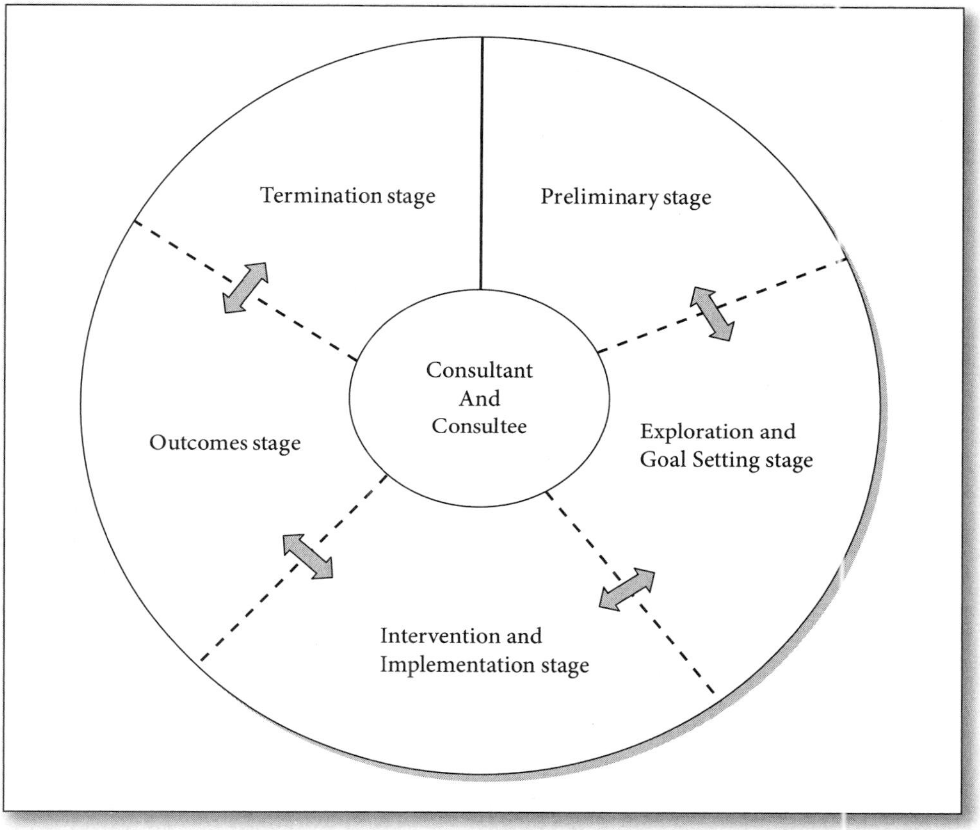

Preliminary Stage

After reading Case 4.1, you can see that while the school would like to examine the need to expand their programs, the staff is unsure of the specific needs and how they could meet their student's needs. This preliminary stage is when the consultee begins the discussion with a possible consultant to determine their needs and also selects a consultant with the expertise to help.

One of the critical pieces in this stage is that a consultee (individual or organization) may contact a consultant without even having a specific end goal for consultation. Len Sperry (2005) suggests that consultants need to gather as much information as possible and not move ahead in the process without attempting to get a clearer picture of what the consultee needs out of the process. Again, the consultee may not know exactly what they want out of consultation, but proceeding without multiple discussions is ill advised. It will be the role of the consultant to discuss with the consultee the general framework of their goal for consultation. This step may lead to the decision that consultation is not needed or that consultant's expertise does not mesh with the consultee's needs. Once a decision has been made to enter into a consultation relationship, the consultant will need to create a contract, negotiate fees, and discuss timelines as discussed in more detail in Chapter 3 of this text.

The preliminary stage is one of the most critical in the consultation process. Not to say that you can't go back and make adjustments, but it is important to not dive into a situation that may have a high probability of failure due to mishandling of the preliminary stage. Dougherty (2009, p. 55) expanded on the work by Wendell L. French and Cecil H. Bell (1999) by reminding consultants to increase the chances of success in the consultation process by not falling into initial traps:

- Promising too much at the beginning of the process
- Failing to realize that your expertise is not in the specified need area of the consultee
- Not recognizing the real problem
- Not stating the specific roles of the consultant (creating boundaries)

Even though you may be very eager to enter into a consulting relationship, please keep these factors in mind and remember that one of the main goals is to do no harm. In 1984, Karen S. Kitchener described this concept of not harming other people as *nonmaleficence*. This will require the consultant to be cognizant of how their interactions with the consultee must be driven by the consultee's needs from consultation and not what the consultant thinks the consultee *should do* to address the issue. For more information on ethical guidelines in consultation, please refer to Chapter 7.

Guided Practice Exercises
Exercise 4.1: Nonprofit

A nonprofit adoption agency has been struggling financially for the past three months, so the director, Mary, decides to seek help and calls you. As a consultant, you agree to meet with Mary at her place of work to discuss the issues that the agency is experiencing.

1. *In this preliminary stage of consultation, what are the most important questions to ask Mary?*

After communicating to Mary that it's important to ask a few questions concerning the situation to be sure you can competently meet her needs, she shares how the agency is running out of funds and she fears it will go under. Mary explains how math and budgeting have never come naturally to her, and she expects her employees to manage the money.

2. *What are some ways you will evaluate whether or not you are qualified to proceed in consulting Mary and her agency?*

Upon deciding you have sufficient knowledge and experience in finance and business, you create a contract. You discuss fees and approximately how long you think your services may be needed, being intentional about mentioning and trying to agree upon a proposed termination date.

3. *How would you handle a situation where the consultee disagrees on a fee or termination date?*

4. *How do you negotiate these differences graciously while maintaining your professional opinion as well as a collaborative approach?*

Exploration and Goal Setting Stage

Once contracts have been finalized (a discussion on how to create a consultation contract is located in the Necessary Skills of a Consultant chapter), the next step in the process is for the consultant to learn about the consultee (individual and/or organization) and work on developing specific goals for consultation. The consultant will learn as much as possible about the consultee and their needs by spending time on-site, interviewing all of the connected people and evaluating all of the available resources of the consultee.

Case 4.2: Hello, My Name Is...

Ahmed was designated to serve as the lead person (consultee) for the school. His first task was to find a local consultant who could help. Ahmed reached out to several local mental health professionals who were trained in addictions and he knew provided consultation services. Ahmed interviewed two consultants who had the expertise to assist in this project. Ahmed would be the first person to say that he really had no idea what to exactly look for in a consultant. Both consultants he interviewed had the education and experience in addictions that would qualify them for the project. Ahmed's decision came down to Kay's potential to "fit" and get along with the other

(Continued)

(Continued)

employees at the school. Ahmed commented on how Kay seemed genuinely interested in the school's concerns and was just so much easier to talk with than the other consultant. Kay wanted to learn as much as possible about the areas of concern and provided Ahmed with clear expectations and descriptions of what her role would be as a consultant. Kay even made the discussion about fees and the contract feel less anxious than the other consultant.

Kay also made a positive impression with the school administrators and other employees during her first week providing consultation services. Kay was more than willing to take time to talk with teachers and other school employees about why she was "in the building" and what her role was as a consultant. Kay was also cognizant of letting the employees talk about what they are seeing and hearing during a typical school day. Kay tried to attend some of the weekly staff meetings to discuss the concerns and needs of the school in relation to the substance abuse issues.

Getting to Know You

Gallessich (1982) and Duane Brown, Walter B. Pryzwansky, and Ann C. Schulte (2011) discussed the very real processes of *formal* and *psychological* entry into an organization. This first section is for the consultant who is external of the organization. The consultant needs to be aware that all of the dynamics of meeting and working with someone for the first time are in play during the consultation process. This is just one of the many opportunities to show off those counseling skills to develop a trusting and meaningful professional relationship with the consultee and other members of the organization (refer back to Chapter 2 for roles of the consultant). Also, just as in traditional counseling, expect to encounter various forms of resistance and reluctance during the process. It will be the consultant's job to be aware of these issues, bring them up, and discuss them in a constructive manner. Remember that although the consultee asked you for assistance, not everyone in the organization may be on board with these changes.

If the consultant is already an employee of the organization, there will still be the adjustment to viewing the person as a consultant and not just a coworker. So, any issues that were lingering between you and your coworkers before you stepped into the role of consultant will STILL be lingering in your new role. These issues may need to be addressed before moving on with the consultation (easier said than done!). Realistically, these personality differences may not have the opportunity to resolve themselves before consultation can begin. One important factor that can assist in the transition to consultant is having the administrators and executives support (direct communication with employees) the consultation role you have taken on. You will need the help and assistance of ALL employees.

One advantage of serving as an internal consultant is that you will already have firsthand knowledge of the organization, its resources and staff (Brown et al., 2011).

Once all of the formalities are out of the way, the consultant can begin the exploration of the consultee's needs and establish some working goals. One clear challenge for the consultant will be to maintain objectivity during the process. This is not a chance for the consultant to "get back" at other coworkers or make changes that they personally always wanted to make in the organization. Remaining neutral and objective will be harder for the internal consultant, but is a critical piece to a successful consultation experience.

We hope you can see that entry (either external or internal) as a consultant can be a very daunting task. Kenwyn K. Smith and Sara J. Corse (1986) state "entry itself is a very complex process. How it is undertaken will powerfully influence the success of later interventions" (p. 254). Howard S. Becker (1967) even contends that the consultant may be expected by groups within the organization to *take sides* in either visible or hidden agendas within the organization. Elizabeth L. Teed and John A. Scileppi (2007) remind consultants that they may be the voice of encouragement the consultee needs to bring up these potential negative issues with the administrators and others in the organization so that these political issues will not be a hindrance in the consultation process. Being able to remain neutral and not get caught up in organization politics will be a very handy tool in your consultation toolbox.

Exploration

> ## Guided Practice Exercises
> ## Exercise 4.2: Exploration

Ahmed and the school administrators charged Kay with the goal of gathering information on the current drugs being abused in the community and what programs could be used in the school to address this growing problem. Ahmed let Kay know that the school needed answers about these new drugs and what they could do to help their students.

After a couple of weeks, Kay presented Ahmed and the school administrators with information about the drug that was actually reaching epidemic proportions in the community. Ahmed's first words after the presentation were "*I didn't realize* that this drug was being used by so many people in the community." Ahmed and the school administrators realized that they would not have been able to get such a clear picture of the substance abuse going on in the local community and how it was affecting the children at their school without Kay's help.

Kay was able to pull together data retrieved from the local police department on recent drug arrests and also talk with addictions counselors at the local substance abuse treatment program to find out about the new drug that had entered the community. Kay continued to gather data to make sure that her information was as accurate as possible and provided the school with any updates.

Discussion Questions

1. *Can you think of other possible community resources that Kay could have used to gather data for Ahmed and the school?*

2. *What types of other information would be helpful to Ahmed and his school in trying to understand this new problem?*

Note: This exercise may be helpful for school counselors in addressing CACREP SC Specialty Standard G2: Knows the signs and symptoms of substance abuse in children and adolescents, as well as the signs and symptoms of living in a home where substance abuse occurs.

As you can see from the case illustration and exercises, there is a lot of work that is completed by the consultant away from the consultee. The consultant is charged with gathering data from as many sources as possible to present to the consultee. Knowing local, state, and national resources is a must for a consultant. Knowing (and keeping in contact) with mental health professionals at local mental health centers and facilities and schools will enable a consultant to keep up with new programs, workshops, and services in the community. Mental health policies are always changing, which mandates that a consultant stay abreast of any changes that could affect the consultee. We have listed several useful websites to help stay informed of mental health policies in the resources section at the end of the chapter.

The consultant is not the only person involved in gathering data from resources. Alex S. Hall and Meei-Ju Lin (1994) explain how the consultee and consultant enter into a collaborative mode to gather information and work together during this stage. The consultee takes an active role in the exploration stage as this may help to clarify needs and produce specific goals.

During exploration, the consultant becomes somewhat of a detective for the consultee—examining information from as many sources as possible and then presenting this information to the consultee to develop concrete goals is the focus during exploration. Will you be able to find out all of the information from the web? No. As you read in Case 4.3, the consultant even made a trip to the local police department to discuss issues related to the consultee's need for help. The resources and possibilities to find and use resources are endless.

Keep a File

An important step in the exploration process (and we tell our students constantly) is to develop working relationships with as many resources as possible. Remember to try not to "burn bridges" with community resources because you never know when you will need their assistance. Also, please remember to offer your help when a resource reaches out to you for assistance. As you work as a consultant over months and years, you will not be able to remember all of the contact information for all of your resources. Please start and maintain a file with contact information for all of your resources. Keeping in regular contact with many of your resources will ensure that you have the correct information and contact person at a site.

Interviews and Observations

Two others components in the exploration stage will be interviews and observations. Once again, you will use your Counseling 101 skills to conduct the needed interviews and observations. Your ability to quickly establish rapport with the interviewee will ensure the greater chances of a successful interview (Gallessich, 1982). Interviews can be either individual or group, depending on the needs of the consultee and the consultant's determination of the most beneficial way to gather interview information. The consultant will need to prepare in advance of the interviews, what type of interview (individual, group, or survey) and what questions need to be asked in the interview.

Guided Practice Exercises
Exercise 4.3: Trips

Entering the Exploration and Goal setting stage of consultation, you begin learning about the nonprofit adoption agency and Mary's role in running it. This consists of making five different visits to the agency to observe all the employees in action, including taking calls from potential clients, reading past financial reports, examining the mission statement, meeting with birth mothers and adoptive families, and staff meetings. Next, you arrange to meet with all eight employees individually, including Mary, to discuss what they understand to be their job description as well as any concerns about their work.

1. *What are the advantages to meeting with the employees individually versus as a group?*

2. *How would you handle an employee who refuses to talk to you or gets defensive?*

3. *What are some clinical skills to incorporate when working with a resistant client?*

Survey interviews can be a set of questions that may explore an employee's thoughts and feelings about an organization (Gallessich, 1982). These can be administered using a hardcopy or electronic format and many use some type of Likert scoring for data collection. The benefit of using surveys is that they can be administered to a large group of individuals without the time and expense of interviewing each person individually or in groups. The con to using surveys is that you will lose the personal touch that comes from face-to-face discussions.

Guided Practice Exercises
Exercise 4.4: Surveys

Imagine that you are entering into the interview and observation stages of consultation. You begin by examining the agency's bank statements from the last year and gather data on significant changes in numbers, which requires Mary's (agency's Director) help. You ask her to provide information on all expenses as well as profits for the last year, which she reports included some very profitable months. Lastly, you conduct a survey of thirty past birth mothers and adoptive families who sought services through the agency.

1. *What are some important questions to ask in these surveys?*

2. *How would the questions differ for the birth mothers and the adoptive families?*

After collecting all the data, you analyze it and prepare to present it to Mary in whole.

3. *What are some ways to present this material to Mary in hard copy form that is not too overwhelming?*

4. *Would you also provide an electronic form of the data? Why or why not?*

The use of observation to gather information in consultation is very similar to observation in traditional counseling. As mental health professionals, we know that behavioral (or direct) observation is not the same (or as easy) as just observing someone in our daily routine. As a consultant, you will need to use your training in behavioral observation when you use this technique in consultation. Smith and Corse (1986) state "since data gathering affects the relationship of the consultant and consultee system, the choices of methods should both maximize the benefit to this relationship and throw light on increasingly precise hypotheses about system dynamics" (p. 260).

Crunching the Data

You have been working hard at collecting all of this data . . . now what?

- Should I just hand over all of this information and let the consultee decipher?
- What should I do with ALL of this information?
- Should I make a fancy presentation to show the consultee?
- Should I decide what to show and not show the consultee?

These are all very real questions that you will need to decide on before going to the consultee with what you have discovered during exploration.

Remember those research design classes you had in graduate school? Now is the time to use that information to crunch the data you have collected into a format that will be easy to comprehend by the consultee. Looking for common themes, significant data points and conclusions are all part of this process. The consultee will many times just want to see the "conclusion" section of your report. That is fine as long as you make sure to include information from all sources. We don't think it is wise for you as the consultant to determine what information to include or leave out. If you provide at least some data from all resources explored, the consultee may actually see something that you missed from a resource. Good or bad, pro or con, let the consultee know about your exploration and resources used in gathering the data. As for the presentation, this will be up to you and what you think the consultee will appreciate. Formal presentations can be advantageous. Just remember to provide the consultee with a hard copy of the data and findings—probably best to go with print copy and electronic version. No matter what you choose, allow time for discussion and open dialogue and understand that official goal setting will be generated by these presentations.

Goal Setting

Now that the oral and written communications have been determined, setting the goal(s) can begin. Goal setting in consultation can be one of the most critical steps in the process. Ask questions such as *Is this actually the correct goal? What happens if this is not the correct goal?* and *Can we change the goal to be a part of the consultation process during goal setting?* Consultants and consultees must be very clear during their discussions about setting goals. Lorna Idol, Phyllis Paolucci-Whitcomb and Ann Nevin (1995) state that during this process, all parties must use language that is understood by all (no jargon) and reduce misunderstandings that are so common in communication. Once again, put all of those Counseling 101 skills to practice! Clarifying, summarizing, and paraphrasing will help you and the consultee know that each other understands the messages that both are trying to convey.

If, during the process, you and the consultee realize that the goal(s) need to be changed, don't panic. Goal revising and updating are part of the continuous process (Hall & Lin, 1994; Gallessich, 1982). Smith and Corse (1986) state that goal revision may be necessary after exploring new data uncovered by the consultation process. So don't assume that the process is a failure if you have to revise the goals of consultation. Just remember to take your time in creating goals at any stage in the process.

As noted earlier, make sure that both you and the consultee completely agree on the established goal. Also make sure that everyone agrees to what their role will be in reaching the goals. Don't leave the goal setting meetings without everyone in agreement on what, when, and where they will complete their tasks for each goal. Hall and Lin (1994) support writing down specific goals to increase the chances of successful consultation. This step may take the most time and be the most arduous step, but well worth the time and effort. I talk to my students about trying to operationally define the goal so that there can be measurable steps along the way of accomplishing the goal; that way, all parties can see how the goal is being met. For example, if the goal of consultation is to create a group-counseling program working with at-risk youth at a local detention center, some of the operationally defined steps could be the following:

Goal 1 will be to establish a group-counseling program at the center.

This goal will be met by the following steps:

- Determine the biggest need(s) of the youth being served at the center.
- Examine resources to meet this need (i.e., group room, time and day of group, who will facilitate the group).
- Discuss with administration what resources are needed to create the group-counseling program.
- Design (or use an existing group-counseling curriculum) and implement the group-counseling program.
- Design (or use already established) assessment to evaluate program.
- Make any necessary changes to program.
- Implement program on a regular basis.

Intervention and Implementation Stage

Guided Practice Exercises
Exercise 4.5: Intervention Time, Which One?

Directions: This exercise will allow you to think of different intervention options that can be used in this case. Don't be afraid to seek out new interventions that could be used to help Ahmed and Kay tackle this growing substance problem in the school.

Kay has helped Ahmed with discovering that a new drug has entered the community and is picking up popularity with the high school students. Kay (the consultant) has provided information to Ahmed and the school administrators about the specific drug and what types of treatment approaches are being used at the community sub-stance abuse centers. With so many options for treatment, Ahmed is feeling a little overwhelmed at deciding on what direction to go into start addressing the issue of substance abuse in his school. While Ahmed wants to clearly address the specific new drug, he (and the school administrators) want to revamp their overall substance abuse curriculum and think this is the best time to do so, with the consultant's help. Kay decides to create a presentation that reviews the current list of top drugs being abused at the school and within the local community. Kay also discusses some of the treatment options that are being used in the local community and leading addiction programs throughout the country. Now Kay will sit down with Ahmed to try to narrow down the specific intervention(s) that will be used at Ahmed's school. Once the intervention is selected, Ahmed and Kay will present the intervention(s) to the school administrators for approval.

Discussion Questions

1. *In what way(s) would you present the information you had gathered, as the consult-ant, to Ahmed? Options could be PowerPoint presentation, simple discussion, written report, etc.*

2. *Would your decision on how to present the information gathered be based on your preference (counseling style) or the needs of the consultee? Explain.*

3. *Using various resources (databases, journal articles, web searches), discuss at least two different interventions that could be used to address the problems of substance abuse at Ahmed's school.*

4. *Get in groups of two for this next exercise. Both of you will take turns in the role of consultant and consultee.*

   A. *When you are the consultant: After researching for possible treatment options, pro-vide the consultee with what you have found. Also go over how you would implement the intervention in the school. Remember to go over issues such as time, cost, who would facilitate the intervention, etc. Remember the list of options provided by Smith and Corse (1982) when deciding on interventions provided earlier in the chapter.*

   B. *When you are the consultee. Listen to the consultant explain the options for the possible intervention to be used in your school. Feel free to ask questions about the how, when and cost of the interventions.*

Intervention

Now that the goals for consultation have been established, the next step is to create possible interventions and implement these interventions to reach the goals. Implementation processes will be different in various settings. As you read about consultation in different settings, you will see that the basic framework is similar, but the focus and direction on the services will differ according to the needs and structure of the specific settings. Interventions will come in all shapes and sizes and can be a daunting task to decide on which one (or group of interventions) to use in a setting. Russ Newman (2010) reminds consultants that they need to be continually gaining new knowledge concerning the consultation interventions field to keep up with the ever changing and fast-paced world. The consultee will look to the consultant for information about different interventions.

The consultant will have many options when deciding on an intervention to use. Keep in mind a buzzword (but incredibly important) concept if deciding on using a formal intervention (i.e., anger management curriculum, stress-reduction curriculum); make sure to know and make decisions based on the *evidence-based* support (Corrigan, Steiner, McCracken, Blaser, & Barr, 2001) for the intervention. Most interventions will have gone through extensive research to examine the effectiveness of an intervention or curriculum. Without evidenced-based support for an intervention or curriculum, the consultant may be put at risk for litigation if an unproven intervention or curriculum is used.

Another factor to consider will be costs of the intervention and costs by the consultee to facilitate the intervention. Gregory D. Chowanec, Donald N. Neunaber, and Mary M. Krajl (1994) remind us that mental health consultants will play a critical role in trying to keep costs down while providing quality services to the consultee. As we all know, many organizations and schools are running on shoestring budgets and will need to get the best intervention while maintaining costs at a manageable level.

There are countless interventions that can be used in the consultation process. Deciding on the intervention is not an exact science and, of course, can be changed if needed. Various interventions will be discussed in the chapters on consultation in various settings throughout the text. With so many to choose from, Smith and Corse (1986, p.262) provide an outline (see Table 4.1) when considering what type of intervention to use in consultation.

As you can see from the decision questions listed in Table 4.1, there are multiple levels of decisions to make when selecting an intervention. The consultant will need to work with the consultee in determining the best approach for the specific needs of the consultee.

Implementation

Implementation of the interventions will be a process that is filled with reevaluation, recycling, and reformation of the interventions. Don't be afraid to admit that the first (or second) intervention may not be working and that there needs to be discussion

Table 4.1 Types of Interventions

* What is the type of organization receiving consultation?

  a. School setting
  b. Mental Health setting
  c. Organizational setting
  d. Higher Education setting

* What will be the philosophical model?

  a. Education and training
  b. Clinical
  c. Mental Health
  d. Behavioral
  e. Organizational

* What will be the actual dynamics of the consultation?

  a. Process consultation
  b. Third-party intervention
  c. Team building
  d. Survey feedback

Source: Adapted from Smith & Corse (1986).

about other intervention options. In fact, having other intervention options already in mind and available will aid in this process and make the transition to another intervention much smoother.

The consultant's role in implementation will vary from site to site and what is best for the consultee. Gallessich (1982) contends that the consultant may not even be involved in the implementation of the intervention. As in traditional counseling, the role of the consultant will be to help facilitate growth in the consultee so that they can make the changes for themselves without having to depend on the consultant for constant help. This is not to say that the consultant will disappear from the scene. The consultant will stay in contact with the consultee to discuss how the intervention is working, if they need to make any small tweaks, and offer general assistance if needed. John R. Bergan and Thomas R. Kratochwill (1990) suggest that the consultant could utilize brief interviews or observations during this time to stay connected and assist the consultee.

Outcomes Stage

So how do you know if all of the hard work that you and the consultee have put into the process is actually working? This is where the outcomes stage comes into view. Brown et al. (2011, p. 126) use the term *formative evaluation* to describe the evaluation of the actual intervention and implementation of the intervention. Gallessich (1982) pointed out that there are a plethora of evaluation instruments to use in evaluating the interventions used in consultation—most importantly, the consultant's familiarity with an evaluation tool and the tool's relevance in measuring the desired intervention. The outcomes stage deals with the consultant gathering data to determine if the intervention is effective. There are several ways to gather this data:

- Surveys
- Observations
- Pretests and posttests and experimental tests (Ketterer, 1981)

Aspects that the consultant will want to evaluate could be

- effectiveness of the intervention,
- overall costs (are they in line with original cost goals),
- time efficiency (is the intervention staying within the established time parameters), and
- support from administrators and staff to continue with intervention.

Guided Practice Exercises
Exercise 4.6: How Do We Know It's Working?

Ahmed has been working with Kay (the consultant) for a couple of months now on the new substance abuse intervention program implemented at Ahmed's school. Kay was able to help in contract negotiations with the mental health/substance abuse facility to provide a licensed addictions counselor to provide weekly substance abuse interventions directly to the students in Ahmed's school. Ahmed and the other school counselors have been working closely with the addictions counselor and providing psychoeducational groups to the parents of the adolescents in their school. Ahmed and the school administrators have heard many positive comments from teachers, parents and even the students on how much they are benefiting from the new focus on substance abuse in the school. Many of the psychoeducational groups are in the afternoon and evenings when parents can attend and not miss as much work.

Ahmed and the school administrators are eager to find out if the interventions are having an effect on the students and parents who are volunteering to participate in the program. Ahmed approached Kay to discuss how they could find out if the intervention is working with the students, parents and teachers. Kay is considering what type of evaluation method would best capture the thoughts about the program and any changes with the students and their substance abuse activity.

Discussion Questions

1. *As the consultant, what you would like to measure?*

2. *How would you measure the variables you listed in question 1?*

3. *Use available resources to conduct a search on relevant measurement instruments that you could use to measure the effectiveness of the intervention(s) you selected in the previous guided exercise.*

If the consultant finds issues with either the intervention or implementation during this outcome stage, discussions should occur with the consultee for any changes that may be made to either issue. This will also be the time for the consultant to serve as support and motivator for the consultee. As we all know, change can be difficult for some. Teed and Scileppi (2007) remind us that with change, some in the organization will benefit while others may not benefit from the changes. The consultant will need to have discussions, early in the process, about the possible pros and cons for the consultee (and organization) of going through with the consultation process. This helps and keeps the struggles associated with change to not be a surprise when they surface.

Termination Stage

Now that the consultation process is winding down, how do you exit the consultation process and consultation relationship? There are two main steps in this stage: final evaluation and termination of services. As in traditional counseling, the process of ending services in consultation needs to start at the very beginning of the consultation activity and be understood by both parties as the ending of the professional relationship. Easier said than done in some situations!

Final Evaluation

The final evaluation phase of the termination stage involves the consultant examining how well the consultation process went with the consultee and any other vested parties. This evaluation is different from the outcomes stage in specifically examining the consultation process as a whole and not the intervention (and implementation of the intervention) as described in the outcomes stage. Typically, a consultant will want to examine one or more of the following issues in their final evaluation:

- Were the overall goals of consultation achieved (Gallessich, 1982)?
- Was the consultant successful in creating an atmosphere that was conducive in supporting and motivating the consultee to participate in the consultation process?
- Did the consultant maintain costs during the process (Gallessich, 1982)?

- Did the consultee feel that the consultant listened to the needs in a respectful and professional manner throughout the process?
- Did the consultant work within the resources and boundaries of the agency/school/organization to help the consultee create beneficial interventions?

As you can see, the evaluation at this point is beneficial to both the consultee *and* consultant. The consultant can use this information to examine strengths and weaknesses in the consultation style that can be addressed before the next consultation assignment. Having data from outside sources can benefit the consultant in discovering those hidden areas of a person's personality that could hinder the professional consultation relationship in the future. Having this data can also highlight personality traits that can be used in future consultation assignments.

This final evaluation is beneficial in providing the consultee and consultant with information about whether the goals of consultation were actually achieved. This is a time for the consultant and consultee to make any final adjustments to the intervention with the consultant's assistance. There is so much already in place at this point so making any last minute changes will not necessitate a complete change in direction or a complete overhaul of the intervention. This is also a chance for the consultant to provide the consultee with data that may provide support for the intervention and all of the consultee's hard work.

Remember that, many times, the consultee will have taken a huge risk by trying to change the way an organization, agency, or school operates and may need a data driven "pat-on-the-back" for all of the hard work during the process. Will every final evaluation be positive and will the consultant and consultee have implemented the perfect intervention? Of course not, but when there are positive results, why not congratulate the consultee for their work? When the final evaluation indicates that the consultation process did not achieve the desired outcomes, this is the opportunity for the consultant to still provide support to the consultee and discuss ways in which the process can be improved in the future. If the goal was not reached or the administrators do not approve the intervention for use in the organization, this does not mean failure. The consultant and consultee will need to look for ways to learn from the process. This learning can be used to create a new way of thinking about the original issue and what can be tried next time. Please don't let all of the hard work be for nothing. Make those changes, discuss new options with administrators, and find new ways to provide the much needed interventions and services!

Saying Goodbye

Termination in the consulting field has some of the same issues as terminating in traditional counseling. Even though consultation services will be very clearly spelled out in the contract, exactly when to terminate can be a tricky decision. Jack Novick (1997) stated that many of the earlier psychotherapists did not even view termination as a phase or step in counseling. Smith and Corse (1986) simplified the process into two steps: (1) the goals were met, or (2) the process failed to reach the goals. Over the years, researchers (Schein, 1969; Gallessich, 1982; Dougherty, Tack, Fullam, & Hammer, 1996) in the field of consultation have proposed guidelines that can be used in the consultation process. Typically, termination will involve the following:

- Acknowledgement that termination of services is approaching
- Reducing support (includes amount of time spent with consultee and amount of information being shared)
- Formal ending of consultation services

The first issue should not be that tricky. The consultee should be made aware of the termination of consulting services during the initial discussions and contract negotiations. The consultant failed in their duties if the consultee is surprised at the end of the process to discover that the consultant will be ending services at a specific date. The consultant will need to keep the consultee abreast of the upcoming end of services, but the final termination date should be agreed upon by both parties (Young, 2009). As in traditional counseling, termination issues are many times the least talked about part of counseling. There is something about ending a relationship (even a professional relationship) that creates anxiety, mixed feelings and avoidance in both the mental health professional and client (Ward, 1984). Now that we know these issues related to counseling, it is even more critical that the consultant begins the discussion about termination early in the consulting relationship. Sometimes, termination may be earlier than discussed due to budgetary issues, discovering that the consultant's expertise may not be the best fit, or the professional consulting relationship is not a productive mesh (Gallessich, 1982). In these and other cases, early termination may be the best option.

Guided Practice Exercises
Exercise 4.7: Time to Say Goodbye

Kay and Ahmed had been working for some time now addressing the substance abuse issue at Ahmed's school. Although there had been some rough times trying to convince administrators to continue with the process, both Kay and Ahmed were feeling very positive about the intervention. While there had been some reevaluations of the process (i.e., working with parents, getting commitment from the students, etc.), the intervention had been in place for several months with no new problems or revisions. Kay realized that the consultation process was starting to come to a conclusion. Kay scheduled a meeting with Ahmed to talk to him about terminating the consultation services and when all of this would happen.

Discussion Questions

1. *What could Kay do in the consultation process so that Ahmed would not be shocked when she called to discuss the termination of services?*

2. *Briefly list the steps you would take as the consultant to prepare for termination of services with Ahmed.*

3. *The chapter talked about what types of issues a consultant may want to evaluate in their final evaluation. Discuss what you think is important in Ahmed's consultation case to evaluate during the termination stage of the process.*

4. *Are you good at goodbyes? Briefly discuss how you would handle the termination of services with Ahmed and the school administrators.*

5. *Are there any multicultural considerations Kay may need to address when entering into and ending the consultation process?*

Reducing support to the consultee is another step in the consultation process. Richard D. Parsons and Joel Meyers (1984) remind the consultant that issues related to dependency by the consultee can surface during this part of the termination process. The consultant will need to be on the lookout for any hint of dependency by the consultee on the consultant and discuss this with the consultee. Having this discussion can be awkward, but necessary. As the consultant reduces their support of the consultee, the consultee will continue to gather strength and knowledge to maintain the changes established in the consulting process. The reducing in support can be a gradual phase out where the consultant could reduce visits with the consultee over a period of time (Gallessich, 1982).

The formal ending in termination is the setting of the actual last day on consulting services and saying goodbyes. We all say goodbye in different ways. Dougherty et al. (1996) brought up an important variable in respecting the consultee's worldview on ending relationships. Having a discussion with the consultee about personal customs on ending relationships will decrease the chances of any awkward goodbyes in the parking lot. As with any ending of a professional relationship, this does not mean that there will never be any other contact in the future. As in counseling, let the consultee know that there will be opportunities for follow-up if needed and also contracting for future consultation services if needed.

Guided Practice Exercises
Exercise 4.8: Hospital

You are a consultant and receive a frantic call one day from the head nurse of the neo-natal unit of a local hospital after another nurse collapsed while holding a newborn baby. The parents of the baby have pressed charges, and the unit is allegedly in chaos. With experience in litigation, you decide to head to the hospital and survey the situation. When you arrive, the head nurse greets you and directs you to a private room. She explains the lawsuit that is underway between the family and the hospital. You ask for clarity concerning what services she is seeking from you. She explains that the hospital has a special protocol for legal situations like this that involves designated lawyers; however, she says she needs your help reconciling nurses in the unit and reestablishing equilibrium and a better crisis plan. She says this scenario was handled poorly, result-ing in more chaos because nurses didn't seem to know what to do with the injured infant and unconscious nurse.

1. *Who is the consultee? Who are the clients? How do these roles differ when working with them?*

You agree to return in two days after everyone has had a day to calm down. Meanwhile, you follow up on the baby's health status. Upon your next arrival to the neonatal unit, you check on the status of the nurse who collapsed and learn she has recovered and is working that day. You first meet with her and then ask to speak with each nurse present the day of the incident individually to hear their experience and decide if they need counseling.

2. *What questions might you ask the nurse who collapsed?*

3. *What questions might you ask the other nurses?*

The nurse who collapsed tells you she is diabetic and collapsed because she forgot to take her morning insulin shot. You ask what accounted for this negligence. She explains she received a speeding ticket on her way to work and when she arrived late, she was asked to attend to an ill baby immediately. When she went to check on the infant, she noticed he was turning blue and began to move him to another incubator, but before she knew it, she was on the floor. She appears very distressed and begins crying.

4. *What are some ways you can comfort this nurse?*

5. *Why might it be important to build rapport with her?*

After speaking with the other four nurses present the day of the accident, you learn they are all frustrated with the nurse who collapsed. However, you also notice that only two of the four nurses mentioned their coworker's diabetes, leading you to suspect that this illness is not public knowledge.

6. *How do you handle this medical information?*

7. *Is the nurse's diabetes confidential information?*

8. *What types of interventions might you implement to facilitate effective group communication among the nurses?*

9. *How can you help the unit process the event effectively?*

10. *How can you be sure to remain objective and not engage in any of the unit's politics?*

11. *How can you involve all the nurses in creating a more effective safety plan?*

Multicultural Considerations

Each stage, phase or step will require the consultant to be cognizant of the client and consultee's diversity and what it means to each person. Progressing through the stages, the consultant will need to continue to engage in open dialogue about how multicultural issues could play a role in any changes (or obstacles) that may be a part of the journey. An example of respecting diversity may be to not schedule meetings (or increase production by working) on days that the consultees may consider the day of rest in their religion. If working with organizations or agencies outside of the United States, a key issue will be to understand and work with their non-U.S. work schedules and workweeks.

Another aspect of diversity issues could be increasing awareness of how any of these changes will affect *all* of their employees and managers. An example could be if the organization decides to move locations or make physical changes to their current locations. The consultant will want to discuss how these changes could impact any of the employees with physical disabilities. The consultant will need to discuss and encourage administrators to be aware and make the location(s) ADA compliant.

Chapter Keystones

- Stages, steps, or phases: They are all advantageous to have a general framework for consulting
- Not all consulting will be exactly linear. Knowing how and when to move to the next steps is the most important step.
- Be vigilant! The more you know about the consultee and clients, the greater the chances for success.
- The first goal a consultee wants to examine might not be the final goal. Evaluate and crunch the data!
- Going back to the drawing board is okay. It's more important to get it right than to finish quickly.
- Termination is a real and much needed part of consultation. Many of the same issues in traditional counseling will surface in consultation termination.

Web-Based and Literature-Based Resources

Websites

Listings of current mental health public policies:

Mental Health America: http://www.mentalhealthamerica.net/go/action/policy-issues-a-z
American Counseling Association: http://www.counseling.org/publicpolicy
Mental Illness Policy Org.: http://mentalillnesspolicy.org

Major public policy acts and programs that will be helpful to review:

Community Mental Health Centers Act in 1963: http://research.archives.gov/description/299383
Omnibus Budget Reconciliation Act in 1981(Health services): http://www.4shared.com/office/fvLJ3op5/Health_Services_and_Resources_.html
National Institute of Mental Health: http://www.nimh.nih.gov/index.shtml

References

Allen, S. J., & Graden, S. J. (2002). Best practices in collaborative problem solving for intervention design. In A. Thomas & J. Grimes (Eds.), *Best practices in school psychology* (4th ed., pp. 565–582). Washington, DC: National Association of School Psychologists.

Becker, H. S. (1967). Whose side are we on? *Social Problems, 14,* 239–247.

Bergan, J. R., & Kratochwill, T. R. (1990). *Behavioral consultation and therapy.* New York, NY: Plenum.

Brown, D., Pryzwansky, W. B., & Schulte, A. C. (2011). *Psychological consultation and collaboration: Introduction to theory and practice* (7th Ed.). Upper Saddle River: Pearson.

Caplan, G., & Caplan, R. B. (1999). *Mental health consultation and collaboration.* Prospect Heights, IL: Waveland.

Chowanec, G. D., Neunaber, D. N., & Krajl, M. M. (1994). Customer driven mental healthcare and the role of the mental healthcare consultant. *Consulting Psychology Journal: Practice and Research, 46*(4), 47–54. doi:10.1037/1061-4087.46.4.47

Corrigan, P. W., Steiner, L., McCracken, S. G., Blaser, B., & Barr, M. (2001). Strategies for disseminating evidence-based practices to staff who treat people with serious mental illness. *Psychiatric Services, 52,* 1598–1606. doi:10.1176/appi.ps.52.12.1598

Dougherty, A. M. (2009). *Psychological consultation and collaboration in school and community settings* (5th ed.). Belmont, CA: Brooks/Cole.

Dougherty, A. M., Tack, F. E., Fullam, C. B., & Hammer, L. A. (1996). Disengagement: A neglected aspect of the consultation process. *Journal of Educational and Psychological Consultation, 7,* 259–274. doi:10.1207/s1532768xjepc0703_5

French, W. L., & Bell, C. H., Jr. (1999). *Organization development: Behavioral science interventions for organization improvement* (6th ed.). Englewood Cliffs, NJ: Prentice Hall.

Gallessich, J. (1982). *The profession and practice of consultation.* San Francisco, CA: Jossey-Bass.

Hall, A. S., & Lin, M.-J. (1994). An integrative consultation framework: A practical tool for elementary school counselors. *Elementary School Guidance & Counseling, 29,* 16–27.

Idol, L., Paolucci-Whitcomb, P., & Nevin, A. (1995). The collaborative consultation model. *Journal of Educational and Psychological Consultation, 6,* 329–346.

Ketterer, R. F. (1981). *Consultation and education in mental health: Problems and prospects.* Beverly Hills, CA: Sage.

Kitchener, K. S. (1984). Intuition, critical evaluation, and ethical principles. The foundation for ethical decisions in counseling psychology. *The Counseling Psychologist, 12,* 43–55.

Newman, R. (2010). Diversifying consulting psychology for the future. *Consulting Psychology Journal: Practice And Research, 62,* 73–76. doi:10.1037/a0018532

Novick, J. (1997). Termination conceivable and inconceivable. *Psychoanalytic Psychology, 14,* 145–162. doi:10.1037/h0079712

Parsons, R. D., & Meyers, J. (1984). *Developing consultation skills: A guide to training, development, and assessment for human services professionals.* San Francisco, CA: Jossey-Bass.

Schein, E. H. (1969). *Process consultation.* Reading, MA: Addison-Wesley.

Smith, K. K., & Corse, S. J. (1986). The process of consultation: Critical issues. In F. Mannino, E. Trickett, M. Shore, M. Kidder, & G. Levin, *Handbook of mental health consultation* (pp. 247–278). Rockville, MD: U.S. Department of Health and Human Services, National Institute of Mental Health.

Sperry, L. (2005). Establishing a consultation agreement. In G. P. Koocher, J. C. Norcross, & S. S. Hill, III (Eds.), *Psychologist's desk reference* (2nd ed., pp. 665–667). New York, NY: Oxford University Press.

Teed, E. L., & Scileppi, J. A. (2007). *The community mental health system: A navigational guide for providers.* Boston, MA: Allyn & Bacon.

Tindal, G., Parker, R., & Hasbrouck, J. E. (1992). The construct validity of stages and activities in the consultation process. *Journal of Educational and Psychological Consultation, 3,* 99–118.

Ward, D. E. (1984). Termination of individual counseling: Concepts and strategies. *Journal of Counseling & Development, 63,* 21–25.

West, J. F., & Idol, L. (1990). Collaborative consultation in the education of mildly handicapped and at-risk students. *Remedial and Special Education, 11,* 22–31.

Young, M. E. (2009). *Learning the art of helping: Building blocks and techniques* (4th ed.). Upper Saddle River, NJ: Pearson.

5

Behavioral and Cognitive- Behavioral Consultation

Introduction

Previous chapters have examined key relational and procedural components of working competently within the consultation paradigm, including insights into the fundamental importance of content knowledge and counseling skills within consultation (Truscott et al., 2012). Another parallel between the consultation and counseling paradigms is the use of evidence-based approaches as a means of conceptualizing consultee/client issues and facilitating change. Behavioral consultation, for example, requires a solid grounding in behavioral theory and practice, particularly Bandura's social learning theory (Bandura, 1977). Here, behavior is learned and current behavior(s) can be replaced with new, more acceptable behavior(s). Structured behavioral assessments are also used by consultants and consultees to help determine a mutually agreed upon path for changing specific behaviors (Ysseldyke, Lekwa, Klingbeil, & Cormier, 2012). At times, the behavioral and cognitive-behavioral models of counseling outlined in counseling texts can appear to be relatively straightforward approaches to understanding client issues and achieving positive therapeutic outcomes. Knowledge of these approaches can also be helpful to you in relation to consultation. Still, we encourage all current and future consultants to remember that the apparent simplicity of a model (any model) can seem more complex, and even inappropriate, when experienced in "real time." As you grow accustomed to the behavioral and cognitive-behavioral models in this chapter, remember that the competent use of these (or any) consultation model requires ongoing attention to the consultation alliance, ethics, and multicultural competencies.

LEARNING OBJECTIVES

After reading the chapter, you will

- Describe the theoretical underpinnings of behavioral and cognitive-behavioral consultation
- Identify the four major behavioral consultation models discussed in this chapter
- Compare and contrast the benefits and challenges of behavioral and cognitive-behavioral approaches to consultation
- Apply behavioral and cognitive-behavioral models to case scenarios

Behavioral Consultation

Historical Perspective

Originally proposed by John Bergan in 1977 and grounded in behavioral psychology's positivistic message (Henning-Stout, 1993), behavioral consultation is highly regarded among mental health, education, and school professionals (Andersen et al., 2010; Anton-LaHart & Rosenfield, 2004; Noell, 1996). Foundationally, behavioral consultation emphasizes scientific research (Andersen et al., 2010), exploring current behaviors, and the principles of behavior change (Gmeinder & Kratochwill, 1998; Martens, 1993). However, prior to the 1960s, consultation drew largely from B. F. Skinner's operant conditioning (Bergan, 1977; Keller, 1981; Piersel, 1985; Russell, 1978; Tharp & Wetzel, 1969), while others favored Pavlov's early-20th-century classical conditioning techniques. As a result, early iterations of behavioral consultation relied heavily on behavioral modification interventions, such as reinforcement, punishment, and shaping (Skinner, 1953).

Bandura's social learning views later challenged operant learning's position that environment alone shapes behavior gained traction in the latter half of the 1960s. As a result, the social learning theory notion that behavior is shaped primarily by observing models within one's environment began to take hold. Social learning theory also diverged from previous learning theories by recognizing that cognition can influence behavior and, thus, behavior change. Still, operant conditioning-based interventions remain entrenched in the consulting protocols of many behavioral consultants, especially among adherents of Bergan's (1977) and Erchul and Martens's (2003) hierarchical view of the consulting relationship (see below).

The evolution of behavioral therapy has also led to disparate views about whether a hierarchical (Bergan, 1977; Erchul, 1992; Erchul & Martens, 2003) or nonhierarchical (Gutkin, 1999) relationship is most appropriate. For clarification, Erchul and Martin's hierarchical view places consultants in control, with strict behavioral interventions alone recognized as the impetus for behavior change. On the other hand, Gutkin's (1996, 1999) view of the relationship as nonhierarchical is more closely aligned with the importance Caplan (1970) placed on creating and maintaining egalitarian consulting relationships. Although this debate remains unsettled and hindered by methodological concerns (Witt, Gresham, & Noell, 1996), there continues to be solid support behind the notion that collaborative relationships are of particular importance (Sheridan & Kratochwill, 2008). Ultimately, Bergan's original model remains valued for its emphasis on bridging pragmatism and empiricism. As a result, the core philosophy of behavioral consultation has evolved from its early reliance on strict behavioral interventions to one more accepting of interventions from a wider array of theoretical perspectives (Kratochwill, Elliott, & Callan-Stoiber, 2002).

The progression of behavior therapy has also directly influenced contemporary descriptions of behavioral consultation. For instance, some view behavioral consultation as a problem solving endeavor (Kratochwill et al., 2002), while others point to the influence of multiple psychological and social science contributors. Examples here include learning theories and the use of behavioral consultation with more diverse settings and populations (Keller, 1981; Vernberg & Reppucci, 1986). Contemporary definitions also recognize behavioral consultation's increased focus on positive relationships and the benefits of structured interviewing (Bergan & Kratochwill, 1990; Sheridan, Kratochwill, & Bergan, 1996). Importantly, each of these holds behavioral consultation's core connection to empiricism, learned behavior, and behavioral change. Essentially, contemporary definitions recognize behavioral consultation's increased focus on positive relationships and the benefits of structured interviewing (Bergan & Kratochwill, 1990; Sheridan, Kratochwill, & Bergan, 1996), positions that adhere to behavioral consultation's grounding in empiricism, learned behavior, and behavioral change (Dougherty, 2009). To simplify, behavioral consultation is founded on several common denominators (Kratochwill et al., 2002; Vernberg & Reppucci, 1986):

- Indirect service delivery methods (i.e., parent/teacher/administrator interviews)
- Grounding in behavior technology principles (i.e., behavior modification)
- Blending of strength-based, problem-solving interventions
- Change involves multiple contexts and settings

Another common feature of behavioral consultation models is the step-wise progression applied to solving a problem (Kratochwill et al., 2002). This sequence includes

- frame problems from behavioral perspective;
- use a functional analysis to clarify antecedent problems and consequences;
- select a target behavior or behaviors;
- design behavior objective(s); and
- construct, implement, and evaluate a behavioral change plan.

In sum, behavioral consultation is grounded in the behavioral therapy tradition(s) and may provide indirect services to a client or system or direct services through training that recognizes the idiosyncratic needs of clients (Keller, 1981; Vernberg & Reppucci, 1986). Several forms of behavioral consultation are available to help best meet consultee needs, including behavioral case consultation, behavioral technology training, and behavioral system consultation. Each of these styles will be discussed in more detail following clarification of the guiding principles of behavioral consultation. In all cases, though, consultants target the development of consultee skills that will facilitate positive behavioral outcomes for the client or system. Overall, behavioral consultation is defined by its scientific view of human behavior, present-centered focus, and grounding in the tenets of behaviorism. Below is a brief overview of prominent behavioral consultation models and their guiding principles.

Guiding Principles of Behavioral Consultation

Scientific Perspective

Behavioral consultation is rooted in a vision of an operationalized methodology and reliance on an empirically rigorous evaluation of chosen and applied interventions interventions (Vernberg & Reppucci, 1986; Bergan & Kratochwill, 1990). This is demonstrated by behavioral consultation's present-centered orientation and behavior change principles.

Present-Centered Orientation

Behavioral consultation is oriented toward present concerns and problems (Kazdin, 2001) and is well suited for delineating current and future desired behaviors (Bergan & Kratochwill, 1990; Kazdin, 2001). Here again, while cognitions (Scheuermann & Hall, 2008) and insight are minimized, past behavior is considered for its potential impact on current consultee issues. Behavioral consultants also maintain the position that problematic behavior and the consultee as a person are not mutually exclusive (Gresham, Watson, & Skinner, 2001). Keeping this in mind will increase the likelihood that the consultant and consultee can create a positive alliance that will lead to them effectively clarifying current problem behaviors and creating evidence-based behavior goals.

Behavior Change Principles

Behavioral consultation believes that the insertion of agreed upon (Bergan & Kratochwill, 1990) learning principles such as reinforcement, shaping, extinction, and modeling promote desired behavioral changes (Kazdin, 2001). These learning principles assist consultants in examining a client or system's behavior and in providing operational direction to the consultant (Bergan & Kratochwill, 1990). In short, the application of learning principles to undesirable or ineffective behaviors will have consequences that lead clients or consultees to adapt to more desirable behaviors.

Process of Behavioral Consultation

Content knowledge specific to behavioral consultation and its distinct forms and functions is, predictably, an expectation for anyone using this method. To that end, we provide an abridged overview of the following behavioral consultation formats: behavioral case consultation, behavioral technology training, and behavioral system consultation. No matter the format, each retains four common principles (Kratochwill, 2008; Vernberg & Reppucci, 1986):

- Use of indirect service interventions
- Integration of learning principles (i.e., behavioral technology) in all aspects of consultation endeavor
- Problem-solving focus
- Empirically vetted interventions

In each instance, a consultant's expertise is used to designate the most effective behavioral strategy for the circumstances while recognizing the consultee's autonomy to implement the selected strategy. In other words, while a consultant's role involves problem clarification, training, and education educational aspects, the consultee is ultimately responsible for making changes. Procedurally, consultants guide consultees through the process through the intentional use of by the use of intentional use of "verbal interaction techniques" (Dougherty, 2009, p. 215). In doing so, behavioral consultants seek to control the direction of the message (source), information input (control), information in the message (content), and the action implied in each message (process). Below is a brief description of the verbal technique categories used in behavioral consultation (Bergan, 1977).

Message Source: Direction of the message (i.e., from consultant or consultee)

Message Content: Information discussed between the consultant and consultee. Consultant generally controls content message(s) through verbal techniques in order to facilitate positive behavioral outcomes. Subcategories include background/environment, behavior setting, behavior, individual characteristics, observation, and plan.

Message Process: Involves the "actionable" dimension of the content message. Examples include specification, evaluation, inference, summarization (i.e., review of previous meeting or current discussion), and validation verbalizations (i.e., "check-out").

Message Control: Involves the direction of input (i.e., consultant or consultee uses message control to provide input or receive input). Subcategories include elicitors (messages intended to obtain a direct response) and emitters (direct responses not intended).

Overall, behavioral consultation places the consultant in the expert role in order to help ensure each element (i.e., problem identification, analysis, implementation, and evaluation) is, to the extent possible, successfully realized. Although consultants should remain sensitive to highlighting key learning principles that could enhance consultee goal attainment, the focus at this point should be on collaboration. For their part, consultees should be expected to

- provide timely, detailed descriptions of each case and associated problems;
- evaluate and decide on efficacy and suitability of consultant recommendation(s), including decision(s) on whether or not to implement the recommendation
- maintain direct service to clients (includes ongoing collaboration with client); and
- maintain a supervisory role (i.e., if consultee has professional authority for others involved in client care)

Behavioral Consultation Approaches

Behavioral Case Consultation

Behavioral case consultation is best exemplified by Bergan's (1997) and Bergan and Kratochwill's (1990) model's historical grounding in operant and classical conditioning principles. Two specific models of behavioral case consultation exist. The first, *developmental case consultation,* assumes a longitudinal view of behavior change, while *problem-centered case consultation* focuses on current behavior. Contemporary trends also recognize the value of learning models that align with the principles of Bandura's 1977 social learning model. The essential feature of behavioral case consultation, however, remains its focus on the direct provision of behaviorally based services to consultees so they may, in turn, effect positive behavioral change with clients on an individual or group basis. This requires that consultants have the base competency to recognize and utilize interventions that can be competently implemented by consultees with various levels of understanding of learning theory principles and methods (Elliott & Busse, 1993).

Behavioral case consultation is also consistent in structure and vision with behavioral consultation's adherence to a four-stage model (Bergan & Kratochwill, 1990). The initial stage, problem identification, is a critical and often deceptively simple (Kratochwill et al., 1995; Kratochwill et al., 2002) stage. Here, consultant-led interviews seek to highlight incongruities between present and desired client behaviors and end when measurable behavior change goals are determined (Kratochwill et al., 2002). Of course, inaccurate or incomplete problem identification could lead to ineffectual interventions and, in some cases, cause irreparable harm to the consultation alliance and process (Bergan & Tombari, 1976).

Problem analysis is the second stage and involves collaboration between the consultant and consultee aimed at uncovering conditions that sustain problematic client behavior. This shared effort involves the two distinct tasks of problem analysis and devising a plan. During problem analysis, effort is directed at understanding the problem in relation to specific conditions (i.e., large case load) or skills (or lack thereof) of the client (i.e., limited training in documentation). The consultant and consultee then together determine the conditions or skills needed by the client to alleviate future problem behavior(s). In the third stage, an intervention is designed to capitalize on consultee assets (Kratochwill et al., 2002). Options may involve discussions with the consultee on how best to implement suggested techniques, educate clients on selected learning principles, or both. It should be remembered that consultants must ultimately cede responsibility for executing the plan to the consultee. Once completed, the treatment plan is formally assessed with the goal of measuring consulting outcomes and determining if and what additional steps are needed for accomplishing the goal(s). This process includes evaluation of goals and plan effectiveness as well as post-implementation planning (Bergan & Kratochwill, 1990).

Treatment evaluation is a three-step process intended to assess consulting outcomes and to determine what, if any, additional steps are needed. Evaluating goal attainment means assessing the degree to which changes in current (observed) behaviors coincide with the desired behavioral changes (goals). This includes evaluation of goals and plan effectiveness as well as post-implementation planning (Bergan & Kratochwill, 1990). Outcomes are defined as *no progress, some progress,* or *accomplishment,* and the results are used as the basis for post-implementation planning. The final stage, post-implementation planning, involves the consultant and consultee working together to design a post-consultation plan that will prevent the reappearance of problem behaviors. Options include continuing the current plan, using alternate, evidence-based interventions; or ending the plan. Final termination of the consulting relationship occurs when the consultation goals have been assessed and the post-implementation plan has been selected. Table 5.1 illustrates this process.

Case 5.1 illustrates another example of this method.

Case 5.1: An Example of Behavioral Case Consultation

A licensed counselor with significant experience in clinical and administrative supervision was hired as a mental health consultant to work with a counselor who is struggling to get the clinicians and mental health paraprofessionals under his supervision to be punctual and competent with their documentation of cases. The counselor is seeking a consult prior to implementing a new course of disciplinary actions he has designed. Together, the consultant and consultee clarify what is meant by "punctual" and "competent" case documentation, complete an analysis of current undesirable and desirable counselor behaviors, and construct a plan that involves rewarding timely and competent documentation by using learning principles (e.g., positive reinforcement and shaping) to help attain the desired behavioral goals of punctual and competent documentation. Following these steps, the consultee executes the plan and, when completed, assesses its effectiveness.

Case 5.2.: Addressing a Child's Inattentiveness Using Behavioral Case Consultation

Consultation

An experienced school counselor was hired as a consultant by a school to work with a teacher who was at "wit's end" with a particular student's inattentive and distracting classroom behaviors. The teacher is seeking a consult with the consultant because he has been ineffective in gaining control of a particularly inattentive and disruptive student. Together, the consultant and consultee first work to define *inattentive* and *disruptive.* Next, they analyze the student's current undesirable and desirable classroom behaviors using functional analysis and create a plan that combines positive and negative reinforcement principles in order to facilitate desired behavioral goals of increased attentiveness and less disruptive behaviors. The teacher (consultee) then implements the plan and evaluates its effect when finished.

Table 5.1 Example of Behavioral Case Consultation Process

Problem Identification

- Consultant leads interview with consultee to uncover current documentation problems and expected/desired documentation skills/requirements.
- Determines measureable behavior change goals.
- **Identified Problem: Limited use of clinical terminology.**

Problem Analysis

- Limited clinical terminology creates issues; has led to third-party reimbursement by agency.
- Consultee acknowledges limited training in clinical terminology.
- Consultee notes challenges in personal life have led to reduced concentration at work.
- **Analysis: Limited knowledge base and personal challenges have contributed to reduced documentation effectiveness. Plan: terminology creates issues that involve staff members and client care.**

Intervention

- Formal training in clinical terminology through seminars and additional clinical & administrative supervision.
- Consultee will spend one hour a week (compensated) reviewing case studies and new files as a means of learning proper terminology and phrasing.
- **Intervention Anticipated Outcome: Consultee will improve clinical vocabulary and documentation skills through reading case files and engaging in additional clinical and administrative supervision.**

Treatment Evaluation

- Evaluation of Goal(s):
- Consultee has successfully engaged in one hour per week of additional clinical and administrative supervision.
- Consultee has had no third-party reimbursement claims filed since interventions began.
- Consultee reports increased efficacy in use of appropriate terminology and sensitivity to implications of documentation on client care.
- **Treatment Evaluation: Consultee has made excellent progress and will continue current plan for one more month.**
- Treatment Outcome: Some Progress on all goals

Post Implementation Planning

- Continue current interventions for increasing knowledge and application of appropriate clinical terminology.
- Given effectiveness of selected interventions, consider implementing quarterly trainings for all members of clinical and administrative staffs.
- Integrate additional training on clinical documentation during initial orientation training for all new staff members.

Exercise 5.1: Using the Behavioral Technology Training Method of Consultation

Respond to the following questions about behavioral case consultation using the dialogue from Cases 5.1 & 5.2, respectively.

1. *What additional information would you want to have at the problem identification stage?*

2. *What counseling skills could you call upon to enhance your ability to clarify the main problem(s)?*

3. *How might this additional or new information influence problem analysis, interventions, and evaluation?*

4. *How would you deal with a consultee who insists that you remain part of "carrying out the plan"? What could this suggest about the consultee? About the consultation alliance? About the consultant's initial role in the process?*

Behavioral Technology Training

Behavioral technology training involves integrating behavioral technology principles into a consultee's professional repertoire. In effect, behavioral technology training is a form of indirect consultation that involves consultees using knowledge acquired from consultants to optimize their own systems (Sheridan & Kratochwill, 2008). Empirically shown to be capable of improving client behaviors (Vernberg & Reppucci, 1986), this training follows the general consulting pattern of assessment, planning, implementation, and evaluation. Overall, behavioral technology training is well regarded and continues to expand outside its initial successes in school settings (Kratochwill & Pittman, 2002; Rosenfield, 2002). T. Steuart Watson and Sheri L. Robinson (1996) highlight several positive outcomes stemming from the understanding and application of this method:

- Optimal opportunities that behavioral programs will be conducted competently
- Increased chances consultees will be able to generalize their use of behavioral technology interventions
- Behavioral technology training can be cost effective and expedient

This method also provides consultants with an opportunity to provide instruction to consultees on learning principles and behavioral technology skills (Bergan & Kratochwill, 1990; Elliot & Busse, 1993; Vernberg & Reppucci, 1986; Watson & Robinson, 1996). As a result, consultants are able to impact consultee systems by training consultees on behavioral technology principles and application. Although targeted initially for school settings, the following items are recognized as keys for using the behavioral technology training format (Rosenfield, 1985):

- Be a content expert in behavioral technology principles and interventions.
- Maintain a practical focus for settings (i.e., classroom) and encourage collaboration between all potential clients (i.e., teachers, counselors).
- Personalize behavioral technology interventions to the extent possible.
- Maintain a multicultural perspective (i.e., language, values).
- Maintain availability to consultees and appreciate consultee work schedules.

Case 5.3 and Exercise 5.2 below illustrate the behavioral technology consultation approach.

Case 5.3: A Case of Behavioral Technology Training

A licensed counselor was hired as a mental health consultant by a state mental health outpatient clinic to help ensure that their in-house clinical supervisors are properly prepared to supervise the clinic's new licensed associated counselor(s). Specific concerns of the clinic's administrators focus on the competent and timely completion of all managed-care documentation. To that end, the consultant provided a 6-hour workshop (two 3-hour sessions) for the agency's designated in-house supervisors on "Enhancing Case Documentation Skills and Competencies." The initial session included a didactic element focused on educating the supervisors on the behavioral technology principles of positive reinforcement and shaping and guidelines for their use. The second session involved a series of experiential exercises where the clinic's supervisors applied the principles of positive reinforcement and shaping in realistic supervisory role-play situations and received feedback from the consultant. As a final step, the consultant sets a time to watch each supervisor implement the techniques with their assigned supervisees and provide immediate feedback.

Exercise 5.2: Using the Behavioral Technology Training Method of Consultation

Using the narrative from Case 5.2, respond to the following questions.

1. *Has the consultant used behavior technology training effectively in this scenario? Describe your reasoning.*

2. *What learning principles do you feel may be particularly effective and/or ineffective given this scenario? Explain your response.*

3. *How might you adapt or reframe what the consultant has done?*

Behavioral System Consultation

Behavior system consultation differs from behavioral case consultation in that it targets an entire social system (Curtis & Stollar, 1996; Lewis & Newcomer, 2002). Essentially, the system is the client and consultees are individuals selected from the system. Consultants again assume the expert role, yet their expertise must extend beyond behavioral technology principles to include the behavior ecology (Jeger & Slotnick, 1982; Willems, 1974) and systems paradigms. Behavior ecology for example, assumes the existence of an interrelated ecological environment (Willems, 1974), while ecological systems theory explores the multiple layers of interconnected systems. At the center is an individual surrounded by a) microsystems include the immediate environment such as a family unit or a classroom; b) mesosystems, the interrelation of multiple microsystems; and c) exosystems, that does not involve the individual as an active participant but does impact the individual; and macrosystems, systems at the cultural level (Bronfenbrenner, 1979). For example, a supervisee struggling with being punctual with paperwork may be facing difficult family issues microsystem (microsystemic) that are impacting concentration and ability to stay on task. As this develops into a problem at work, it becomes mesosystemic as multiple microsystems are impacted. Further, the supervisee may have a significant other who is having difficulty at work, a potential stressor that could indirectly impact the supervisee's concentration and performance (exosystem). Finally, macrosystemic issues may be at play, such as multicultural concerns that need to be examined. In other words, the issues confronting a consultee are interrelated to some degree and should be conceptualized and addressed as such.

We also know that the behavioral system model values collaboration. However, it needs to be reiterated that consultees have final decision making authority. This authority requires that consultees supply consultants with consultant's information and insights that could benefit each step of the process leading to accomplishing the system's overall goals. This information may center on problem definition, system boundaries, data collection, and feedback on potential interventions. In effect, consultants apply behavioral technology principles to the subsystems in order to optimize desired behaviors between and among them and, ultimately, optimize the functioning of the system as a whole.

Overall, behavioral system consultation consists of system definition, assessment, intervention, and evaluation. The first step, system definition, seeks to identify a system's structure and process. This includes system variables such as geographical location (macrosystem), demographics (macrosystem), administrative manuals and guidelines (exosystem), and facility schematics (exosystem). The second step, identifying the system's process dimension, refers to operationalizing member behaviors. Dougherty (2009) outlines the key foci of this step:

- Assessment: Focus on measuring behaviors of all members of the system
- Interventions: Focus on identifying a system's response to change
- Evaluation: Focus on determining the system's quality
- Communication: Focus on the manner and direction of communication between and among system members

Clarity on the structural and process elements of system definition leads to system assessment. Here, consultant and consultee unite to determine links between structure and process. Assessment of the gathered information then allows the consultant and consultee to visualize specific intervention needs within the system (Maher, 1981) and set up an intervention aimed at removing structural and process barriers.

System evaluation is the final stage. Specific tasks include evaluating whether a program was run effectively, determining if it accomplished the stated system change goals, and deciding which interventions were tied to outcomes and identify necessary future alterations (Dougherty, 2009).

Case 5.4: An Example of Behavioral System Consultation

A state mental health outpatient clinic hired a licensed counselor as a mental health consultant to ensure their clinical staff is properly trained on current managed-care documentation guidelines. These concerns arose from an internal audit that found gaps in proper documentation among the clinical staff and, in several key instances, the paraprofessional staff (i.e., case managers). The consultant and the selected consultee, the clinic's executive director, met to define the clinic's structure and process. The structure is defined quickly due to a clear organizational chart. On the other hand, considerable time is spent defining the process. Here, they explore the interactions between the system's (i.e., clinic) and subsystems (i.e. administration, clinical staff, and paraprofessional staff) in relation to how they communicate, as well as evaluation procedures and the problem-solving capabilities of each. After several discussions, they identified the system's inherent hierarchy as the primary concern. Specifically, poor communication between the administrative and clinical staffs has led to confusion, misunderstandings, and frustration concerning specific documentation timelines, procedures, forms, and overall responsibilities. Overall, several instances of strained alliances between employees at different organizational levels were also highlighted as a concern.

Identification of these key concerns led to a joint determination between the consultant and consultee to target the communication problems among the subsystems. To do so, they proposed two items. First, each subsystem will move to formal bimonthly meetings and will include a liaison representing each of the clinic's subsystems in order to open lines of communication, facilitate transparency, and refocus attention on the fact that the clinic's success is rooted in the combined efforts of all the clinic's subsystems. Second, the establishment of monthly luncheon seminars (with lunch provided by the executive director) will be led by the director of clinical services. In addition to insights and trainings into required managed care issues, seminar topics will be solicited from all staff and addressed (time permitting) during the seminar. For example, documentation and related treatment issues and new initiatives (i.e., new forms, managed-care guidelines, timelines, etc.) may be addressed with the clinical and paraprofessional staffs. Prior to the executive director meeting with the full staff, the consultant agrees to attend that meeting with the full staff and offer feedback on how to address the targeted meetings with the staffs of each subsystem prior to full implementation. On the advice of the consultant, the executive director agrees to attend each subsystem's monthly staff meeting to address how well the chosen objectives are being implemented. Employee surveys will be used at 3- and 6-month intervals to gauge the efficacy of the two initiatives in facilitating targeted changes.

Exercise 5.3: Behavioral System Consultation

Respond to the following questions based on the narrative from Case 5.3.

1. *What are the similarities and differences between this approach and the case and behavioral technology approaches?*

2. *Do you agree with the consultant's use of the expert role in this scenario? If yes, what elements do you agree with how might you build on the consultant's successes? If you disagree, which elements do you disagree with and how would you approach this situation differently?*

3. *Describe the narrative from the behavior ecology and ecological systems theory points of view. What are the key features of each? How might they influence how you utilize the "expert" role?*

(Continued)

(Continued)

4. *How would you describe the culture of the organization? What strengths and limitations might you have in working within the behavioral system consultation approach?*

Conjoint Behavioral Consultation

Conjoint behavioral consultation (CBC), with its distinctive shared consultee role, is increasingly popular in school settings (Sheridan, 2000; Sheridan & Kratochwill, 2008). This role, which unites parents and teachers in the consultee role, is well suited for identifying and addressing the interplay of the key constituencies of home, school, and community (Auster, Feeney-Kettler, & Kratochwill, 2006; Kratochwill, Elliott, & Carrington Rotto, 1995; Semke & Sheridan, 2012) that impact a child's needs (Sheridan, 1993) and development (Sheridan & Kratochwill, 2008). This knowledge better allows parents and teachers to focus on the specific needs of the child together.

Aside from adding *conjoint* to its design, CBC remains procedurally consistent (Guli, 2005) with the original behavior models of Bergan (1977) and Bergan and Kratochwill (1990). The consultant's role continues to parallel traditional behavioral models with a focus on both process and outcome dimensions. This consistency provides a foundation for consultants knowledgeable about traditional behavioral consultation models, yet they must remain cognizant of the distinct challenges and opportunities associated with the addition of the conjoint consultee framework. Conversely, CBC distinguishes itself conceptually from the base behavioral models not only by the unified parent–teacher consultant role, but in its adoption of the ecological systems paradigm. This is evidenced by the CBC model's appreciation of the interrelated influences of home, school, and community on the child and the shared nature of the consultee role (Sheridan, 2000) in helping the client. Another distinction is the CBC vision of positive, collaborative relationships between schools and families that are grounded in shared effort, mutual respect, and cultural competence (Sheridan & Kratochwill, 2008). As a result, CBC's focus on shared effort and responsibility between parents and teachers is aimed at optimizing outcomes for both parties.

It also bears repeating that the CBC's adoption of Bronfenbrenner's (1979) ecological system's theory requires that consultants address deficiencies in their understanding of the system's framework (Sheridan, Kratochwill, & Bergan, J. R., 1996). Failure to do so would clearly inhibit, if not fully impede, the potential efficacy of the CBC approach. In the case of behavioral case consultation, for example, the identification of a child's inattentive behavior in the classroom would result in the application of targeted learning principles to decrease the unwanted behavior within the context of the classroom. The CBC model, however, would involve the consultant gathering data from consultees (parents and teachers) about a child's home, school, and community that could be impacting the child's inattentiveness in the classroom (Sheridan et al., 2012). This helps provide a more contextualized view of the child (and the behavior) in relation to the child's overall environment.

Research on CBC further illustrates its potential and limitations. On the benefit side, the CBC model is responsive to multicultural issues (Guli, 2005; Sheridan, Eagle, & Doll, 2006) with consultants showing high rates of goal attainment (Sheridan, Eagle, Cowan, & Mickelson, 2001). Other research indicates consultee preferences for the shared consultee (i.e., parent and teacher) approach over the traditional behavioral models (Freer & Watson, 1999). Alternatively, the shared consultee role assumes inherent interpersonal and contextual challenges such as interpersonal disagreements or logistical challenges that could impede timely and constructive communication. One example is Priscilla F. Grissom, William P. Erchul, & Susan M. Sheridan's 2003 finding that indicates the tendency of parents to dominate the consulting dyad. In sum, while the research on the CBC approach is promising, current methodological and conceptual limitations remain and should be addressed in part through an increased use of qualitative research designs (Brown, Pryzwansky, & Schulte, 2011). The vignettes below help draw distinctions between how a consultant may address a child's inattentiveness using the behavioral case consultation (BCC), behavioral systems consultation (BSC), and CBC points of view.

Case 5.5: Addressing a Child's Inattentiveness Using Conjoint Behavioral Consultation

An experienced school counselor who uses the conjoint behavioral consultation model was hired by a middle school principal to address what a first-year teacher defines as a difficult student's "inattentive and disruptive" classroom behavior following the holiday break. The first item on the agenda was clarifying that the consultant role is a joint teacher–parent endeavor. Fortunately, the teacher and student's parents were willing to share this role in the best interest of the child. The consultant then set up a meeting with the consultant (parent[s]–teacher) to identify the problem. Next, they worked together to analyze the student's atypical "inattentive and disruptive" classroom behaviors and the timing of the new behaviors. Working together, the consultants shared information that strongly suggested the child's recent classroom behaviors may be related to the unexpected death of his grandmother during the holiday break. Based on this information, the consultees designed a change in his school schedule where he will have 30 minutes each week to talk to the school counselor. Moreover, the teacher has stated that he will express sympathy and empathy to the student about the loss of his grandmother at an appropriate time at school. His parents also agree to seek out a mental health professional to help their child process the loss of his grandmother. Importantly, the teacher and parents agree to correspond by electronic mail on a daily basis for a period of 2 weeks and then on Fridays until they both agree the student's classroom behaviors have compensated appropriately. Finally, the parent–child consultee team will meet in person for 30 minutes on a biweekly basis to evaluate the interventions and clarify the need for future contact.

> ### Case 5.6: Addressing a Child's
> ### Inattentiveness Using Behavioral System Consultation
>
> An experienced school counselor was hired as a consultant by a rural school system to work with their elementary school faculty on classroom management issues. This hiring was in response to multiple complaints from teaches, several of whom had never worked in a rural school setting, about a lack of student attentiveness and disruptive behaviors. The consultant and the selected consultee, the school system's superintendent, meet to define the school's structure and process. Understanding the process takes more time and includes exploring interactions between the system's (school's) subsystems (administration, faculty, paraprofessional, and custodial staffs) in relation to how they communicate, how each is evaluated, and the problem-solving capabilities of each. After several discussions, they identified the system's inherent hierarchy as the main problem. Specifically, a closer examination of the school's structure revealed the school's designated organizational flowchart had given way to a strong alliance between the principal and a small number of senior teachers. This alliance had led to poor communication, confusion, and resentment among the other subsystems that appeared to be manifesting in reduced faculty engagement in the classroom—actions that could have direct bearing on student attentiveness and disruptive behaviors.
>
> Identification of the structural problems and their possible impact on teacher engagement and, by extension, increased student inattentiveness and disruptions, led to an agreement between the consultant and consultee to implement three interventions. To address the structural inequities, the superintendent will hold monthly meetings with principals from each school in order to reinstill the school system's intended administrative (and authoritative) structure and to enhance communication and clarity of the school's mission at the highest levels of the system. In order to address the process challenges, each subsystem will hold a monthly meeting led by an elected member of the subsystem, with all members able to place items on the meeting agenda for discussion. Finally, a monthly meeting will be held to address concerns from all of the school's subsystems. Each subsystem will elect a liaison to represent their position and a secretary will be elected from among the subsystems to take minutes. Prior to any of these meetings, the consultant agrees to attend the first session of all meetings and to offer feedback on how to improve communication and engagement on all levels. Evaluation of the perceived sense of engagement among the school subsystem, particularly that of faculty classroom engagement and perceptions of student inattentiveness and disruption, will be collected with surveys at 3-, 6-, and 9-month intervals.

Cognitive-Behavioral Model of Consultation

By the 1970s, the influence of cognitive-behavioral therapy (CBT) had grown considerably. This approach differs from behavioral consultation with the recognition that cognition influences behavior. Simply stated, CBT posits that cognition guides one's affective and behavioral responses to a situation or event. Thus, problem development or nondevelopment lies within this sequence. The CBC paradigm was also helped in the 1980s with the development of models that honor traditional operant and classical conditioning positions while integrating key aspects of Bandura's (1971, 1976, 1977, 1978) social learning theory, including the following:

- Recognition of behavior, environment, and cognition influences behavioral change.
- Observational learning of current or historical models is a primary determinant of new behavior (departure from operant conditioning).
- The cognitive variables of *self-efficacy* and *appraisal* influence behavior.
  - Self-efficacy: one's level of confidence in the ability to perform a specific task
  - Appraisal: the value one places on task or goal achievement
- Self-regulation and creativity allow individuals to confront, adjust, and adapt to (behavior) change.

Several additional elements guide the cognitive-behavioral model. In brief, these key CBT dimensions include

1. Human behavior is influenced by a multitude of internal, external, antecedent, and present-centered variables, including cognitions, schools, family, culture, and biology.

2. Behavioral antecedents include cognition(s), a key distinction from the behavioral model.

3. Behavior is purposeful and may serve observable or nonobservable functions.

Cognitive-Behavioral Consultation and the Consultation Alliance

The relational component of the CBC model, particularly the notion of control within the relationship, has spurred considerable debate. Briefly, while Bergan (1977) and others (Bergan & Kratochwill, 1990) viewed control as an essential and overt element of the consultation relationship, Gallessich (1982) viewed control as having an implicitly manipulative quality. We hold that a more collaborative role is fundamental to effective consultation in that both consultant and consultee should be similarly engaged in, and benefit from, the consultation alliance and process. In that vein, Ann Schulte and Susan S. Osborne (2003), in describing the notion of the equal power–equal value relationship, believe the following variables must exist for this type of relationship to occur:

1. Voluntariness

2. Equality between and among participants

3. Equal commitment and responsibility for goal setting

4. Equal sharing of resources

5. Equal decision making responsibility for problem identification and interventions

More recently, Brown et al. (2011) suggested that the equal power–equal value relationship should include involves two additional variables. The first includes interactions based in "honesty, empathy, and trust" (p. 49), with the second being the idea that both consultant and consultee benefit from their interactions.

Before moving on, we again want to highlight the potential conceptual and pragmatic benefits of applying Bordin's working alliance model in this context. For example, the collaboration for change principle that guides Bordin's model is consistent with the notion of the equal power–equal value relationship model. Both models also agree on the principle of shared effort, particularly in regard to goal setting, decision making, and communication based on trust and respect. Some variations do exist, of course. For example, consultants should remain sensitive to power dynamics in their interactions with consultees (individual, group, systems). In general, though, the working alliance model remains a sensible and pragmatic means for conceptualizing and addressing the relational (and procedural) aspects of CBC.

Cognitive-Behavioral Consultation and Problem Identification

Problem identification is initiated by consultees noting problematic behavior or lack of expected behavior(s). Initially stated in general terms, problem identification evolves into a detailed problem description based on what can be seen and measured, with care taken to frame problems in behavioral terminology. Input from consultees is then used to ascertain and address identified problems and deficits. This sequence also recognizes that some problems are unobservable, yet may play a crucial role in one's behavior.

The second step of problem identification is a functional behavioral assessment (FBA). This method involves identifying essential cognitive, emotional, and contextual data that illuminates vital behavioral antecedents that could assist in selecting appropriate interventions. Using direct, Using direct, indirect (or in combination), the FBA first seeks to identity the *how* and *when* of behaviors. This information is then used to create a hypothesis about other conditions that could factor into behavior.

The second phase employs direct or indirect strategies develop a theory regarding the role physiological, cognitive, and contextual variables may play in the occurrence and maintenance occurrence and maintenance of behavior (Malott & Trojan Suarez, 2004). Simply stated, the second phase of the FBA is to identify past issues and implications. Given this goal, the use of an A-B-C model of antecedent(s), behavior(s), and consequence(s) is often favored. More recently, Ronald C. Martella, J. Ron Nelson, and Nancy E. Marchand-Martella (2003) advocated for the inclusion of *setting events*, or factors that alter the interplay among the variables. Absent information on setting events, the FBA may lack details about behavior that could lead to flawed interventions and unreliable and invalid outcome evaluations. Thus, proper documentation is necessary in order to ensure the most accurate and detailed accounting of information. Paul E. Touchette, Rebecca F. MacDonald, and Susan N. Langer (1985) also note that direct assessments can help link key contextual factors (i.e., setting, timeframe), and with behaviors, behavior occurrences and the timing and setting of the behavior, contextual factors (i.e., clinic, home, school), nature of the activity, and shared outcomes. Examples of direct assessments include scatter plots for tracking behaviors (Martella et al., 2003) as well as the ABC and Four Factor (setting + ABC) models. Still, direct assessments often miss important details. Therefore, indirect assessments such as personal interviews should be used whenever possible to collect information missed during direct assessments so the most accurate and complete accounting of the behavior(s) is available.

Cognitive-Behavioral Consultation and the Intervention Process

Implementing specific behavioral strategies requires an understanding of the problematic behavior(s) in need of change, followed closely by setting appropriate objectives. Here, direct and indirect assessment techniques such as scatter plots and personal interviews are used to design and implement measurable and attainable short, medium, and long-range change(s) in behavior. While collaborative in nature, consultation during this initial phase may involve the consultant teaching about and facilitating the construction of these goals to help ensure the chosen behavioral objectives promote long-term behavior change.

Cognitive-Behavioral Consultation and Intervention Selection

Cognitive-behavioral interventions are largely grounded in the social, operant, and classical learning traditions, further highlighting the need for consultants to maintain an intentional approach to intervention selection. This broad conceptual base allows consultants and consultees the opportunity to select from a range of techniques that best suit the dynamics of the selected goals and dynamics of the participants. At the same time, consultants should avoid interventions that are overly restrictive and intrusive (Martella et al., 2003), procedurally or logistically complex, or that may add unwanted environmental distress. In other words, interventions should be, to the extent possible, simple, nonintrusive, and ethical. Interventions aimed at reducing inappropriate behaviors, for example, could include aversive strategies aimed at removing a negative reinforcer. Aversive strategies may include non-exclusionary timeouts, response cost methods, or restitution (Martella et al., 2003; Walker, Shea, & Bauer, 2004). In a clinical mental health, setting a response cost scenario could involve a clinician being required per their third-party payer guidelines to submit a "session note" within 24 hours of each client contact. Clinicians that fulfill this requirement each month are "rewarded" with a two hour discretionary time (i.e., time off) that can be applied the following month pending administrative approval.

Consultants should also be sensitive to using negative reinforcement strategies that could have unwanted or harmful consequences. Using the example of a disruptive student, a teacher directing a disruptive student to the assistant principal's office to be disciplined for inappropriate classroom behavior may be reinforcing the unwanted behavior by "rewarding" the student who seeks relief from their current distress in the situation. Another option for reducing unwanted behavior is the use of differential reinforcement. A teacher using differential reinforcement would reinforce student behavior that differs from prior negative behavior or reinforce even the most subtle behavior(s) that aligns with appropriate classroom behavior. In either case, the goal is to highlight positive options to prior negative behavior by supporting suitable behavior or not acknowledging unacceptable behavior. For example, a teacher may offer verbal and nonverbal support to a disruptive student who raised a hand instead of interrupting the teacher. Alternatively, the teacher may ignore the student who is waving a hand wildly to gain the attention of the teacher.

Behavioral principles are also used for increasing acceptable behaviors. As a refresher, these may include modeling, cueing, the Premack's Principle (i.e., performing a less desirable act to access a more desirable activity), and self-management strategies. Self-management strategies, for example, require clearly defined behavior goals in order to select the most appropriate type and timing of intervention. Because of the transitory nature of self-management strategies (Alberto & Troutman, 2003), behavioral contracts and interventions that maintain a self-reinforcing quality (Brown 2011), and recognize the dynamic between consultee and their environment, and can influences one's self-management strategies are suggested. For example, a new mental health counselor encountering the significant documentation requirements of a licensed practitioner could develop an internal dialogue focused on disparaging the managed-care system instead of client needs. Given that proper documentation and client care are entwined, the need to develop and maintain an appropriate internal narrative surrounding managed care and its link with client care is crucial. Case 5.7 provides an example of using self-management to address a common counselor grievance.

Case 5.7: Example of a CBT Behavioral/Contingency

Consultee identified Issue:

In order to improve my documentation, I will design and follow a personal behavioral contract consisting of the following:

If, by the end of the month, I have completed and submitted all required documentation and . . .

If I have received no informal or formal concerns from my supervisors or colleagues regarding my documentation,

Then, I will reward myself by attending a matinee of my selection or . . . I will reward myself to a meal at my favorite restaurant (including dessert!).

Then, I will record my behaviors on a contract in order to monitor my behavior over the course of the next year.

Case 5.8: Cognitive-Behavioral
Strategies Related to Documentation Problems

- **From:** "I can't believe the amount of paperwork required by managed-care companies and the time it takes to stay even with deadlines, much less setting up a treatment plan that follows their guidelines. It's like the client isn't as important as the diagnosis. It feels like all I'm doing is paperwork, which certainly isn't what I intended to do as a counselor."
- **To:** "I will plan a day trip to see friends or family at the end of each month if I have received no formal or informal warnings or reprimands concerning my paperwork."
  - "I will stay a half hour later after work and review current documentation standards in relation to my error(s) each time I am reprimanded for unacceptable documentation." *(Self-punishment)*
  - "I will work to better understand the third-party payer's documentation guidelines in order to optimize the treatment I'm providing for my client and ensure my client has access to the services he/she needs." *(Restructuring dialogue)*
  - "In order to improve my documentation skills, I will review key documentation words and phrases each Sunday evening for 15 minutes and will recite them out loud in relation to issues I've encountered with clients. I will continue this practice internally as I complete my formal documentation responsibilities with clients." *(Self-instruction)*

Exercise 5.4: Where Do I Stand?

Respond to the following questions based on your current understanding on behavioral and cognitive behavioral methods of consultation. Be sure to compare and contrast your responses with your classmates.

1. *How comfortable do you believe you would be if asked to focus exclusively on a consultee's cognitions? How about strictly the consultee's emotions?*

2. *Identify and describe key similarities and differences between each of the behavioral and cognitive behavioral models discussed in the chapter.*

3. *What method(s) do you believe would best fit your skill set(s), knowledge base, and professional style? Discuss your response.*

Each strategy has challenges and benefits. For example, restructuring the clinician's internal dialogue should consider the totality of the statement. Consider the statement again:

I can't believe the amount of paperwork required by managed-care companies and the time it takes to stay even with deadlines, much less setting up a treatment plan that follows their guidelines. It's like the client isn't as important as the diagnosis. It feels like all I'm doing is paperwork, which certainly isn't what I intended to do as a counselor.

The statement notes concern with the amount of documentation and a perception that the personhood of a client is minimized by formal diagnostic labels. It also notes a sense of disappointment and frustration that paperwork is such a substantial aspect of the clinician's responsibility. Qualitative changes to the counselor's internal dialogue require clarification of the most pertinent issue(s) while recognizing more complex narratives may be involved. In short, concerns about the quantity of documentation needed, while important, may be secondary to core schemas that view labeling (formal diagnosis) as unnecessarily stigmatizing or having to document according to prescribed guidelines (agency, managed care). The later may also signal a previously held aversion to hierarchies or authority. Another possibility is the new clinician's personal struggle of adapting to the realities of working so closely with and (possibly within) the managed-care system. Restructuring internal dialogue should therefore consider the potential complexity of any statement given that negative or ineffectual internal dialogues could reduce one's ability to successfully design, apply, and maintain suitable internal self-reinforcing and punishment statements. The implications of failing to create more effective internal dialogues extend well beyond the consulting endeavor and could influence job performance, job satisfaction, and personal wellness. Self-instruction involves a procedural element that ultimately relies on individual self-direction, yet is also vulnerable to the internal dialogues emanating from the individual's core schemas.

The use of behavioral or contingency contracts also requires monitoring internal dialogue given that contracts require clarification regarding style (behavioral or contingency), level of collaboration, procedure, goal and objective setting, timing and sequencing (goal/objective discussion/feedback, contract re-design/termination). Contracts implemented poorly or incorrectly could have critical flaws, including such as culturally insensitive or unreasonable goals. Ultimately, conceptualizing, implementing, maintaining, and evaluating contracts requires attention and sensitivity to issues related to design, procedure, personal and cultural dynamics, and outcome implications.

Antecedent events, which include those of a physical, cognitive, and psychological or emotional nature, are increasingly recognized as pertinent to creating effective treatment plans and selecting appropriate interventions treatment plans and specific interventions (Walker et al., 2004). For example, physiological antecedents such as hunger, sleep, and emotional or psychological issues like anxiety or depression could have critical implications. For instance, a normally well-behaved student has for the last two weeks been late for class, failing to complete homework, and has been in at least one witnessed inappropriate verbal altercation with a teacher. This altercation led to the student being disciplined by the assistant principle with a half-day in-school suspension, albeit without inquiring about any changes in the student's life that could provide insights into the qualitative change in behavior. Had the administrator done so, he or she may have learned that the student's parents had recently separated and the father (who is now taking her to school) sometimes forgets breakfast in the morning. Failing to consider the potential impact of an antecedent could and lead to inappropriate discipline. In this case, knowledge of the student's personal crisis may have resulted in a lesser form of discipline and a referral to the school counselor.

Observation and Assessment

A final element of CBC involves observing and assessment. In short, the consultant follows up the intervention by assessing its impact. Here again, though, while consultants may offer general support or guidance, it is the consultee who bears the ultimate responsibility for assessing the accuracy and efficacy of the intervention(s). In short, consultants compare baseline data of goals, objectives and behavior occurrences collected prior to implementation of the intervention with data gathered from the intervention. Collaborative efforts, meanwhile, would differ slightly in that all parties involved would have roles in executing the intervention. A critical parallel between consulting and collaborative efforts are periodic meetings where progress is assessed and changes, if necessary, are determined and implemented.

Multicultural Considerations

It will not surprise you that we again point out the fundamental importance of multicultural competence (Newell, 2012). Insensitivity to multicultural considerations at any point in the consulting relationship or process could quickly, and perhaps permanently, diminish the consultation alliance or otherwise well-reasoned goals, objectives, and interventions. The models and interventions outlined in this chapter are no exception. For example, while attentiveness to relational dynamics is suggested in order to appeal to a wider range of cultures (Sheridan, 2000; Sheridan et al., 2006), between and within- group similarities and differences is vital for consultants using behavioral or cognitive-behavioral consultation models (or any model for that matter). This awareness may be particularly useful with groups who feel marginalized, although awareness without collaboration could be just as detrimental to the process (Dougherty, 2009; Hoffman et al., 2006). For example, a consultee hailing from a collectivistic cultural background but who personally holds a more individually oriented worldview may find behavior goals and interventions that involve family as infringing on the personal right to autonomy.

The cognitive-behavioral consulting (CBC) approach, is also considered effective with client populations who tend to link thoughts, feelings, and behaviors and value personal responsibility for their behaviors (Beck & Weishaar, 2008; Persons, Burns, & Perloff, 1988) and for groups that are oriented toward action, planning, and the future. Because the CBC model is grounded in Eurocentric principles, though, consultants must consider the model's inherent future and individualistic orientation biases. This may involve goals, objectives, and interventions that accentuate a consultee's primary value system in relation to time as well as individual or collectivistic goals, and interventions. For example, a consultant working with a 15-year-old White male from the United States may find the consultee agreeable to goals that promote individual achievement, while a 15-year-old from a more collectivistic society, may prefer goals that are aligned with his family's vision that personal achievement correlates with family ideals of success. The key in any multicultural scenario (and doesn't every scenario involve cultural considerations?), of course, is for consultants to recognize potential congruencies and incongruencies between outcome goals and culture and adapt accordingly. In the prior example, the consultant could, for instance, reframe the individualistic-oriented goals and intervention used with the American student as a group or family intervention to better reflect the Japanese student's (and culture's) collectivistic-value system (C. Skinner, Skinner, & Burton, 2009). No matter the preferred orientation, identifying cultural value systems is done collaboratively between the consultant and consultee and must be cultivated so problems that arise can be dealt with directly, openly, and with respect for potential between and among group similarities and distinctions.

The culturally competent use of the behavioral and cognitive-behavioral models requires avoiding a rush to judgment on consultee behavior, potential interventions, and appropriate change goals. It is certainly reasonable to suggest that discussions with consultees on goals and objectives could reveal previously unrecognized cultural factors connected to a consultee's current problematic behavior. Sensitivity to language issues is another key consideration, as the use of professional terminology or slang may confuse or alienate consultees (Sheridan, 2000). Awareness of these variables could strengthen the consultation bond or facilitate changes to previously selected goals that are better aligned with the consultee's cultural values and expectations. Again, it is expected that consultants will consider all possibilities (cultural and otherwise) prior to settling on new goals, such as the notion that consultees who have assimilated well into their environment may not recognize subtle cultural dynamics known to other family members or others in their community (i.e., generational differences) and agree to goals that may unwittingly upset the school or family's entrenched values or rules and potentially cause distress for the consultee. Prematurely settling on new behavior goals without considering culture may also mitigate opportunities to gain valuable insights from the consultee about personal behavior and, in many cases, highlight unseen cultural dynamics. Therefore, failing to build a quality alliance and fully assess consultee behavior (and/or, cognitions, emotions, and antecedents) could easily weaken the consultation alliance or result in the selection of ineffective or inaccurate goals. Overall, consultation, like counseling, requires not only the requisite content knowledge, but a willingness to engage in active self-reflection in order to provide culturally and ethically competent consultation services.

Chapter Keystones

- Behavioral consultation is based on the notion that behavior is observable and can be changed through the use of learning principles. Fundamental goal is behavioral change.
- Behavioral consultation formats include behavioral case consultation, behavioral technology training, and behavioral system consultation.
- Behavioral consultation is used in varied settings and is the most commonly researched consultation framework.
- Behavioral consultation emphasizes collaboration between consultant and consultee and aims to change behavior through evidenced-based problem solving.
- Behavioral consultation is recognized as an effective consultation approach that emphasizes scientific rigor and evidence-based interventions, structured formats, behavioral change (i.e., learning) principles, and a present-centered and practical approach (Erchul & Shulte, 1996; Martens & DiGennaro, 2008).
- Emphasis on detailed, structured assessment facilitates more precise goal identification leading to more effective, measurable interventions that support and advance the efficacy of the behavioral consultation paradigm.
- Behavioral consultation identifies and promotes evidence-based interventions that are best suited to the skills, knowledge base, and goals of the consultee.
- Potential limitations challenges associated with behavioral consultation models include the following:
  - Challenge of applying behavioral methods in the natural environments of consultees (Kazdin, 2001) or the sense that manipulation is involved on part of the consultant
  - Limited attention to the consultation alliance as well as the consultee's affective or cognitive experiences related to implementing behavioral interventions
  - Potential limits of verbal communication with consultees as a means of facilitating true behavior change (Witt et al., 1996)
  - Slowness to integrate ecological and systems models
  - Complexity of some interventions, as well as foreclosure on known intervention, could mitigate opportunities for anticipated behavioral change(s)
  - Lack of empirical evidence supporting several key tenets of behavior consultation, including behavioral consultation's cost efficiency; expert stance less effective than a collaborative one; and new behaviors inherently sustainable (Watson & Sterling-Turner, 2008)
  - Slowness to adopt other recognized approaches such as ecological and system-level models
- Consultants using the cognitive-behavioral consultation (CBC) approach emphasize collaboration and shared problem solving instead of a position of expert
- Cognitive-behavioral consultation (CBC) recognizes that
  - behavior is influenced by internal and external factors;
  - behavioral antecedents can be impacted by cognitive, environmental, biological, and cultural factors; and
  - behavior is purposeful, yet the actual purpose may not be immediately known.

Web-Based and Literature-Based Resources

Websites

Consulting Psychology Journal: Practice and Research (2013): http://www.apa.org/pubs/journals/cpb/index.aspx

Division 13 of the American Psychological Association, The Society of Consulting Psychology (2013): http://www.apadivisions.org/division-13/index.aspx

Journal of Educational & Psychological Consultation (2013): http://www.tandfonline.com/toc/hepc20/current

Suggested Readings

Akin-Little, K. A., Little, S. G., Bray, M. A., & Kehle, T. J. (Eds). (2009). *Behavioral interventions in schools: Evidence-based positive strategies.* Washington, DC: American Psychological Association.

Altschaefl, M. R. (2013). Problem-solving (behavioral) consultation: School-based applications. In A. M. Dougherty (Ed.), *Casebook of psychological consultation and collaboration* (6th ed.). Belmont, CA: Brooks/Cole.

Beck, A. T., & Weishaar, M. E. (2008). Cognitive therapy. In R. J. Corsini & D. Wedding (Eds.). *Current psychotherapies* (8th ed., pp. 263–294). Belmont, CA: Thomson.

Bronfenbrenner, U. (1979). *The ecology of human development.* Cambridge, MA: Harvard University Press.

Persons, J. B., Burns, D. D., & Perloff, J. M. (1998). Predictors of dropout and outcome in cognitive therapy for depression in a private practice setting. *Cognitive Therapy and Research, 12,* 557–575.

Sheridan, S. M., & Kratochwill, T. R. (2008). Conjoint behavioral consultation (2nd ed). New York, NY: Springer.

References

Akin-Little, A., Little, S. G., Bray, M. A., & Kehle, T. J. (Eds.). (2009*). Behavioral interventions in schools: Evidence-based positive strategies.* Washington, DC: American Psychological Association.

Alberto, P. A., & Troutman, A. C. (2003). *Applied behavior analysis for teachers* (6th ed.). Englewood Cliffs, NJ: Prentice Hall.

Andersen, M. N., Hofstadter, K. L., Kupzyk, S., Daly, E. J., III, Bleck, A. A., Collaro, A. L., . . . Blevins, C. A. (2010). A guiding framework for integrating the consultation process and behavioral analytic practice in schools: The treatment validation consultation model. *Journal of Behavioral Assessment and Intervention in Children, 1*(1), 53–84.

Anton-LaHart, J., & Rosenfield, S. (2004). A survey of preservice consultation training in school psychology programs. *Journal of Educational & Psychological Consultation, 15,* 41–62.

Auster, E. R., Feeney-Kettler, K. A., & Kratochwill, T. R. (2006). Conjoint behavioral consultation: Application to the school-based treatment of anxiety disorders. *Education and Treatment of Children, 29,* 243–256.

Bandura, A. (1971). Psychotherapy based on modeling principles. In A. E. Bergin & S. L. Garfield (Eds.), *Handbook of psychotherapy and behavioral change: An empirical analysis* (pp. 653–708). New York, NY: Wiley.

Bandura, A. (1976). Self-reinforcement: Theoretical and methodological considerations. *Behaviorism, 4,* 135–155.

Bandura, A. (1977). *Social learning theory.* Englewood Cliffs, NJ: Prentice Hall.

Bandura, A. (1978). The self system in reciprocal determinism. *American Psychologist, 33,* 344–358.

Barlieb, D. (2003). Applying a solution focus to consultation. In R. L. Dingman & J. D. Weaver (Eds.), *Days in the lives of counselors* (pp. 144–150). Needham Heights, MA: Allyn & Bacon.

Bergan, J. R. (1977). *Behavioral consultation.* Columbus, OH: Merrill.

Bergan, J. R., & Kratochwill, T. R. (1990). *Behavioral consultation and therapy.* New York, NY: Plenum Press.

Bergan, J. R., & Tombari, M. L. (1976). Consultant skills and efficiency and the implementation and outcomes of consultation. *Journal of School Psychology, 14*(1), 3–14.

Bordin, E. S. (1983). A working alliance model of supervision. *The Counseling Psychologist, 11,* 35–42.

Bronfenbrenner, U. (1979). *Ecology of human development: Experiments by nature and design.* Cambridge, MA: Harvard University Press.

Brown, D., Pryzwansky, W. B., & Schulte, A. C. (2011). *Psychological consultation and collaboration: Introduction to theory and practice.* Boston, MA: Pearson.

Bruner, J. (1990). *Acts of meaning.* Cambridge, MA: Harvard University Press.

Caplan, G. (1964). *Principles of preventive psychiatry.* New York, NY: Basic Books.

Caplan, G. (1970). *The theory and practice of mental health consultation.* New York, NY: Basic Books.

Center for Effective Collaboration and Practice. (1998). *Addressing student problem behavior: Conducting a functional behavior assessment.* Retrieved from http://www.air.org/cecp/fba/problembehavior2.main2.htm

Curtis, M. J., & Stollar, S. A. (1996). Applying principles and practices of organizational change to school reform. *School Psychology Review, 25,* 409–417.

De Shazer, S. (1985). *Keys to solution in brief therapy.* New York, NY: Norton.

Dougherty, A. M. (2009). *Psychological consultation and collaboration in school and community settings.* Belmont, CA: Brooks/Cole.

Elliott, S. N., & Busse, R. T. (1993). Effective treatments with behavioral consultation. In J. E. Zins, T. R. Kratochwill, & S. N. Elliott (Eds.), *Handbook of consultation services for children* (pp. 179–203). San Francisco, CA: Jossey-Bass.

Erchul, W. P. (1992). On dominance, cooperation, teamwork, and collaboration in school-based consultation. *Journal of Educational & Psychological Consultation, 3,* 363–366.

Erchul, W. P., & Martens, K. (2003). *School consultation: Conceptual and empirical bases of practice* (2nd ed.). New York, NY: Plenum Press.

Erchul, W. P., & Shulte, A. C. (1996). Behavioral consultation as a work in progress. *Journal of Education and Psychological Consultation, 7,* 345–354.

Freer, P., & Watson, T. S. (1999). A comparison of parent and teacher acceptability ratings of behavioral and conjoint behavioral consultation. *School Psychology Review, 28,* 672–684.

Gallessich, J. (1982). *The profession and practice of consultation.* San Francisco, CA: Jossey-Bass.

Gmeinder, K. L., & Kratochwill, T. R. (1998). Short-term, home-based intervention for child noncompliance using behavioral consultation and a self-help manual. *Journal of Educational & Psychological Consultation, 9,* 91–117.

Gredler, M. E. (2008). *Learning and instruction: Theory into practice* (6th ed.). Upper Saddle River, NJ: Prentice Hall.

Gresham, F. M., Watson, T. S., & Skinner, C. H. (2001). Functional behavioral assessment: Principles, procedures, and future directions. *School Psychology Review, 30,* 156–172.

Grissom, P. F., Erchul, W. P., & Sheridan, S. M. (2003). Relationships among relational communication processes and perceptions of outcomes in conjoint behavioral consultation. *Journal of Educational & Psychological Consultation, 4,* 157–180.

Guli, L. A. (2005). Evidence-based parent consultation with school-related outcomes. *School Psychology Quarterly, 20,* 455–472.

Gutkin, T. B. (1996). Patterns of consultant and consultee verbalizations: Examining communication leadership during initial consultation interviews. *Journal of School Psychology, 34,* 199–219.

Gutkin, T. B. (1999). Collaborative versus directive/prescriptive/expert school-based consultation: Reviewing and resolving a false dichotomy. *Journal of School Psychology, 37,* 161–190.

Henning-Stout, M. (1993).Theoretical and empirical bases of consultation. In J. E. Zins, T. R. Kratochwill, & S. N. Elliott (Eds.), *Handbook of consultation services for children* (pp. 15–45). San Francisco, CA: Jossey-Bass.

Hoffman, M. A., Phillips, E. L., Noumair, D. A., Shullman, S., Geisler, C., Gray, J., . . . Zeigler, D. (2006). Toward a feminist and multicultural model of consultation and advocacy. *Journal of Multicultural Counseling and Development, 34,* 116–128.

Individuals with Disabilities Education ACT (IDEA) Public Law 105-117. (1997). Washington, DC: U. S. Government Printing Office. Retrieved from http://www2.ed.gov/offices/OSERS/Policy/IDEA/the_law .html

Jeger, A. M., & Slotnick, R. S. (Eds.). (1982). *Community mental health and behavioral ecology: A handbook of theory, research, and practice.* New York, NY: Plenum Press.

Kahn, B. B. (2000). A model of solution-focused consultation for school counselors. *Professional School Counseling, 3,* 248–254.

Kazdin, A. E. (2001). *Behavior modification in applied settings* (6th ed.). Pacific Grove, CA: Wadsworth/ Thomson.

Keller, H. R. (1981). Behavioral consultation. In J. C. Conoley (Ed.), *Consultation in schools: Theory, research, and procedures* (pp. 59–99). New York, NY: Academic Press.

Kim, B. (2001). Social constructivism. In M. Orey (Ed.), *Emerging perspectives on learning, teaching, and technology.* Retrieved January, 19, 2013, from http://epltt.coe.uga.edu/index.php?title=Social_Constructivism

Kratochwill, T.R. (2008). Best practices in school-based problem-solving consultation: Applications in prevention and intervention systems. In A. Thomas & J. Grimes (Eds.), *Best practices in school psychology* (5th ed., pp. 1673–1688). Bethesda, MD: National Association of School Psychologists.

Kratochwill, T. R., & Bergan, J. R. (1990). *Behavioral consultation in applied settings: An individual guide.* New York: Plenum Press.

Kratochwill, T. R., Elliott, S. N., & Busse, R. T. (1995). Behavioral consultation: A five-year evaluation of consultant and client outcomes. *School Psychology Quarterly, 10,* 87–110.

Kratochwill, T. R., Elliott, S. N., & Callan-Stoiber, K. (2002). Best practices in school-based problem-solving consultation. In A. Thomas & J. Grimes (Eds.), *Best practices in school psychology* (4th ed., pp. 583–608). Washington, DC: National Association of School Psychologists.

Kratochwill, T. R., Elliott, S. N., & Carrington Rotto, P. (1995). Best practices in school-based behavioral consultation. In A. Thomas and J. Grimes (Eds.), *Best practices in school psychology* (3rd ed., pp. 519–537). Washington, DC: National Association of School Psychologists.

Kratochwill, T. R., & Pittman, P. H. (2002). Expanding problem-solving consultation training: Prospects and frameworks. *Journal of Educational & Psychological Consultation, 13*(1/2), 69–95.

Lewis, T. J., & Newcomer, L. L. (2002). Examining the efficacy of school-based consultation: Recommendations for improving outcomes. *Child & Family Behavior Therapy, 24,* 165–181.

Maher, C. A. (1981). Interventions with school social systems: A behavioral-systems approach. *School Psychology Review, 10*(4), 499–510.

Malott, R. W., & Trojan Suarez, E. A. (2004). *Principles of behavior* (5th ed.). Upper Saddle River, NJ. Prentice Hall.

Martella, R. C., Nelson, J. R., & Marchand-Martella, N. E. (2003). *Managing disruptive behavior in the schools.* Boston, MA: Allyn & Bacon.

Martens, B. K., & DiGennaro, F. D. (2008). Behavioral consultation. In W. P. Erchul & S. M. Sheridan (Eds.), *Handbook of research in school consultation* (pp. 147–170). New York, NY: Erlbaum.

Martens, B. K. (1993). A behavioral approach to consultation. In J. E. Zins, T. R. Kratochwill, & S. N. Elliot (Eds.), *Handbook of consultation services for children* (pp. 65–86). San Francisco, CA: Jossey-Bass.

Newell, M. L. (2012). Transforming knowledge to skill: Evaluating the consultation competence of novice school-based consultants. *Consulting Psychology Journal: Practice and Research, 64,* 8–28.

No Child Left Behind (NCLB) Act of 2001, Pub. L. No. 107-110, § 115, Stat. 1425 (2002). Retrieved from http://www2.ed.gov/policy/elsec/leg/esea02/107-110.pdf

Noell, G. H. (1996). New directions in behavioral consultation. *School Psychology Quarterly, 11,* 187–188.

Parsons, R. D., & Kahn, W. J. (2005). *The school counselor as consultant: An integrated model for school-based consultation.* Belmont, CA: Brooks/Cole.

Piaget, J. (1972). *The psychology of the child.* New York, NY: Basic Books.

Piersel, W. C. (1985). Behavioral consultation: An approach to problem solving in educational settings. In J. R. Bergan (Ed.), *School psychology in contemporary society* (pp. 331–364). Columbus, OH: Merrill.

Reynolds, C. R., Gutkin, T. B., Elliot, S. N., & Witt, J. C. (1984). *School psychology: Essentials of theory and practice.* New York, NY: Wiley.

Rogoff, B. (1990). *Apprenticeship in thinking: Cognitive development in social context.* New York, NY: Oxford University Press.

Rosenfield, S. A. (1985). Teacher acceptance of behavioral principles. *Teacher Education and Special Education, 8*(3), 153–158.

Rosenfield, S. A. (2002). Developing instructional consultants: From novice to competent to expert. *Journal of Educational & Psychological Consultation, 13*(1/2), 97–111.

Russell, J. L. (1978). Behavioral consultation: Theory & process. *Personnel and Guidance Journal, 56,* 346–350.

Scheuermann, B. K., & Hall, J. A. (2008). *Positive behavioral supports for the classroom.* Upper Saddle River, NJ: Pearson.

Schulte, A. C., & Osborne, S. S. (2003). When assumptive worlds collide: A review of definitions of collaboration and consultation. *Journal of Educational & Psychological Consultation, 14*(2), 109–138.

Semke, C. A., & Sheridan, S. M. (2012). Family-school connections in rural educational settings: A systematic review of the empirical literature. *School Community Journal, 22*, 21–46.

Sheridan, S. M. (2000). Considerations of multiculturalism and diversity in behavioral consultation with parents and teachers. *School Psychology Review, 29*, 344–353.

Sheridan, S. M., Bovaird, J. A., Glover, T. A., Garbacz, S. A., Witte, A., & Kwon, K. (2012). A randomized trial examining the effects of conjoint behavioral consultation and the mediating role of the parent-teacher relationship. *School Psychology Review, 41*, 23–46.

Sheridan, S. M., Eagle, J. W., Cowan, R. J., & Mickelson, W. (2001). The effects of conjoint behavioral consultation: Results of a 4-year investigation. *Journal of School Psychology, 39*, 361–385.

Sheridan, S. M., Eagle, J. W., & Doll, B. (2006). An examination of the efficacy of conjoint behavioral consultation with diverse clients. *School Psychology Quarterly, 21*, 396–417.

Sheridan, S. M., & Kratochwill, T. R. (2008). *Conjoint behavioral consultation: Promoting family-school connections and interventions* (2nd ed.). New York, NY: Springer.

Sheridan, S. M., Kratochwill, T. R., & Bergan, J. R. (1996). *Conjoint behavioral consultation: A procedural manual*. New York, NY: Plenum Press.

Simonsen, B., & Sugai, G. (2009). School-wide positive behavior support: A systems level application of behavioral principles. In A. Akin-Little, S. G. Little, M. A. Bray, & T. J. Kehle (Eds.), *Behavioral interventions in schools: Evidence-based positive strategies* (pp. 125–140). Washington, DC: American Psychological Association.

Skinner, B. F. (1953). *Science and human behavior*. New York, NY: Macmillan.

Skinner, C. H., Skinner, A. L., & Burton, B. (2009). Applying group-oriented contingencies in the classroom. In A. Akin-Little, S. G. Little, M. A. Bray, & T. J. Kehle (Eds.), *Behavioral interventions in schools: Evidence-based positive strategies* (pp. 157–170). Washington, DC: American Psychological Association.

Tharp, R. G., & Wetzel, R. J. (1969). *Behavior modification in the natural environment*. New York, NY: Academic Press.

Touchette, P., MacDonald, R., & Langer, S. (1985). A scatterplot for identifying stimulus control of problems. *Journal of Applied Behavior Analysis, 18*, 343–351.

Truscott, S. D., Kreskey, D., Bolling, M., Psimas, L., Graybill, E., Albritton, K., & Schwartz, A. (2012). Creating consultee change: A theory-based approach to learning and behavioral change processes in school-based consultation. *Consulting Psychology Journal: Practice and Research, 64*(1), 63–82.

Turco, T. L., Skinner, C. H., & Wilcoxon, S. A. (1991). An analysis of consultee verbal responses to structured consultant questions. *Texas Association for Counseling and Development Journal, 19*(1), 23–32.

Vernberg, E. M., & Reppucci, N. D. (1986). Behavioral consultation. In E. V. Mannino, E. J. Trickett, M. F. Shore, M. G. Kidder, & G. Levin (Eds.), *Handbook of mental health consultation* (pp. 49–80). Rockville, MD: National Institute of Mental Health.

Vygotsky, L. (1978). *Mind in society*. Cambridge, MA: Harvard University Press.

Walker, J. E., Shea, T. M., & Bauer, A. M. (2004). *Behavior management: A practical approach for educators* (8th ed.). Englewood Cliffs, NJ: Prentice Hall.

Watson, T. S., & Robinson, S. L. (1996). Direct behavioral consultation: An alternative to traditional behavioral consultation. *School Psychology Quarterly, 11*, 267–278.

Watson, T. S., & Sterling-Turner, H. (2008). Best practices in direct behavioral consultation. In A. Thomas & J. Grimes (Eds.), *Best practices in school psychology* (5th ed., pp. 1661–1672). Bethesda, MD: National Association of School Psychologists.

Willems, E. P. (1974). Behavioral technology and behavioral ecology. *Journal of Applied Behavioral Analysis, 7*, 151–156.

Witt, J. C., Gresham, F. M., & Noell, G. H. (1996). What's behavioral about behavioral consultation? *Journal of Educational and Psychological Consultation, 7*, 327–344.

Ysseldyke, J., Lekwa, A.J., Klingbeil, D., & Cormier, D.C. (2012). Assessment of ecological factors as an integral part of academic and mental health consultation. *Journal of Educational and Psychological Consultation, 22*(1/2), 21–42. DOI:10.1080/10474412.2011.649641

Solution-Focused Consultation

Introduction

The behavioral and cognitive-behavioral models described previously offer a view of consultation that is grounded in the modernist philosophy that reality is objective and knowable. Solution-focused counseling, on the other hand, is rooted in a postmodern philosophy, a view that believes reality and knowledge are, and remain, subjective. Consultants interested in this approach should understand two key paths within constructive theory: *constructivism* and *social constructivism*. Constructivists believe that individuals create their own knowledge and reality, while social constructivists regard knowledge and reality as being created through and within dialogue and interaction with others. As posited by John Sommers-Flanagan and Rita Sommers-Flanagan (2012), "everything is perspective and perspective is everything" (p. 370). As a result, consultants taking the constructivist perspective would attend closely to the consultee or client's inner dialogue while a consultant holding a social constructionist view would do so and, in addition, attend closely to the interactions and dynamics between a consultee and his or her environment. These basic tenets will be explored in more detail later in the chapter.

Historically, Steve de Shazer (1985) and his wife Insoo Kim Berg, are widely credited for recognizing the potential benefits of social construction within the counseling paradigm. This eventually led to the development of solution-focused brief therapy (SFBT). From a conceptual and operational standpoint, SFBT neutralizes historical influences, dismisses diagnostic labeling, and takes a strength-based, collaborative (Caplan, 1993) approach to solving current and future concerns. The innate influence of social and environment variables in one's subjective interpretations is also a core element, a position that underscores the need for consultants to be culturally competent while remaining attuned to the subjective nature of the individual's experiences and interpretations.

The philosophy and pragmatism of the solution-focused approach has led several consultation scholars and researchers to work on adapting the approach to consultation (Barlieb, 2003; Brown, Pryzwansky, & Schulte, 2011; Kahn, 2000). This model, defined as *solution-focused consultee consultation* (SFCC), draws largely from the views of de Shazer and the conceptual framework of Caplan's consultee-centered case consultation (see Chapter 5). This chapter provides an overview of this model.

LEARNING OBJECTIVES

After reading the chapter, you will be able to

- Understand the key tenets of the solution-focused paradigm and the framework and process of the solution-focused consultee consultation (SFCC) model
- Discriminate between the modernist and postmodernist philosophies
- Describe the philosophical underpinnings of constructivism and social constructivism and their connection with solution-focused consultation
- Compare and contrast solution-focused consultee consultation with behavioral and cognitive-behavioral consultation philosophies
- Describe the role and responsibilities of the consultant and consultee in solution-focused consultation
- Apply solution-focused techniques to applicable cases

Current Perspectives

The use of postmodern philosophies may seem a bit disorienting at first to those can be deceptively complex to those most familiar with the modern philosophies. In this case, readers are strongly encouraged to understand each philosophy in form and function prior to engaging in consultation with models from either approach. This is both an ethical and pragmatic necessity and one more complex than suggesting than transitioning from a model grounded in objectivity to one based in subjectivity is easily digested and applied. For one author of this text, the notion that a clear and viable solution to a problem would appear with little more than a solid rapport with clients was quickly dispelled. Rather, it became apparent that while the subjectivity element was conceptually intriguing, applying this philosophy required additional knowledge, experiences, and supervision.

This perspective is included with the hope of illustrating that, while the SFCC approach to consultation is an interesting and potentially invaluable approach, consultants must understand not only the relational and procedural dynamics of the model, but also its guiding philosophical tenets. Ultimately, perhaps the most appropriate suggestion is to attend to the theory or model as a whole, from its philosophical underpinning to termination. Trying to cherry-pick aspects of a model (or philosophy) or technique (i.e., miracle question, finding exceptions) you find especially appealing only ends up providing an incomplete therapeutic or consultation picture. Without the perspective of a postmodernist philosophy (i.e., SFCC), the subjective reality of a consultee's perspective on a problem and their thoughts on viable solutions may remain unclear or unknown.

Solution-Focused Consultee Consultation

Working Alliance (Relationship)

Although current writings on the consultation alliance are limited, the SFCC model is known to recognize the social constructivism vision of social interaction as a means of attaining knowledge and understanding. The cornerstone of these interactions, and thus communication (Rogoff, 1990), is intersubjective compatibility—or an understanding among individuals or groups that is grounded in the shared cultural, social, and environment factors that influence worldviews (Brown et al., 2011). Predictably, this perspective requires cultural competence, active listening, and a willingness to encourage clients as they acquire a more affirming perspective of current problems or concerns and construct new realities. This includes the willingness of consultants to highlight even the slightest evidence of progress toward problem resolution. In short, the SFCC approach to the relational element of consultation recognizes that positive social interactions with well-informed, culturally competent individuals are key to promoting new knowledge attainment (Gredler, 1997; Berg, 2001).

The Solution-Focused Consultee Consultation Process

As noted, the SFCC parallels SFBT conceptually and operationally, with the notable exception of placing the miracle question after goals are set. The following sections detail specific stages of the SFCC model.

Initial Phase

The initial meeting in SFCC involves dialogue aimed squarely at solutions. Consultants seek to empower consultees by emphasizing their assets and previous successes that will facilitate problem resolution (Brown et al., 2011). This requires language that is both free of professional jargon that could impede problem solving and sensitive to cultural and social histories. In the solution-focused therapy model, for example, de Shazer (1985) suggests challenging clients to examine the aspects of their existence they would like to continue. This challenge could also be used at the outset of SFCC once a consultee has clarified a new goal. It is imperative to note, though, that this effort may require helping a consultee transition from a modernist to a postmodern view of the problem. Once done, this forward-looking perspective can help instill confidence and efficacy as consultees begin the process of recognizing positive aspects of themselves as they move toward problem resolution. Still, transitioning to a solution-focused mindset is challenging and, in some cases, inconceivable to consultees who possess entrenched negative schemas or an external locus of control. In such cases where progress seems unfeasible to consultees, consultants may take extra care to express faith in a client's problem-solving ability, remain respectful of their core desire to change, and assume they are knowledgeable about their own environment and motivated (Brown et al., 2011; Berg, 2001).

Several options exist within the SFCC model for identifying and changing current negative perspectives. One example involves the search for exceptions. This technique illustrates the SFCC view of the inevitability of change while challenging clients to conceptualize their life without the burden of the current problem (de Shazer, 1985; Berg & Miller, 1992). Another widely used technique involves helping consultee's envisioning new realities devoid of past problems (Kahn, 2000), a technique more commonly known as the *miracle question*. Specifically, miracle questions challenge individuals to create a context where the problem is no longer viewed as a barrier for the client. Examples of how to phrase the miracle question include

If a miracle occurred last night when you were sleeping and your problem went away, what would your life be like today?

What would be different?

Who else would notice that a change has taken place?

Dialogue surrounding the cognitive and emotional elements of this new reality would follow, with attention focused on the objectives leading to completion of the stated goals (Parsons & Kahn, 2005). At its core, however, the SFCC model recognizes that problem identification is valid only when subjectively viewed as such by the consultee. Goal setting commences once the problem is clearly identified.

Forming Goals and Scaling

Solution-focused consultation allows consultees to set goals individually, while constructing effective objectives to meet the goals remains collaborative. According to Richard D. Parsons and Wallace J. Kahn (2005), "goals of commission" (p. 211), or problem solving goals, are the primary goal-setting objectives in SFCC. Here, dialogue with consultees should lead to the identification of practical, solution-focused tasks and goals. One particularly useful means of getting a baseline reading of a client's view of a problem is by using a scaling technique. For example, a consultant could ask, "On a scale of 1 to 10, with 10 being the most severe, how would you rate the problem right now? What would it take to see that problem decrease this week?" Remember, active listening is critical in scaling questions as change is assessed by listening to the consultants' rating *and* by distinctions in how they are giving meaning to the problem:

Consultant: *If a miracle occurred last night when you were sleeping and your problem was no longer a problem, how would you tell?*

Consultee: *Well, my student would not be having behavior problems in class and would be sitting still and working without me having to tell him more than once.*

Consultant: *Ok, the student would be behaving more appropriately in class without you having to remind him more than once. Is that a goal you would like to set for our work together?*

Consultee: *Yes, that sounds like a great idea.*

Consultant: *So, on a scale of 1 to 10, where is the problem right now?*

Consultee: *Well, I would say that it is at a 9—the student/he has been really bad lately.*

Consultant: *Sounds like his behavior is a real challenge. How do you think you might be able to help move it down a little, say to an 8 or 7?*

Consultee: *I need him to follow the classroom rule of staying in your assigned seat unless otherwise directed. He tends to get antsy and move around after a few minutes, so I guess I could try to encourage him when he stays seated for periods of time.*

Consultant: *That sounds like a great goal and the positive encouragement is a useful way of encouraging his positive behavior and rule following. It sounds to me like the goal is to have him follow classroom rule of staying in your assigned seat and the task you will use is encouraging statements when he does stay seated. Is that correct?*

Consultee: *Yes, that's what I would like to do and see happen.*

Subsequent sessions may find the consultant continuing to employ scaling questions as a way of assessing their view of the problem over time. The SFCC consultant would view consultee answers as key to understanding the degree to which the problem has been resolved or not. Using this technique, subsequent sessions may find the consultant employing a scaling intervention by asking the consultee to rate the level of progress on a scale of 1 to 10 with 1 being little or no progress and 10 being goal attainment. Consultee answers provide key insights and should be addressed specifically. For example, if the consultee above rated events 1 week after the initial meeting a 5, the consultant would inquire as to the consultee's interpretation of what 5 means in relation to the problem and their cognitive and emotional experiencing of the situation. At times, consultants may recognize discrepancies between a client's emotional or cognitive response and the scaling number selected. Appropriate confrontation in these circumstances could lead to more intentional dialogue regarding the consultee's subjective experiences and perceptions of goals, tasks, and interventions associated with problem resolution. Finally, SFCC dismisses the notion of resistance. Instead, the SFCC consultant frames all discourse with the consultees as essential information that provides current insight and understanding of their subjective experiences and perceptions— knowledge that can be used to reframe or create new solutions to the current problem(s).

Finding a Solution

For starters, consultants should hold a baseline notion that solutions are more likely when the consultation alliance is strong and the consultation environment is safe and free of personal agendas and values. That said, consultants have several options for helping consultees toward solutions. As mentioned, the use of *scaling* and the *miracle question* are core brief strategic family therapy (BSFT) and SFCC features. The *exception question*, which attempts to diffuse entrenched or fatalistic cognitions and highlight consultee assets, is another option. In general, each of these possibilities "activates a problem-solving mindset" and "helps [clients] look beyond the problem" (Nichols & Schwartz, 2007, p. 253). Duane Brown, Walter B. Pryzwansky, and Ann C. Schulte (2011) also suggest having the consultee "appoint" an observer who can provide feedback on a specific problem. Questions from consultants would then be designed to elicit exemptions, such as items that help illustrate consultee strengths. In all cases, consultants point out even the most seemingly minor client assets or behaviors that indicate progress—a view that some consultees, especially those expecting immediate progress or who tend to blame others—may find hard to fathom. Ultimately, the SFCC method reasons that goal attainment is derived primarily from consultees parlaying their own (perhaps dormant or previously unknown) strengths into goal directed actions that result "in a more self-reinforcing and empowering internal locus of control" (Parsons & Kahn, 2005, pp. 210–211).

Termination of Initial Session

First-session outcomes are of critical importance, so consultants and consultees should work hard at the outset to share their perceptions about any issue that could influence problem resolution. For example, questions such as, questions such as, *Did (consultee) clarify specific solutions that would facilitate goal attainment?* or *Did you not identify specific solutions that would lead to you attaining your goal?* In the first example, consultants would simply encourage the consultee to carry out the solution. If the latter materializes, implementing any of the previously noted strategies may help the consultee transition out of a ineffective, problem-focused orientation that is impeding a their ability to focus on solutions. In these and other cases, use of a *summary message* that reframes a consultee's experience in a more encouraging way is often especially helpful. Specifically, a summary message may contain praise for positive consultee actions, provide context to the consultee's problems, and propose homework for consultees to complete for the next session (Nichols & Schwartz, 2007). Here again, any advancement toward goals are met with encouraging dialogue and specific comments aimed at accentuating successes.

Consultees who hold firmly to the notion that problems are unsolvable can be challenging and frustrating, yet SFCC requires that consultants maintain a pragmatic and supportive tone. This may often include techniques such as asking goal-directed questions, identifying exceptions, developing tasks or solutions, and/ or highlighting indicators of progress (Parsons & Kahn, 2005). If SFCC techniques ultimately fail to liberate the consultee from a problem-focused orientation, alternatives such as bibliotherapy, observing other professionals, dialoguing with parents dealing with similar work or home concerns, or keeping a personal journal to track insights as well as emotional and cognitive responses can be suggested by consultants (Brown et al., 2011).

Below is a list of solution-focused questions and comments gathered from several authors (Brown et al., 2011; Parsons & Kahn, 2005; Nichols & Schwartz, 2007):

- Have there been times in the past when this problem didn't exist or wasn't as severe or difficult as it is today?
- You have described your life without the problem you brought here today. Is that your goal for our work together?
- How were you able to do that? What benefits have you gotten?
- Miracle Question . . .
  - Suppose you went to sleep tonight and a miracle occurred and when you awoke your problem was resolved. What is the first thing that you would notice is different? What other things would you notice? Would anyone besides you know a miracle occurred?
- I am impressed with efforts you have made to stay on track and achieve your goal.
- How well did the strategy work? Are there ways to improve the strategy that you selected? What have you learned this last week?

Follow-Up Sessions

Follow-up sessions in the SFCC model are based on consultee actions (or inaction) following their initial session. For example, after a consultee attempted a solution to an identified problem, dialogue would center on the results, perceived improvements, and needed adjustments to the goal (Brown et al., 2011). If no solution has yet been identified, dialogue would center on the consultee's cognitive or emotional responses to the perceived problems and a renewed attention to viable solutions. Predictably, termination follows goal attainment or the consultee's stated belief in personal efficacy as an autonomous problem solver. As in any professional counseling and consultation relationship, of course, consultants using SFCC should monitor their consultant–consultee dynamic to prevent the emergence of dependency.

Multicultural Considerations

The postmodern philosophy, along with the key tenets of constructivism and social constructivism, has important multicultural implications for consultants. Of particular importance is recognizing that the consultee's construction of a problem is rooted in personal interpretation of a problem, while the social constructivist perspective holds that a consultee's problem is an interplay of this view in relation to the influence of others. As a result, consultants must also adapt to the consultee's perspective of individual culture and place or role in it—regardless of what the consultant, through research or personal experience, believes and/or knows to be factually true about the consultee's culture. It also illustrates to consultees is working from their own sense of the "truth". For example, a consultant using the SFCC approach must set aside (but not dismiss) personal knowledge and experience in order to discern the consultee's perception of a problem and help the consultee discern the appropriate course of action for resolving it. Alternatively, the SFCC approach would consider a consultee's subjective understanding of how, for example, individual experiences (cultural and otherwise) have led to the construction of "fairness" prior to addressing exceptions. This could be especially challenging for consultants with considerable professional experience and content knowledge about the problems and environmental conditions in which consultees are experiencing problems.

Consultants who are able to make this transition will likely appreciate the SFCC vision of gaining the clearest insight into the consultee's subjective view of current problems. Doing so requires that consultants be able and willing to confront their own biases or current understandings of what they "know" in favor of the consultee's perspective on the problem and on the best course of action for resolving the problem. In other words, consultant and consultee must be on the same page. That is, the page which articulates the consultee's perception of the problem, the variables involved in triggering or maintaining the problem, and the best means of resolving the problem. Therefore, gaining access and remaining attuned to the consultee's worldview is a requisite for the culturally competent application of the SFCC approach.

Chapter Keystones

- Solution-focused consultee consultation (SFCC) is grounded in de Shazer's (1985) brief-solution-focused therapy model.
- SFCC is predicated on a postmodernist theory of social constructivism, a belief conceptually distinct from the modernist perspective of the other models detailed in this text.
- Subjectivity remains a hallmark of the postmodernist and social-constructivist philosophies.

- Understanding how or what a consultee perceives as a problem (and a potential solution) requires that consultants consider only how the consultee perceives the problem was influenced by environmental factors.
- SFCC draws from BSFT techniques, include finding exceptions, the miracle question, scaling questions, and conceptualizing clients' narratives based on their perceptions (i.e., social constructivism).
- SFCC closely parallels BSFT, with a key distinction being SFCC's placement of the miracle question after goal setting.
- Understanding and competent use of SFCC requires an understanding of the distinctions between the modern and postmodern perspectives.
- The SFCC approach can be used with individuals, groups, parents, and teachers (Brown et al., 2011).

Guided Practice Exercises
Exercise 6.1: An Initial Session

Find/link with a partner for this exercise. Imagine that one of you is a counselor that is struggling with a very difficult client; the other partner will serve as a consultant. Simulate an initial solution-focused consultation session. Be sure to (a) incorporate a miracle question, (b) set goals (incorporating scaling questions for baseline "data"), and (c) include a challenge to the consultee.

Because it is a simulated situation, it is likely that the session will be fairly brief (approximately 10–15 minutes). However, you can go for longer, if you would like. Once you have finished the session, discuss what happened. Identify the three required elements.

What was the miracle question? What goals were set? What was the challenge to the consultee? Focus on the strengths of the session and consultee's actions.

An option to this exercise is to include a third person (before the session begins), who can serve as an observer and provide feedback regarding the elements that were witnessed.

Guided Practice Exercises
Exercise 6.2: The Miracle Question Contest

Think of as many different ways of stating a "miracle question" as possible. This can be an individual or small-group activity.

The person/group with_____ wins.

- the most number of different questions
- the most creative way of asking a miracle question

- the most subtle way of asking a miracle question
- the most humorous miracle question
- the most concise, yet effective miracle question

Guided Practice Exercises
Exercise 6.3: Self-Reflection and Group Discussion

Spend time alone exploring your personal understanding to each question. Consider not only your emotional and cognitive responses, but also your own view of how problems are resolved and the implications of this view for your work as consultant. Following your own reflections, find a partner or two and discuss your responses to the questions and challenge your partner(s) to elaborate on their responses.

1. Describe the key differences between the modern and postmodern philosophies and their potential influence on the consultant model you feel is more amenable to your personal philosophy of change.

2. Numerous intervention options are available to you as a consultant. Choose two from each model and provide an example of when each would be indicated and/or potentially counterindicated. Be sure to consider cultural and ethical and legal issues.

3. Describe the key similarities and distinctions between solution-focused consultant and de Shazer's brief-solution-focused therapy models. Which are you more comfortable with and why?

Web-Based and Literature-Based Resources

Websites

Association for the Quality Development of Solution Focused Consulting and Training: http://www.asfct.org
SOL World: Sharing and building Solution Focused practice in organisations: http://www.solworld.org

Suggested Readings

Barlieb, D. (2003). Applying a solution focus to consultation. In R. L. Dingman & J. D. Weaver (Eds.), *Days in the lives of counselors* (pp. 144–150). Needham Heights, MA: Allyn & Bacon.
De Jong. P., & Berg, I. K. (2013). *Interviewing for solutions*. Belmont, CA: Brooks/Cole.
Kahn, B. B. (2000). A model of solution-focused consultation for school counselors. *Professional School Counseling, 3*(4), 248.

References

Bandura, A. (1977). *Social learning theory.* Englewood Cliffs, NJ: Prentice Hall.

Barlieb, D. (2003). Applying a solution focus to consultation. In R. L. Dingman & J. D. Weaver (Eds.), *Days in the lives of counselors* (pp. 144–150). Needham Heights, MA: Allyn & Bacon.

Berg, I. K., & Miller, S. D. (1992). *Working with the problem drinker: A solution-focused approach.* New York, NY: Norton.

Brown, D., Pryzwansky, W. B., & Schulte, A. C. (2011). *Psychological consultation and collaboration: Introduction to theory and practice.* Boston, MA: Pearson.

Caplan, G. (1964). *Principles of preventive psychiatry.* New York, NY: Basic Books.

Caplan, G., & Caplan, R. B. (1993). Mental health consultation and collaboration. New York, NY: Basic Books.

de Shazer, S. (1985). *Keys to solution in brief therapy.* New York, NY: Norton.

Gredler, M. E. (1997). *Learning and instruction: Theory into practice.* Upper Saddle River, NJ: Prentice Hall.

Kahn, B. B. (2000). A model of solution-focused consultation for school counselors. *Professional School Counseling, 3,* 248–254.

Nichols, M. P., & Schwartz, R. C. (2007). *The essentials of family therapy.* Boston, MA. Allyn & Bacon.

Parsons, R. D., & Kahn, W. J. (2005). *The school counselor as consultant: An integrated model for school-based consultation.* Belmont, CA: Brooks/Cole.

Rogoff, B. (1990). *Apprenticeship in thinking: Cognitive development in social context.* New York, NY: Oxford University Press.

Sommers-Flanagan, J., & Sommers-Flanagan, R. (2012). *Counseling and psychotherapy theories in context and practice: Skills, strategies, and techniques* (2nd ed.). Hoboken, NJ: Wiley.

Vygotsky, L. (1978). *Mind in society.* Cambridge, MA: Harvard University Press.

7

Ethical and Legal Aspects of Consultation

Introduction

Which code of ethics do I need to follow?

The discussion of ethics in counseling can be a semester-long conversation. Many times, beginning counselors are very confused about what is ethical behavior for a counselor. This confusion escalates when you add consultation to the counseling and ethics equation. Fortunately, professional organizations such as the American Counseling Association (ACA, 2005), the American Mental Health Counseling Association (AMHCA, 2010), and the National Association of Social Work (NASW, 2008) all provide a detailed "Code of Ethics" which contain specific sections on consultation to guide mental health professionals–consultants in their daily professional activities. In addition, the American Psychological Association (APA, 2010) and the American School Counselor Association (ASCA, 2004) provide their members with a code of ethics that is followed in their professional activities.

Even with these professional guidelines, many times counselor–consultants find themselves questioning if they are acting in an ethical manner when working with their client or organization.

Understanding Ethical and Legal Codes in Consultation

An individual serving in a consultation role faces ethical issues just as they would if they were serving in a mental health or educational role. However, the codes of ethics of various professional organizations (e.g., American Counseling Association,

LEARNING OBJECTIVES

After reading this chapter, you will be able to

- Locate and apply the ethical and legal codes used in counseling–consultation
- Describe and explain the ethical principles that will guide you in your role as consultant
- Through guided exercises, discuss and explore ethical issues and how they pertain to the world of the counselor as consultant

American Psychological Association, National Association of Social Workers) never seem to be specific enough for those fulfilling a consultation role. This is due, in part, to the complex nature of the consultation role. Multiple people can be involved in your work as a consultant (e.g., the consultee or consultees), and multiple people can be affected by the work that a consultant does (the consultee and client).

Consulting relationships are certainly helping relationships, but the complex triadic connections may impede individuals in consulting roles from readily having clear-cut guidelines to follow. Is a consultant's responsibility to the consultee, the client system, or both? Is it possible to have a conflict of interest with a consultee? Jody L. Newman in 1993 indicated that since consulting relationships are different from counseling ones, then they require special ethical considerations. It is a mistake to assume that the knowledge and skills required for effective counseling are the same as those required for effective consultation (Newman, 1993).

Organizations such as the American Counseling Association (ACA) have come a long way over time in adapting their codes of ethics to incorporate elements related to consultation (see Table 7.1 on page 157), but there is still much room for individual situational interpretation by consultants in the field. Codes of ethics in consultation have been overlooked over time and very little has been written in this area. Counselors serving as consultants have found themselves in a bit of a gray area, having specific codes of ethics in which to follow as counselors, but not much specific direction when taking on consultative responsibilities. This gray area creates complicating issues both ethically and legally.

Professional ethics (even when consultation is mentioned) and law have overlapping topics, but that doesn't mean that the focuses of each are equal (McCarthy & Sorenson, 1993). Without clarity in consultation ethics, counselors may find themselves at risk professionally and legally. Consultants could be sued for malpractice, breach of contract, or other action (or lack thereof). Courts may very well refer to a profession's code of ethics when weighing decisions regarding an individual's behavior (e.g., What would constitute malpractice?).

In the end, however, the legal principles that apply to counselors, psychologists, and social workers, for example, also apply to those professionals when they serve as consultants (McCarthy & Sorenson, 1993). A lack of awareness of the law is not a reason for violating well-established legal principles. It may be legal to engage in some consultative behaviors, but that doesn't mean that the behavior is ethical. Correspondingly, some consultative behaviors may be ethical but not necessarily legal. It is important for consultants to learn about the laws that affect their practices.

Most professionals in the field are bound by specific state laws related to their profession. It is recommended that all professionals make themselves aware of the laws that professionally bind them within their respective state. Martha M. McCarthy and Gail Paulus Sorenson (1993) indicate that much federal statutory law impacts public and private federally-aided institutions and that federal constitutional law affects public education employees like school counselors, school psychologists, school social workers.

The Development of Ethical Guidelines in Consultation

Douglas R. Gross and Sharon E. Robinson (1985) indicate that the history of professional consultation dates back to the 1940s and 1950s. Somewhat later, in 1978, the *Personnel and Guidance Journal*, a precursor of the *Journal for Counseling and Development*, published two special issues that addressed consultation. These issues provided specific elements related to consultation in the counseling profession: concepts, models, procedures, and theories. At the time in which Gross and Robinson published their article (1985), they indicated that the ethical standards for consultation were too vague, too generic, or missing. They labeled consultation as a "Developing Role."

Newman (1993) noted that there were no formal guidelines or codes related to consultation for the counseling profession in the early 1990s. At the time, most organizations had hints of "consultation" in their respective codes of ethics but only minimal mentions. In 1992, A. Michael Dougherty indicated that the American Association of Counseling and Development (AACD; an earlier name for ACA), the National Board for Certified Counselors (NBCC), and the American School Counseling Association (ASCA) all mentioned consultation in their respective codes of ethics, but that the mentions were minimal. Even other professionals (early childhood professionals) have noted there are no specific behavioral guidelines for consultants from the helping professions: Examples cited (Wesley & Buysse, 2006) were the American School Counseling Association (ASCA) and the National Association of Social Work (NASW).

Historically, ACA and the APA have provided limited guidance in each respective ethical code (Newman, 1993). In an earlier version of ACA's code of ethics from 1981, there were six specific mentions of consultation and only one was different from the standards related to counseling relationships (Gross & Robinson, 1985). In an earlier version of the APA's Ethical Principles of Psychologists (1981), "Consulting Relationship" and "Consulting" each appear only twice in the document (Gross & Robinson, 1985).

It was agreed by some that the ethical codes were not adequate for consultants (Dougherty, 1992; Newman, 1993), not much effort had been put forth toward ethical issues and procedures for consultation, and that this was a neglected area (Gross & Robinson, 1985). Many professionals at the time stressed the need for ethical guidelines for consultants. Along the way, both ACA and APA appointed task forces to develop standards for training in consultation (Newman, 1993).

There is not a specific course requirement in consultation for counseling programs accredited by the Council for the Accreditation of Counseling and Related Educational Programs (CACREP), but the CACREP standards do contain requirements related to knowledge in consultation skills (Davis, 2004). Some counselor education programs require a course in consultation as part of their standard course of study—to address CACREP standards that mention consultation knowledge and skills—but also because they see the value of training helping professionals in this specific activity related to indirect service.

Prior to codes being established, each counselor serving as a consultant was responsible for interpreting appropriate professional consulting behavior (Wesley & Buysse, 2006). It has been suggested that the lack of a common set of standards can be attributed to the reality that consultants are represented by different professions and different backgrounds (Gross & Robinson, 1985). It is not proposed that there be one set of common ethical standards for consultants because there will always be consultants from each of the respective helping professions and each profession will maintain its own set of ethical codes. However, there can be some common elements.

Codes of ethics tend to be general in nature and do not specify requirements related to courses of action in consultation. Patricia W. Wesley and Virginia Buysse (2006) suggest that the codes should reflect current professional conditions and concerns in their respective fields. They suggest that there are typically (a) consultant issues, (b) relationship issues, and (c) process issues. Some professional organizations are increasing their attention to consultation in their respective ethical codes. Some have specific statements related to ethical consultative behavior but most focus on general guidelines.

Since most of the professional codes of ethics are readily available via Internet websites, we have listed the respective websites in the resource section later in the chapter. You are encouraged to visit these websites to learn more about how consultation is viewed and included in professional codes of ethics.

Many organizations' codes of ethics make reference to seeking consultation when faced with an ethical dilemma as well as presenting actual guidelines for consultation. The former (references made) are directives or suggestions for practice (what to do in specific situations: "a professional should seek consultation") and are not guidelines related to the practice of consultation. The statements typically end with a direction to seek consultation and do not provide information for the actual consultant or for what should occur during this consultation. Although useful components of the ethical guidelines, these references to consultation are not the focus of our discussion related to ethical guidelines for consultative behaviors.

Ethical Principles

The theoretical and pragmatic tenets of professional ethics and ethical decision making required of counseling professionals are also central to the provision of competent consultation. Counselors acting in the role of a consultant must be able to discern a reasonable course of action from recognized ethical standards within their profession.

In the counseling discipline, American Counseling Association's (ACA, 2005) ethical code constitutes the overarching ethical and legal standards of practice that is to be followed. Still, while ethics in relation to consultation parallel those of counseling in that they are standards of conduct, ethical issues and competent ethical decision making is seldom a clear cut process in the actual practice of consultation. However, counselors and consultants are well served by drawing on the six core moral principles that guide the ethical decision making of professional counselors and other mental health professionals. These principles are respect for autonomy, nonmaleficence, beneficence, justice, fidelity, and veracity. An abridged version of each principle is paraphrased from the writings of Theodore P. Remley and Barbara Herlihy (2010) and applied to consultation:

- *Respect for autonomy* is defined as fostering self-determination of a consultee. Consultants respect a consultee's right to determine a personal belief system and course of action. Consultants work to facilitate independent decision making and mitigate the development of consultee dependence. Such respect for autonomy can be seen in the following case illustration.

Case 7.1: Respect for Autonomy

As Tony was walking out of the building after a long day of providing consulting services for a local agency, he thought to himself, "If I had a dollar for every time a consultee asked me to just tell them what to do." Tony's current consultee was similar to others he had worked with in the past. Initially the consultee was very excited about having Tony come in and provide consultation services. As time went on, many of the consultees realized that Tony was there to *help* facilitate change and not swoop in and tell them exactly what to do to be a successful agency. Tony would remind this new agency (as he has in the past working with previous agencies) that the final decision to make the changes was ultimately up to the people in the agency. Tony was very aware of the possibility of the agency to become dependent on his recommendations and leadership. He made his actions very transparent and continued to remind the agency that they are in charge and responsible for their own decision making concerning the issues at hand.

- *Nonmaleficence* is defined as do no harm and constitutes the view that even inadvertent harm done to a client is unacceptable and, thus, all actions taken by the consultant must be based on the standard of nonmaleficence.
- *Beneficence* is the converse of nonmaleficence and involves the active promotion of the holistic wellness of the consultee.
- *Justice* involves the consultant's commitment to equality in all consulting professional relationships, including the exclusion of bias and discrimination in word and deed.
- *Fidelity* requires that consultants fulfill their responsibility to uphold trust in any professional relationship, such as maintaining confidentiality. Case illustration 7.2 provides an example of a consultant working in the school system.

Case 7.2: Fidelity

Roberta, a school counselor at an elementary school, is working with Ms. Jackson, a third-grade teacher at her school. Ms. Jackson requested Roberta's help with developing some classroom behavior-management strategies because she has sent several children from her classroom to the principal's office for their misbehavior. The principal has expressed displeasure with the manner in which Ms. Jackson has handled her classroom but has not offered any assistance or suggestions. Ms. Jackson believes that the principal does not like her, and will soon be completing a negative evaluation of her performance for her personnel file. Ms. Jackson is expecting to receive a formal reprimand and has asked for Roberta's help not only to appear proactive but to also find strategies to help her work with the misbehaving children.

Roberta has observed Ms. Jackson in her classroom on a couple of occasions and has met with her one time to review the observation and discuss strategies and ideas. She feels like they are making decent progress in a short amount of time, discussing the children who are primarily causing the problems, and what role Ms. Jackson is playing in the relationship. The have agreed that the children are partially responsible, but that Ms. Jackson has played a part in the problem as well. This role, and what to do about it, was the majority of what Roberta and Ms. Jackson discussed during their meeting.

Today, the principal stopped Roberta in the hall and inquired about her work with Ms. Jackson, "How is it going?" she asked.

Roberta wasn't sure how the principal knew this bit of information—that she was consulting with Ms. Jackson. More importantly, however, she hadn't been given permission by Ms. Jackson to discuss the matter. Roberta knew that any information could contribute to a negative evaluation for Ms. Jackson, and she felt like she and Ms. Jackson were making some significant progress. Roberta couldn't help but think about how the principal was her (Roberta's) administrator and direct supervisor as well. On one hand, she felt obligated to report her own work activities—but more importantly, she felt responsible for upholding the confidentiality of her consultee and remaining silent with respect to their work.

- *Veracity* equates with truthfulness, as would be evidenced by a consultant's forthrightness with a consultee in detailing their concerns regarding potential outcomes expected of their professional relationship. Case Illustration 7.3 provides an example of the sometimes difficult and delicate work of a consultant when evaluating an organization.

Case 7.3: Veracity

Stephanie, a licensed professional counselor and counselor educator, was asked to consult with a children's shelter in a beautiful, yet isolated region of the country regarding the organization's desire to become a CACREP- and APA-approved clinical training site for graduate and postgraduate-level PhD counselors and psychologists. During her initial meeting with the organization's administrative and clinical leadership, Stephanie provided informed consent and obtained written agreement of these parameters from both the administrative and clinical leadership. While working to clearly define the problems and concerns to be addressed, it became clear to Stephanie that the administrative and clinical leadership shared many of the same goals, including the inclusion of both master's- and doctoral-level counselors-in-training (CIT) from CACREP-accredited counseling programs and clinical psychology students from APA-accredited programs, respectively. Additionally, both leaders expressed their aspirations to be the "go to" regional clinical training facility. Other items noted specifically by the administrator included the potential financial incentives for the interns, housing, third-party reimbursement for intern services, and marketing strategies for recruiting from programs across the United States.

Stephanie spent the following two days interviewing the clinical and administrative staffs of the organization and learned several key facts. These included the administrative leadership's belief that interns were expected to be primary-service providers and maintain up to 15 hours of billable services per week and that the organization had the clinical infrastructure (i.e., licensed clinical staff, office space, administrative support, supervision) to provide training for a mix of up to five counseling and clinical psychology interns. However, after extended discussions with the clinical director, Stephanie learned that the organization had only one licensed mental health professional (a licensed clinical social worker), had no staff properly trained in clinical supervision, and was planning to place interns immediately into several settings, including poorly coordinated, school-based counseling programs which lacked formal policy agreements with the schools. Additionally, the clinical director, who held a bachelors of arts degree in psychology, reiterated their interest in immediately using interns to help "shore up" their billable service hours due to their tenuous financial situation after the downturn in the economy. Finally, Stephanie learned that the organization had little to no insight into CACREP- and APA-accrediting standards or the requirements of receiving formal approval to place interns at their organization. Moreover, the clinical director requested that perceived interns begin at the beginning of the next fall academic term, a time frame of only 3 months.

Challenge: Identify the moral principles that Stephanie will encounter in writing her formal report to this organization, while paying special consideration to the principle of **veracity***.*

While consultants should consider each of these ethical principles in their decision making, as dictated by the specific ethical standards for consulting in the ACA ethical code (2005, p. 11, Section D.2.a through D.2.d), their deliberations should also include consideration of morality issues (i.e., right vs. wrong; Corey, Corey, & Callahan, 2007). Thus, consultants, like counselors, are strongly urged to consider the influence and potential implications of mandatory ethics, aspirational ethics, principle ethics, and virtue ethics. Ultimately, the application of these principles, whether individual or in combination, obligates consultants as it does counselors to maintain a solid grasp on professional ethical codes and a personal understanding of the professional and personal views that guide their ethical decision making. In that sense, several options are available.

Principle ethics, for example, form the nucleus of the collective moral belief system of a profession. With this perspective, a consultant who is frustrated with a perceived lack of a quality working alliance with a consultee may reflect on the principle of veracity, or truthfulness. In doing so, the consultant would address concerns regarding the quality of the alliance in hopes of strengthening the alliance and, ultimately, ensuring that the goals of the consulting contract are successfully met. *Virtue ethics,* on the other hand, diverge from principle ethics based on the notion that professional ethics includes the idea of personal character. In this sense, the equation changes from one of "How should I approach a situation?" to "What role do I play?" In essence, virtue ethics connects the consultant to the reflective practitioner model in the sense that it challenges the professional "to look at who you are" instead of "what you do" (Remley & Herlihy, 2010, p. 10).

Another interpretation of ethical standards is *mandatory ethics,* or the view that ethical compliance is based on following the standard as written. Several concerns have been voiced about this approach, including the notion that this view meets the "letter but not the spirit" (Remley & Herlihy, 2010, p. 11) of ethical standards. In other words, consultants aspire to meet the minimum level of compliance, a practice that while valid in the sense that ethical code is followed, remains incongruent with the professional notion of "best practice." Other authors (Pope & Vasquez, 2007) suggest that those using virtue ethics as their primary ethical guide risk falling prey to denying, minimizing, or even rejecting the intent of the standard or the issues therein (Pope & Vasquez, 2007). Conversely, consultants who use *aspirational ethics* seek to conduct themselves at the highest levels of professional practice. Consultants with this disposition seek to bridge the important concepts of "best practice" and "reflective practitioner." For example, a consultant using the mandatory ethics may frame a decision as "It can't be unethical if I don't see it as an ethical issue" (Remley & Herlihy, 2010, p. 11). On the other hand, consultants using the aspirational ethics as a guide would reflect on how their own worldview (values, ethics, beliefs) may influence their view of the ethical question under consideration and, in conjunction with the requisite ethical standards of their profession, are likely to respond in a manner that best facilitates the goals of the consultee while ensuring the actions of the consultant and consultee are compliant with the letter and spirit of all relevant ethical standards. Ultimately, consideration of the six moral principles, together with the noted styles of ethical decision making and standards set forth by the ethical standards of appropriate professional ethical codes, are part and parcel to the guiding principles of consultation ethics. These principles are outlined below.

Ethical Principle I: Professional Competencies

Professional counselors serving in the role of consultant are expected to attain and abide by the standards for professional competence set forth in the ACA code (2005): counseling professionals who serve as consultants. In the ACA code, professional competence is addressed in several instances, including standards specific to consultation activities. Section C.2.a through C.2.g of the 2005 ACA ethical code, for example, outlines the education, continued training, supervision, and awareness of personal and professional wellness and limitations (Newman, 1993) considered instrumental to the professional competence of counselors. However, these qualities are evident in the dedicated standards for counselors serving as consultants (ACA, 2005, D.2.a through D.2.d), led by the competency standard (D.2.a):

D.2.a. Consultant Competency

Counselors take reasonable steps to ensure that they have the appropriate sources and competencies when providing consultation services. Counselors provide appropriate referral resources when requested or needed.

Exercise 7.1 will allow you to explore an issue for consultants when they are performing multiple roles.

Exercise 7.1: Can I Do Both?

A well-educated and highly experienced licensed professional counselor, Sarah, who has over 15 years working as a mental health counselor in a rural outpatient clinic, was asked by a colleague at another agency to take on the role of sole consultant for their new school-based counseling program in a larger, urban school system. This particular program seeks to mesh the clinical services of an agency and need for mental health services. After deliberating for a few days, Sarah accepts the consulting offer based on her years of experience as an agency counselor and begins negotiations in good faith on a contract with her colleague's agency.

Discussion Questions

1. *Is this ethical behavior on the part of Sarah?*

2. *Describe your answer with backing evidence from one or more of the ethical codes.*

Ethical Principle II: Client Welfare

The responsibility to foster and protect a client's welfare is an explicit function of professional counselors serving in the role of consultants. This requirement is firmly embedded in the ACA ethical code and the ethical codes of allied mental health disciplines (i.e., APA, 2002) and illustrates the importance of the welfare of clients and any unforeseen others who may be impacted. In either case, the ACA ethical code D.2.b requires that "counselors attempt to develop with their own consultees a clear understanding of problem definition, goals for change, and predicted consequences of interventions selected" (2005, p. 11). Following this standard helps ensure client welfare in the sense that consultees are aware of and engaged in each factor of the consultation process and along with informed consent (D.2.d), understand their right to terminate consultation without penalty.

In fact, the first standard in the ACA (2005) ethical code, Section A, standard A.1.a, states, "the primary responsibility of counselors is to respect the dignity and to promote the welfare of clients" (p. 4). A rather predictable beginning, in many respects, yet client welfare requires a discerning and learned awareness and understanding of the ACA code, ethical decision making, and one's own worldview and sense of morality. Without this perspective, decisions made within the context of consultation have not been fully vetted by the consultant and, as such, may have the potential to mitigate or even negate positive consulting outcomes. For example, client welfare is first expressed within ACA standards A.1.a, through A.1.e, which includes client welfare in relation to treatment records (A.1.b), collaborative treatment planning (A.1.c), efficacy of social support groups (A.1.d), and consideration of reasonable client employment opportunities (A.1.e). It also extends to key interpersonal behaviors, such as not engaging in behaviors that could be deemed as sexual harassment (C.6.a).

In each case, consultants must possess the content knowledge and skills necessary to discern the often nuanced set of circumstances facing the consultee, not only the standard as written, but to consider the moral principles underlying their decision making. For example, if a consultant believes an individual consultee or organization has set unreasonable productivity goals for their employees, a consultant may need to balance the client's right to determine their own productivity standards (respect for autonomy) with the need to provide a truthful assessment of reasonable productivity hours based on the organizational structure, programming needs, and current staffing availability (veracity). Not doing so could result in consultees feeling discounted and ultimately working toward productivity standards that could reduce their effectiveness and, in some cases, lead to impairment or burnout.

Several other areas of client welfare should be noted by consultants. For example, informed consent remains a core element of ethical consulting. In the ACA code, standard D.2.d addresses the traits and issues counselors are to address with consultees prior to engaging in consulting services and, when necessary, readdress or clarify issues on an on-going basis so the consultees remain aware of their rights. Several moral principles are also applied in this standard, not the least of which is veracity (truthfulness) in the sense that consultees must be made aware of, and give their consent, before entering into a consulting relationship. As an example, a private practitioner who is considering a consulting contract with a local mental health agency to assist with the establishment of a school-based mental health program must make abundantly clear, through the proper disclosure of informed consent parameters, the distinctions between the consultant's role and responsibilities as a private practitioner and those of the role as consultant to the agency.

Another example, which pits a client's legitimate need for treatment with a consultant's moral position on diagnosing, involves standard E.5.d of the ACA ethical code. This standard allows counselors to "refrain from making and/or reporting a diagnosis if they believe it would cause harm to the client or others" (ACA, 2005, p. 12). Should consultants be asked specifically to assess and report on the efficacy of a consultee or organization's diagnostic or treatment procedures, careful consideration should be given to this standard so the consultants' personal view of diagnosis and medical model does not compromise their overall assessment and recommendation. Exercise 7.2 is designed to help you understand the importance of proper diagnoses and the role of the consultant.

Exercise 7.2: My Consultee Isn't Being Ethical!

Directions: This exercise will require you to think about the consultee's behaviors and determine if the behaviors are unethical. You can use one of the Professional Code of Ethics listed above to review and make your determination if the consultee's behaviors are ethical.

Case: You are working with a consultee (Wade) dealing with how to properly submit insurance claims for his clients. Wade describes to you the problem he has with many of his clients in that they may not actually exhibit the threshold of symptoms to be diagnosed with a billable psychological disorder. He states that, on several occasions, he has considered and even "up-coded" a client's diagnosis so that he could have the insurance provide payment for his counseling services. Wade explains that many of his clients would not be able to receive counseling unless their insurance pays for these services. He goes on to say that he feels extremely bad that these clients could go without counseling services and feels that he is doing the right thing by providing diagnoses that will enable payment by the client's insurance company.

Discussion Questions

1. *Is Wade acting in an ethical manner?*

2. *Give your reasons for your answer to number one.*

3. *Discuss your thoughts on the illegal practice of up coding and down coding.*

4. *Now what? What should you do as a consultant with this information?*

5. *Can you find help in the professional code of ethics? List the possible sections that pertain to this type of ethical issue.*

In other instances, you may utilize assessment measures in your consulting work. In doing so, Section E of the ACA code of ethics, "Evaluation, Assessment, and Interpretation," is utilized. Standard E.1.a, E.1.b, and E.2.a, through E.2.c, require sensitivity to ensure that the counselor is properly trained and competent in the use of the intended instrument (E.2.a through E.2.c), that assessments do not harm the client (E.1.b), and that informed consent has been provided (E.3.a) and consultees are aware of how and to whom the results will be discussed (E.3.b).

The agreement of a fee schedule for consultation is, of course, a requisite area for consideration and is noted consistently in the ACA code of ethics. In terms of fees, however, counselors acting as consultants do have choices. There is the more common fee-for-service paradigm, in which case all fees would be discussed during informed consent (D.2.d). When you provide consulting services, you should consider the ACA Standards A.10.a through A.10.e. These standards dictate the establishment of fees, nonpayment for service, and the options for bartering and receiving gifts in lieu of monetary payment. While counselors are clearly within their rights to charge market-value fees for their consulting services, consideration should be given to Standards A.10.a through A.10.e, which provides parameters for receiving compensation for consulting services. Because in many cases counselors taking on the role of consultant may be well versed with the individual practitioners and organizations in their area, various payment options should be considered, including the provision of reduced fee or pro-bono consulting services (ACA, 2005).

Consultation competency also extends to the often challenging decision to recognize and address the termination of a consulting relationship and proper referral (D.2.a). Termination of consultation services is a right of both parties involved in a consulting endeavor, yet several ethical issues may arise. For example, the ACA ethical code prohibits counselor–consultants from abandoning clients (A.11.a). In cases where the counselor–consultant concludes the benefits of the service have been exhausted, steps are then taken to provide referrals to professionally and culturally appropriate sources (A.11.b), avoid fostering dependence (A.11.b), and ensure that open communication lines and appropriate administrative issues are addressed (A.11.d). To that end, the counselor–consultant must consider that, similar to counseling relationships, termination of a consulting partnership may entail a range of issues that could affect future personal and professional relationships, and only some of which may have been formally resolved during the contractual period. Simply stated, client welfare must remain a central feature of all counselor–consultant interactions and potential outcomes.

Ethical Principle III: Confidentiality

Despite some contradictory evidence concerning its therapeutic implications (Muehleman, Pickens, & Robinson, 1985; Taube & Elwork, 1990), noted counseling ethics scholars Remley and Herlihy (2010) argue that "confidentiality has become such an internalized norm in the counseling profession that it is rarely questioned" (p. 108). Evidence supporting their claim is apparent in the widespread acknowledgment of confidentiality in the ACA ethical code. Predictably, confidential communication within the consulting paradigm parallels that of the clinical, education, supervision, and assessment components of the code. Exercise 7.3, will help you begin to more fully appreciate the challenge of maintaining confidentiality while consulting.

Exercise 7.3: I Think We Need to Talk

Over the course of a 3-day consulting job, Ed, a licensed professional counselor, is acting as an external consultant to a struggling mental health organization in a different state than he practices. During the evenings, after the formal consulting work has been done, Ed is asked to accompany several of the employees out for dinner and drinks. Hoping to build on the positive professional relationships that have so far been built, Ed accepts the offer. Over the course of the evening, and after a few drinks, one employee expresses clear reservations about how the organization's "books are being kept". When asked to clarify, the employee simply stated, "Well, I don't think the money is going where it's supposed to all the time, but I can't prove it." This was the only statement of this kind made to Ed over the course of the evening.

Discussion Questions

1. *Based on the current ACA standards, what do you believe is the ethical course of action for Ed as he returns to the organization the following morning for the final day of consulting work in which the primary meetings are with the organization's key administrators, including those in the accounting and development departments?*

When should confidentiality be addressed? Confidentiality, and its legal cousin, privileged communication, should be stated at the outset. However, because privilege is determined by individual states, consultants must research the privileged communication laws in the states in which they are licensed or will be consulting. If the counselor–client relationship changes to a counselor–consultant (or vice versa), the process should be repeated as much as deemed necessary by the counselor. Under the informed consent standard specific to consultation (D.2.d), counselor–consultants are obligated to disclose limits to confidentiality.

Just as importantly, counselor–consultants who find themselves in changing roles, such as a judicial or administrative role, must take steps to clarify any confidentiality changes occurring as a result of their altered roles and responsibilities (ACA, Standard D.1.d). This is relevant information, but this statement alone provides limited context to consultee(s) relative to several key elements of confidentiality. To address this potential gap, counselor–consultants are urged to review standards B.1.a through B.1.d and B.2.a through B.2.d. These standards are necessary in order to make consultees aware of confidentiality in its entirety, including diversity issues, limitations, minimal disclosure, and legal implications. However, standard B.3.c, "Confidential Settings", requires counselors to "discuss confidential information only in settings in which they can reasonably ensure client privacy" (ACA, p. 8). By following this standard, counselor–consultants have a solid baseline to begin processing issues related to confidentiality and privilege.

The pragmatic realities of confidentiality can weigh heavily on a counselor–consultant. There is a potential quandary faced by a counselor–consultant working for an organization if they are asked to report client information. In such cases, while this disclosure may be a boon for the organization, revealing confidential information is incongruent with the ACA (and APA, 2002) ethical code and places the consultant in an awkward position. Under the banner of best practices, the appropriate recourse for counselors is to follow the current ACA (2005) ethical code regarding confidentiality and minimal disclosure (ACA, standard B.2.d), understand the state laws regarding confidentiality and privileged communication (ACA, standard B.2.c), and clearly and precisely state the parameters and limitations of confidentiality and privilege during the entry stage of the consultation process, primarily through initial and on-going statements associated with informed consent procedures.

Ethical Principle IV: Public Statement Parameters

The moral principle of veracity (truthfulness) undergirds the ethical parameters related to public statements made or implied by counselor–consultants. Here again, we begin by emphasizing the need for counselor–consultants to adhere to professional boundaries of competence for consulting (ACA, Standard D.2.a). From there, counselor–consultants have several ACA ethical standards to address when considering or acting on public statements regarding their consulting work. For starters, ACA standard C.7.a (2005) requires counselors to clarify any public statement as their personal view in order to negate the perception they are speaking for other professionals. Prior to making any public statement, however, the counselor–consultants should review their record of professional training and credentials, both historically and currently. In particular, their assessment should include a review of ACA Standard C.4.a through C.4.f (2005). These standards outline the framework for counselors to follow in making public statements and are consistent with the behaviors for consultants. Guidelines include honest statements regarding professional credentials (C.4.b), education level and accreditation (C.4.c, C.4.d), and active professional memberships (C.4.f). Once verified, a review of ACA standards C.6.a through C.6.c, which specifically addresses the public responsibilities of counselors. More specifically, it states care is to be taken to ensure accuracy in "public lectures, demonstrations, radio or television programs, prerecorded tapes, technology-based applications, printed articles, mailed material, or other media" (ACA, p.10), including reports and behaviors with constituents. Examples of these constituents could include insurance companies, the legal system, or other professionals with whom client documents are shared (C.6.a, C.6.b). If questions do arise concerning how to properly represent yourself professionally, you should apply the standards found in C.6.c. As an example, the standards under C.6, particularly those specific to reports to third parties (C.6.b) and media presentations (C.6.c) are increasingly relevant given the rapid technological advances in communication. As noted earlier, the combination of the 24-hour news cycle and proliferation of social media now allows one's thoughts and feelings to be broadcast in real time. As such, counselor–consultants must refrain from any form of communication, such as Facebook or Twitter postings, that may illuminate one's personal feelings toward a consultee or organization, tempting as it may be when circumstances become challenging. Moreover, those seeking a competitive advantage in the consulting marketplace should refer closely to the parameters within standard C.6.c. In doing so, consultants will be shielded from accusations of professional misconduct (i.e., ethical violation) while appealing to a wider audience through a diverse range of media outlets.

Ethical Principle V: Social and Moral Responsibility

The ACA (2005) ethical code has embedded standards for expected parameters for moral behavior as well as guidelines for addressing concerns with professionals viewed to have acted incongruently with these standards. This applies, of course, for counselors serving in a consulting capacity. There are potential ethical hazards for a consultant related to their personal characteristics or needs and, in some cases, with related ACA ethical code standards. These include

- role change from facilitating client development to decision maker (A.5.e),
- requesting favors from clients (A.10.e),
- fostering dependence of consultee for financial gain,
- lack of awareness of personal limitations,
- failure to address a consultee's compliance,
- real or potential lack of ethical/legal issues,
- failure to consider consultee readiness prior to the start of formal consulting activity,
- losing professional objectivity with consultee/enmeshment in organizational politics,
- impressing one's value system on a consultee (A.4.b),
- improper reporting of consulting results (E.4),
- disrespect to other professionals (D.1.a), and
- opposition to evaluation (i.e., supervision).

Although space constraints limit a full exploration of all potential ethical dilemmas in this area and how they are covered under current professional ethical codes, you will see that professional organizations have clearly considered and worked to provide appropriate ethical parameters for such behaviors and guidelines for addressing real or potential ethical lapses.

As a baseline for this discussion, consultants are referred to the Section A.4.a and A.4.b, "Avoiding Harm," a clear reference to upholding the core principle of nonmaleficence. Standard A.4.b, for instance, requires counselors guard against personal and cultural encapsulation in order to maintain their focus on client goals. Appropriate social and moral behavior most obviously also extends to interpersonal behaviors and communications. For example, ACA standard A.5.a forbids consultants from sexual or romantic relationships with consultees. However, counselor–consultants must remember that behaviors that could be deemed sexual harassment are also expressly prohibited (C.6.a). It is important to note that this standard also extends to the responsibility of counselor–consultants to act in a responsible manner if they encounter inappropriate sexual conduct. Counselor–consultants unsure on how to proceed when faced with these types of issues should refer to Section H.2.a through H.2.g of the ACA ethical code. Under the above circumstances, for instance, responses could range from an informal discussion wherein concerns about the perceived unethical behavior would be shared with the alleged offender (H.2.b) to making a formal written complaint describing the alleged incident to the appropriate licensing board (H.2.c).

Similar concerns may arise given ACA standard A.5.d, "Potentially Beneficial Interactions." While this standard could in many respects provide a wide berth for professionals in their decision making regarding client interactions, let us take this opportunity to signal caution. Failure to consider both short- and long-range implications in such matters could complicate the consulting relationship or procedures in inconceivable ways. An equally important consideration under this principle is the notion of counselor–consultant impairment. Under Section C of the ACA ethical code, counselors are required to continually reflect on their personal holistic wellness (i.e., mental, physical, emotional). If any of these personal areas become real or potential barriers to the competent provision of services, they are to seek assistance to rectify the problem(s).

In situations where impairment is clear, options involve limiting, suspending, or terminating professional services until they have rectified the problem. Another key aspect of the ACA impairment standard requires that professionals help colleagues they perceive as impaired and, if necessary, "intervene as appropriate to prevent imminent harm to clients" (ACA, 2005, C.2.g, p. 10). Given the central importance of professional competence, it must be noted that impairment does not necessary equate with a lack of competence. Still, the social and moral actions of consultants in relation to client welfare are expected to showcase the highest standards of professional behavior and practice.

Ethical Principle VI: Professional Relationships

Counseling professionals are ethically and legally obligated to maintain respectful relationships with professionals from their own and other disciplines, including their "traditions and practices" (ACA, 2005, D.1.a, p. 18). While that element may appear rather predictable, consultation activities are likely to place counselors in situations and environments requiring an awareness of applicable ethical standards and a means to competently resolve these issues in a professional manner and with the client's fundamental interest at heart. For example, one of the authors was a member of a consulting team led by an expert in education consulting that also included a university president and a former dean of a college of education. Each member of the team brought a unique perspective, yet over the course of discussions between both the consulting team and organization (i.e., consultee), there became the realization of a range of different ethical, legal, procedural, and financial variables were being discussed from different, and sometimes conflicting, perspectives. Once realized, steps were taken to clarify the ethical and legal obligations of each member of the team, as well as in relation to the insights and information provided to the client. In doing so, the author, the only licensed counselor on the consulting team, remained aligned with the ACA ethical code.

Specifically, standards D.1.a, D.1.c, and D.1.e, respecting the views and expertise of other professionals (D.1.a), provided a counseling perspective on how best to serve the clients in relation to the suggestions of the other consultants and client goals (D.1.c) and guided the work to clarify potential ethical and legal concerns from the counseling perspective that arose during discussions (D.1.e). In the case of the latter, for example, several suggestions were amended in order to ensure that all ethical and legal obligations were met in terms of the procedural and administrative elements of the client's goals. Stated more simply, counseling professionals need to develop and maintain respectful, ethically responsive relationships with all those they consult with (and for) while remaining cognizant that the client is the center of any consulting activity. Exercise 7.4 will explore the possible confusing roles of being a colleague or consultant.

Exercise 7.4: Am I a Consultant?

Directions: This exercise will again require you to think about the consultee's behaviors and determine if the behaviors are unethical. You can use one of the professional codes of ethics listed above to review and make your determination if the consultee's behaviors are ethical.

Case 1:

Thelma has been a school counselor at a middle school for 18 years. She has enjoyed her work with the students, teachers, and administration. School counselors wear many "hats" throughout the school year, and Thelma has been no exception to this standard. One role that she particularly values is her role as consultant to the teachers at her school. She has felt that her time, expertise, and opinion have been valued greatly by the staff. Throughout the years, she has helped numerous teachers become more effective classroom behavior managers—simply by working with the teachers to develop better strategies and approaches.

She has heard other school counselors grumble throughout her career, reporting that the staff at their respective schools has complained about how they (the counselors) use their time. The staff report never seeing those counselors, and believe that they don't really do very much at their respective schools. Thelma knows this isn't the case—that the other counselors are working very hard—and believes that the staff members at the respective schools just aren't aware of what the counselors are doing. Thelma believes that the school counselors probably could improve their perceived status by spending more time actively consulting with the teachers and administrators. She has considered offering herself as a consultant to these other counselors to help them address and improve their own consultation behaviors.

(Continued)

(Continued)

One day, while Thelma briefly returned to her office in between a meeting with the principal and her next classroom guidance lesson, Mr. Robinson, an eighth-grade social studies teacher, knocked on her office door. Thelma was busy gathering her materials for the classroom guidance activity. After the classroom lesson, she was scheduled to run a small group counseling session back in her office.

"Thelma," he said, "do you have a minute? It's the end of my planning period, and I don't have much time."

"Sure, come on in. What's up?" Thelma had known Mr. Robinson for a few years now. He had been teaching at the school for a short while, and was well respected (or was it feared?) by the students he taught. He was also a coach for the school's basketball team and was a particularly tall and imposing figure, much larger than any of the students (or fellow staff) at the school.

"I'm having some trouble with one of the kids in my homeroom. He's driving me crazy, and I can't seem to get a handle on what to do with him." As he said this, Mr. Robinson was rubbing his face as if he were tired, half grunting his statement.

"Who is it?" Thelma asked.

"It's that new kid, Michael, the one that transferred in a month or so ago. He's all over the place, disrespectful, constantly out of his seat, making noises, distracting everyone." Mr. Robinson was gesturing wildly with his hands and arms, attempting to display his interpretation of Michael's behavior for Thelma. As he gestured, he inadvertently knocked a coffee cup that was displayed on a shelf by Thelma's office door. It shattered on the floor.

"Ah, (explicative)!" he said a little too loudly with gritted teeth. "Sorry", he said gruffly, "I'll clean it up." He bent down and began picking up the pieces of the fractured cup. Thelma went over to help. It took a couple of minutes to retrieve a broom and dustpan and collect all of the fragments from the floor. As they were finishing, Mr. Robinson glanced at his watch and used another "four-letter word."

"Can you come by my room the next chance you get, just to take a look at him?" he asked hurriedly.

Thelma was thinking about all of the things that she needed to address in the remainder of the day and was contemplating how she might possibly squeeze in a classroom visit to help the visibly frustrated teacher–coach.

"Please, Thelma," he pleaded as he looked at his watch again, backing out the door, "I'm desperate. This kid is a piece of work. What else could you be doing that is more important?" Apparently, Thelma thought, Mr. Robinson didn't have a problem with speaking what he was thinking.

"Okay," she could barely get out before he started out the door, "I'll try to come around fifth period, but . . ."

"Great. Thanks." he said. And he was gone.

Near the end of fifth period, Thelma was able to find a few minutes to visit Mr. Robinson's room. She had cut her group session a little short to make time. As she was walking down the hall toward his room, she could see him speaking to Michael (the student in question) out in the hall. The door to the classroom was shut, and Michael had his back against the wall, looking up at Mr. Robinson. Mr. Robinson was leaning toward Michael, fairly close, and had his right index finger pointing directly into Michael's face. He wasn't touching Michael, but he was jabbing his finger very close to Michael's nose. The closer Thelma got to the pair, the more she could make out of their muffled conversation. Mr. Robinson's tone was harsh, but he wasn't speaking loudly enough to create any attention from the other classrooms on the hall. Michael was staring back at Mr. Robinson with a look of indifference.

When Thelma was close enough to be able hear what was being said, Mr. Robinson finished his last statement and looked down at her.

"Can you take this gentleman to the office for me? I need to get back to class", and he opened his door and walked back into his classroom.

Discussion Questions

1. *What should Thelma do?*

2. *Based on what you know so far, could Mr. Robinson be called her consultee?*

3. *What responsibility does Thelma have to him?*

4. *Would this change, based on your interpretation of whether or not Mr. Robinson is a consultee?*

5. *Does she take Michael to the office, or do something else?*

6. *Does she speak to the administration about Mr. Robinson's behavior?*

7. *Does she speak to Mr. Robinson about his behavior?*

(Continued)

(Continued)

8. *Does she speak to Michael about his behavior?*

9. *Does she continue to consult (or consider consultation) with Mr. Robinson?*

Multicultural Considerations

As would be expected of any effective counseling professional, competent consultation also requires an active awareness and consideration of cultural variables. While it could be argued that the need for multicultural competence is implied in the section on consultation ethics, we refer back to standard A.2.c (ACA, 2005, p. 4), "Developmental and Cultural Sensitivity," that requires counselors and, by extension, consultants, to remain cognizant of the developmental and cultural sensitivities of clients. Additional thought should be given to standard A.4.b, which expects counselors to be respect the unique qualities of each client and remain "aware of their own values, attitudes, beliefs, and behaviors" in order to refrain from "imposing values that are inconsistent with counseling goals."

Consultants must remain cognizant of their worldviews so as to not taint the consulting process with their own personal value systems. Finally, competencies are required of consultants who choose to utilize and interpret assessment measures in their work (E.1.a, E.2.b). It should also be noted that gaps in one's knowledge do not necessarily equate with a lack of competence. In such cases, counselors simply consult with other professionals such as peers and professionals with specialized supervision training. In general, though, consultants may be best served by applying the premises and dimensions of the multicultural counseling competencies (Arredondo et al., 1996) to their consulting interactions. Failure to include or advocate for the unique and wide-ranging diversity elements of a consulting activity could have a dramatic impact on the relational or procedural elements of consultation and, by extension, the final outcomes of one's consulting efforts.

Chapter Keystones

- Be familiar with the consultation section of the professional code of ethics that you will use in your career.
- Consultation without ethics has the potential to jeopardize the consultant–consultee relationship and have legal implications.
- Understand the six core moral principles of ethical decision making.
- Know how to apply ethical principles to professional consultation.

Table 7.1 American Counseling Association's Code of Ethics: Excerpts Outlining Consultation (2005)

D.2. Consultation

D.2.a. Consultant Competency

Counselors take reasonable steps to ensure that they have the appropriate resources and competencies when providing consultation services. Counselors provide appropriate referral resources when requested or needed. (See C.2.a)

D.2.b. Understanding Consultees

When providing consultation, counselors attempt to develop with their consultees a clear understanding of problem definition, goals for change, and predicted consequences of interventions selected.

D.2.c. Consultant Goals

The consulting relationship is one in which consultee adaptability and growth toward self-direction are consistently encouraged and cultivated.

D.2.d. Informed Consent in Consultation

When providing consultation, counselors have an obligation to review, in writing and verbally, the rights and responsibilities of both counselors and consultees. Counselors use clear and understandable language to inform all parties involved about the purpose of the services to be provided, relevant costs, potential risks and benefits, and the limits of confidentiality. Working in conjunction with the consultee, counselors attempt to develop a clear definition of the problem, goals for change, and predicted consequences of interventions that are culturally responsive and appropriate to the needs of consultees. (See A.2.a, A.2.b)

B.8. Consultation

B.8.a. Agreements

When acting as consultants, counselors seek agreements among all parties involved concerning each individual's rights to confidentiality, the obligation of each individual to preserve confidential information, and the limits of confidentiality of information shared by others.

B.8.b. Respect for Privacy

Information obtained in a consulting relationship is discussed for professional purposes only with persons directly involved with the case. Written and oral reports present only data germane to the purposes of the consultation, and every effort is made to protect client identity and to avoid undue invasion of privacy.

B.8.c. Disclosure of Confidential Information

When consulting with colleagues, counselors do not disclose confidential information that reasonably could lead to the identification of a client or other person or organization with which they have a confidential relationship unless they have obtained the prior consent of the person or organization or the disclosure cannot be avoided. They disclose information only to the extent necessary to achieve the purposes of the consultation. (See D.2.d)

Source: Reprinted from The American Counseling Association. Reprinted with permission. No further reproduction authorized without written permission from the American Counseling Association.

Web-Based and Literature-Based Resources

Websites

American Counseling Association (ACA) Code of Ethics (2005); Sections on Consultation (B.8.a, B.8.b, B.8.c, D.2.a, D.2.b, D.2.c, D.2.d): http://www.counseling.org/Resources/CodeOfEthics/TP/Home/CT2.aspx

American Psychology Association, Code of Ethics Office: http://www.apa.org/ethics/index.aspx

American Psychological Association Ethical Principles of Psychologists and Code of Conduct: 2010 Amendments; Standards 3.07, 3.10, 4.04, 4.05, 4.06, 6.07: http://www.apa.org/ethics/code/index.aspx

American School Counseling Association (ASCA) Ethical Standards for School Counselors (2010), Sections: C.2, D.2, F.1.g, F.2.b: http://asca2.timberlakepublishing.com//files/EthicalStandards2010.pdf

Center for Ethical Practice: http://www.centerforethicalpractice.org

Codes of Ethics with Specific Sections on Consultation: American Mental Health Counseling Association's Code of Ethics (Revised 2010) Section F, Consultant: https://www.amhca.org/assets/news/AMHCA_Code_of_Ethics_2010_w_pagination_cxd_51110.pdf

National Association of Social Work (NASW) Code of Ethics (2008); Sections 2.05, 3.01, 5.01: http://www.socialworkers.org/pubs/code/code.asp

National Board for Certified Counselors Code of Ethics (2005); Section F, See Consulting: http://www.nbcc.org/Assets/Ethics/nbcc-codeofethics.pdf

Contact Information

APA Code of Ethics Office:
750 First Street, NE • Washington, DC • 20002-4242
Phone: 202-336-5930 • TDD/TTY: 202-336-6123
Fax: 202-336-5997
ACA Ethics and Professional Standards Department:
1-800-347-6647, ext. 314 or
E-mail: ethics@counseling.org

References

American Counseling Association. (2005). *ACA Code of Ethics.* Alexandria, VA: Author.

American Mental Health Counseling Association. (2010). *AMHCA Code of Ethics* (REVISED 2010). Retrieved from https://www.amhca.org/assets/news/AMHCA_Code_of_Ethics_2010_w_pagination_cxd_51110.pdf

American Psychological Association. (2010). *Ethical principles of psychologists and code of conduct (2010 amendments).* Washington, DC: Author.

American School Counseling Association. (2004). *Ethical standards for school counselors.* Alexandria, VA: Author.

Arredondo, P., Toporek, R., Brown, S. P. Jones, J., Locke, D. C., Sanchez, J., & Stadler, H. (1996). Operationalization of the multicultural counseling competencies. *Journal of Multicultural Counseling and Development, 24,* 42–78.

Becker, T. F., & Glaser, E. M. (1979). *Portraits of 17 outstanding organizational consultants.* Los Angeles, CA: Human Interaction Research Institute.

Corey, G., Corey, M. S., & Callanan, P. (2007). *Issues and ethics in the helping professions* (7th ed.). Pacific Grove, CA: Brooks/Cole.

Davis, K. M. (2003). Teaching a course in school-based consultation. *Counselor Education and Supervision, 42*, 275–285.

Dougherty, A. M. (1992). Ethical issues in consultation. *Elementary School Guidance and Counseling, 26*, 214–220.

Gross, D. R., & Robinson, S. E. (1985). Ethics: The neglected issue in consultation. *Journal of Counseling and Development, 64*, 38–41.

McCarthy, M. M., & Sorenson, G. P. (1993). School counselors and consultants: Legal duties and liabilities. *Journal of Counseling and Development, 72*, 159–167.

Meara, N. M., Schmidt, L. D., & Day, J. D. (1996). Principles and virtues: A foundation for ethical decisions, policies, and character. *Counseling Psychologist, 24*, 4–77.

Muehleman, T., Pickens, B. K., & Robinson, F. (1985). Informing clients about the limits to confidentiality, risks, and their rights: Is self-disclosure inhibited? *Professional Psychology: Research and Practice, 16*(3), 385–397.

National Board for Certified Counselors. (2005). *National Board for Certified Counselors Code of Ethics.* Retrieved from http://www.nbcc.org/Assets/Ethics/nbcc-codeofethics.pdf

Newman, J. L. (1993). Ethical issues in consultation. *Journal of Counseling and Development, 72*, 148–156.

Remley, T. P., & Herlihy, B. (2010). *Ethical, legal, and professional issues in counseling* (3rd ed.). Upper Saddle River, NJ: Pearson.

Pope, K. S., & Vasquez, M. J. T. (2007). *Ethics in psychotherapy and counseling: A practical guide* (3rd ed.). San Francisco, CA: Jossey-Bass.

Taube, D. O., & Elwork, A. (1990). Researching the effects of confidentiality law on patients' self-disclosures. *Professional Psychology: Research and Practice, 21*, 72–75.

Wesley, P. W., & Buysse, V. (2006). Ethics and evidence in consultation. *Topics in Early Childhood Special Education, 26*, 131–141.

Consultation in Mental Health Settings

Introduction

The development of consultation in mental health settings is largely attributed to the views and writings of Gerald Caplan (1964, 1970, 2004; Caplan & Caplan, 1999). Caplan envisioned consultation as a vital form of service delivery rather than a distinct professional discipline. Caplan also reasoned that communities and their constituents (individuals, groups, systems) that attend to the well-being of others can help prevent the development of mental illness, mitigate future psychological distress, and enhance the psychological wellness of the community—all while reducing the need for direct mental health services (Albee & Fryer, 2003). To do so, however, requires effective consultation between mental health and professionals such as educators, law enforcement, and church leaders (Caplan, 1964).

This chapter provides a more detailed rendering of mental health consultation, from its historical and conceptual influences to contemporary applications. In doing so, we highlight the range of consultation approaches available for mental health professionals and, as always, the need to have the requisite content knowledge, skills, and ethical and cultural competence required prior to engaging in any form of (mental health) consultation. And, as with any professional endeavor, expect a learning curve even if and when you have extensive experience as a clinician, supervisor, administrator, or educator. As one author noted, the best consultation experience he had was being the "rookie" among a group of knowledgeable and talented consultants (educators, administrators, and private consultants) who illustrated in word and deed the subtleties and interrelatedness of the consultation alliance and process over the entirety of a consultation event. For this author, it was a gratifying and humbling experience to make a professional contribution while bearing witness to the talents and wisdom of a group of experienced consultants. However, perhaps no greater lesson arose from that experience than the realization that competent consultation requires sensitivity to and consideration of the environmental context in which one's professional knowledge, skills, and experience are applied, received, and used (or dismissed!). So, prepare, be open to opportunities, seek out mentors, observe, and enjoy.

LEARNING OBJECTIVES

After reading this chapter, you will be able to

- Recognize key historical, contemporary, and multicultural issues, individuals, and events related to the development and practice of mental health consultation models
- Have an understanding of the process of mental health consultation
- Define mental health consultation and distinguish between the client-centered case consultation, consultee-centered case consultation, program–centered administrative consultation, and consultee-centered administrative consultation approaches
- Have opportunities to examine and discuss different consultation scenarios using different mental health consultation approaches

Historical Background

Mental health consultation grew out of the post-World War II community mental health movement's belief that community-based social service organizations were crucial stakeholders in the prevention of mental illness (Caplan, Caplan, & Erchul, 1994). This perspective recognized the need for consultation between individuals and community-based professionals and organizations, a view felt to be best suited in the context of a collaborative and egalitarian consultation relationship (Gutkin & Curtis, 1990; Schulte & Osborne, 2003). This collaborative view is central to Caplan's position that hierarchies are a potential detriment to a consultee's personal or professional autonomy and the ability or willingness to hear, internalize, or use a consultant's suggestions. On the other hand, egalitarian relationships offer challenges of their own, such as the need for consultants to possess the requisite interpersonal skills necessary to build and sustain positive consultation alliances (Maher, 1993).

There are several key contributors to the prominence and sustainability of the mental health consultation approach. The introduction of the National Mental Health Act of 1946, for example, created the National Institute of Mental Health (NIMH) and increased public awareness and support for preventative, community-based mental health services. Years later, the Mental Retardation Facilities and Community Health

Centers Construction Act of 1963 funded the construction of community mental health facilities and formally recognized consultation and education as instrumental elements of community-based services. Yet another boost to the preventative approach was recognition that the prevailing views held within the medical consultation model were medical consultation viewpoint largely counterintuitive to the preventative ideals of Caplan's model. Two factors primarily facilitated this transition. First, the community-based approach expanded the range of professionals deemed competent to provide consultation. Second, intrapsychic and environmental variables were recognized by Caplan as vital to resolving consultee problems and that failure to consider these qualities could hamper treatment. These factors also featured prominently in Caplan's emergence as the seminal authority on consultation for decades to come.

Caplan's early view of mental health consultation drew from his work with a team of psychiatrists and allied mental health professionals who treated Israeli children following World War II. This physically, emotionally, and geographically challenging setting helped galvanize Caplan's belief that the medical model treatment protocol being applied with these children was incapable of effectively addressing their immense needs. However, this setting also provided Caplan with a first-hand accounting of the benefits derived when mental health specialists and other caregivers created and maintained open dialogue with patients, an experience he later applied directly to his vision of mental health consultation. In essence, Caplan's model diverged from the individual-treatment orientation of the medical model to one where working with larger groups of workers could serve an exponentially larger number of people. Caplan's views were so prescient that today consultation is also referred to as *Caplanian consultation* and the Caplanian model (Dougherty, 2009). Among the most valuable were his beliefs that:

- working closely with direct service staff instead of individual clients allows for an exponentially larger number of clients to be served,
- honest, compassionate dialogue with workers can offset distorted views of clients and lead to more sensitive and effective interventions, and
- providing on-site services helps contextualize the multifaceted issues encountered by patients (i.e., children) and the treatment teams.

Caplan also deemed consultation most effective as a direct interaction between a consultant and consultee when set within the consultee's professional environment and recognizes the consultee's perception of events as the baseline for consultation. Caplan (1970) articulated this consultation vision in his seminal text *The Theory and Practice of Mental Health Consultation* and other writings (Caplan 1964, 1977). These views helped reshape consultation (and consultants) as being "objective, not sympathetic" (Dougherty, 2009, p. 178). In other words, problems addressed in consultation should be viewed as external to the consultee or client versus the client being considered the problem. Helping consultants reframe problems was especially helpful in reconnecting staff members with their clients and that, in turn, allowed new treatment possibilities to emerge (Knotek & Sandoval, 2003).

Caplan later migrated to the United States to continue his work at Harvard University's School of Public Health and Medicine. It was here, often in concert with Erich Lindemann, that Caplan refined the model he now labeled *mental health consultation*. Numerous advances and insights occurred during this period. Particularly significant were his positions that mental health consultation is primarily preventative and that consulting relationships are fundamentally collaborative and egalitarian. Other advancements included the acceptance of consultation as amenable to group and noncrisis contexts. All told, this helped pave the way for a broader range of professionals with specific expertise to provide services within established community-based systems such as schools, hospitals, and social service agencies. The following sections examine mental health consultation in detail, including overviews of some prominent mental health consultation approaches.

Foundations of Mental Health Consultation: Key Points and Approaches

Although true to many of Caplan's original ideas, contemporary versions of consultation generally place less importance on psychodynamic influences. Gerald Caplan and Ruth B. Caplan in 1993 defined mental health consultation as:

> a process of interaction between two professional persons-the consultant, who is a specialist, and the consultee, who invokes the consultant's help in regard to a current work problem with which he is having some difficulty and which he has decided is within the other's area of specialized competence. The work problem involves the management or treatment of one or more clients of the consultee, or the planning and implementation of a program to cater to such clients. (p. 1)

From this definition, one can see Caplan's view of consultation as a shared effort that encourages consultee ownership in all aspects of the process. A full rendering of Caplan's core assumptions for consultation is found in 1993's *Mental Health Consultation and Collaboration*. The following is a paraphrased listing of core assumptions of the mental health consultation model endorsed by Caplan and Caplan (p. 179).

> Mental health consultation is conducted by one professional (consultant) who provides specialized expertise to another professional (consultee).

> Consultee problems are related to the client's mental health, the provision of mental health services, or environmental factors impeding the provision of mental health to the client.

> Consultants have no administrative responsibility for the consultee, nor bear professional responsibility to alter consultee behaviors with clients or final client outcomes.

> Consultees bear no obligation to accept information from consultants.

The consulting relationship is either nonhierarchical and egalitarian or coordinate. Consultee autonomy in respected at all times.

The collaborative, egalitarian essence of consultation relationships is bolstered by the consultant's outside expertise.

Consulting relationships are, per consultee, intermittent and ultimately discontinued to avert consultee dependency on consultants. In group settings, peer support is used to avert dependency.

Consultation is longitudinal and anticipated as the complexity of consultee skills, client cases, duties, or organizations increase.

Despite their broader expertise, consultants address only the presenting concerns of the consultee.

The two goals of consultation are to facilitate (a) consultee competence with mental health related issues of individuals, groups, and organization and (b) consultee ability to solve future related problems.

Although the well-being of consultants is important, consultation is intended as a means of improving consultee competence.

Personal issues, such as consultee thoughts, feelings, and attitudes and values, are dealt with indirectly.

When relevant to the consultee's presenting problem, personal attitudes are addressed only as they relate to the consultee's conceptualization and resolution of the presenting problem(s).

Consultants must remain cognizant of the abundance of potential mitigating circumstances experienced by consultees, such as a crisis event that may require role flexibility.

The paragraphs below provide a quick summation of the unique aspects of mental health consultation (Brown, Pryzwansky, & Schulte, 2011) that consultants should possess.

First, mental health consultation views environmental and intrapsychic variables as instrumental in behavior change. Here, Caplan viewed environmental and intrapsychic factors as having interpretive and change agent qualities, a position that underscores the multisystemic and ecological nature of consultee and client behaviors and problems. These factors could manifest in any consultation situation, so consultations must give them consideration in relation to areas such as client characteristics, consultee skills and worldview (i.e., beliefs and attitudes), quality of consultant–consultee or consultee–client communication, and organizational and environmental factors. For example, consideration would be given to contextual factors such as the consultee's worldview and intrapsychic factors (i.e., a consultee's affective or cognitive state) that could, independently or together, impede or compel behavioral change. The notion of an intrapsychic variable directly impacting consultee and client behaviors is illustrated in Guided Exercise 8.1.

Guided Practice Exercises
Exercise 8.1: Addressing a
Consultee's Affective and Cognitive States

You have been hired as a mental health consultant to work with Janine, a 26-year-old licensed counselor, who works with adult survivors of domestic violence at an outpatient mental health clinic in a large city, to help her address the following case.

In her last session with Kendra, a 23-year-old survivor, Kendra described to Janine for the first time several instances of sexual assault in addition to the physical abuse she has endured for 2 years from her husband. Upon hearing this information, Janine recalls thinking, "This is so wrong. I have to get her to recognize that she doesn't deserve this and that she should get out of this situation right away! It's bad enough the physical abuse is occurring, but the sexual assault is the last straw!" Outwardly, this information caused Janine to become visibly upset and state forcefully to Kendra that her partner's behavior is unacceptable, which caused Kendra to quickly minimize the sexual behaviors of her husband. Kendra did not speak of the sexual issues the remainder of the session.

Discussion Questions

1. *Describe possible affective and cognitive dimensions of Janine's experience and response to Kendra's story.*

2. *In your consult, how would you address Janine's affective experience in this scenario? How about the cognitive elements of Janine's responses?*

3. *What additional strategies might you use to enhance Kendra's chances for positive therapeutic outcomes?*

Next, the choice and design of interventions used in mental health consultation can be multifaceted. As such, sensitivity to potential biases (i.e., philosophical, cultural, professional) are central to the choice and design of any intervention. Consultants must realize these and other potential limits to the interventions they design (individually and with consultees). Third, mental health consultants should refrain from engaging in the implementation of interventions and allow consultees the autonomy to implement the interventions. Caplan (1970) is clear that responsibility for implementing interventions lies with the consultee while consultants are challenged to cultivate consultee engagement in problem identification and resolution. The end result is to facilitate consultee ownership in their problems that will promote engagement in selecting and implementing interventions aimed at problem resolution. Knowledge gained from these actions can be generalized to clarifying and solving future problems. However, consultee intrapsychic variables should be monitored given they could influence how a consultee interprets the success or failure of an intervention and their willingness to generalize it as a means for solving future problems to solve future issues. Fourth, mental health consultation should be considered a supplemental form of providing mental health service provision, not a distinct discipline within the larger mental health paradigm. For example, addressing skill deficits are better suited for clinical supervision (Brown et al., 2011), while addressing core knowledge deficits is a primary role of educators. Overall, consultation is one of many services at the disposal of mental health professionals and can be utilized in combination with or separate from other mental health service delivery options.

Caplan's recognition of consultee intrapsychic variables also acknowledges the potential complexity of any consulting endeavor (Pinkerton & Temple, 2000). However, while addressing consultee attitudes or emotions toward clients is viable, it is better to do so indirectly. (1970; Caplan & Caplan, 1999). For example, a consultant may not directly confront a consultee who made statements that imply a heterosexist bias. Instead, indirect dialogue, such as the use of metaphors (Caplan & Caplan, 1999), is used as a way to maintain a collaborative relationship, mitigate potential consultee defensiveness, and focus on the current problem. Since consultees are under no obligation to accept or employ a consultant's suggestions, indirect methods are considered less likely to trigger consultee reactance responses that would inhibit their sense of autonomy and keep them from working to resolve problems or continue on with current problematic behaviors.

The Consultation Process

Caplan (1970) describes the consultation process as having the following components: (a) relationship development, (b) individual/organizational, (c) assessment, (d) interventions, and (e) follow-up and evaluation. The following sections address each in more detail.

The Consulting Alliance (Relationship)

The consultation relationship or alliance (see Chapter 2) is foundational to the mental health consulting process. Depending on the format, this could include alliances with individuals, groups, or organizations as a whole. In all cases, Caplan urges patience and professionalism, as consultation relationships require empathy, tolerance, and flexibility. Still, while Caplan viewed consulting relationships as collaborative and nonhierarchical, trust is a dynamic and unpredictable variable. Careful monitoring is needed to ensure consultees perceive their autonomy and professional insights are sought out, valued, and integrated throughout the process. Consultants should also work to ensure the development and maintenance of nonhierarchical, egalitarian consulting relationships. While consultants do not possess administrative authority over consultees (Caplan, 1970), consultees who sense a power imbalance may feel more constrained and less inclined to engage in the process. Kathryn Evans, Heather Law, Roisin Turner, Andrew Rogers, and Keren Cohen (2011), for example, found that the nonhierarchical relationship approach of a mental health consultant was viewed by the staff as gratifying and enhanced their (consultee) willingness to engage in the consultation process. Conversely, the absence of these qualities may decrease a consultee's sense of ownership in the process. Thus, consultants must fashion a relationship with consultees that encourages open discourse and assimilates consultee knowledge and skills while promoting consultee ownership of the problem and autonomy regarding the implementation of interventions. Verbal and behavioral assurances of confidentiality are also critical for getting consultees to openly discuss problems at the individual, group, and/or organizational level.

Assessment

While assessment differs according to the type of consultation, the collaborative, nonhierarchical approach remains constant. For example, in contrast to structured clinical assessment approaches, consultation assessments are generally less formal and structured. Further, a clinical interview often involves structured documents with formalized questions. Consultation assessments, on the other hand, may favor less formal (yet professional) dialogue with the consultee. Consultants blend active listening and focused questions aimed at "widening and deepening" (Caplan, 1970, p. 59) the consultee's understanding of the problem and potential resolutions. Consultants also need to remain sensitive to establishing and maintaining a nonhierarchical relationship and an awareness of the multidimensional nature and implications of their recommendations.

Assessment involves consultants exploring problems directly with the consultee in order gain the clearest understanding of the issues confronting a consultee understanding of influences. This information is vital to both problem conceptualization and resolution. Distinctions do occur, of course. For example, a client-centered consultation would involve a meeting with the consultee's client to gather information, while in consultee-centered consultation the consultant would rely almost exclusively on data from the consultee. Another example involves how questions are framed. For instance, indirect questions can facilitate reflective thinking in hopes of stimulating a broader understanding of the problem and facilitating ownership in designing and implementing solutions. In all cases, information is used to increase the consultee's understanding of the problem and of potential solutions.

Interventions

Conceptualizing and recommending appropriate interventions requires consideration of the intervention's focus (i.e., client, consultant, program or policy), technique (questions, education, modeling), and complexity. For instance, consultants using consultee-centered consultation may create and implement interventions without the consultee's knowledge if they perceive consultees lack the necessary knowledge. In client-centered consultation, consultants may have a consultee to provide a written conceptualization of a case based on a specific theoretical paradigm. In another context, a consultant using the program-centered consultation approach with an agency's entire clinical staff may need to be particularly flexible in their choice of interventions and how they are applied. For example, a training on ethics in the workplace may require the seminar be given at different times and in different locations to accommodate all of the agency's clinical staff. It is important to remember that here again the consultee bears the responsibility for taking action against the identified problem.

Evaluation and Follow-Up Contact

The central notion of evaluating consultation interventions lies in seeking to optimize the consultee's professional competence. Consultants must therefore recognize the multifaceted nature of the evaluation and follow-up processes. The multifaceted nature of these dimensions also helps explain why mastery of mental health consultation is oftentimes more elusive than mastery of psychotherapy (Iscoe, 1993). It is also crucial for consultants to reflect on the multicultural dimensions of the consultation relationship and process. This will help them better recognize factors that could promote or impede successful consulting outcomes. The consultation process also demands and benefits from consultants grounded in ethical (see Chapter 4) and multicultural competencies that mitigate the chances that blame for unmet goals would be placed solely on the consultee (Martin & Curtis, 1981). At all time, then, interventions should be ethical reasoned, empirically supported, and implemented for the purpose of facilitating positive change.

Types of Mental Health Consultation

Caplan outlines four distinct consultation strategies that fall within two divisions. These are *client-centered consultation, consultee-centered consultation, program-centered consultation,* and *consultee-centered administrative consultation* (Caplan & Caplan, 1993). The two divisions are separated by consultation goals. The first division consists of consultation efforts directed at specific client cases or administrative concerns, while the second assumes a more systemic outlook.

Client-Centered Consultation

Client-centered consultation is mental health consultation in its most recognizable form (Caplan, 1970). Here, consultants assume an expert stance and seek the creation of an effective treatment plan for the consultee's client, with psychoeducation and skill development as secondary goals. To that end, consultants directly assess clients, select the appropriate diagnosis, and offer treatment suggestions. The primary goal of the consultant, then, is two-fold (Dougherty, 2009). First, to determine if a specialist referral is needed. Second, to determine the most efficient way a consultant assist the client given the current setting and environmental dynamics. Here, consultees are called upon to provide the consultant with substantive client and environmental information they perceive as potential impediments to successful outcomes. This information is also crucial in helping consultants understand the multidimensional nature of the variables facing the consultee and, if needed, modify recommendations to suit these challenges.

Client-centered consultation's prescriptive nature (Hylander, 2012) is also seen in subsequent steps as consultants next gather all available personal, institutional, and cultural information on the consultee and client. This is followed by the creation of specific, written recommendations to consultees on how to address the identified problems. It is expected that consultees will also use the document as a way to broaden their professional competencies and efficacy. Face-to-face meetings are suggested, but whether or not direct contact occurs, the consultant's report should be clear, pragmatic, and free of professional jargon and bias. Once again, consultees bear the responsibility of implementing the consultant's suggestions, although consultants remain available whether or not the consultee implements any or all of the consultant's recommendations. Guided Exercise 8.2 builds on the scenario from Exercise 8.1 to illustrate the client-centered case consultation.

Guided Practice Exercises
Exercise 8.2: Client-Centered Case Consultation With Janine

In her last session with Kendra, a 23-year-old survivor, Kendra described to Janine for the first time several instances of sexual assault in addition to the physical abuse she has endured for 2 years from her husband. Upon hearing this information, Janine recalls thinking, "This is so wrong. I have to get her to recognize that she doesn't deserve this and that she should get out of this situation right away! It's bad enough the physical abuse is occurring, but the sexual assault is the last straw!" Outwardly, this information caused Janine to become visibly upset and state forcefully to Kendra that her partner's behavior is unacceptable, which caused Kendra to quickly minimize the sexual behaviors of her husband. Kendra did not speak of the sexual issues the remainder of the session.

Consultant Response Using Client-Centered Case Consultation

Stephen is a licensed professional counselor who is consulting with Janine, a licensed associated counselor, about a client named Kendra who she is seeing on an outpatient basis for issues related to domestic violence. Janine reported that Kendra is a 23-year-old married woman who is seeking counseling to help her deal with domestic violence issues. Janine stated that until last week, Kendra had been a compliant and engaged client. Currently, Kendra has been late for the past three sessions and has spoken only superficially of her concerns. Janine noted that Kendra's reduced engagement coincides with her (Janine) "confronting" Kendra on her concerns about her statements of sexual assault in her marriage.

Upon hearing Janine's more detailed description of the case, Stephen finds that while Kendra's case is both personally and professionally challenging for Janine, he believes Kendra and Janine can continue to build on a strong working alliance that will eventually provide the safety Kendra needs to explore the negative patterns in her relationship and steps that can be taken to be address her emotional and physical safety needs. Stephen also believes Janine is competent to continue seeing this client and to assist her in dealing with the different types of abuse she is encountering in her marriage and the implications they may be having in other areas of her life. Stephen then completed a written report detailing steps for helping Janine inform Kendra of the correct procedures for reporting sexual assault and domestic violence to the proper authorities. The report also suggested continued individual counseling with Janine and a referral for Kendra to a partner violence support group that meets biweekly at the clinic. This information was provided to Janine during a final consultation meeting and Janine agreed to follow the recommendations. Stephen then sets up a meeting with Janine in 2 weeks to assess the agreed upon recommendations.

Discussion Questions

1. *Do you agree with the consultant's recommendations? What would you change, adapt, or add?*

2. *What additional recommendations or interventions might be useful in this scenario?*

3. *This scenario does not include the consultant meeting directly with the client. If you were the consultant, would you assess the client directly or follow the pattern used above? Explain your decision.*

Consultee-Centered Case Consultation

Also referred to as mental health consultation and Caplanian consultation, *consultee-centered case consultation* focuses on the problem(s) a consultee is having with a specific client in his or her work environment. The main goal of consultee-centered case consultation is to improve consultee professional functioning with current clients and with future clients presenting with similar issues. As with client-centered consultation, the focus remains on the current case. The secondary goal remains client improvement.

The assessment process in consultee-centered case consultation emphasizes communicating directly with the consultee. This distinction from the client-centered model is necessitated by the importance of gaining the consultee's subjective understanding of the difficulties with the client. During the assessment consultants listen for affective or cognitive incongruencies in the consultee's narrative about the client. This enables consultants to trace the source of the difficulties and place it or them into one of four descriptors developed by Caplan (lack of skill, lack of knowledge, lack of confidence, lack of objectivity), each of which requires a distinct consultee response. These sources will be addressed in more detail below.

Consultee-centered case consultation provides consultants with role options such as expert, detective, and educator (Dougherty, 2009). The detective role, for instance, involves active listening and questioning to help discern cognitive and affective problems facing the consultee. Consultants assuming the expert role listen and discuss the case with the consultee from the vantage point of one with expertise in mental health, while the educator supplies the consultee with information and training that can help resolve problems with the present case and similar future scenarios. Regardless of the role selected, consultee-centered case consultation is more directive than the client-centered approach. In addition, consultee problems are based on a subjective view of the client. Thus, consultants work to resolve problems based solely on the consultee's subjective assessment of the client (Caplan & Caplan, 1993).

Overall, the principle role of the consultee in consultee-centered case consultation is to describe the case in detail to the consultant. In theory, skilled questioning by the consultant would expand the consultee's understanding of the potentially disruptive role of cognitions and emotions in case conceptualization (Caplan & Caplan, 1993). Yet because the consultee is again the dedicated change agent, they maintain the autonomy to integrate or completely nullify consultant suggestions.

Lack of Skill

Skill deficits differ from knowledge deficits. Thus, consultees may show substantial content knowledge, yet lack the skills needed to address the problem. Caplan believed consultants should generally steer clear of addressing skill deficiencies. His reasoning included his view that skill deficiencies fall primarily within the realm of supervision (clinical or administrative) and that the presence of a consultant from outside the consultee's environment is inherently limited in their institutional knowledge and culture. Thus, the role of the consultant is to engage the consultee in a systematic examination of the perceived problems, attempted solutions, and possible future solutions. Based on the consultee's input and perceptions, consultants are better able to ascertain the type and level of skill(s) deficits impeding the consultee's progress in the case. The information also allows for exploring skill(s) development and the implications in the therapeutic relationship and process. This is followed by consultants recommending available means to gain the necessary skill(s), with primary consideration given to options within the consultee's work setting such as clinical supervision or evidence-based professional journals, or even shadowing colleagues to experience the distinct ways other professionals use the identified skill(s). In the event on-site resources are unavailable, recommendations may include additional coursework from credible or accredited academic institutions (including web-based courses) or training seminars and professional conferences. Consultants may occasion work to rectify consultee skill deficits (Dougherty, 2009), although this is suggested only after careful consideration of alternative interventions or services.

Lack of Knowledge

Lack of knowledge signals a consultee who possesses insufficient factual or theoretical knowledge necessary to provide clinically and culturally competent mental health services to a client. When knowledge deficits are identified, consultants should work to fill the consultees' knowledge gap so their content knowledge allows them to competently engage current and future cases with similar issues. In addition to drawing from their expertise, consultants may follow recommendations similar to those with skill deficits, such as additional individual or group supervision, attendance at seminars and professional conferences, and immersion in applicable evidence-based professional journals. It should be noted that Caplan also viewed excessive knowledge deficits as indicative of core systemic problems. Yet given the time commitment and fiscal burdens often associated servicing more extreme knowledge deficits, Caplan suggested consultants address these types of deficiencies, and possible solutions, with the organization's senior management.

Lack of Confidence

Consultee lack of confidence may arise from several sources, including inexperience (broadly or specific to a current case) or intrapsychic traits. Like knowledge deficits, Caplan felt confidence problems were poorly suited for consultation. When confidence problems surface in specific consultee actions or inaction, consultants have a responsibility to provide short-term support and encouragement while helping them identify appropriate support within their work setting that can help them with specific confidence problems.

Lack of Objectivity

Lack of objectivity as the problem source is considered only after lack of knowledge and skill have been refuted (Erchul, 1993). Nevertheless, lack of objectivity can be a multifaceted problem that arises when a consultee loses perspective on a particular case. Variables consistent with a lack or loss of objectivity include prominent themes, discrepancies, assumptions, and biases that frame the consultee's narrative of the case. Others may have trouble setting or maintaining professional boundaries. Still others may hail from organizations that are closely aligned with specific philosophies that discourage alternate viewpoints. Consultees from respected organizations may be even less inclined to own their loss of objectivity when they are unable to resolve problems on their own (Brown et al., 2011). And while a lack of objectivity can be a product of poor cultural awareness, there remains the possibility that a consultee is aware of their lack of objectivity yet remain resistant to address the issue given the matter concerns a core personal value. In any of these scenarios, consultees may react defensively to any suggestion, implied or otherwise, that challenges their professional judgment or capabilities. Accordingly, exposing and addressing objectivity problems are also a natural threat to the collaborative, egalitarian nature of the alliance and consultants are encouraged to consider the current strength of the alliance prior to (and during) addressing objectivity concerns with a consultee. When it is time to engage the consultee, indirect diplomacy is a valued approach given that the personal and professional integrity of the consultee is essential (Caplan, 1993). In some cases, however, a loss of objectivity requires a referral to another mental health professional.

According to Caplan, the five categories associated with a lack of objectivity include (1) direct personal involvement, (2) simple identification, (3) transference, (4) characterological distortion, and (5) theme interference. Loss of objectivity related to *direct personal involvement* includes problems arising when the consultant relationship transitions inappropriately from professional to personal, generally due a subjective emotional response to a client. In this case, we cite the following set of ACA ethical standards as particularly vulnerable to violation by a consultee whose objectivity problems are related to direct personal involvement.

- A.4.a. Avoiding Harm
- A.5.a. Current Clients
- A.5.b. Former Clients
- A.5.c. Non-professional Interactions
- A.5.d. Potentially Beneficial Interactions
- A.5.e. Role Changes in the Professional Relationship
- C.2.g. Impairment

In cases involving direct personal involvement, Caplan (1970) favors two approaches that follow the edict of protecting the relationship and client integrity by using indirect strategies. First, consultants can focus attention on the client or consultant through a fictitious story or parable that involves the main character's struggle to maintain appropriate boundaries. A second option involves consultants modeling objectivity by designing dialogue that expands consultee awareness of a client outside a single focus or characteristic.

In *simple identification*, consultants identify with some aspect of a client's story even if the consultant may not readily acknowledge or even recognize the connection and its negative impact on objectivity. In other words, simple identification extends beyond empathy and involves a loss of objectivity because of a strong, often unrecognized connection to a specific client trait. *Transference* occurs when consultees ascribe feelings and attitudes to clients based on prior relationships. In doing so, objectivity is lost as the consultee is unable to discern the reality of the client's situation. If not recognized, these patterns are likely to manifest in future cases. *Characterological distortions* involve a consultee's innate personality traits (Caplan, 1970) that alter reality, impair objectivity, and diminish effective service delivery. Given the distortions are enduring personality traits, consultants are advised to support, encourage, and model objectivity instead of working to alter ingrained personality traits.

Theme interference reveals itself surreptitiously, often when consultants or consultees can find no reason for a client's lack of progress. Caplan and Caplan (1993, 1999) assert that theme interference, which involves a consultee framing a new situation through a preconceived (often negative or biased) view, is relatively common in work settings. Once framed in this manner, the die is cast—failure or disappointment is imminent, unavoidable, and destined to repeat itself. The certainty of this negative result provokes a loss of objectivity and often leads to poorly chosen interventions (Erchul & Schulte, 1993). Reducing theme interference is best done through interventions that are aimed at full, not partial, resolution of the theme blocking objectivity. Used individually or in combination, theme interference strategies entail accepting the premise of the client's theme and working with the client in order to prevent foreclosing on the inevitability of that theme. In doing so, a consultee's personal problems are resolved, objectivity is restored, and a sense of professional competence is reignited. Interventions used to accomplish this task include verbal focus on the client, parables, nonverbal focus on the client, and nonverbal focus on the relationship. An abridged summary of each method is below.

Verbal focus on the client uses direct dialogue between a consultant and consultee to deconstruct a client's case and facilitate a discussion on alternate potential outcomes. As an example, a consultant may acknowledge negative aspects of a case without adopting the consultee's notion that negative outcomes are inevitable. This tack illustrates objectivity while challenging consultees to examine alternatives beyond the defeatist position implied by the theme interference.

Parables involve the creative use of storytelling to address theme interference and restore objectivity. Consultants may draw from their actual life events to weave a fictitious yarn that includes the identified theme (Caplan & Caplan-Moskovich, 2004), thereby providing a narrative where the consultant and consultee can indirectly examine the consultee's prevailing sense of inevitable failure in current themes and assist the consultee in expanding the minds to other possibilities and, by extension, alternative (and more positive) endings.

Nonverbal focus on the case alludes to the consultant taking a professional, yet relaxed tone when discussing the details of a consultee's case. By explicitly addressing consultee concerns in a serious, professional demeanor, consultees are modeled a broader sense of potential outcomes and, in particular, those free of the notion that negative outcomes are inevitable. *Nonverbal focus on the relationship*, on the other hand, assumes that just as a consultee can displace thoughts and feelings about past relationships onto current clients, so too can the consultee transfer thoughts and feelings from past relationships onto the consultant. The same can be true for consultee themes that lead to objectivity problems. Guided Exercise 8.3 illustrates this point.

Guided Practice Exercises
Exercise 8.3: A Case of
Consultee-Centered Case Consultation

A mental health consultant is called in to work with a licensed associate counselor who has been working with adult clients in a rural outpatient mental health clinical for 3 months. This is the counselor's first job after graduate school. The counselor (i.e., consultee) quickly turns to a client he has been seeing for 4 months and has had eight sessions with on a biweekly basis. The consultee also noted that "We get along well, yet he is not a good historian and his story lacks detail." However, we have been able to set some goals together, although he is less willing to talk about how to accomplish them. The consultee quickly highlights his current concerns about a 22-year-old male client who has begun making statements about self-harm, including "what I guess would be suicidal statements because he talked about not wanting to wake up sometimes and he could use sleeping pills to make it happen." The consultee also stated, "I don't know really what to do with these statements. I certainly know this is an important issue because I had a close friend who committed suicide a few years ago, but it's not like his life is all that bad, really. He's got a new girlfriend and he told me he just got a new job he likes. There's no reason to want to die over these issues. I mean, we've all had bad times." For the remainder of the initial session, the consultant listens and seeks to gain and clarify details about the case and how the consultee is experiencing the client and the current situation. In this case, the consultee is engaged and provides a solid accounting of the client's story and his (consultee) experiences with this case.

Discussion Questions

1. *How would you describe the current state of the consultation alliance? What do you base your position on?*

2. *How would you categorize the consultee's concerns (i.e., lack of knowledge, skill, confidence, objectivity)? Provide evidence to support your position.*

3. *Would you say the consultee upheld his responsibility in this case? Provide evidence to support your response.*

4. *Based on your response to question 2, describe the type of intervention(s) you would utilize and provide your reasoning for your selections and/or actions.*

5. *Do you believe there is any evidence of theme interference? If yes, describe your position and suggest a possible intervention to address it.*

6. *What techniques or procedures would you use with this consultee?*

Author's Response

1. How would you describe the current state of the consultation alliance? What do you base your position on?

   a. *The alliance has several positive qualities. The consultee has shown an inherent trust in the consultation process and consultant's expertise by actively providing details of a case that troubles him on both a personal and professional basis. More information is needed to ascertain the agreement on future tasks suggested by the consultant to address these concerns, but the trend toward a positive bond is positive.*

2. How would you categorize the consultee's concerns (i.e., lack of knowledge, skill, confidence, objectivity)? Provide evidence to support your position.

   a. *Several consultee difficulty areas are present.*

      i. *Lack of knowledge or skill: Consultee appears to lack key information and assessment skills regarding self-harm and proper assessment procedures for lethality.*

      ii. *Lack of self-confidence: Consultee's limited job experience could be a contributor to this consultee's low level of professional efficacy in dealing with "real-time" issues of suicidality, including both the recognition of self-harm and suicidal statements, how to assess for lethality, and the procedures needed to ensure client safety and those of others.*

      iii. *Lack of professional objectivity: Potential factors include possible loss of objectively due to transference or theme interference. For example, consultee may be blocked from effectively addressing client's suicidal statements due to unresolved issues stemming from his friend's suicide.*

3. Would you say the consultee upheld his responsibility in this case? Provide evidence to support your response.

   a. *Yes. The consultee's primary responsibility is to provide detailed information regarding the case and any difficulties being experienced. In this case, the consultee provided information regarding his concerns about the client's self-harm and suicide statements. Although more implicit, the consultee also provided important details suggesting his personal difficulties in trying to make sense of the client's experience.*

4. Based on your response to discussion question 2, describe the type of intervention(s) you would use and provide your reasoning for your selections and/or actions.

a. *Lack of Knowledge or Skill: I would provide critical content, theoretical informa-tion, and review of basic counseling techniques necessary to fill or bridge gaps in the consultee's knowledge base or procedural aspects of assessing lethality. This will be done in a strength-based approach that aims to maintain or build a strong alliance while increasing the consultee's professional efficacy.*

b. *Lack of Self-Confidence: Consultee's initial distress about the situation suggest a clear lack of confidence in dealing with a suicidal client—a situation not uncommon to an inexperienced counselor. In this case, I would encourage the consultee and highlight his positive attributes (i.e., clinical skills/experiences). Additional suggestions would include consulting with peers and his clinical supervisor.*

5. Do you believe there is any evidence of theme interference? If yes, describe your position and suggest a possible intervention to address it.

a. *Transference or Theme Interference: The consultee in this case appears to have unresolved issues surrounding suicide that may be causing a lack of objectivity. It may be that this barrier manifests as consultee appearing less confident and or lacking in skill or knowledge. I would work to clarify if a transference distor-tion or theme interference is present. In this case, theme interference is appar-ent. To that end, I would dialogue with the consultee about the specifics of the case in a manner that would refocus the consultee on the clinical aspects of the case instead of his own emotional and cognitive experiences of the case. The intention here is to minimize theme interference clouding the consultee's assess-ment of the client and ability to work effectively with him and with future cli-ents experiencing similar issues. It should be noted, however, that reducing theme interference assumes a 3 to 4 week timeframe and specified procedure of theme assessment, consultant intervention, ending, and follow up (Caplan & Caplan, 1993).*

6. What techniques or procedures would you use with this consultee?

a. *While several techniques could be effective (i.e., verbal focus on the client, theme interference reduction), I am drawn to the use of a parable for this con-sultee. My reasoning is that this consultee has readily engaged with the consult-ant and in the consultation process, suggesting that he would engage in a dialogue with the consultant about a fictitious case that had similar themes. In doing so, I would use a nonverbal focus on the case in order to help reduce the consultee's anxiety about the case and illustrate that the case is one that can be dealt with effectively. This could also help expand the consultee's awareness of potential client outcomes without focusing on his own affective and cognitive issues that may be impeding his work with this client and future clients present-ing with similar concerns.*

Program-Centered Administrative Consultation

Program-centered administrative consultation involves the consultant entering the work setting in the role of content expert. Although time limited, the consultant works with administrators on topics related to the mental health features of their program or some facet of the organization's performance. Effective with program-centered administrative consultation will involve consultants blending their core counseling skills with knowledge and skills in data collection and action planning (i.e., writing clinical/technical/administrative reports and recommendations). Overall, the primary goal of program-centered administrative consultation is the creation of a well-thought-out action plan with recommendations targeted at resolving problems related to mental health programming or organizational functioning. Additionally, all consultee reports should include recommendations that address the breadth of the problems defined at the outset and be intelligible to all constituents of the organization. A subsequent follow-up meeting should then be scheduled so feedback can be provided regarding the implementation of the recommendations. A secondary goal is improving consultees' functioning by equipping them with new and more effective interventions to help resolve similar problems in the future. Once again, consultants remain connected and interested, yet as in client-centered consultation, the consultee is the responsible change agent.

In this context, the consultee is generally the organization's administrator who is charged with hiring the consultants. More specifically, the consultee's role is to assist the consultant in problem definition, coordination of data collection, and approval of activities available within the organization. The level of contact between the consultant and consultee, however, is determined by the consultant. Overall, the consultee's tasks are to continually inform the consultant of the nuances of the organizational system and provide the consultant with on-going feedback to ensure recommendations are best suited to meet the mission of the organization's programs or improve organizational functioning. Guided Exercise 8.4 provides an example of this approach.

Guided Practice Exercises
Exercise 8.4: A Case of
Program-Centered Administrative Consultation

Jolene is a mental health consultant who is working with the head administrator of a rural mental health clinic (Candace) and the lead counselor of a juvenile justice program at a rural mental health clinic (Bill). The focal point of consultation is the critical relationship between the agency program and the court system—a relationship that has led to a well-received juvenile justice counseling program. The coinciding appointment of a new head administrator at the mental health agency and the election of a new judge overseeing the juvenile population has led to disruptions in the program that have distressed employees of both organizations. Jolene was hired to provide recommendations on how to restart the program and, by extension, renew a previously successful professional relationship between agency and courts.

Prior to meeting with the agency administrators and counselors, Jolene researched all aspects of the previous programs and, to the extent possible, relationships between the agency and courts. This included a full day at the agency and another at the courts interviewing the administrators, counselors, and the new judge and her employees in order to gain an understanding of their views of the previous program and perceptions of the program going forward. Jolene was also able to interview three former clients of the program and their parents or guardians.

Results of these interviews highlighted several key points. First, the former program administrator, counselors, and judge held consistent views on how to address the mental health and behavioral problems of the juveniles that presented before the courts and worked closely together to provide these services under the mandate of the court. Second, the clients and parents or guardians felt the program was sensitive to juvenile offenders as individuals and were supportive of the program's focus on services that addressed their mental health and behavioral problems. Third, the interviews highlighted that while the counselors from the program were retained, the new administrator and judge hold dissimilar views on treating juvenile offenders. As a result of the interviews, Jolene created a set of recommendations that were shared with each of the constituents involved in the program (administrators, counselors, judge and her staff).

Consultant Report

The juvenile justice program has a history of successes tied to astute programming, competent clinicians, and positive relationships between the agency and court systems. Due to recent changes in the agency's administrative and program leadership and the election of a new judge, communication between these two primary constituencies has been interrupted and caused disruptions to the program. This has also disrupted the previously strong working alliance between the program and courts. The current mental health administrators and counselors perceive the new judge and her staff as more "punitive" in their orientation and, ultimately, less open to addressing the mental health aspects of the juveniles presenting before the judge. Moreover, while the new judge is open to counseling mandates, she and her staff have emphasized stricter behavioral parameters for mandated clients under the supervision of the courts (i.e., probation). To address these concerns, I am recommending the following actions:

1. The administrator of the juvenile justice program and the judge should hold focused meetings with their respective staffs aimed at clarifying previous programming efforts between the two organizations and identifying current and future goals for such programs.

Once the program staff and the judge and her staff have clarified their individual positions, a meeting between the mental health agency and courts will occur. The meeting is to clarify the position of each agency with a primary goal of reimplementing the previously successful collaborative program between the mental health agency and court. The meeting should seek to clarify all aspects of the program, including fiscal, supervisory, clinical, evaluative, logistical, jurisdictional responsibilities, and reporting mandates. Attention also needs to be given to the previous successful elements of the program, including the positive impact of strong alliances among administrators, counselors, court system employees (judge/judge's staff/probation office).

Jolene then followed up 2 months later and saw that the agency and courts had indeed met, clarified their positions and ideological differences, had restructured the program according to agree upon goals, and within the last two weeks have begun implementing the juvenile justice program at the agency based on court referrals.

Discussion Questions

1. *Do you believe the proper amount of data was collected by the consultant prior to setting the meeting? Explain your response.*

2. *Do you believe the proper amount of analysis was done in this case? Explain your position.*

3. *Would you address any other issues surrounding this program going forward? If so, what issue and what is your reasoning?*

4. *Do you believe enough consideration was given by the consultant to the various alliances in this scenario (i.e., consultant–consultee, agency–courts, etc.)? Support your response.*

5. *Do you agree with the consultant's report? What changes might you make to enhance or clarify the report? Support your answer.*

Consultee-Centered Administrative Consultation

The intent of *consultee-centered administrative* consultation is to optimize the functioning of the organization's personnel (Erchul & Schulte, 1993) and policies. To that end, administrative consultation is more educational (Mendoza, 1993), longitudinal, and attuned to enhancing the entire organizational staff's leadership qualities and professional competencies (Erchul & Schulte, 1993; Meyers, Meyer, Proctor, & Huddleson, 2012). The overall goal of this model is to create changes that will result in enduring organizational change (Caplan et al., 1994). An example of such an outcome would be an administrative staff, that after consultation, is more capable of identifying and implementing policies and programs that help the organization achieve its stated mission.

Consultants using this method most often assume the expert role. In this model, the expert role assumes the consultant will able to recognize overt and subtle relational, programmatic, administrative, and cultural nuances that could be adversely affecting the organization. This would also involve the development of a productive consultation alliance with the identified consultee and commitment to building quality working alliances with employees at all organizational levels. To that end, Dougherty (2013) points out that consultee-centered administrative consultation requires that consultants possess "skills required for program-centered administrative consultation, including expertise in group consultation and specialized knowledge of social systems, administrative procedures, and organizational theory" (p. 197).

Consultee identification is especially critical in this approach given that the administrator may want to include one or more consultees in the process and interactions and interventions may be in individual, group, or organizational formats. Consultants must also recognize and state clearly that their role is that of an unbiased change agent (Dougherty, 2013) so employees understand that consultation is not designed to favor particular individuals or entities within the organization. In complex situations, such as consulting with large and diversified organizations, more than one consultation may be employed. Oftentimes, however, several members of the organization's administrative staff engage the consultant in identifying problems, a process that provides a better overall understanding of the organization's programs and perceived problems as well as possible solutions.

Once the consultees are clarified, consultants proceed in a manner that includes their initial entrance into the organization setting, alliance building activities with consultees, assessment of the organization's culture, intervention planning, implementation of individual, group, or organizational interventions, and evaluation and follow-up. This focus on the organizational system as a whole allows the consultant to assess and highlight issues that could inhibit or inspire program performance and the overall health and functioning of the organization. Here, consultants should consider the input of all consultees and be willing to create interventions that are "important to the staff and related to changes the staff would like to make" (Dougherty, 2013, p. 198). This involves constant attention to creating and maintaining strong alliances with consultees in hopes these quality interactions will, in part, encourage them to successfully implement the consultant's recommendations. Yet, because of the voluntary nature of consultation, consultants must consider that employees may limit or even outright decline to share their knowledge and insights even when asked to do so by an administrator.

Interventions are generated only after the consultant has taken in the entirety of the organization's social system and issues have been identified. These concerns are then relayed directly and clearly to all identified consultees, who are ultimately responsible for using their own understanding of the issue and personal resources to address the issues (Caplan & Caplan, 1993). In all instances, consultants should remain impartial and recommend interventions only after fully considering how their interventions and recommendations would enhance a consultee's ability to improve overall organizational functioning through administrative or policy advancements. Guided Exercise 8.5 outlines a more detailed example of the consultee-centered administrative approach.

> ## Guided Practice Exercises
> ## Exercise 8.5: An Example of Consultee-Centered Administrative Consultation

A counselor educator was hired to consult with a small rural mental health agency about their interest in establishing a nationally recognized internship program for graduate students from mental health training programs. Based on funding from a start-up grant, the vision of the agency's executive director is to build a unique training and research site for future mental health professionals while helping them meet the rapidly expanding mental health needs of their community. The agency's executive director believed that graduate-level interns could be in place by the beginning of the next fall school term (a period of 1 year). Specifically, the executive director was interested in the administrative process and policies necessary to create an agency internship program that would attract graduate students from graduate- and postgraduate-level psychology, counseling, and social work programs nationwide.

The executive director's goals of creating a training and research dimension to the agency requires substantial programmatic and policy additions and changes to the agency. These goals would also require the interplay of administrative and clinical staffs among numerous academic, clinical, and school settings. These factors led the consultant to choose the consultee-centered consultation approach. Because of the multiple constituencies and specialties involved, the consultant expanded the consulting team, with the agency's approval, to include a current college president, a former dean of a college of education, and an educational consultant with fundraising expertise in educational and private settings. This ensured the consultation team had the experience and expertise to address all dimensions of the principal consultee's (i.e., executive director) vision. Further, the executive director required that the staff attend at least one meeting with the consulting team and strongly encouraged them to provide their insights so that all "angles are covered." As a result, a series of meetings were scheduled over a 2-day initial consulting period. The first day's schedule included a 3-hour morning meeting with the agency's administrative and clinical leadership teams, respectively, to discuss the agency's mission, current policies and programs, and goals and concerns for and about the proposed training and research program. A 2-hour afternoon meeting was scheduled with the agency's full clinical and paraprofessional staff, followed by a tour led by the clinical director of their on-site and off-site facilities and programs.

Data From Meetings

The morning meeting with the leadership teams highlighted the executive director's vision to design a "cutting edge" training and research program that would make the agency a respected "destination site" for mental health trainees from multiple disciplines. According to the executive director, the agency would allow interns opportunities to engage in the full range of service delivery and administrative tasks related to their clinical and research areas. A secondary goal would be to expand the service delivery in the agency's area, a location that is geographically isolated. According to the clinical director, the agency currently employs five master's-level mental health clinicians (three social workers and two counselors) in their school-based mental health program, although only one (a social worker) is licensed and none have formal training as supervisors. According to the agency's clinical director, first they would like to hire two clinical interns and a dedicated research intern. The meeting with the principal consultee and his administrative and clinical leadership teams was informative and productive.

The meeting with the clinical staff was also productive. According to the clinical staff, this year marks their third year serving as school-based mental health clinicians in the local elementary, middle, and high schools. At each level, the clinicians report steadily increasing caseloads as the program became more integrated into the school culture. They report general concerns about needing clarification on documentation and the option for individual supervision in addition to the 2-hour weekly staffing meeting. They also report feeling stressed and fatigued by the increased workload, frustrated by the lack of raises within the last year, and, in several cases, the extended commute from their homes to the agency and school sites. Overall, they report they enjoyed their jobs and the services the agency provides for the community. While they felt interns could help reduce their case loads, they expressed considerable reservations about the administration's vision to create and maintain a prominent internship site given the agency's size, geographical isolation, and limited clinical and fiscal resources.

The next morning the consulting team met with the administrative and clinical leadership teams to process what they had learned from their meetings. The consultants highlighted the key positives and concerns that they heard or deduced from each meeting and allowed the leadership teams to respond. After a final summary by the principal consultee and leader of the consultation team (counselor educator) about their perception of the key points and vision for the program, the consultation team met alone to discuss and frame their recommendations that were to be presented at a final afternoon meeting with the agency's leadership team. Prior to stating their recommendations, the consulting team agreed on follow-up phone calls one time per month for the next 3 months to assess progress and deal with any new issues. A face-to-face meeting with the team and consultees will be conducted at the end of the 6-month period to assess progress and make any additional adjustments. Both the principal consultee and consultation team agreed to this sequence.

Consultant's Recommendations

The creation and maintenance of a nationally recognized internship program with clinical and research components for graduate-level mental health trainees involves a variety of organizational and policy issues related to licensing, accreditation and supervision that will add considerable requirements and bureaucracy to an agency of limited size and facing additional budget constraints due to a poor economy. The social culture within the agency and its employees appears generally positive. Specific concerns among the clinical staff were increased service delivery requirements (increased caseloads/documentation) and long home-to-work commute times with no appreciable pay increase. Employees, both administrative and clinical, appear to find their jobs rewarding and are pleased to work for the agency. Overall, the primary consultant, in conjunction with the other members of the consulting team, recommends the following:

1. *Mission and vision* statement(s) should be expanded to include a graduate-level training and research component.

2. *Develop a cohort* of appropriately licensed staff. Consider additional funding to provide for the necessary formal academic and clinical requirements of attaining and maintaining professional licensure.

3. *Develop policy manuals* in keeping with the appropriate accrediting and licensing agencies (i.e., psychology, counseling, social work).

4. *Assess current personnel,* at all levels, to determine educational and practical job requirements and expectations to achieve the desired vision; work to create an agency culture conducive to integrating diverse types of mental health trainees and facilitating their personal and professional development.

5. *Invest* in current personnel and new hires to achieve the desired level of organizational expectations and success.

6. *Accreditation* will be needed through proper national associations (i.e., CARF).

7. *Educating* current and future staff in the necessary mental health program accreditation (i.e., counseling–CACREP) standards that must be followed.

8. *Seek funding* to provide the following:
   * continuing education, training and licensing requirements for current staff;
   * intern stipends, including housing and other living expense needs;
   * an attractive package for "faculty sabbaticals," similar to the above mentioned areas of need;
   * technology enhancements and upgrades; and
   * on-going assistance for consulting fees and expenses.

9. *Seek funding* from a variety of sources for the above mentioned areas:
   * State and federal grants
   * Private foundations and individuals
   * Organizations such as AARP and Veteran's Administration
   * Businesses and corporations, with a special pitch regarding the economic impact of the agency: for example, highlight how the increased staff credentials and internship and research program would help meet the needs of agency and community constituents and how money spent on agency services is less expensive than serious crime and incarceration, thus an economic benefit to the community it serves

10. *Pursue technology enhancements and upgrades* to accommodate the opportunity to communicate with interns (and their programs, professors, or supervisors)

11. *Develop an inventory* of potential participating institutions

12. *Develop a strategy* for further alliances within local, regional, and state agencies

13. *Engage in board development, training and education* to revisit the mission and to develop a strategic master plan for the agency that includes the internship and research component

Discussion Questions

1. *Do you believe the consultant's decision to hire additional consultants was justified? Explain your position.*

2. *Do you believe the social system of the agency, schools, and communities they served were given their just due by the consultants? If no, what would you do differently and why?*

3. *Do you believe enough time was spent building positive alliances between the consultants and consultees? What evidence supports your position?*

4. *Do you believe the consultants addressed interventions that addressed the individual, group, and organizational levels appropriately? Support your response and include any changes you believe should be considered.*

Current Trends

Mental health consultation continues to expand from the early consulting paradigm's deficit orientation to a growth model that recognizes and attends to consultee strengths. Importantly, the core notions of prevention and indirect interventions remain fundamental features of this philosophical change. An example of this movement is the recognition of cognitive change as a dimension of successful consulting outcomes. No matter the focus, the push to increase and strengthen the empirical breadth and depth of mental health consultation remains constant (Perry & Linas, 2012; Kaufmann, Perry, Hepburn, & Duran, 2012).

The paradigm shift experienced in mental health consultation is perhaps most easily noted by the expansion of the consultee-centered consultation approach. Specifically, consultee-centered consultation has evolved from its psychodynamic origins to one that frames problem definition through a constructivist framework. As a result, dialogue between the consultant and consultee involves gaining the consultee's subjective interpretation of the problem (Sandoval, 2004). Another trend is its broader applicability outside of mental health. For example, consultants in school systems are applying the model to help teachers enhance classroom instruction outcomes (Babinski, Knotek, & Rogers, 2004; Knotek, Rosenfield, Gravois, & Babinski, 2003), while other schools are training "instructional consultants" (Rosenfield, Silva, & Gravois, 2008) in response to the increased need for evidence-based instruction (Brown et al., 2011).

The consultee-centered approach is also being expanded and applied to specialized populations. Examples include the use of this approach within medical and mental health communities (Sears, Rudisill, & Mason-Sears, 2006), hospice programs (Lindenberg, 1996), and business communities (Shosh, 1996). A more recent development is the implementation of early childhood mental health consultation (ECMHC), a model designed to "increase the ability of childcare staff/programs and families to prevent, identify, and manage social and emotional problems in young children" (Conners-Burrow, Whiteside-Mansell, McKelvey, Amini-Virmani, & Sockwell, 2012, p. 256). The available research suggests the ECHMC model is effective with enhancing teacher functioning and the emotional development of children (Perry, Dunne, McFadden, & Campbell, 2008). Like other emerging theories, ECMHC has empirical gaps such as it has not yet been "manualized" (Kaufmann et al., 2012, p. 281) and much of the current data has not been published in peer-reviewed journals. Still, this model recognizes the need for effective consultation with underserved and marginalized populations. Combined with the advocacy consultation work of Drum & Valdes (1988), consultation can highlight its value as a means of facilitating connections and services between known community-based consumers of mental health consultation such as mental health agencies and schools (Dahir & Stone, 2012; Lewis, Lewis, Daniels, & D'Andrea, 2011).

Although noted previously, we briefly revisit the ecological perspective given that it continues to gain traction in mental health consultation. Simply stated, the ecological perspective explores the relationship between humans and their environment. Applied to consultation, consultants would consider behavior as inherently influenced by some blend of individual and environmental factors. In general, then, a consultation issue is based on incongruencies between the consultee and environment. Only when we understand the individual in relation to personal environment can consultants fully appreciate a consultee's behavior and work to change it.

Trends in mental health also include paradigm and contextual shifts. Although far from exhaustive, we've included information below for areas we believe contemporary consultants should have knowledge and competencies in order to remain competitive with other mental health professionals as consultation providers.

Table 8.1 Meyers School-Based Consultation Approach

Level	Focus	Example
Level I	Child	Consultant works with teacher to address a child's disruptive classroom behavior.
Level II	Teacher	Consultant works with teacher to clarify classroom behavior rules.
Level III	System	Consultant provides in-service trainings about current research on classroom behavioral management and strategies

School-Based Counseling: Prelude to School-Based Mental Health Consultation?

Historically, Caplan's views on consultation were not viewed as widely applicable to the school environment. However, Joel Meyers and other scholars (Meyers, 1973; Meyers, Parsons, & Martin, 1979; Parsons & Meyers, 1984) have long considered consultation as applicable to schools settings. Using many of Caplan's (1970) core ideas, including a nonhierarchical view and respect for client autonomy (Meyers, 1981), Meyers (1973) developed a three-tiered consultation system for use in school settings. Meyers also believes both in the use of direct interventions and that consultants and consultees have a mutual responsibility for implementing interventions (Meyers, 1973; Meyers et al., 1979). It is also critical that consultants be sensitive to the distinctive culture of the school and its employees toward mental health services and the school-based mental health clinician. For example, a school culture where mental health issues are stigmatized (Weist, Myers, Hastings, Ghuman, & Han, 1999) will require a consultant to consider relationships and actions in relation to the school's (and perhaps entire school district's) sociocultural milieu. These issues will be addressed in more depth in the chapter on educational settings (Chapter 9). Table 8.1 below offers an overview of Meyer's school-based consultation approach.

Consultation in Groups

Caplan's early negative views of consultation in groups were attributed mainly to his notion that group dynamics were unpredictable, could threaten a consultee's professional integrity, and his limited confidence in vicarious learning. Still, challenges to his views (Altrocchi, 1972) prompted a reanalysis of his early views and led to his belief that groups can offer consultees a critical support system, cost-saving measures, and opportunities to expand their professional competencies (Caplan, 1977; Caplan & Caplan, 1993, 1999). Of critical importance, however, is the recognition that the practice of group-based consultation fundamentally requires competencies in group dynamics. In short, group consultation can be a dynamic, complex undertaking and should be considered only when the requisite education, training, and appropriate professional credentials are possessed by the counselor–consultant (see ACA, 2005; see C.2.a. Boundaries of Competence & C.2.b. New Specialty Areas of Practice). Likewise, counselor–consultants must be cognizant of the paradigm shift between the provision of group therapy and group consultation as well as the need to transition from an individual-oriented consultation endeavor to one involving a group.

Collaboration

The broader range of mental health professionals who work and provide consultation within school systems also prompted Caplan to reassess his original framework. Especially influential was Pryzwansky's (1974) reasoned argument regarding the efficacy of joint responsibility for action, a view that challenged the position that the consultee held full responsibility for taking action. Caplan retained certain core truths about his early model, however, including the belief that consultants in the expert role retain full decision-making authority, clarifying the form of consultation as the first step, and the belief in collaboration as a primary consideration when internal issues predominate. Thus, when collaboration is used, the consultee relinquishes full authority for refusing to implement consultant recommendations given that both are now responsible for effective implementation and outcomes. Still, Caplan's flexibility illustrates his willingness to recognize the conceptual limits of his early views and adapt to the notion of collaboration as "a process complementary to, but different from, consultation" (Dougherty, 2009, p. 199), a process he later termed *mental health collaboration*. Overall, Caplan's embrace of the limits of his original view of mental health consultation, along with his acceptance of collaboration as a viable form of mental health service delivery, rate as key changes in the mental health consultation paradigm.

Executive Coaching and Consultation

It is imperative that counselor–consultants be aware of all service delivery options. In that vein, we note the increasing popularity of coaching (Auerbach, 2001), particularly executive coaching and consultation, among mental health professionals. It is not hard to see why mental health consultants are drawn to these methods. Coaching, for example, involves providing individuals with skills, knowledge, and opportunities to enhance their personal efficacy (Peterson & Hicks, 1996). In a recent example, mental health consultants acting as coaches have worked to bolster student and teacher efficacy (Cappella et al., 2012). In addition, Sperry (2004) posits that the specific functions of an executive coach address skill, performance, and development, with a fourth key role being that of advisor.

Although widely explored in the psychological literature, coaching as a unique form of service delivery and discipline (Auerbach, 2001) is relatively new to many counseling professionals (Corey, Haynes, Moulton, & Muratori, 2010; Griffiths & Campbell, 2008; Peltier, 2001), particularly executive consultation (de Haan & Duckworth, 2012). Yet, while uncertainty remains regarding the parameters of coaching (Diedrich, 1996), it is not difficult to find parallels between counseling and executive coaching and consultation. Like clinicians, executive coaches attend to professional relationships

Table 8.2 Keys to Successful Coaching

Keys to Successful Coaching

1. Capitalize on your strengths.
2. Take an active, directive role.
3. Become polytheoretical.
4. Be very clear about who the client is.
5. Understand the business world.
6. Be clear about the differences between psychotherapy and coaching.
7. Be equally clear about the similarities between coaching and psychotherapy.
8. Conduct individual outcome evaluations for every client.
9. Continue to build your skills.

(Kilburg, 2000), ethics (Passmore, 2009), cultural awareness (Coultas, Bedwell, Burke, & Salas, 2011; Hodgson & Crainer, 1993), and individual (Gregory, Levy, & Jeffers, 2008) and group settings (Carr & Peters, 2013). Thus, as the coaching paradigm continues its expansion into the mental health arena, consultants must take the time to understand its parameters and potential impact on the practice of consultation in different settings currently serviced by professional counselors of all specialties.

So what exactly is executive coaching and consultation? Generally speaking, executive coaching is an action-oriented intervention with multiple formats. Still, the distinction between executive coaching and psychotherapy remains controversial, particularly with regard to professional training (Berglas, 2002; Dean & Meyer, 2002). Those less captivated with the idea of formal psychological training for executive coaches suggest that psychological training can be gained outside formal psychological training programs and that, in some cases, such training could have minimal effect or even negative implications (Garman, Whiston, & Zlatoper, 2000; Kilburg, 2004). Although this discussion exceeds the parameters of this text, counselor–consultants should be cognizant of these controversies given the surge of licensed mental health professionals providing mental health delivery based on the executive coaching and consultation model along with individuals from other disciplines such as business and education who are successfully utilizing the coaching-consultation model.

William H. Berman and George Bradt (2006) created a model of executive coaching that outlines four types of coaching: (1) facilitative coaching, (2) restorative coaching, (3) developmental coaching, and (4) executive consulting. Facilitative coaching is a time limited and direct-intervention focused on "core leadership competencies" (p. 245). Restorative coaching is another time-limited strategy aimed at mitigating personal, contextual, and organizational barriers to success and generating new strategies. Developmental coaching offers an often lengthier approach of addressing the interpersonal concerns of identified clients that could mitigate positive organizational outcomes. Finally, executive consultation involves "a consultive, relationship-based service provided by seasoned consultants who serve as advisors and objective sounding boards to senior executives" (p. 245). In other words, the goal of the executive consultant is to optimize an executive's success. This role, like that of a consultant, involves content expertise, active listening and communication skills, an ability to synthesize multiple dimensions (i.e., theoretical, pragmatic, personal, contextual, political, organizational), creativity, and the ability to be an active and direct participant in the process (Berman & Bradt, 2006; Kilburg, 2000). What seems clear at this point is that the counselor–consultant should be aware of the similarities and distinctions between counseling, coaching, and consultation given that the coaching paradigm continues to draw more adherents and expand its literature base.

Although executive coaching and consultation offer several benefits, it is imperative to ascertain if you are eligible to provide executive coaching or consultation. For example, in at least one author's state, the coaching credential requires full licensure as a professional counselor and a specialized coaching endorsement (which requires additional training and regular continuing education requirements). In this author's state, absent these state-sanctioned endorsements, the "coach" would be considered to be practicing without a valid counseling license and is subject to potential ethical and legal problems. To simplify, always seek out and attain the proper credentials prior to engaging in any new form of mental health service delivery. Overall, though, mental health professionals who are properly trained and accredited as coaches appear well-situated to challenge those outside the mental health arena in the open marketplace. Thus, we strongly encourage readers to investigate this quickly expanding paradigm not only to maintain their content base but to remain competitive within the consultation arena as new forms of service delivery arise. Table 8.3 illustrates the key skill sets of executive coaches and consultants.

Multicultural Considerations

The diversity among and between consultees, programs, and organizations presents unique benefits and challenges for mental health consultants. For instance, the psychodynamic foundation of Caplan's mental health consultation model makes the client-centered and consultee-centered models especially well-suited for exploring and addressing diversity issues. The nonhierarchical relationship is quite amenable to clients with distinct perspectives, particularly those who value privacy (Ingraham, 2003, 2004). In addition, the contemporary version of the consultee-centered model provides opportunities for safe discourse in which consultees can create new, more culturally sensitive narratives that can help them problem solve and enhance their professional and personal functioning. Ultimately, mental health consultation is positively situated for providing culturally competent consultation at all levels. Additionally, the postmodern reinterpretation now gaining prominence in consultee-centered consultation shows the adaptability of Caplan's ideas among and between distinct levels, cultures, and professional orientations.

While cultural competence is implied in the professional interactions of mental health counselors and consultants at the individual level, the notion of cultural competence within organizational settings often receives less attention. Kenneth Fung, Hung Tat Lo, Rani Srivastava, & Lisa Andermann (2012), for instance, noted the following characteristics of organizational competence: organizational commitment, values, governance and leadership, partnerships within the community, flexibility and availability of services for specialized populations, workforce development issues, availability and integration of diversity initiatives within an organization (Center for Mental Health Services, 1997; Hernandez, Nesman, Mowery, Acevedo-Polakovich, & Callejas, 2009; National Quality Forum (NQF), 2009; U.S. Department of Health and Human Services, Office of Minority Health, 2001). Awareness, however, is only part of the process. Recommendations for new cultural initiates in an organization should rely on accurate personal and organizational cultural assessments. Moreover, prominent issues within organizations such as the "glass ceiling" (Smith, 2000) and sexual harassment (Stockdale, 1996) must also be considered. Rosinski (2003) goes further, listing seven prominent organizational cultural factors that consultants should monitor. These include a sense of power and responsibility, time management, definition of identity and purpose, organizational structure, territory and boundary issues, communication, and organizational ways of thinking. According to Fung et al. (2012), culturally competent recommendations include the following:

1. True organizational change requires consideration of the organization's unique culture.

2. Cultural competence initiatives should connect to clinically based objectives of facilitating positive outcome among all potential organizational employees.

3. Cultural initiatives should be measureable and accountable.

4. Programs and initiatives should involve as many employees and their families as possible.

5. Collaboration with a broad range of community based organizations and individuals is critical to the development of a "systemic and coordinated impact and sustainable change" (p. 177).

Chapter Keystones

- Mental health consultation is rooted in the work of Gerald Caplan (see also, Caplan & Caplan 1993, 1999; Caplan & Moskovich, 2004).
- Key consultation approaches include client-centered case consultation, consultee-centered case consultation, program-centered case consultation, and consultee-centered case consultation. These are based on two distinct levels (case, administrative) and foci (client, program).
- Multicultural and ethical competencies must be maintained throughout the consultation process. Mental health consultants must remain aware of the cultural and ethical codes in relation to several different contexts. Examples include consultation with individuals, groups, schools, mental health organizations (staff, administrators, clinicians).
- Trends in consultation, such as collaboration, coaching, group, and school-based mental health require content knowledge and skills prior to providing consultation services.
- Benefits of mental health consultation include improved, expanded service delivery and refocused attention on the benefits of the consultee's emotional and psychological health (Caplan et al., 1994).

- Criticisms include lack of operational definition of mental health consultation, its lack of a strength based and preventative orientation, limited recognition of consultee competencies (Caplan & Caplan, 1993), minimal attention to the health of the consultation alliance, tendency of consultants to be overly directive and hierarchical in service delivery, and a lack of empirical support (Knotek et al., 2003).

Web-Based and Literature-Based Resources

Suggested Readings

Caplan, G. (1970). *The theory and practice of mental health consultation.* New York, NY: Basic Books.

Caplan, G., & Caplan, R. B. (1999). *Mental health consultation and collaboration.* San Francisco, CA: Jossey-Bass.

Yalom, I. D. (with Leszcz, M.). (2005). *The theory and practice of group psychotherapy* (5th ed.). New York, NY: Basic Books.

References

Adelman, H. S., & Taylor, L. (2000). Promoting mental health in schools in the midst of school reform. *Journal of School Health, 70*(5), 171–178.

Albee, G. W., & Fryer, D. M. (2003). Praxis: Toward a public health psychology. *Journal of Community & Applied Social Psychology, 13,* 71–75.

Altrocchi, J. (1972). Mental health consultation. In S. E. Golann & C. Eisdorfer (Eds.), *Handbook of community mental health* (pp. 477–508). New York, NY: Appleton-Century-Crofts.

American Counseling Association (2005). ACA Code of Ethics. Alexandria, VA: Author.

Auerbach, J. (2001). *Personal and executive coaching: The complete guide for mental health professionals.* Ventura, CA: Executive College Press.

Babcock, N. L., & Pryzwansky, W. B. (1983). Models of consultation: Preferences of educational professionals at five stages of service. *Journal of School Psychology, 21,* 359–366.

Babinski, L. M., Knotek, S. E., & Rogers, D. L. (2004). Facilitating conceptual change in new teacher consultation groups. In N. M. Lambert, I. Hylander, & J. H. Sandoval (Eds.), *Consultee-centered consultation: Improving the quality of professional services in schools and community organizations* (pp. 101–113). Mahwah, NJ: Erlbaum.

Beck, A. T., & Steer, R. A. (1987). *BDI, Beck Depression Inventory: Manual.* San Antonio, TX: Psychological Corporation.

Benjamin, M., & Curtis, J. (1981). *Ethics in nursing.* New York, NY: Oxford University Press.

Berglas, S. (2002). The very real dangers of executive coaching. *Harvard Business Review, 80*(6), 86–91.

Berman, W. H., & Bradt, G. (2006). Executive coaching and consulting: "Different strokes for different folks." *Professional Psychology: Research and Practice, 37*(3), 244–253.

Brown, D., Pryzwansky, W. B., & Schulte, A. C. (2006). *Psychological consultation and collaboration* (6th ed.). Boston, MA: Allyn & Bacon.

Brown, D., Pryzwansky, W. B., & Schulte, A. C. (2011). *Psychological consultation and collaboration: Introduction to theory and practice.* Boston, MA: Pearson.

Caplan, G. (1961). *An approach to community mental health.* New York, NY: Grune & Stratton.

Caplan, G. (1964). A conceptual model for primary prevention. In D. A. van Krevelen (Ed.), *Child psychiatry and prevention.* Bern, Switzerland: Verlag Hans Huber.

Caplan, G. (1970). *The theory and practice of mental health consultation.* New York, NY: Basic Books.

Caplan, G. (1977). Mental health consultation: Retrospect and prospect. In S. C. Plog & P. I. Ahmed (Eds.), *Principles and techniques of mental health consultation* (pp. 9–21). New York: Plenum.

Caplan, G., & Caplan, R. B. (1993). *Mental health consultation and collaboration.* San Francisco, CA: Jossey-Bass.

Caplan, G., & Caplan, R. B. (1999). *Mental health consultation and collaboration.* Prospect Heights, IL: Waveland. (Original work published in 1993).

Caplan, G., Caplan, R. B., & Erchul, W. P. (1994). Caplanian mental health consultation: Historical background and current status. *Consulting Psychology Journal: Practice & Research, 46,* 2–12.

Caplan, G., & Caplan-Moskovich, R. B. (2004). Recent advances in mental health consultation and mental health consultation. In N. M. Lambert, I. Hylander, & J. H. Sandoval (Eds.), *Consultee-centered consultation: Improving the quality of professional services in schools and community organizations* (pp. 21–35) Mahwah, NJ: Erlbaum.

Capella, E., Hamre, B. K., Kim, H. Y., Henry, D. B., Frazier, S. L., Atkins, M. S., & Schoenwald, S. K. (2012). Teacher consultation and coaching within mental health practice: Classroom and child effects in urban elementary schools. *Journal of Consulting and Clinical Psychology, 80*(4), 597–610. doi: 10.1037/a0027725

Carr, C., & Peters, J. (2013). The experience of team coaching: A dual case study. *International Coaching Psychology Review, 8*(1), 80–97.

Center for Mental Health Services. (1997). *Cultural competence standards in managed mental health services: Four underserved/underrepresented racial/ethnic groups.* Washington, DC: Substance Abuse and Mental Health Services Administration.

Collins, B. G., & Collins, T. M. (2005). *Crisis and trauma: Developmental-ecological intervention.* Lahaska, PA: Lahaska Press.

Conners-Burrow, N., Whiteside-Mansell, L., McKelvey, L., Amini-Vermani, E., & Sockwell, L. (2012). Improved classroom quality and child behavior in an Arkansas early childhood mental health consultation pilot project. *Infant Mental Health Journal, 33*(3), 256–264.

Corey, G., Haynes, R., Moulton, P., & Muratori, M. (2010). *Clinical supervision in the helping professions: A practical guide* (2nd ed.). Alexandria, VA: American Counseling Association.

Coultas, C. W., Bedwell, W. L., Burke, C. S. & Salas, E. (2011). Values sensitive coaching: The DELTA approach to coaching culturally diverse executives. *Consulting Psychology Journal: Research and Practice, 63*(3), 149–161.

Dahir, C. A., & Stone, C. B. (2012).*The transformed school counselor* (2nd ed.). Belmont, CA: Brooks/Cole.

Dean, M. L., & Meyer, A. A. (2002). Executive coaching: In search of a model. *Journal of Leadership Education, 1,* 1–15.

de Haan, E., & Duckworth, A. (2012). Signalling a new trend in executive coaching outcome research. *International Coaching Psychology Review, 8*(1), 6–16.

Diedrich, R. C. (1996). An interactive approach to executive coaching. *Consulting Psychology Journal: Practice & Research, 48*(2), 61–66.

Dougherty, A. M. (2000). *Psychological consultation and collaboration. A casebook.* Belmont, CA: Wadsworth/Thomson Learning.

Dougherty, A. M. (2009). *Psychological consultation and collaboration in school and community settings* (5th ed.). Belmont, CA: Brooks/Cole.

Dougherty, A. M. (2013). *Psychological consultation and collaboration in school and community settings* (6th ed.). Belmont, CA: Brooks/Cole.

Drum, D. J., & Valdes, L. E. (1988). Advocacy and outreach: Applications to college university centers. In D. J. Kurpius & D. Brown (Eds.), *Handbook of consultation: An intervention for advocacy and outreach* (pp. 38–60). Alexandria, VA: American Association for Counseling and Development.

Erchul, W. P. (1993). Selected interpersonal perspectives in consultation research. *School Psychology Quarterly, 8,* 38–49.

Erchul, W. P., & Schulte, A. C. (1993). Gerald Caplan's contributions to professional psychology: Conceptual underpinnings. In W. P. Erchul (Ed.), *Consultation in community, school, and organizational practice* (pp. 3–39). Washington, DC: Taylor & Francis.

Evans, K., Law, H., Turner, R., Rogers, A., & Cohen, K. (2011). A pilot study evaluating care staffs' perceptions of their experience of psychological consultation within a mental health setting. *Child Care In Practice, 17*(2), 205–219. doi:10.1080/13575279.2010.541423

Fisher, M., & Ireland, C. A. (2010). Acting as the consultant advisor in a crisis situation: Consultancy and advising in forensic practice: Empirical and practical guidelines. In C. A. Ireland & M. J. Fisher (Eds.), *Consultancy and advising in forensic practice: Empirical and practical guidelines, forensic practice* (pp. 91–107). Leicester, UK: Wiley.

Fung, K., Lo, H., Srivastava, R., & Andermann, L. (2012). Organizational cultural competence consultation to a mental health institution. *Transcultural Psychiatry, 49*(2), 165–184. doi: 10.1177/1363461512439740

Garman, A. N, Whiston, D. L., & Zlatoper, K. W. (2000). Media perceptions of executive coaching and the formal preparation of coaches. *Consulting Psychology Journal: Research and Practice, 52*, 201–205.

Gilliland, B. E., & James, R. K. (2013). *Crisis intervention strategies*. Belmont, CA: Brooks/Cole.

Granello, D. H., & Granello, P. F. (2007). *Suicide: An essential guide for helping professionals and educators.* Boston, MA: Allyn & Bacon.

Gregory, J., Levy, P., & Jeffers, M. (2008). Development of a model of the feedback process within executive coaching. *Consulting Psychology Journal: Practice and Research, 60*, 42–56. doi: 10.1037/1065-9293.60.1.42

Griffiths, K., & Campbell, M. A. (2008). Semantics or substance? Preliminary evidence in the debate between life coaching and counselling. *Coaching: An International Journal of Theory, Research and Practice, 1*(2), 164–175. doi:10.1080/17521880802328095

Gutkin, T. B., & Curtis, M. J. (1990). School-based consultation: Theory, techniques, and research. In T. B. Gutkin & C. R. Reynolds (Eds.), *The handbook of school psychology* (2nd ed., pp. 577–611), New York, NY: Wiley.

Gutkin, T. B., & Curtis, M. J. (1999). School-based consultation theory and practice: The art and science of indirect service delivery. In C. R. Reynolds & T. B. Gutkin (Eds.). *The handbook of school psychology* (3rd ed., pp. 598–637). New York, NY: Wiley.

Henning-Stout, M. (1993).Theoretical and empirical bases of consultation. In J. E. Zins, T. R. Kratochwill, & S. N. Elliott (Eds.), *Handbook of consultation services for children* (pp. 15–45). San Francisco, CA: Jossey-Bass.

Hernandez, M., Nesman, T., Mowery, D., Acevedo-Polakovich, I. D., & Callejas, L. M. (2009). Cultural competence: A literature review and conceptual model for mental health services. *Psychiatric Services, 60*(8), 1046-1050. doi:10.1176/appi.ps.60.8.1046

Hodgson, P., & Crainer, S. (1993). *What do high performance managers really do?* London, UK: Pitman.

Hylander, I. (2012). Conceptual change through consultee-centered consultation: A theoretical model. *Consulting Psychology Journal: Practice and Research, 64*, 29–45.

Ingraham, C. L. (2003). Multicultural consultee-centered consultation: When novice consultants explore cultural hypotheses with experienced teacher consultants. *Journal of Educational and Psychological Consultation, 4*, 329–362.

Ingraham, C. L. (2004). Multicultural consultee-centered consultation: Supporting consultees in the development of cultural competence. In N. M. Lambert, I. Hylander, & J. H. Sandoval (Eds.), *Consultee-centered consultation: Improving the quality of professional services in schools and community organizations* (pp. 133–170). Mahwah, NJ: Erlbaum.

Iscoe, I. (1993). Gerald Caplan's conceptual and qualitative contributions to community psychology: Views from an old timer. In W. P. Erchul (Ed.), *Consultation in community, school, and organizational practice* (pp. 87–98). Washington, DC: Taylor & Francis.

Kaufmann, R. K., Perry, D. F., Hepburn, K., & Duran, F. (2012). Assessing fidelity for early childhood mental health consultation: Lessons from the field and next steps. *Infant Mental Health Journal, 33*(3), 274–282.

Kilburg, R. R. (2000). *Executive coaching: Developing managerial wisdom in a world of chaos.* Washington, DC: American Psychological Association.

Kilburg, R. R. (2004). Trudging toward Dodoville: Conceptual approaches and case studies in executive coaching. *Consulting Psychology Journal, 56*, 203–213.

Knight, J. A., & Kleespies, P. M. (1999, August 22). *The Boston assessment of suicide ideation correlates (BASIC): Development of a suicide risk assessment for veterans.* Paper presented at the 107th annual Convention of the American Psychological Association, Boston, Massachusetts.

Knotek, S. E., Rosenfield, S. A., Gravois, T. A., & Babinski, L. M. (2003). The process of fostering consultee development during instructional consultation. *Journal of Educational and Psychological Consultation, 14,* 303–328.

Knotek, S. E., & Sandoval, J. (2003). Current research in consultee-centered consultation. *Journal of Educational and Psychological Consultation, 4,* 243–250.

Kübler-Ross, E. (1969). *On death and dying.* New York, NY: Macmillan.

Lewis, J. A., Lewis, M. D., Daniels, J. A., & D'Andrea, M. J. (2011). Community counseling: A multicultural-social justice perspective (4th ed.). Belmont, CA: Brooks/Cole.

Lindemann, E. (1944). Symptomatology and management of acute grief. *American Journal of Psychiatry, 101,* 141–148.

Lindenberg, S. P. (1996). Highlight section: The mental health counselor and hospice. In W. J. Weikel & A. J. Palmo (Eds.), Foundations of mental health counseling (2nd ed., pp. 229–231). Springfield, IL: Thomas Books.

Maher, C. A. (1993). Providing consultation services in business settings. In J. E. Zins, T. R. Kratochwill, & S. N. Elliott (Eds.), *Handbook of consultation services for children* (pp. 317–328). San Francisco, CA: Jossey-Bass.

Martin, R. P., & Curtis, M. (1981). Consultants' perceptions of causality for success and failure of consultation. *Professional Psychology, 12,* 670–676.

Martin, T., & Doka, K. (2000). *Men don't cry . . . Women do: Transcending gender stereotypes of grief.* Philadelphia, PA: Brunner/Mazel.

Mendoza, D. W. (1993). A review of Gerald Caplan's theory and practice of mental health consultation. *Journal of Counseling and Development, 71,* 629–635.

Meyers, A. B., Meyers, J., Graybill, E. C., Proctor, S. L., & Huddleston, L. (2012). Ecological approaches to organizational consultation and systems change in educational settings. *Journal of Educational & Psychological Consultation, 22*(1/2), 106–124. doi:10.1080/10474412.2011.649649

Meyers, J. (1973). A consultation model for school psychological services. *Journal of School Psychology, 11,* 5–15.

Meyers, J. (1981). Mental health consultation. In J. C. Conoley (Ed.), *Consultation in schools* (pp. 35–58). New York, NY: Academic Press.

Meyers, J. (1989). The practice of psychology in the schools for the primary prevention of learning and adjustment problems in children: A perspective from the field of education. In L. A. Bond & B. E. Compas (Eds.), *Primary prevention and promotion in the schools* (pp. 391–422). Newbury Park, CA: Sage.

Meyers, J., Parsons, R. D., & Martin, R. (1979). *Mental health consultation in the schools.* San Francisco, CA: Jossey-Bass.

Mills, C., Stephan, S. H., Moore, E., Weist, M. D., Daly, B. P., & Edwards, M. (2006). The President's New Freedom Commission: Capitalizing on opportunities to advance school-based mental health services. *Clinical Child and Family Psychology Review, 9*(3), 149–161. doi: 10.1007/s10567-006-003-3

Miron, M. S., & Goldstein, A. P. (1978). *Hostage.* Kalamazoo, MI: Behaviordelia.

Myer, R. A., & Moore, H. (2006). Crisis in context theory: An ecological model. *Journal of counseling & Development, 84,* 139–147.

National Quality Forum. (2009). *A comprehensive framework and preferred practices for measuring and reporting cultural competency: A consensus report.* Washington, DC: Author.

Parsons, R. D., & Meyers, J. (1984). *Developing consultation skills.* San Francisco, CA: Jossey-Bass.

Passmore, J. (2009). Coaching ethics: Making ethical decisions–novices and experts. *The Coaching Psychologist, 5*(1), 6–10.

Peltier, B. (2001). *The psychology of executive coaching: Theory and application.* New York, NY: Brunner-Routledge.

Perry, D. F., Dunne, M. C., McFadden, L., & Campbell, D. (2008). Reducing the risk for preschool expulsion: Mental health consultation for young children with challenging behaviors. *Journal of Child and Family Studies, 17,* 44–54.

Perry, D. F., & Linas, K. (2012). Building the evidence base for early childhood mental health consultation: Where we've been, where we are, and where we are going. *Infant Mental Health Journal, 33*(3), 223–225. doi:10.1002/imhj.21331

Peterson, D., & Hicks, M. (1996). *Leader as coach: Strategies for coaching and developing others.* Minneapolis, MN: Personnel Decisions International.

Pinkerton, R., & Temple, R. D. (2000). Mental health consultation and psychology internship training. *Professional Psychology: Research and Practice, 31,* 315–320.

Pryzwansky, W. P. (1974). A reconsideration of the consultation model for delivery of school-based psychological services. *The American Journal of Orthopsychiatry, 44*(4), 579–583.

Pryzwansky, W. P. (1977). Collaboration or consultation: Is there a difference? *Journal of Special Education, 11,* 179–182.

Rogers, J. R. (2001). Suicide risk assessment. In E. R. Welfel & R. E. Ingersoll (Eds.), *The mental health desk reference* (pp. 259–263). New York, NY: Wiley.

Rosenfield, S. A., & Gottfredson, G. D. (2006). *2006 IC effectiveness study updates.* Retrieved November 30, 2009, from http://www.icteams.umd.edu/IESupdates.html

Rosenfield, S. A., Silva, A., & Gravois, T. A. (2008). Bringing instructional consultation to scale: Research and development of IC and IC teams. In W. P. Erchul & S. M. Sheridan (Eds.), *Handbook of research in consultation* (pp. 203–223). New York, NY: Erlbaum.

Rosinski, P. (2003). *Coaching across cultures: New tools for leveraging national, corporate, and professional differences.* London, UK: Nicholas Brealey.

Sandoval, J. (2004). Conceptual change in consultee-centered consultation. In N. M. Lambert, I. Hylander, & J. H. Sandoval (Eds.), *Consultee-centered consultation: Improving the quality of professional services in schools and community organizations* (pp. 37–44). Mahwah, NJ: Erlbaum.

Schulte, A. C., & Osborne, S. S. (2003). When assumptive worlds collide: A review of definitions of collaboration and consultation. *Journal of Educational and Psychological Consultation, 14*(2), 109–138.

Sears, R., Rudisill, J., & Mason-Sears, C. (2006). *Consultation skills for mental health professionals.* Hoboken, NJ: Wiley.

Shosh, M. (1996). Counseling in business and industry. In W. J. Weikel & A. J. Palmo (Eds.), *Foundations of mental health counseling* (2nd ed., pp. 232–241). Springfield, IL: Thomas Books.

Slaikeuu, K. A. (1990). *Crisis intervention: A handbook for practice and research* (2nd ed.). Boston, MA: Allyn & Bacon.

Smith, D. (2000). *Women at work: Leadership for the next century.* Upper Saddle River, NJ: Prentice Hall.

Sperry, L. (2004). *Executive coaching: The essential guide for mental health professionals.* New York, NY: Brunner-Routledge.

Stockdale, J. S. (1996). *Sexual harassment in the workplace: Perspectives, frontiers, and response strategies.* Thousand Oaks, CA: Sage.

Stroebe, M. S., Hansson, R. O., Schut, H., & Stroebe, W. (Eds.). (2008). *Handbook of bereavement research and practice: Advances in theory and intervention.* Washington, DC: American Psychological Association.

U.S. Department of Health and Human Services, Office of Minority Health. (2001). *National standards for culturally and linguistically appropriate services in health care: Final report.* Washington, DC: Author.

Van Orden, K. A., Witte, T. K., Gordon, K. H., Bender, T. W., & Joiner, T. E. (2008). Suicidal desire and the capability for suicide: Tests of the interpersonal psychological theory of suicidal behavior among adults. *Journal of Consulting and Clinical Psychology, 76,* 72–83.

Weist, M. D., Myers, C. P., Hastings, E., Ghuman, H., & Han, Y. L. (1999). Psychological functioning of youth receiving mental health services in the schools versus community mental health centers. *Community Mental Health Journal, 35,* 69–81.

Consultation in Education (or School System) Settings

Introduction

School environments present myriad opportunities and challenges for consultation, from the diversity of classroom and school cultures to the varying problems, needs, and goals of a wide range of stakeholders. In one recent study, 80% of school counselors had consulted with school personnel (Perera-Diltz, Moe, & Mason, 2011). Consultation occurring in school settings, herein defined as school-based consultation, is recognized as an expedient and cost-efficient method (Dougherty, 2013) for fostering positive academic achievement (American School Counselor Association [ASCA], 2005) and emotional growth of students (Sheridan et al., 2009). This chapter is designed to review the paradigm of consulting in schools—a setting where a consultant's skills and knowledge will be routinely challenged by the unique cultural, ethical, and systemic dimensions within school settings. Guided Exercise 9.1 provides an opportunity to engage school-based constituents in a way that can enhance your content knowledge of school-based consultation services while gaining valuable insights from professionals in the field.

Guided Practice Exercises
Exercise 9.1: Evidence-Based Professional Interview

The school consultation literature offers a wealth of evidence based theories, interventions, and approaches. For the counselor-in-training, however, the amount of information can easily overwhelm. In other cases, assigned readings and assignments become tasks to be completed, resulting in a good grade (hopefully) but little if any knowledge has been internalized. To help address this discrepancy, complete the following:

1. *Set up an interview with a teacher at a local school. To prepare for the interview, read at least five evidence-based studies that address issues specific to that teacher's responsibilities (i.e., 5th-grade teacher, yearbook advisor, etc.).*

2. *Construct a minimum of five questions based directly on the articles you've read. You may, for example, design a question to better understand a teacher's personal experience in comparison to what is written in the literature. Be sure to consider teacher roles and responsibilities with and to students, parents, and administrators.*

3. *Write a three-page paper that synthesizes the information you've read with the information gathered from your interview.*

4. *During class, break into triads and discuss the three key points you took from your interview and how this information has caused you to alter (or has helped solidify) your perceptions consulting with teachers. Be prepared to support your position.*

Consultants working in and with school systems are often afforded quick access to those with direct authority over the lives of students (Gutkin, 2012), further highlighting the need for ethically and culturally competent consultants (American Counseling Association [ACA], 2005; ASCA, 2005). Helping fuel the increased need for and interest in school consultation and collaboration are societal ills (Meyers, Meyers, & Grogg, 2004), increased school accountability and reform (Adelman & Taylor, 2007), and educational testing (Braden & Tayrose, 2008; Kanel, 2007). Oftentimes, school-based consultants will find themselves working alongside medical and allied health professionals (Steen & Noguera, 2010; Truscott, & Albritton, 2007) or as a link between the schools and community (Portman, 2009). Thus, it is easy to see why schools are viewed as "microcosms of community life" (Dougherty, 2013, p. 268) and a setting with considerable consultation possibilities.

Before you read on, remember that schools multi-dimensional and interrelated to some degree. That is, they are systemic in nature. Thus, we strongly encourage anyone interested in school-based consultation to use every available opportunity to experience classroom environments that address the needs of mainstream students as well as those placed in special needs and gifted program classrooms (Knotek, Kovac, & Bostwick, 2011). Additional suggestions are to attend in-service days and parent–teacher conferences, read each school's policy and procedure manuals, and consider each potential consultee's experience from an individual and systemic perspective. By doing so, all school consultation interventions become grounded in the reality of the school as a dynamic and diverse setting (think ecological and systemic models).

LEARNING OBJECTIVES

At the end of this chapter, you will be able to

- Identify and distinguish between distinct approaches to school-based consultation and collaboration
- Identify potential roles of key stakeholders in school-based consultation and collaboration
- Identify key considerations when working with teachers, school administrators, school systems, parents, and outside advocates of the school (i.e., donors)
- Recognize and offer ethical interventions in response to multicultural variables that could influence the choices made by school-based consultants
- Critically examine school-based consultation scenarios using guided exercises

Historical Background

School-based consultation traces its origins back nearly a century (Merrell, Ervin, & Gimpel, 2006). Early iterations of present day school-based consultation, such as interventions targeting the learning and mental health of school-age children are consistent with the work of school psychologists in the 1920s (Bramlett & Murphy, 1998). Not until the 1950s and 1960s, however, did consultation gain widespread recognition within the schools. Key contributors to this shift included federal legislation such as the 1954 Thayer Conference (Dougherty, 2013) and influential reports by professional counseling organizations such as the report by the Joint Committee on The Elementary School Counselor (Joint Committee, 1966). Credit is also given to Harold F. Cottingham's (1956) view that school-based counselors as consultants have systemic value and Verne Faust's (1968) attention to parental influence on the school success of children. In the latter view, Faust emphasizes the importance of consultants working directly with teachers and parents to address issues ranging from student behavior to academic concerns.

The 1970s witnessed an increased attention to group consultation efforts such as in-service teacher training programs (Dinkmeyer & Caldwell, 1970; Fullmer & Bernard, 1972) and federal laws advancing school consultation with special needs students (e.g., Public Law 94-142, Education of All Handicapped Children Act). Dinkmeyer and Carlson (1973) helped further this position with their view of school-based consultants as having the power to effect positive change within the school environment. Despite concerns about inadequate training, collaboration continues to gain acceptance as a distinct form of service delivery in school settings (Newman, 2010). What is not disputed is the view of school-based consultation as a valuable and essential form of service delivery in the schools.

Increased academic and testing standards, such as those associated with the No Child Left Behind Act (NCLB), have also changed the academic landscape (Adelman & Taylor, 2007). School counselors are increasingly assigned the role of test administrator, a position in direct conflict with the responsibilities of a professional school counselor (ASCA, 2005). This is especially disconcerting given the evidence that while nearly 20% of American youth experience mental health concerns, only one quarter of those needing professional care receive it (Greenberg et al., 2003). School personnel must also provide accommodations that comply with the Individuals with Disabilities Education Act (IDEA; Pub. L. 108-446, 2004). As such, school-based consultants must be knowledgeable and responsive to problems associated with IDEA. For instance, a school-based consultant should possess, at a minimum, an understanding of the distinctions and similarities between visible and invisible disabilities and the potential problems, barriers, and solutions associated with each. School personnel, while certainly aware of the complex and multilayered needs of students, are increasingly called upon to implement services that stretch school personnel and constrain already limited budgets.

From individual student issues to system-wide problems, school settings present school-based consultants with a litany of issues and problems. All attempts by school-based consultants to address these dynamic and multidimensional problems requires general content knowledge about schools, and a willingness and ability to learn about and embrace the nuances of each school's culture in order to understand the problem within the context of the system in which it exists. In short, consultants must be knowledgeable about, and able to respond to, a dynamic set of individual and systemic issues, circumstances, and stakeholders.

School-Based Consultation and Collaboration

The academic success of students and school personnel unites the school-based consultation and collaboration perspectives, yet disagreements remain as to the exact distinctions between consultation and collaboration in the schools (Kurpius & Fuqua, 1993). One position holds that consultation and collaboration have distinct goals, roles, and assumptions. For example, Duane Brown, Walter B. Pryzwansky, and Ann C. Schulte (2011) posit that while a school-based consultant works in conjunction with the consultee, the responsibility for action lies with the teacher (i.e., consultee). With the collaborative approach, the consultant and consultee have joint responsibility for successful outcomes throughout the process. Alternatively, Richard D. Parsons and Wallace J. Kahn (2005) view collaboration as a widely applicable "style" of consultation (p. 32). Here, collaboration falls on a continuum from least collaborative, defined as *provisional service,* to the style known as *coordinate service* where the consultant and consultee maintain an egalitarian relationship. The goal with the coordinate service style is sharing diagnostic observations and coequally owning and developing intervention strategies. In both cases, though, barriers to successful consultation, exist including limited-time parameters (Gutkin & Curtis, 1999) and disinterested or philosophically opposed school administrators (Gutkin & Bossard, 1984). These events, while predictable to some degree, require consultants to have the skills and knowledge to assess and select the most suitable approach for addressing the issues at hand.

Consultation With Teachers

High academic standards are central to educators and comprise just one reason that teacher consultation and collaboration continues to gain prominence. The appeal of teacher consultation is rooted in its ability to address current and future issues (Cook & Friend, 2010; Dahir & Stone, 2012). In other words, teacher consultation can address a multitude of behavioral, academic, social, and emotional and psychological issues (Tysinger, Tysinger, & Diamanduros, 2009) occurring within school settings that may, for example, frustrate classroom efficiency (Hughes, 2000; Pohlman, Hoffman, Dodds, & Pryzwansky, 1998). Additional positive indicators include the self-efficacy of the teacher (Stenger, Tollefson, & Fine, 1992), location of the consultant, and proactive delivery of consultation services (Brown et al., 2011). On-going technological advances also hold potential benefits for consultation with teachers and within the schools (Dahir & Stone, 2012; Roach, Kratochwill, & Frank, 2009).

Obstacles to positive teacher consultation outcomes also exist. Consultee expectations can be potential obstacles to successful teacher consultation (Tysinger et al., 2009). Here again, we call attention to the critical consultant–teacher alliance (see Chapter 2) teacher perceptions of the consultant could inhibit or promote positive outcomes (Brown et al., 2011). Other examples include the need to ensure teachers are oriented to the theoretical base of consultation and trained to implement recommended interventions (Hershfeldt, Pell, Sechrest, Pas, & Bradshaw, 2012; Sterling-Turner, Watson, & Moore, 2002). To that end, Francis E. Lentz, Sarah J. Allen, and Kristal E. Ehrhardt (1996) suggested creating a template of change agents (i.e., students, teachers, peers, parents) and intervention types. For example, a teacher using a contingency-based intervention may use positive reinforcement in response to a positive student behavior, while an antecedent-based approach may choose assertiveness training as an intervention as a preventative measure against future inappropriate classroom behavior. Additional limitations could include disparate professional orientations between teacher and consultation time concerns (Johnson, Pugach, & Hammitte, 1988), and availability of administrative support (Gutkin & Bossard, 1984).

Another factor in teacher consultation involves selecting the most appropriate type of service delivery. This aspect differs from previous examples of consultation. Whereas the consultation approach would normally hold the teacher (i.e., consultee) responsible for implementing recommended interventions (and the resulting outcomes), teacher consultation allows the consultant and teacher to coordinate their efforts and assume mutual responsibility for outcomes. This form of service delivery is particularly well-received by those in special education (Cramer, 1998; Trolley, Haas, & Patti, 2009). School-based consultants should remain aware that school-based consultation involving students with special needs will almost assuredly involve a multidisciplinary team approach to address the care and comfort of a special needs student (Dougherty, 2013). For example, a consultant asked to collaborate with a teacher about an anxious student with autism may find himself or herself in the company of a treatment team featuring a teacher, family member, school counselor, school-based mental health counselor, and possibly even the principal. The fact remains that no matter the circumstances, teacher consultation requires flexibility, cultural competence, and the willingness to work in tandem with the teacher or a multidisciplinary treatment team.

Guided Practice Exercises
Exercise 9.2: Consultation With Teachers

Amy is a fifth-grader whose behavior in class has escalated within the two weeks from intermittent inappropriate curse words to the more recent direct verbal abuse aimed at her classmates and the teacher. According to her teacher, all attempts at discipline have been rebuffed. Amy is known to the school as a student of high intelligence and is placed in the gifted classroom. Prior to this two week period, there have not been behavior concerns. Amy was referred to the counselor and has complied with each of the four sessions scheduled with her school counselor.

According to the school counselor, Amy's responses were "surface oriented" and she denied her behavior was disruptive. She did note, however, that kids were "teasing" her because she was adopted. After the four appointments with the school counselor, Amy stated she didn't see why she had to keep coming here and did not view her behavior as disruptive. At this time, the school counselor contacted the teacher and suggested they take on a teacher–consultant relationship to see if they could address Amy's behavioral issues in a different manner. The teacher agreed due to his worry over Amy's falling grades.

Because the only identifiable concern made by Amy was her frustration with being teased about being adopted, the focus of consultation centered on helping Amy address her classmates and teachers in an appropriate manner while learning to respond assertively to teasing or bullying by her classmates. After discussing how to approach the situation, the teacher and consultant decided on an approach based in social reinforcement. Here, the teacher's role would be to provide positive verbal and social reinforcement when she heard or saw Amy interact with or speak respectfully to classmates. His responsibility also extended to reinforcing the classroom and school rule against bullying and teasing. The school counselor's role was to visit (starting with Amy's class) each of the three fifth-grade classrooms and provide a guided exercise on bullying prevention. Over the course of the week, the teacher and school counselor–consultant would take notes on Amy's behavior, dialogue on her progress, and process their respective roles in trying to help Amy address her recent behavioral problems.

One week later, after the consultant's classroom activity and intermittent reinforcement from the teacher, Amy's aggressive verbal behavior toward her classmates and her teacher dissipated and her concentration on her studies returned to normal. While she still expressed frustration about being "teased" she stated that she "gets" that she can't use " bad language" and shouldn't yell at her classmates and teacher.

This positive outcome is helped by several factors. For instance, the teacher and consultant took a proactive stance on working together to address Amy's behavior. This is indicative also of a quality alliance and the fact that the consultant is able to quickly engage the teacher in a shared intervention that targets Amy but can be generalized to her classmates. Finally, Amy's status as an academically gifted student does not shield her from (and in certain cases may lead to) being bullied or reacting negatively to it. In short, school-based consultants must be able and willing to address issues such as bullying in different contexts (i.e., verbal, physical, social media) in a developmentally appropriate manner.

Consultation With School Administrators

The use of consultation and collaboration in the schools can expand services to students exponentially. This does, of course, require the approval and support of school administrators. Research suggests, for example, that change in the schools is largely contingent on the level of support (or lack thereof) of school administrators (Bryan & Griffin, 2010; Knotek, 2012). This lends empirical support to what we would argue is the rather intuitive notion that school-based consultants should be prepared to work with all types of administrators. Of course, this requirement will undoubtedly be complicated by the role, responsibilities, and nuances of the administration's personnel, philosophy, and culture (for starters!). It is encouraging to note that research does indicate increasing support for school consultation among administrators (Dahir & Stone, 2012). Examples of situations for which school administrators may seek out consultants include issues pertaining to specific programming (Jacob & Hartshorne, 2003), school violence and crises, school reform (Colbert, Vernon-Jones, & Pransky, 2006), diversity (Pena, 1996; Sander, Sharkey, Olivarri, Tanigawa, & Mauseth, 2010), testing, and problematic behaviors (Luiselli, 2002). School-based consultants should also be sensitive to the need for systemwide (i.e., schoolwide) programming and services (Adelman & Taylor, 2007; Anderson-Butcher et al., 2010). It should also be noted that school administrators are generally accomplished multitaskers and, as such, consultants should be prepared to be creative as to how and when they engage them. Several strategies have been suggested for assisting those who wish to engage school administrators (Bahr & Kovaleski, 2006; Curtis & Stollar, 2002; Rafoth & Foriska, 2006; Rotheram-Borus, Bickford & Milburn, 2001):

- Be clear on how the program is introduced
- Be knowledgeable about resource allocation
- Consider stakeholder relationships
- Attend to impact of evidence-based research on program(s)
- Assimilate primary prevention programs into schools
- Consider schoolwide programming goals
- Be open to suggestions for collaboration with external consultants

Guided Practice Exercises
Exercise 9.3: An Example of Administrative Consultation

You are a respected former school counselor with over 20 years of services to your local school and community as a middle school counselor. Your current position is clinical supervisor of a local mental health agency. As a member of the local mental health community, you have been generally aware that the smaller district in a neighboring city has experienced a notable decline in the number of middle school students the last 5 years. On a Friday morning, the principal from this poorly performing middle school calls and requests that you come to her school and consult with her about this continuing trend and you agree to do so. What led you to accept the offer to consult with the principal was her statement to you over the phone. In essence, this is what she said:

Ms. X, I would like to request that you be hired as an outside consultant at my school. I'm not sure how that works, but I know I need some help. As a former school counselor and now mental health clinician, I know you are at least minimally aware of the difficulties our town has faced recently with the closing of the textile mills and subsequent unemployment. Since I've seen you at professional meetings, I know you are also aware of the alarming trend in our drop-out rate after the eighth grade. I don't want to let that past disagreement get in the way of drawing on your experience and skills. I know my teachers are as distressed as I am about this situation, yet the attitude and general mood of my school has become very distrustful of me and my leadership team—a trend I wish to address and stop immediately because it's negatively impacting every level of employee and student we have at the school. I've recently even had parents contact me about comments their children are making about the bad attitude of teachers. However, I have tried several in-service activities and that only seems to make matters worse. As a long-time educator and now school counselor, I was hoping you would take on this consultation opportunity with us and see if you can assist me in understanding what is happening and change course.

Discussion Questions

Based on that short scenario only, respond to the following questions:

1. *Based only on the information provided, who do you initially perceive is the consultee?*

2. *What type of consultation framework do you believe is best suited for this scenario given who contacted you and the issues that were described (i.e., school based consultation/collaboration; a mental health consultation/collaboration approach)?*

3. *What do you perceive to be the issues in this scenario?*

4. *Identify the stakeholders you feel are central to changing the current negative culture at the school.*

5. *What will be required of the consultee(s) once identified? What will be the responsibilities of the consultant?*

6. *Describe this scenario from a system's perspective and provide three examples of how the breakdown in morale has impacted the school system as a whole.*

7. *Based on the type of consultation you use, provide two reasonable, evidence-based interventions you feel may be warranted if, upon assessing the situation first hand, you perceive the situation to be as described by the principal.*

8. *Based on the information provided, what benefits and challenges might there be in terms of establishing a strong consultation alliance? Be sure to address all three dimensions of the alliance as you support your response.*

Consultation With Parents

It is well known that family plays a critical role in the academic, social, and behavioral elements of a child's life (Carlson & Trapani, 2006; Riley, 1996). Consultation scholars also recognized the potential positive impact of consulting with parents (Sheridan, 1993). More recent consultation research indicates that creating and maintaining successful working relationships between parents and schools is bolstered when a consultation holds a more inclusive view of different family structures (Dahir & Stone, 2012; Finello, 2011; Miller & Kraft, 2008). Specifically, parental consultation aims to increase parental understanding of how to best facilitate the child's development and help mitigate the child's emotional distress and behavior problems in school settings (Guli, 2005). When successful, parental consultation has been shown to moderate in-school behaviors and emotion problems (Golden & Cook, 2010) and increase parental engagement in school and family functioning (Muro & Kottman, 1995; Sheridan, 1993). Despite these successes, consultation with parents can be a disappointing experience, particularly when parents do not engage or drop out of services (Downing & Downing, 1991).

Conceptually, parental consultation is influenced mainly by social learning theory (Bandura, 1977, 1978, 1986), mental health consultation (Caplan, 1970), and systems theory (Bateson, 1972; Capra, 1982). A more recent addition to the conceptual framework of parental consultation has been the application of an ecological perspective. Among the most popular parent consultation models to date, and one that also assumes an ecological approach, is Conjoint Behavioral Consultation (CBC; Sheridan & Kratochwill, 2008; see Chapter 5). Of particular value is the CBC model's insistence on establishing positive, collaborative relationships between the consultant and family within the context of the school setting. This is done to help clarify and address student problems and, hopefully, stimulate student growth and achievement. Overall, school-based consultants generally use case consultation to address, identify, and resolve student problems with parents.

Consultants must also consider that many parents may respond more positively to the collaboration model's vision of shared responsibility and egalitarian relationships (Finello, 2011). In these situations, consultants should take care to ensure that each step of the process remains a joint effort with the parent(s). Moreover, the increasing prominence of home-schooling, a paradigm bolstered by federal legislation intended to benefit parents who have children with disabilities (Cook & Friend, 2010), offers potential benefits and challenges to utilizing parental collaboration. For instance, while home–school collaboration involves efforts to build strong alliances with parents in order to engage them in efforts to enhance their child's academic achievement (Raines & Dibble, 2011), limited parental engagement often obstructs progress (Manz, Mautone, & Martin, 2009). To combat this problem, researchers (Bryan & Griffin, 2010) and professional organizations (ASCA, 2013) emphasize the importance of school based mental health professionals developing positive parent–school alliances. It seems reasonable that school-based consultants could also benefit from this approach. Following this preventative approach would help consultants engage parents in a joint effort where the opinions of all participants are solicited, respected, and used in determining a positive path forward for the child's academic success and the health of the family system as a whole (Esler, Godber, & Christenson, 2008).

Alternative approaches to consulting with parents include parent education and training. Parent education is knowledge focused and generally seeks to improve parenting, improve communication skills, and enhance parental sensitivities to their child's developmental needs. The goal of parent education is to lead parents toward more creative and developmentally appropriate strategies for increasing positive interactions with their children (Hoard & Shepard, 2005). Parent education interventions are ultimately designed to address a specific strategy or skill that will increase the chances their children will fare better in their academic lives (Sheridan et al., 1996). For example, the consultant can provide a seminar for parents who use aggressive language with their children. In the seminar, consultants could provide assertiveness training in order to provide the parent(s) with a more productive way of communicating with their child.

The second approach, parent training, suggests that parents can be taught outside the didactic approach favored in the parent education model. Three distinct types of parent training approaches have been identified (Kramer, 1990). These include a Rogerian-based approach termed *parent effectiveness training*, (Gordon, 1970), the Adlerian approach (Carlson et al., 2006), and behavioral approaches based on Bandura's writings on social learning (Becker, 1971). Empirical support demonstrating the fidelity of parent training approaches remains in the early stages (Hoard & Shepard, 2005). Regardless of the format (consultation, collaboration), theoretical approach, or method (i.e., home–school collaboration, parent case consultation, parent education), school-based consultations should recognize the systemic, multicultural, and dynamic nature of any parental consultation endeavor and be intentional in its selection and application.

School-Based Mental Health Consultation

In our introduction we noted the impact of societal, curriculum, and testing advancements (Adelman & Taylor, 2007; Braden & Tayrose, 2008; Greenberg et al., 2003;

Gutkin, 2009) on the school counselor's ability to address the increasing mental health needs of our nation's youth. One increasingly popular method of providing mental health services within the school setting is the school-based mental health model, herein defined as *school-based counseling*. Originating in the 1970s (Armbruster, 2002), school-based counseling programs were designed to address the increasingly unmet mental health and behavioral issues of school-age children and adolescents (Catron & Weiss, 1994; Leaf et al., 1996). Allowing licensed mental health professionals to counsel students in school settings allows school administrators the opportunity to address badly needed mental health services for their students while allowing them to refocus their attention on their mandated academic roles and responsibilities (DuPaul, 2007).

School-based counselors are well situated to take on the role of a school-based mental health consultant. For example, they are likely to hold licensure as a professional counselor and, as such, will possess a knowledge base, skill set, and experiences specific to this distinctive type of mental health service delivery. Further, school-based counselors who elect to consult are likely to be well versed regarding various environmental and cultural dimensions that are unique to their schools. Examples may include an increased awareness of cultural dimensions related to school functions, insights into school functions insights into strategies for accessing teachers and administrators, and/or insights into when and how best to be "heard" by faculty and administrators (i.e., faculty meetings). Finally, it should be remembered that although the development and maintenance of positive alliances with all levels of school personnel requires patience, flexibility, and initiative (Adelman & Taylor, 1998), school-based counselors also routinely interact with their client (the student), parents, and families. Therefore, school-based mental health consultants must retain a systemic perspective of their work in the schools.

From a conceptual and operational perspective, school-based counseling programs are, in effect, an illustration of a collaboration model between mental health agencies and school systems (Weist, 2005). Within the school-based counseling movement exist two distinct formats, the school-based health clinic (SBHC) and independent school-based mental health program model (ISBMHP). Employees of an SBHC may be hired by the school or be contracted with an outside agency. Service delivery is based within the school setting and includes preventative and early intervention general and mental health care services (Armbruster, 2002). Funding sources often include a combination of school, local, state, and federal entities (Armbruster, 2002; Hoganbruen, Clauss-Ehlers, Nelson, & Faenza, 2003). The alternative ISBMHP model contracts with community-based mental health agencies to provide counseling for students (Paternite, 2005). Clearly benefits and challenges exist with each model, yet school-based counselors themselves are, in many ways, ideally positioned to transition their knowledge, skills, and experiences within the school setting into a consultation or collaborative role with school administrators, teachers, and parents. Our review of the school-based counseling literature, however, suggests that the notion of a school-based counselor as consultant is a largely untapped form of service delivery for counselors interested in consultation as a method of mental health service delivery.

Today, school-based counseling remains a growing specialization area within the mental health paradigm (Weist, 2005). Thus, it seems clear to us that school-based consultants, particularly those able to blend clinical mental health and school counseling experiences, knowledge, and skills, are uniquely qualified to provid consultation on clinical and perhaps (depending on background) administrative problems that arise. At this stage, we would encourage those interested in this type of consultation service to become well versed in the mental health consultation approaches (especially consultee-centered case consultation & consultee-centered administrative consultation) while remaining attuned to the inherent cultural, ethical, and systemic elements of any school-based interaction. Guided Exercise 9.3 helps to illustrate this type of consultation scenario.

Guided Practice Exercises
Exercise 9.4: School-Based Mental Health Consultation

You are a licensed professional counselor and school-based counselor at a local elementary school in your home community. Your employer, Blue Mountain Mental Health, Inc., has placed you, at your request, at a school with over 90% of students receiving free or reduced lunch. Soon after you arrived for work, a teacher mentioned that a 14-year-old male student had just presented at school with clear evidence that he has not taken his ADHD medicine for at least one day. That day, you heard several other teachers mention their concerns and feelings of helplessness having to deal with him once again given his anxious behavior and inattentiveness that derails class dialogue. One teacher even commented, "I know it's terrible, but it's impacting several of the kids in my class because they're friends—but it's really important. I'm trying to prepare them for the upcoming state testing and he's getting in the way no matter what I try!" Even the school counselor expressed "fatigue" and lamented that he is barely able to get to each classroom for his guidance lessons more than once every two months, much less try and keep track of the wellness of each individual student—especially given "my orders to be the testing supervisor again."

Now, break into triads in class.

One individual will play the role of a school-based counselor brought on to create and implement a full day in-service program on recognizing and addressing suspected or known cases of ADHD in the school. A second will play the role of the school's principal who is the person who contacted you to provide the in-service. The third individual is in the role of the parent of a 13-year-old female student with ADHD and is now a children's advocate for the local children's shelter. Together, you are to use the consultation literature to create a 20-minute role play for the following class period that is intended to foster a better awareness of the possible signs and symptoms of abuse as well as one's roles in cases of suspected and/or substantiated cases of abuse or neglect. Considerations may include but are not limited to the following:

1. *Who is the consultee in this scenario?*

2. *What type of service should the consultant utilize? Describe how you arrived at this decision.*

3. *Should parents or any other vital stakeholder in student wellness and achievement be targeted for services? Why or why not?*

   - *Would an individual or group–team consultation approach be more efficient or effective?*

   - *Why or why not? If yes, what would be the makeup of the group (i.e., students/ parents/teachers/administrators)?*

4. *What diversity and ethical issues are evident or implied in this scenario?*

5. *What would a reasonable and competent counselor as consultant consider as positive outcomes for a project of this type?*

6. *Is a school-based mental health counselor (i.e., someone from outside the school setting- albeit working primarily in the school) the best option as a consultant or would a consultant with direct knowledge of the school system (i.e., school counselor) be more appropriate (and perhaps effective)? Support your answer.*

Instruction-Based Consultation

Instructional consultation (IC) was conceived as an early intervention model that uses evidence-driven concepts and interventions to increase quality classroom learning environments (Rosenfield, 2008). In other words, consultants work with teachers or groups to clarify and reduce obstructions to optimal classroom learning environments. Initial versions of the IC model drew comparisons with behavioral consultation (Rosenfield 2002), although its bilateral attention to process and content has led to comparisons with the consultee-centered consultation approach. Still, the quality of the relationship remains a core value of the model no matter if the consultant chooses the role of a collaborator, educational trainer, advocate, detective, observer, or data collector (Dougherty, 2009). Because IC interventions often challenge consultees to revamp their teaching in style and substance, heavy emphasis is placed on the relationship components of trust and sharing.

In its original, individual-based form, the IC model's procedure involved (a) creation of a collaborative relationship, (b) problem identification, (c) classroom observation of the defined problem, (d) assessment of curriculum, (e) planning of new curriculum, and (f) termination. However, the reinterpretation of the IC model from the ecological- and team-approach perspectives (Gravois, Groff, & Rosenfield, 2009) has resulted in a model with a more distinctive social constructivist, systems-oriented flair. This reorientation also seeks to move the teacher from a student learning-deficit perspective to a strength-based focus (Rosenfield, 1987). For example, consultants can use dialogue as a means of helping the consultee generate new ideas and solutions that will improve teaching methods and classroom environment. This is also consistent with the social constructivist influenced consultee-centered consultation approach (Knotek, Rosenfield, Gravois, & Babinski, 2003). Overall, the IC team approach redefines how consultants and consultees work in tandem to conceptualize student learning problems, facilitate meaningful dialogue, and work together to redesign interventions that promote optimal classroom efficiency. Along with the student's academic achievement, successful IC outcomes can help promote a collaborative, strength-based, problem-solving focus among all constituencies within the school.

It is also important to be aware of the recent trends associated with the IC model. Of particular interest is the model's reformulation to one more consistent with consultee-centered consultation. Other trends involve the recognition of the need for, and inclusion of, evidence-based assessments like the curriculum-based assessment (CBA; Burns, 2004; Wizda, 2004) model. For instance, in contrast to the model's original belief that problems were based solely on student learning deficits, the CBA model can provide a systematic analysis of "the instructional needs of a student"(Dougherty, 2009, p. 275) and creation of instructional methods that can optimize a student's academic successes. Additionally, the CBA model is used throughout the consulting process to highlight the need for changing current intervention(s) in order to optimize student academic achievement (Gravois

& Gickling, 2002). Another trend is the use of language to facilitate successful outcomes (Rosenfield, 2004). In this case, consultants may need to equip consultees (teachers) with language consistent with the transition from the deficit-model underpinnings of the early IC format to language more closely aligned with a strength based approach along with the consultee-centered model's social constructivist's paradigm. Finally, consultants must help consultees be cognizant of the IC model's ability to help them (Ingraham, 2008) adapt to changing societal and school demographics. One example is the use of school interpreters to help non-native English speaking students and families. Absent this perspective, the consultee–teacher may struggle to adapt to the notion of creating, applying, and maintaining new instructional narratives.

Response to Intervention

Response to intervention (RTI) arose out of the Individuals with Disabilities Education Improvement Act (IDEIA). In short, RTI is a problem-solving framework that utilizes multilevel assessments to gather evidence of behavioral, academic, social, or emotional problems with students (Forman & Selman, 2011). Based on the assessment information, evidence-based interventions target issues at the individual and systemic levels (Schellenberg & Grothaus, 2011) with an overall goal of facilitating healthy and productive learning environments and maximizing student outcomes. Evidence-based interventions include three tiers (Sanetti & Kratochwill, 2009). Tier 1 interventions address the student body as a whole. Tier 2 interventions focus on at-risk students, while Tier 3 interventions are directed at students in need of more intense services (Sulkowski, Wingfield, Jones, & Coulter, 2011).

Consultants interested in RTI should also be cognizant of its criticisms (Li & Vazquez-Nuttall, 2009), including concerns about its "culturally sensitive appropriateness and quality of interventions for some populations" (Dougherty, 2013, p. 295). In short, school-based consultants need to remain vigilant about RTI as it gains recognition among consultants. At this point in its development, it is possible to draw parallels between RTI and consultation and collaboration. The points listed below are based on Dougherty's (2013) recent review of the RTI literature (Erchul, 2011; Gruman & Hoelzen, 2011; Kratochwill, 2008; Ryan, Kaffenberger, & Carroll, 2011). We have drawn on this review to highlight similarities and differences. These include the following:

- Consultation and RTI focus on problem solving; however, the focus of consultation is the teacher–consultee, while RTI focuses on the student.
- Consultation and RTI are both preventative and use evidence based interventions.
- Consultation can be internal or external, while RTI is set within the school.
- RTI is often team oriented; consultation is less team oriented.
- Consultation is voluntary; RTI participation may be mandatory.
- Consultation can be more general in nature than RTI.

Systems-Focused Consultation

There should be little doubt at this point of the need for consultants to be knowledgeable about the systemic paradigm. For example, interventions targeting individual students could be fundamentally shortsighted given that multiple systems (see Figure 8.1) could impact their academic attainment. To date, researchers One positive effect of this view is that it increases the potential that view schools systemically and, as a result, as a valuable tool for assessing (Adelman & Taylor, 2007) and conceptualizing the issues and needs of individuals and organizations. The potential they will be viewed as disparate elements to the health of students, parents, school personel, and school systems are considered together. In other words, as a whole. The systems approach to consultation provides consultants with a holistic perspective that considers and organizational change (Reschly & Christenson, 2012), multicultural and social justice issues (Tomes, 2011; Williams & Greenleaf, 2012), and their own skill development (Forman & Selman, 2011) together instead of as disparate elements.

While counselors receive training in systems theory during their graduate program, school-based consultants can easily over- or underidentify with a specific aspect or individual within a system and, in doing so, foreclose on an intervention without full consideration of it's the potential implications on the school or the student's family system. Conceptually at least, systems-based consultation guards against this type of error. Still, the use of a systems-based consultation approach implies the consultant possesses the ability and skills to accurately conceptualize the interactions of multiple interconnected individuals and systems—and the ability to engage all potential stakeholders to ensure that appropriate intervention(s) are identified and properly implemented.

Group Consultation

Time constraints are a common complaint for those working in school settings. One way to increase efficiency while increasing service options is to provide group consultation. Several popular methods of group consultation are discussed briefly below. As a rule, though, consultants interested in utilizing group consultation methods must have competencies in group development dynamics, ethics and legal issues, and multicultural issues.

Issue groups are designed to focus on a single or limited number of topics. Conceptually, issue groups are designed to offer a group of professionals (i.e., teachers) from similar environments or programs (i.e., 4th-grade teacher, resource instructor) the opportunity to safely discuss topical concerns related to the school setting. Consultants function as the group leader and are responsible for introducing relevant topics, discussion questions, and ideas; facilitating dialogue; and transitioning among and between topics (Cohen & Osterweil, 1986).

Peer consultation centers on the idea that a group of similarly trained professionals will be able to problem solve together. Topics can be specific or broad, individual or systemic, with group efforts paying dividends through increased engagement of group members. Maureen C. Pugach and Lawrence J. Johnson (1988) suggested that such engagement is especially pertinent in that it can help similarly oriented professionals engage in a shared activity and experience together the development, implementation, and success of a specific action or goal.

Task groups, predictably, have a clear directive on what aspect of the student is to be addressed and resolved. Task groups also follow the known group stages of development, so consultants must have competencies in group development, dynamics, and ethics. Another type, *C groups*, were developed to create a more personal connection between teachers (Dinkmeyer & Carlson, 1973), with the goal of utilizing these relationships for creating safe environments where strong relationships that would facilitate personal and professional growth and change. Within these groups lie interpersonal exchanges that promote self-assessment aimed at reframing problem situations and seeking solutions on one's own and with help from the group as needed. Such insights are often in response to positive levels of group cohesiveness. In a nutshell, Don C. Dinkmeyer and Jon Carlson envision this as a group of teachers engaged in a joint effort to identify and resolve a common concern.

A final group type, the *case-centered group*, often includes case presentations in a group setting with colleagues. As any counselor-in-training intern can attest to, there are advantages and disadvantages to this method. Advantages include opportunities for increasing one's knowledge base, improved case conceptualization, and improved communication with your colleagues (Cohen & Osterweil, 1986). Conversely, disadvantages may include increased anxiety, group conflicts, and the tendency for consultees to have discussions about their case derailed or diminished by one or more group members. Another main concern is that the group will begin addressing the personal issues of the attendees instead of focusing on the cases being discussed. As with other forms of consultation and collaboration, though, specific skills, competencies, and content knowledge are expected. In the case of group consultation formats, this fact is punctuated by the consultation having competencies in group work.

Multicultural Considerations

School-based consultation formats place consultants in contact with individuals, families (Sheridan, 2000), groups, and schools (and school employees), each of which holds a nearly limitless potential combination of cultural variables that could influence outcomes (Dahir & Stone, 2012; Ramirez & Smith, 2007). Equally important is recognizing within and between group diversity (Ramirez & Smith, 2007) and, when using a postmodern theory, remembering the shift from objective to subjective realities. If not, even the most obvious cultural dimension could be overlooked or diminished. Gerri S. Moseley-Howard (1995), for instance, suggested that understanding the impact of culture on a child's educational success and behaviors, as well as parental and family dynamics (Brown, 1997; Minke, 2006; Steen & Noguera, 2010) requires:

- being cognizant of systemic influences on the child,
- assessing the child's environment and acculturation level,
- being sensitive to positive dimensions and dynamics of a consultee's (or their family/school's) culture,
- maintaining focus on developmental and cognitive qualities of the consultee(s), and
- being mindful of cultural factors that could impact assessment and interventions.

There remain numerous useful tips for developing and maintaining multicultural competence in (and outside) schools. Lee (1995), for example, argues that consultants should be aware of the following six factors influencing race and ethnicity:

- The consultee's view of kinship
- Roles and status
- Sex-role socialization
- Language
- Religion and spirituality
- Ethnic identity

In the literature on consulting with parents, Julia Bryan and Cheryl Holcomb-McCoy (2010) suggest consultants maintain sensitivity to historical and current societal issues that could impact the consultation alliance and process. Examples here include

- consultee power differentials,
- the expert role,
- validation of shared efforts between consultant–consultee,
- help for parents to explore their cultural history, and
- use of strength-based dialogue and interventions to promote parental competence.

And as a final illustration of how consultant–consultee communication could influence the alliance and process of consultation, Carter (1991) argues that culturally competent consultants must consider

- the consultation hierarchy,
- the identity of the consultee(s) and stakeholders,
- basic communication and listening skills, and
- consultee autonomy and right of refusal.

You will no doubt find some value in all the factors cited. In the end, it is up to the individual to cultivate and nourish their own "cross-cultural consultation style" (Brown et al., 2011, p. 136). To do so, we encourage the reader to stay abreast of current consultation literature, diversify personal and professional experiences, and engage in active and on-going self-reflection as a means of developing and nurturing a professional identity anchored in multicultural competence.

Chapter Keystones

- The methods of consultation in schools are varied, yet all remain aimed at optimizing the academic and personal development and success of students.
- Consulting in the schools can accommodate different paradigms, including mental health approaches, systemic and ecological approaches, as well as those that focus on facilitating student success by consulting individually and in conjunction with parents, teachers, school administrators, interdisciplinary and agency individuals and organizations.
- Consultation and collaboration in the schools require sensitivity and attention to diversity, time constraints of school personnel, school climate and environment, and the range of family structures, rules, dynamics.
- School based consultants must work hard to develop and nurture positive interdisciplinary and interagency relationships.

Web-Based and Literature-Based Resources

Websites

American School Counselor Association: http://www.schoolcounselor.org
American School Counselor Association National Model: http://www.ascanationalmodel.org
National Association of School Psychologists: http://www.nasponline.org

Suggested Readings

Gysbers, N. C., & Henderson, P. (2012). *Developing & managing your school guidance & counseling program* (5th ed.). Alexandria, VA: American Counseling Association.
Meyers, A. B., Meyers, J., Graybill, E. C., Proctor, S. L., & Huddleston, L. (2012). Ecological approaches to organizational consultation and systems change in educational settings. *Journal of Educational & Psychological Consultation, 22*(1–2), 106–124. doi:10.1080/10474412.2011.649649
Sandoval, J. (2013). *Crisis counseling, intervention and prevention in the schools.* New York, NY: Routledge.

References

Adelman, H. S., & Taylor, L. (1998). Reframing mental health in schools and expanding school reform. *Educational Psychologist, 33*(4), 135–152.
Adelman, H. S., & Taylor, L. (2007). Systemic change for school improvement. *Journal of Educational and Psychological Consultation, 17,* 55–77.
Albert, L. (1996). *Coping with kids* (2nd ed.). Circle Pines, MN: American Guidance.
Allen, K. (2011). Introduction to the special issue: Cognitive behavioral therapy in the school setting. *Psychology in the Schools, 48*(3), 215–222.
American Counseling Association. (2005). *ACA code of ethics.* Alexandria, VA: Author. American School Counselor Association (2005). *ASCA national model: A framework for comprehensive school programs* (2nd ed.). Alexandria, VA: Author.
Anderson-Butcher, D., Lawson, H. A., Iachini, A., Bean, J., Flaspohler, P. D., & Zullig, K. (2010). Capacity-related innovations resulting from the implementation of a community collaboration model for school improvement. *Journal of Educational and Psychological Consultation, 20,* 257–287.

Armbruster, P. (2002). The administration of school-based mental health services. *Child and Adolescent Psychiatric Clinics of North America, 11*(1), 23–41.

Bahr, M. W., & Kovaleski, J. F. (2006).The need for problem-solving teams. *Remedial and Special Education, 27,* 2–5.

Bandura, A. (1977). *Social learning theory.* Englewood Cliffs, NJ: Prentice Hall.

Bandura, A. (1978). The self-system in reciprocal determinism. *American Psychologist, 33,* 344–358.

Bandura, A. (1986). *Social foundations of thought and action: A social cognitive theory.* Englewood Cliffs, NJ: Prentice Hall.

Bateson, G. (1972). *Steps to an ecology of mind.* New York, NY: Ballantine.

Becker, W. C. (1971). *Parents are teachers.* Champaign, IL: Research Press.

Braden, J. P. (2002). Best practices for school psychologists in educational accountability: High stakes testing and educational reform. In A. Thomas & J. Grimes (Eds.), *Best practices in school psychology* (4th ed., pp. 301–319). Bethesda, MD: National Association of School Psychologists.

Braden, J. P., & Tayrose, M. P. (2008). Best practices for school psychologists in educational accountability: High stakes testing and educational reform. In A. Thomas & J. Grimes (Eds.), *Best practices in school psychology* (5th ed., pp. 557–588). Bethesda, MD: National Association of School Psychologists.

Bramlett, R. K., & Murphy, J. J. (1998). School psychology perspectives on consultation: Key contributions to the field, *Journal of Educational and Psychological Consultation, 9,* 29–55.

Broughton, S. F., & Hester, J. R. (1993). Effects of administrative and community support on teacher acceptance of classroom interventions. Journal of Educational and Psychological Consultation, 4, 169–177.

Brown, D. (1997). Implications of cultural values for cross-cultural consultation with families. *Journal of Counseling and Development, 76,* 29–35.

Brown, D., Pryzwansky, W. B., & Schulte, A. C. (2011). *Psychological consultation and collaboration: Introduction to theory and practice.* Boston, MA: Pearson.

Bryan, J. A., & Griffin, D. (2010). A multidimensional study of school-family-community partnership involvement: School, school counselor, and training factors. *Professional School Counseling, 14,* 75–86.

Bryan, J., & Holcomb-McCoy, C. (2010). Collaboration and partnerships with families and communities: The school counselor's role. [Special issue]. *Professional School Counseling, 14.*

Buerkle, K. I., Whitehouse, E. M., & Christenson, S. L. (2009). Partnering with families for educational success. In T. B. Gutkin & C. R. Reynolds (Eds), *The handbook of school psychology* (4th ed., pp. 655–680). Hoboken, NJ: Wiley.

Burns, M. K. (2004). Curriculum-based assessment in consultation: A review of three levels of research. *Journal of Educational and Psychological Consultation, 15,* 63–78.

Caplan, G. (1970). *The theory and practice of mental health consultation.* New York, NY: Basic Books.

Caplan, G., & Caplan, R. B. (1993). *Mental health consultation and collaboration.* San Francisco, CA: Jossey-Bass.

Capra, F. (1982). *The turning point: Science, society, and the rising culture.* New York, NY: Simon & Schuster.

Carlson, C., & & Trapani, J. N. (2006). Single parenting and step-parenting. In G. G. Bear & K. M. Minke (Eds.), *Children's needs III: Development, prevention, and intervention* (pp. 783–797). Bethesda, MD: National Association of School Psychologists.

Carlson, J., Watts, R. E., & Maniacci, M. (2006). *Adlerian therapy: Theory and practice.* Washington, DC: American Psychological Association.

Carter, R. T. (1991). Cultural values: A review of the empirical literature and implications for counseling. *Journal of Counseling and Development, 70,* 164–173.

Catron, T., & Weiss, B. H. (1994). The Vanderbilt school-based counseling program: An interagency, primary-care model of mental health services. *Journal of Emotional and Behavioral Disorders, 2*(4), 247–253.

Cohen, E., & Osterweil, Z. (1986). An "issue-focused" model for mental health consultation with groups of teachers. *Journal of School Psychology, 24*(3), 243–256.

Colbert, R. D., Vernon-Jones, R., & Pransky, K. (2006). The school change feedback process: Creating a new role for counselors in education reform. *Journal of Counseling and Development, 84,* 72–82.

Cook, L., & Friend, M. (2010). The state of the art of collaboration on behalf of students with disabilities. *Journal of Educational and Psychological Consultation, 20,* 1–8.

Cottingham, H. F. (1956). *Guidance in the elementary school: Principles and practice.* Bloomington, IL: McKnight & McKnight.

Cramer, S. F. (1998). *Collaboration: A successful strategy for special educators.* Boston, MA: Allyn & Bacon.

Curtis, M. J., & Stollar, S. A. (2002). Best practices in system-level change. In A. Thomas & J. Grimes (Eds.), *Best practices in school psychology* (4th ed., pp. 223–243). Washington, DC: National Association of School Psychologists.

Dahir, C. A. & Stone, C. B. (2012). The transformed school counselor (2nd ed.). Belmont, CA: Brooks/Cole.

Dinkmeyer, D., & Caldwell, E. (1970). *Developmental counseling and guidance: A comprehensive school approach.* New York, NY: McGraw-Hill.

Dinkmeyer, D., & Carlson, J. (1973). *Consulting: Facilitating human potential and change processes.* Columbus, OH: Merrill.

Dougherty, A. M. (2009). *Psychological consultation and collaboration in school and community settings* (5th ed.). Belmont, CA: Brooks/Cole.

Dougherty, A. M. (2013). *Psychological consultation and collaboration in school and community settings* (6th ed.). Davis, CA: Brooks/Cole.

Downing, J., & Downing, S. (1991). Consultation with resistant parents. *Elementary School Guidance and Counseling, 25,* 296–301.

DuPaul, G. J. (2007). School-based mental health: Current studies and future directions. In S. W. Evans, M. D. Weist, & Z. N. Serpell (Eds.). *Advances in school-based mental health interventions: Best practices and program models* (vol. 2, pp. 21.1–21.15). Kingston, NJ: Civic Research Institute.

Erchul, W. P. (2011). School consultation and response to intervention: A tale of two literatures. *Journal of Educational and Psychological Consultation, 19,* 95–105.

Esler, A. N., Godber, Y., & Christenson, S. L. (2008). Best practices in supporting home-school collaboration. In A. Thomas & J. Grimes (Eds.), *Best practices in school psychology* (5th ed., pp. 917–936). Bethesda, MD: National Association of School Psychologists.

Faust, V. (1968). *The counselor-consultant in the elementary school.* Boston, MA: Houghton Mifflin.

Finello K. M. (2011). Collaboration in the assessment and diagnosis of preschoolers: Challenges and opportunities. *Psychology in the Schools, 48,* 442–453.

Forman, S. G., & Selman, J. S. (2011). Systems-based services delivery in school psychology. In M. A. Bray & T. J. Kehle (Eds), *The Oxford handbook of school psychology* (pp. 628–646). New York, NY: Oxford Press.

Freer, P., & Watson, T. S. (1999). A comparison of parent and teacher acceptability ratings of behavioral and conjoint behavioral consultation. *School Psychology Review, 28,* 672–684.

Fullmer, D. W., & Bernard, H. W. (1972). *The school counselor consultant.* Boston, MA: Houghton Mifflin.

Golden, L., & Cook, K. (2010). The parent consultation center. *The Family Journal: Counseling and Therapy for Couples and Families, 18,* 423–426.

Gordon, T. (1970). *Parent effectiveness training.* New York, NY: Wyden.

Gravois, T. A., & Gickling, E. E. (2002). Best practices in curriculum-based assessment. In A. Thomas & J. Grimes (Eds.), *Best practices in school psychology* (4th ed., pp. 885–898). Bethesda, MD: National Association of School Psychologists.

Gravios, T. A., & Gickling, E. E. (2008). Best practices in instructional assessment. In A. Thomas & J. Grimes (Eds.), *Best practices in school psychology* (5th ed., pp. 503–518). Bethesda, MD: National Association of School Psychologists.

Gravois, T. A., Groff, S., & Rosenfield, S. A. (2009). Team-based services as value-added consultation. In C. R. Reynolds & T. B. Gutkin (Eds.), *Handbook of school psychology* (4th ed.). New York, NY: Wiley.

Greenberg, M. T., Weissberg, R. P., O'Brien, M. U., Zins, J. E., Fredericks, L., Resnik, H., & Elias, M. J. (2003). Enhancing school-based prevention and youth development through coordinated social, emotional, and academic learning. *American Psychologist, 58,* 466–474.

Gruman, D. H., & Hoelzen, B. (2011). Determining responsiveness to school counseling interventions using behavioral observations. *Professional School Counseling, 14*(3), 183–190.

Guli, L. A. (2005). Evidence-based parent consultation with school-related outcomes. *School Psychology Quarterly, 20,* 455–472.

Gutkin, T. B. (2009). Ecological school psychology: A personal opinion and a plea for change. In T. B. Gutkin & C. R. Reynolds (Eds.), *The handbook of school psychology* (4th ed., pp. 463–496). Hoboken, NJ: Wiley.

Gutkin, T. B. (2012). Ecological psychology: Replacing the medical model paradigm for school-based psychological and psychoeducational services. *Journal of Educational and Psychological Consultation, 22,* 1–20. doi: 10.1080/10474412.649652

Gutkin, T. B., & Bossard, M. D. (1984). Impact of consultant, consultee, and organizational variables in teachers' attitudes toward consultation services. *Journal of School Psychology, 22*(3), 251–258.

Gutkin, T. B., & Curtis, M. J. (1999). School-based consultation theory and practice: The art and science of indirect service delivery. In T. B. Gutkin & C. R. Reynolds (Eds.), *The handbook of school psychology* (3rd ed., pp. 598–637). New York, NY: Wiley.

Gutkin, T. B., & Curtis, M. J. (2009). School-based consultation: The science and practice of indirect service delivery. In T. B. Gutkin & C. R. Reynolds (Eds.), *The handbook of school psychology* (4th ed., pp. 591–635). Hoboken, NJ: Wiley.

Hershfeldt, P. A., Pell, K., Sechrest, R., Pas, E. T., & Bradshaw, C. P. (2012). Lessons learned coaching teachers in behavior management: The PBISplus coaching model. *Journal of Educational and Psychological Consultation. 22,* 280–299.

Hoard, D., & Shepard, K. N. (2005). Parent education as parent-centered prevention: A review of school-related outcomes. *School Psychology Quarterly, 20,* 434–454.

Hoganbruen, K., Clauss-Ehlers, C., Nelson, D., & Faenza, M. M. (2003). Effective advocacy for school-based mental health programs. In M. D. Weist, S. W. Evans, & N. A. Lever (Eds.), *Handbook of school mental health: Advancing practice and research* (pp. 45–59). New York, NY: Plenum.

Hughes, J. N. (2000). The essential role of theory in the science of treating children: Beyond empirically supported treatments. *Journal of School Psychology, 38,* 301–330.

Ingraham, C. L. (2008). Studying multicultural aspects of consultation. In W. P. Erchul & S. M. Sheridan (Eds.), *Handbook of research in school consultation* (pp. 269–291). New York, NY: Erlbaum.

Jacob, S., & Hartshorne, T. S. (2003). *Ethics and law for school psychologists* (4th ed.). Hoboken, NJ: Wiley.

Johnson, L. J., Pugach, M. C., & Hammitte, D.J. (1988). Barriers to effective special education consultation. *Remedial and Special Education, 9,* 41–47.

Joint Committee of the Association for Counselor Education and Supervision & American School Counselor Association. (1966). Preliminary statement committee on the elementary school counselor: The elementary school counselor. *The Personnel and Guidance Journal, 44,* 658–661. doi: 10.1002/j.2164-4918.1966.tb03576.x

Kanel, K. (2007). *A guide to crisis intervention* (3rd ed.). Pacific Grove, CA: Brooks/Cole.

Kennedy, E. K., Frederickson, N., & Monsen, J. (2008). Do educational psychologists "walk the talk" when consulting? *Educational Psychology in Practice, 24,* 169–187.

Knotek, S. E., Kovac, M., & Bostwick, E. (2011). The use of consultation to improve academic and psychosocial outcomes for gifted students. *Journal of Applied School Psychology, 27,* 359–379.

Knotek, S. E., Rosenfield, S. A., Gravois, T. A., & Babinski, L. M. (2003).The process of fostering consultee development during instructional consultation. *Journal of Educational and Psychological Consultation, 14,* 303–328.

Kramer, J. J. (1990). Training parents as behavior change agents: Successes, failures, and suggestions for school psychologists. In T. B. Gutkin and C. R. Reynolds (Eds.), *The handbook of school psychology* (2nd ed., pp. 683–702). New York, NY: Wiley.

Kratochwill, T. R. (2008). Best practices in school-based problem-solving consultation: Applications in prevention and intervention systems. In A. Thomas & J. Grimes (Eds.), *Best practices in school psychology* (5th ed, pp. 1673–1688). Bethesda, MD: National Association of School Psychologists.

Kurpius, D. J., & Fuqua, D. R. (1993). Introduction to the special issues. *Journal of Counseling and Development, 71*, 596–597.

Leaf, P. J., Alegria, M., Cohen, P., Goodman, S. H., Horwitz, S. M., Hoven, C. W., . . . Regier, D. A. (1996). Mental health service use in the community and schools: Results from the four-community MECA study. *Journal of the American Academy of Child & Adolescent Psychiatry, 35*(7), 889–897.

Lee, C. C. (1995). School counseling and cultural diversity: A framework for effective practice. In C. C. Lee (Ed.), *Counseling for diversity: A guide for school counselors and related professionals* (pp. 3–17). Boston, MA: Allyn & Bacon.

Lentz, F. E., Allen, S. J., & Ehrhardt, K. E. (1996). The conceptual elements of strong interventions in school settings. *School Psychology Quarterly, 11*(2), 118–136.

Li, C., & Vazquez-Nuttall, E. (2009). School consultants as agents of social justice for multicultural children and families. *Journal of Educational and Psychological Consultation, 19*, 26–44.

Luiselli, J. K. (2002). Focus, scope, and practice of behavioral consultation to public schools. *Child & Family Behavior Therapy, 24*, 5–21.

Manz, P. H., Mautone, J. A., & Martin, S. D. (2009). School psychologists' collaboration with families: An exploratory study of the interrelationships of their perceptions of professional efficacy and school climate, and demographic and training variables. *Journal of Applied School Psychology, 25*, 47–70.

Merrell, K. W., Ervin, R. A., & Gimpel, G. (2006). *School psychology for the 21st century: Foundations and practices.* New York, NY: Guilford Press.

Meyers, J., Meyers, A. B., & Grogg, K. (2004). Prevention through consultation: A model to guide future developments in the field of school psychology. *Journal of Educational and Psychological Consultation, 5*, 257–276.

Miller, D. D., & Kraft, N. P. (2008). Best practices in communication with and involving parents. In A. Thomas & J. Grimes (Eds.), *Best practices in school psychology* (5th ed., pp. 937–951). Bethesda, MD: National Association of School Psychologists.

Minke, K. M. (2006). Parent-teacher relationships. In G. G. Bear & K.M. Minke (Eds.), *Children's needs III: Development, prevention, and Intervention* (pp. 73–85). Bethesda, MD: National Association of School Psychologists.

Moseley-Howard, G. S. (1995). Best practices in considering the role of culture. In A. Thomas & J. Grimes (Eds.), *Best practices in school psychology* (3rd ed., 337–345). Washington, DC: National Association of School Psychologists.

Muro, J. J., & Kottman, T. (1995). *Guidance and counseling in the elementary and middle schools: A practical approach.* Madison, WI: WCB Brown & Benchmark.

Newman, R. (2010). Diversifying consulting psychology for the future. *Consulting Psychology Journal: Practice And Research, 62*, 73-76. doi:10.1037/a0018532

Parsons, R. D., & Kahn, W. J. (2005). *The school counselor as consultant: An integrated model for school-based consultation.* Belmont, CA: Brooks/Cole.

Paternite, C. E. (2005). School-based mental health programs and services: Overview and introduction to the special issue. *Journal of Abnormal Child Psychology, 33*(6), 657–663. doi: 10.1007/s10802-005-7645-3

Pena, R. A. (1996). Multiculturalism and educational leadership: Keys to effective consultation. *Journal of Educational and Psychological Consultation, 7*, 315–325.

Perera-Diltz, D. M., Moe, J. L, & Mason, K. L. (2011). An exploratory study in school counselor consultation engagement. *Journal of School Counseling, 9*(13). Retrieved from http://www.jsc.montana.edu/articles/v9n13.pdf

Pohlman, C., Hoffman, L. B., Dodds, A. H., & Pryzwansky, W. B. (1998). Utilization of school-based professional services: An exploratory analysis of perceptions of mentor teachers and student teachers. *Journal of Educational and Psychological Consultation, 9*(4), 347–365.

Portman, T. A. A. (2009). Faces of the future: School counselors as cultural mediators. *Journal of Counseling & Development, 87,* 21–27.

Pugach, M. C., & Johnson, L. J. (1988). Peer collaboration. *Teaching Exceptional Children, 20*(3), 75–77.

Rafoth, M. A., & Foriska, T. (2006). Administrator participation in promoting effective problem-solving teams. *Remedial and Special Education, 27,* 130–135.

Raines, J. C., & Dibble, N. T. (2011). *Ethical decision making in school mental health.* New York, NY: Oxford University Press.

Ramirez, S. Z., & Smith, K. A. (2007). Case vignettes of school psychologists' consultations involving Hispanic youth. *Journal of Educational and Psychological Consultation, 17,* 79–93.

Reschly, A. L, & Christenson, S. L. (2012). Moving from "context matters" to engaged partnerships with families. *Journal of Educational and Psychological Consultation, 22,* 62–78.

Riley, R. W. (1996). Improving America's schools. *School Psychology Review, 25,* 477–484.

Rosenfield, S. A. (1987). *Instructional consultation.* Hillsdale, NJ: Erlbaum.

Rosenfield, S. A. (2002). Developing instructional consultants: From novice to competent to expert. *Journal of Educational and Psychological Consultation, 13*(1&2), 97–111.

Rosenfield, S. A. (2004). Consultation as dialogue: The right words at the right time. In N. M. Lambert, I. Hylander & J. H. Sandoval (Eds.), *Consultee-centered consultation: Improving the quality of professional services in schools and community organizations* (pp. 337–347). Mahwah, NJ: Erlbaum.

Rosenfield, S. A. (2008). Best practices in instructional consultation and instructional consultation teams. In A. Thomas & J. Grimes (Eds.), Best practices in school psychology (5th ed., pp. 1645–1659). Bethesda, MD: National Association of School Psychologists.

Rosenfield, S. A., Silva, A., & Gravois, T. A. (2008). Bringing instructional consultation to scale: Research and development of IC and IC teams. In W. P. Erchul & S. M. Sheridan (Eds), Handbook of research in school consultation (pp. 203–223). New York, NY: Erlbaum.

Roach, A. T., Kratochwill, T. R., & Frank, J. L. (2009). School-based consultants as change facilitators: An adaptation of the concerns-based adoption model (CBAM) to support the implementation of research-based practices. *Journal of Educational and Psychological Consultation, 19,* 300–320.

Rotheram-Borus, M. J., Bickford, B., & Milburn, N. G. (2001). Implementing a classroom-based social skills training program in middle childhood. *Journal of Educational and Psychological Consultation, 12*(2), 91–111.

Ryan, T., Kaffenberger, C. J. & Carroll, A. G. (2011). Response to intervention: An opportunity for school counselor leadership. *Professional School Counseling, 14,* 211–221.

Safran, S. P., & Safran, J. S. (1998). Prereferral consultation and intervention assistance teams revisited: Some new food for thought. *Journal of Educational and Psychological Consultation, 8,* 93–100.

Sander, J. B., Sharkey, J. D., Olivarri, R., Tanigawa, D. A., & Mauseth, T. (2010). A qualitative study of juvenile offenders, student engagement, and interpersonal relationships: Implications for research directions and preventionist approaches. *Journal of Educational and Psychological Consultation, 7,* 89–97.

Sanetti, L. M. H., & Kratochwill, T. R. (2009). Toward developing a science of treatment integrity: Introduction to the special series. *School Psychology Review, 38,* 445–459.

Schellenberg, R. C., & Grothaus, T. (2011). Using culturally competent responsive services to improve student achievement and behavior. *Professional School Counseling, 14,* 222–230.

Sheridan, S. M. (1993). Models for working with parents. In J.E. Zins, T.R. Kratochwill, & S. N. Elliot (Eds.), Handbook of consultation services for children (pp. 110–133). San Francisco: Jossey-Bass.

Sheridan, S. M. (2000). Considerations of multiculturalism and diversity in behavioral consultation with parents and teachers. *School Psychology Review, 29,* 345–353.

Sheridan, S. M., Eagle, J. W., & Doll, B. (2006). An examination of the efficacy of conjoint behavioral consultation with diverse clients. *School Psychology Quarterly, 21,* 396–417.

Sheridan, S. M., & Kratochwill, T. R. (2008). *Conjoint behavioral consultation: Promoting family-school connections and interventions* (2nd ed.). New York, NY: Springer.

Sheridan, S. M., Warnes, E. D., Woods, K. E., Blevins, C. A., Magee, K. L., & Ellis, C. (2009). An exploratory evaluation of conjoint behavioral consultation to promote collaboration among family, school, and pediatric systems: A role for pediatric school psychologists. *Journal of Educational and Psychological Consultation, 19,* 106–129.

Steen, S., & Noguera, P. A. (2010). A broader and bolder approach to school reform: Expanded partnership roles for school counselors. *Professional School Counseling, 14,* 42–52.

Stenger, M. K., Tollefson, N., & Fine, M. J. (1992). Variables that distinguish elementary teachers who participate in school-based consultation from those who do not. *School Psychology Quarterly, 17,* 47–77.

Sterling-Turner, H. E., Watson, T. S., & Moore, J. W. (2002).The effects of direct training and treatment integrity on treatment outcomes in school consultation. *School Psychology Quarterly, 16,* 56–67.

Sulkowski, M. L., Wingfield, R. J., Jones, D., & Coulter, W. A. (2011). Response to intervention and interdisciplinary collaboration: Joining hands to support children and families. *Journal of Applied School Psychology, 27,* 1–16. doi: 10.1080/15377903.2011.565264

Tomes, Y. I. (2011). Building competency in cross-cultural school psychology. In T. M. Lionetti, E. P. Snyder, & R. W. Christner (Eds.), *A practical guide to building professional competencies in school psychology* (pp. 35–49). New York, NY: Springer.

Trolley, B. C., Haas, H. S., & Patti, D. C. (2009). *The school counselor's guide to special education.* Thousand Oaks, CA: Corwin.

Truscott, S. D., & Albritton, K. (2011). Addressing pediatric health concerns through school-based consultation. *Journal of Educational and Psychological Consultation, 21,* 169–174.

Tysinger, P. D., Tysinger, J. A., & Diamanduros, T. (2009). Teacher expectations on the directedness continuum in consultation. *Psychology in the Schools, 46,* 319–332.

Weiss, H. (1996). Family-school collaboration: Consultation to achieve organizational and community change. *Human Systems, 7,* 211–235.

Weist, M. D. (2005). Fulfilling the promise of school-based mental health: Moving toward a public mental health promotion approach. *Journal of Abnormal Child Psychology, 33*(6), 735–741.

Weist, M. D., Lever, N. A., & Stephan, S. H. (2004).The future of expanded school mental health. *Journal of School Health, 74*(6), 191.

Weist, M. D., Sander, M. A., Walrath, C., Link, B., Nabors, L., Adelsheim, S., . . . Carrillo, K. (2005). Developing principles for best practice in expanded school mental health. *Journal of Youth and Adolescence, 34*(1), 7–13. doi:10.1007/s10964-005-1331-1

Whitaker, C. R. (1992). Traditional consultation strategies: Finding the time to collaborate. *Journal of Educational and Psychological Consultation, 3,* 85–88.

Williams, J. M., & Greenleaf, A. T. (2012). Ecological psychology: Potential contributions to social justice and advocacy in school settings. *Journal of Educational and Psychological Consultation, 22,* 141–157.

Wizda, L. L. (2004). An instructional consultant looks to the future. *Journal of Educational and Psychological Consultation, 5,* 277–294.

10

Consultation in Career Counseling Settings

What's the difference between a career consultant, a career coach, a career development facilitator, and a career counselor?

Introduction

There are career-related activities that people other than career counselors engage in and provide for clients. It can be confusing for the general population to hear about . . . career counselors . . . career coaches . . . career development facilitators. They are different people claiming to be in different professions, sometimes doing very similar things. Granted each profession has different training requirements and different credentialing, but they may all be engaged in career consultation activities and providing the same types of services to a client.

After reading this chapter, you will be able to

- Distinguish between the credentials of a career counselor, a career coach, and a career development facilitator
- Describe some of the current trends in consultation in career development settings
- Give sound feedback and critique (using current best practices) on résumés and cover letters
- Offer helpful suggestions and feedback regarding job interviewing
- Make suggestions for networking, including the use of technology resources like LinkedIn
- Design and plan career training and career education activities
- Describe all of the different settings in which a career consultant may work
- Explain the rationale for career consultants being knowledgeable about program evaluation
- Plan a program evaluation
- Specify the multicultural and diversity issues of consultation in career counseling

Direct Services: An Important Distinction in Career Consultation

The consultation activities mentioned in this chapter are common to all of the career-related professions, and the majority of the activities are perhaps better defined as direct services to a client. Direct services to clients are not typical of a traditional idea of consultation. Consultation is typically an indirect service provided by a consultant to a client. The tendency is to label these direct service activities as counseling activities. However, the consultation activities mentioned in this chapter are not counseling activities because of the focus of the relationship. Counseling is a professional relationship that empowers diverse individuals, families, and groups to accomplish mental health, wellness, education, and career goals . . . Counseling is a collaborative effort between the counselor and client. Professional counselors help clients identify goals and potential solutions to problems which cause emotional turmoil, seek to improve communication and coping skills, strengthen self-esteem, and promote behavior change and optimal mental health . . . Counseling is a personal opportunity to receive support and experience growth during challenging times in life. Individual counseling can help one deal with many personal topics in life, such as anger, depression, anxiety, substance abuse, marriage and relationship challenges, parenting problems, school difficulties, and career changes (American Counseling Association [ACA], 2013, para. 1).

Career consultants are providing a service to clients that assists with accomplishing career goals, but it is not a collaborative activity and it does not blend personal concerns with career concerns. The service provided is a one-way exchange of information, rather than a two-way exchange. Career consultation activities are the provision of advice or expert opinions (e.g., reviewing, critiquing, and editing a client's résumé) and don't require a graduate degree in counseling. Other career related professionals (non-counselors) are competent and qualified to provide the same activities. These types of activities can, and certainly do, happen within the context of career counseling. However, we would like to distinguish and label these activities *as consultation activities* rather than counseling activities. Career counselors provide these types of consultation services—but they also provide counseling services (and may be blended with consultation activities). To simplify things, throughout this chapter, you may find us referring to *career consultants*, rather than career counselors, career coaches, or career development facilitators.

This chapter attempts to review what we consider to be the current trends in career consultation activities common across career development professions—hopefully providing you with some practical ideas for providing career consultation services. We discuss some of the settings in which career consultants may find themselves working, and we devote some time to program evaluation activities. Program evaluation is extremely important in any type of counseling and consultation, but because career counselors typically provide so many programs, information sessions, and activities, it is even more crucial that they be familiar with this necessary skill. Last, but not least, we cover multicultural and diversity considerations in career consultation.

Current Trends

Self-Identification

As a profession, counseling has always carried a certain stigma for those who seek it—usually regardless of what type of counseling it is. This is true even for career counseling. Historically, many career development professionals have experimented with defining themselves in different ways. Career counselors will sometimes adopt a title of *career consultant*, simply because the term *counselor* has been known to drive clients away (Egodigwe, 2003). In the end, the career consultant may not do anything different than a career counselor.

The confusing part is that career coaches and career development facilitators (each having different training, standards, and credentials) will also sometimes refer to themselves as career consultants. From an outsider's (or potential client's) perspective, a career consultant may be the same thing as a career counselor, a career counselor may be the same thing as a career coach, and a career coach may be the same thing as a career development facilitator (Gerstner, 2012). With respect to *career consultation activities*, for the most part, they may be right. There aren't necessarily any differences. We may all engage in some of the same consultation activities, regardless of training, standards, and credentials. In the interest of clarity, we will make some distinctions among

- Career Counselors
- Career Coaches
- Career Development Facilitators

before we describe some of the currently trending consultation activities. It should be noted that there are other titles (e.g., career advisor), but they aren't associated with any clearly defined profession—and they will not be addressed.

Career Counselors

According to the National Career Development Association (NCDA, 2009), a career counselor has at least a master's degree in counseling and likely holds a state or national credential. A career counselor may

- conduct individual and group personal counseling, connecting personal and career issues;
- create a supportive environment;
- administer and interpret assessments and inventories (regarding career interests, work values, abilities, skills, personality characteristics or traits, etc.);
- gather information;
- introduce, teach, and facilitate decision-making skills;
- utilize computer-based systems or Internet services related to career planning;
- develop individual career plans for their clients;
- provide emotional support related to crises and transitions (career related or not)
- **teach clients job search strategies, skills, and techniques, including networking, résumé writing and critiquing, interview techniques, and salary negotiation;**
- **assist clients with exploring continuing education options and prepare them to pursue opportunities; and**
- **present and consult with the general public on career development information and resources (NCDA, 2009).**

The services mentioned above in boldface font are what we would consider consultation activities of a career counselor.

Career Coaches

Career coaches have been around since the late 1980s, according to the International Coach Federation. The "coaching market" has grown considerably over the years, and there are at least 50,000 part-time and full-time career coaches (Center for American Nurses, 2007). It is estimated that the market is currently worth around $2 billion globally (Passmore, Holloway, & Rawle-Cope, 2010). In the past, career coaches were known as mentors, management consultants, and human resource specialists, just to name a few (Hagevik, 1998). In the early iterations of career coaches, many had therapeutic backgrounds and they operated from outside organizations, like an external consultant. As the profession has changed, and coach training has become more available, more coaches now work within organizational settings (Passmore et al., 2010).

Pieter Koortzen and Rudolf M. Oosthuizen (2010) have described what they believe to be the differences between coaching and counseling. They report that the length of sessions and depth of material covered are some of the primary differences.

Coaching sessions, they say, can last anywhere from a few minutes to a few hours, where counseling sessions are typically in 45 to 50 minute time blocks. They also claim that career coaches can be more directive than counselors and that the relationship between a coach and the client is more collegial. Career coaches, in theory, do not go into the same amount of depth of issues as a counselor would.

Few states require licensure for a person to claim that they are a career coach. Sometimes career coaches are career counselors who have renamed or rebranded themselves, but they could also be former executives, sport coaches, self-proclaimed experts, or graduates of newly formed career coaching training programs (Hagevik, 1998). There are multiple professional coaching organizations that offer courses and certifications to become a career coach. As a result, career coaches can vary greatly in experience and level of expertise. Although coaches need a certain level of coach-specific training to claim a coaching credential, there is no specific level of education required to be a coach.

The Center for Credentialing and Education (CCE), an affiliate of the National Board for Certified Counselors (NBCC), created the Board Certified Coach (BCC) credential in an attempt to establish standards for coaching competency and accountability. Someone who holds a BCC credential has

- met educational and training requirements (these are different depending on whether you already have an advanced degree and what the degree is);
- passed an exam that is *coach specific*;
- documented experience in the field as a coach;
- a professional colleague who will serve as a reference for skills and abilities;
- agreed to abide by a code of ethics for coaching; and
- agreed to pursue continuing education hours related to coaching (CCE, 2013).

Because of the variance in training provided for coaches, it is difficult to specify what ALL career coaches do. Some of the activities can include the following:

- Strengthen relationships and improve communication
- Examine life choices
- Explore career options
- Set goals and monitor progress toward goals
- Provide focus to career growth
- Enhance satisfaction in current role
- Improve job performance
- Provide suggestions to move their clients to the "next level" of their career (Koortzen & Oosthuizen, 2010)

Career Development Facilitators

A career development facilitator (CDF), or global career development facilitator (GCDF), is another credential offered and managed by the Center for Credentialing and Education (CCE). The obtainment of this credential does not require an advanced degree. Global career development facilitators provide career facilitation and guidance—and reportedly work alongside those career development professionals with more education and training (CCE, 2013). They are employed in any career development setting in which they incorporate career information or skills in their work with students, adults, clients, employees, or the public. They work in settings that can include government employment agencies, K–12 schools, colleges and universities, corporate human resource departments, and private consulting firms. A GDCF must complete 120 hours of a career development curriculum. The training includes content regarding: labor market information and resources, planning processes, basic helping skills, career development models and theories, informal and formal assessment approaches, diversity and specific population needs, development and maintenance of an effective career resource center, training and program promotion, case management and referral, ethical issues, technology, and job searching and employability skills (CCE, 2013).

Some of the GCDF's tasks include the following:

- Conduct career groups
- Train individuals about conducting a job search
- Coordinate a career development center
- Serve as a career development case manager
- Conduct intake interviews
- Provide occupational and labor market information
- Work as an employment or placement specialist

The "Career Consultant"

There are common career consultation activities among the career counselor, the career coach, and career development facilitator, and this is where we would like to provide some direction and instruction (from this point, we will simply refer to the career consultant, as opposed to any particular career development professional). A career consultant may find themselves working with clients on

- résumé writing and editing,
- cover letter writing and editing,
- how to act in an interview,
- job search strategies,
- networking, and
- improving worker satisfaction.

We will cover some of the current trends related to these consultation activities.

Résumé Writing

For most job seekers, the résumé is the main document which is sent to a potential employer. It is the first step in applying for a position—and the first chance for making an impression upon a potential employer. The primary purpose of a résumé is to allow a client to make it past the first round of applicant reviews and secure an interview.

The document should be designed with the intention of capturing the reader's attention and convincing them that the writer has the perfect credentials, training, and experience for a job. It is an advertisement for the applicant.

Résumés should look professional, be well written, and highlight the past and present skills that are specific to the job that is sought. It is encouraged that each résumé sent out be custom made for the reader or prospective employer. A consultant should encourage their client to research the "client system" (the prospective employer) to which they are applying in order to best tailor the résumé to that organization and position. The writer should work toward connecting the academic, past, and present professional experiences to the position.

The résumé should be well organized, logical in its presentation, and free from any typos, spelling errors, and grammatical errors. Having simple errors in these areas are an easy way to halt an applicant's progress in the job search process. Overall, the presentation should be easily scannable by the reader to determine whether or not the applicant might make a good fit within the organization (whether they meet all of the criteria requested for someone in the future position).

A simple font with a serif typeface is usually suggested, because it is believed to be easier to read (e.g., Times New Roman, not Arial). All fonts that might be considered juvenile are strongly recommended to be avoided. A 12-point font is recommended (absolutely no less than 10pt) to make the document easy to ready with younger or older sets of eyes. If printed, résumés should be submitted on white or off-white paper (no other colors are encouraged), and a high quality, cotton-fiber paper is highly recommended. We recommend the inclusion of the client's name and page number at the bottom of each page, including the total number of pages if more than one page. Most word processing software has this feature. If a printed, or hard copy, version of the documents is submitted, they are usually submitted without being stapled. If the person in the position of sifting through résumés is looking at multiple résumés at one time, it could be easy to separate the pages and shuffle the order of documents.

There are different kinds of résumés: chronological, functional, and hybrid (a combination of chronological and functional).

Chronological Résumé

The chronological résumé is the most commonly used form of a résumé. It essentially lists professional experiences from the most recent experiences through the rest of the relevant work experiences (i.e., a reverse chronological format). The drawback to a chronological résumé is that it makes it very easy for a reader to notice employment gaps, career changes, or lack of experience.

Functional Résumé

A functional résumé is a form of résumé that is most often used by persons who either don't have a great deal of work experiences or who have gaps in their employment for one reason or another. This form of résumé is typically organized by skills or competencies, rather than by events or experiences. The drawback to a functional résumé is that it is not used very often, and some readers who are used to a chronological format will therefore not understand the different presentation.

Hybrid or Combination Résumé

A hybrid résumé format is a combination of styles of the chronological format and the functional format. It lists both the sequence of events in terms of experiences but also organizes information by skills or competencies. The section of chronological information may not have a great deal of detail so that the functional section of information can go into greater detail regarding specific skills or competencies that are intended to be highlighted. This format of résumé is particularly useful for those that have worked for a long period of time and may have had similar jobs in different organizations. It allows the writer to streamline their information to make it concise as possible. It is also particularly useful for those that may be changing career paths or field. They can still highlight their past work history, while at the same time extracting specific elements that would be relevant to their newly chosen path. The drawback to the hybrid résumé format is similar to that of the functional résumé format, in that the reader may not be used to a different way of presenting information in a résumé. The drawback for this format, however, may be a little less than the drawback for the functional format, simply because the hybrid format still provides basic sequencing of events in a writer's life.

Case 10.1: Doug Hammers a Sale Home

Doug has a bachelor's degree in chemistry. However, when he graduated from college 20 years ago, he immediately began work as a house construction contractor. When the housing market declined, there was less work for him. Seven years ago, he decided to stop doing construction work and purchase (and then manage) a small local hardware store. It was a familiar business to Doug. As a building contractor, he was extremely familiar with nearly all of the tools and products sold.

He enjoys the sales part of his business and has experienced a moderate degree of success over the last 7 years, but he doesn't enjoy the long hours and is ready to move on to something else. He is no longer interested in the building industry.

His primary interest is in sales and he expresses a great desire to try his hand at pharmaceutical sales. A career consultant works with Doug on his résumé. They agree that Doug would benefit from a functional or combination format résumé that focuses the reader's attention to Doug's experience in sales, his college degree in chemistry, and his ability to get things done on time as a contractor. They discuss the idea to include some information on his chronological history of positions just to illustrate that he has been continuously employed, but that they really want to focus the résumé's keyword use on *sales*, *chemistry*, and *project management*.

Electronic Submissions

The method in which résumés are submitted is another factor to consider when working with clients on their résumés. Certainly, there is the old-fashioned, printed-on-paper method of sending out résumés to prospective employers. However, because of the increased availability and use of technology, many clients will send their résumés out in an electronic format. A writer needs be careful in terms of the electronic format that is submitted ("format" meaning something different in this context). Even though the writer may be drafting the document using Microsoft Word, and the reader will read it using Microsoft Word, there are still differences between versions of the software. The reader may also be using a Mac as opposed to a PC. Software differences, hardware differences, or difference in both can affect the way in which a résumé looks to the reader. Since the visual (or aesthetic) impression is important in a résumé, it is not recommended that the writer send out their résumé in a "raw" software format. It is recommended that they convert the résumé into a format that preserves the way in which the document looks, but yet still makes it easy to open and read. A Portable Document Format (or PDF) works well for this purpose. The more recent versions of most word processing software (e.g., MS Word, Apple Pages, Open Office, Google Docs) will easily convert a document into PDF format.

Some organizations will request a résumé in a basic text format. They make this request for a specific reason: They are using their own computers to organize, categorize, and eliminate applicant résumés. The résumé-reading software easily sifts through the information of a multiple-page résumé to extract information that might determine whether or not the writer's specified skills and experiences match the available position. This type of technology has changed the way that some people write résumés, with less worry about repetition and length of information, and more focus on the increased use of specific keywords. Using the right keywords can increase the writer's chances for being seen as the right fit for a position. Kayda Norman (2012) suggests that people who use résumé-reading software input specific keywords or keyword phrases. If a résumé doesn't contain the appropriate keywords or keyword phrases, then the writer's name won't come up in searches and may not be contacted for a position. If there is a position that is advertised, we generally recommend making an attempt to use the same language, or keywords, that are used within the advertisement (provided that they are accurate with respect to the writer's own experiences or skills).

Basic text résumés require that the information by typed appropriately in paragraph format (no columns or templates). Creative visual elements are completely eliminated from basic text résumé, because they may keep the software from reading the document correctly. The words used are the most important features. Basic text résumés should not contain any symbols, bullets, underlining, boldface font lettering, or graphics (Akpan & Notar, 2012). A writer could use a chronological, functional, or hybrid format, but the information should be presented in the most straightforward manner. Length is not really a concern in basic text résumés.

Résumé Content

Because chronological résumés are the most often used and accepted, we will cover the basic content contained in chronological résumés and the order in which we suggest presenting it. However, it is recommended that the organization of the material within the résumé mirror the requested requirements for the job being sought. For example, if the first requirement for a position is a graduate degree and licensure in a specific area (and the client/applicant has that degree and licensure), then the first information presented on the résumé should be the applicant's education experiences and credentials. If one of the first requirements for a position is 5 years of experience in the field, then education might be presented after the writer's experience.

Heading

This section should be at the top of the first page, and it contains the client's

- Name
- Address
- Telephone number: This can be any type of number (mobile, landline, VoIP). It simply needs to be a number at which the client can receive calls and messages about job opportunities.
- E-mail address: It is recommended that this be a permanent and professional-looking e-mail address (not a student e-mail address or any address that might be considered less than professional looking).

Defining or Branding Statement

This statement is just below the heading and replaces what used to be known as a career objective. The current trend in résumé writing is to forego the statement of what is pursued and utilize this space to direct the reader's attention to qualification highlights. We suggest that clients use this space to define (or "brand") themselves in a way that utilizes specific keywords relevant to their experiences and the position sought. The intention is further support that the client is the perfect fit for the desired position. Other résumé writers may suggest a summary of qualifications here.

Education

Using reverse chronological order, the writer specifies the most recent degree first, if there is more than one degree. If the writer attended college, he or she should specify

- the name of the college or university;
- the city and state of the institution;
- the name of the degree (no abbreviations);
- the dates of attendance;
- major and minor (if applicable); and
- grade point average (GPA) on a 4-point scale, only if it is a GPA above 3.0. Also, if the writer has been out of school for more than a few years, this should be left off.

Licensure or Industry-specific Credentials

If the writer is licensed or credentialed in any area, this should specified here including information about the license or credential, when it was issued, who issued it, and possibly an expiration date of the credential, if applicable.

Academic or Professional Honors or Awards

If the writer has received any accolades, honors, or awards for academic or professional work, these should be highlighted here. It should specify what the accolade was, when it was received, and who issued it, if relevant.

Experience

This section should primarily focus on highlighting a client's work (and other) experiences that demonstrate the applicant is a good fit with the position sought. Not every position ever held needs to be included here, and the section could be entitled "Experience, selected." Like most other elements on a résumé, the most recent experiences should be listed first and presented in reverse chronological order. With each citation, list

- organization name;
- city and state of organization;
- position held or title: This section can and should include paid or nonpaid positions (e.g., internship, volunteer, etc.);
- month and year of start and end of experience (present activities should end with *present*);
- bulleted work tasks (with quantifiable results, if possible): Start the bulleted points with action-oriented verbs. Present activities or roles should be written in present tense, past activities or roles in past tense. It is suggested that no more than three to four bulleted points be written per position.

Core Competencies and Trade Skills

Use this section to highlight basic or trade-specific skills of the client. An effort should be made to include language and specific keywords from the client's experiences that are relevant and desired for the targeted position. The section can simply contain a list of bulleted terms, phrases, or keywords.

Other sections within a résumé may include: consultation activities, grants obtained, presentations made, publications, and community service. However, these types of activities are less common and might be more appropriate on a curriculum vita, which is a comprehensive document and used more often in academic settings. A lot of the features from a vita are similar to a résumé, but the writer of a vita makes an attempt to summarize all professional activities. With résumés, a writer attempts to be more concise and focused. Résumés are usually anywhere from one to three pages, depending of the age and experience of the subject. With a vita, a writer is not concerned with length of the document.

Regardless of whether a résumé or vita is the focus, the writer should not present any false information. False information, or lying, on a résumé is a sure way of losing a position in the present or future (Akpan & Notar, 2012). The inclusion of references (or even the statement "References available upon request") is not suggested as the space in a résumé is sometimes in high demand. We believe that the space used to include this statement or information could be used in better ways (either incorporating more keywords within the document or reducing the overall length). References can easily be provided when requested later in the process. With respect to references, clients should contact the person listed as a reference to request permission for their inclusion. Family members and clergy should not be used as references (Akpan & Notar, 2012).

Exercise 10.1: Résumé Review and Revision

Exchange your résumé with a classmate (either a paper copy or digital copy) and receive the classmate's in return. Review and critique the document. Write your editorial suggestions, critiques, and comments directly on the document (if using digital versions of their document, use the track changes function of your software). Once the reviews are complete, exchange them and schedule a time to meet to review the critiques. Discuss the suggestions you made and the suggestions your classmate made. Revise your own document based on the feedback you receive. You don't need to incorporate every suggestion made by your peer (some suggestions you may not agree with), but you should make an honest effort to improve your document.

Cover Letter Writing

Most résumés should be accompanied by, and sent out with, a cover letter. Like a good résumé, a cover letter should be tailor written to specific positions that are sought. The cover letter is a chance for the writer to highlight key elements from a résumé that are the most important and most relevant. The cover letter is intended to express the writer's interest in the position and how the qualifications match the open position (Akpan & Notar, 2012). It logically presents how the applicant would be the perfect fit for the position. The cover letter details how the writer fulfills requirements in a way that may not be easily discerned from the résumé. It may describe specific accomplishments and strengths, and also how a person's skills and experiences fit the position (Norman, 2012).

Like the résumé, the cover letter (if printed) should be sent out on a high-quality paper (cotton-fiber paper is recommended). White or off-white paper is preferred, and the writer should use a basic font that matches the font type and size (10 or 12 point is recommended) of the résumé. The cover letter should be entirely free of spelling and grammatical errors and should present content in a concise and straightforward manner. The writer cannot assume that the person reading the cover letter (or résumé) knows industry-specific or organization-specific terminology.

For example, there can be different roles and responsibilities for someone holding the same job title in different organizations (Norman, 2012).

A client or applicant should make the best effort to research the organization to which he or she is applying and find out as much information as possible about it. If a specific job advertisement (if there is one) does not specify to whom the letter should be addressed, then this should be part of the information researched. A cover letter is best addressed to someone specific and not "To whom it may concern" or "Dear hiring manager." Address the hiring authority by name and personalize the cover letter.

We recommend a general format for the content of a cover letter. The first paragraph should be written in a way that expresses a client's interest in a position. The client can describe how (or from whom) he or she learned of the position. The specific job title and position number (if available) should be cited.

The middle part of the letter should be written to express the client's reason for interest in the position. The client should make an attempt to address each job requirement or preference and how the qualifications match each one (point by point, and as many as possible or reasonable). This area of the letter is where the client can highlight specific elements from the résumé, areas to which the reader of the document should be most interested in with respect to the position.

In the final part of the letter, the client should express appreciation for consideration for the position and a passive invitation to meet regarding the position. The end of the letter should contain the client's signature, telephone number, and e-mail address. We've heard of other career consultants recommending that a client close the letter by specifying a contact time to discuss their documents with the hiring authority. However, we believe that this approach is too aggressive. Sometimes, the person in the position of reviewing documents is working within a hiring schedule. A client contacting them before they are ready to proceed may not be welcomed or seen as a positive trait. A client can write a passive invitation for contact and still be assertive in the pursuit of a job. If enough time has passed since the documents have been submitted, and the client has not heard anything, contacting the hiring authority could be helpful and informative.

Job Interviews

A client should prepare for an interview by researching the prospective organization to as much as possible. An applicant should

- review the organization's website if they have one
- perform a general online search looking for any news or information about the organization or its products, and
- make inquiries within personal networks.

It might be helpful, depending on the nature of the business, to know who the organization's competitors are (Norman, 2012). A client can additionally prepare by having at least three to five good questions about the position ready to ask near the end of the interview.

A career consultant can assist the client with preparation by simulating some of the questions that may be asked by the interviewers (role-playing) and providing feedback regarding the client's performance. Many career consultants working in larger organizations will arrange group mock interviews to provide role-playing with feedback and critique on a larger scale, serving more clients at one time.

A career consultant can also provide some assistance with interview preparation by giving some tips related to the client's dress. Some examples include the following:

- Conservative "business dress" is recommended. Matching coats and pants (a suit) is suggested. For women, if a skirt is worn, the skirt should cover the thighs when seated.
- If a suit is worn, black, dark blue, or gray is recommended.
- Nails should be clean and trimmed to a professional length.
- Neutral color undergarments should be worn and should complement the suit.
- For women, moderate use of makeup is recommended.
- Spend the time and money to have garments tailored to fit. Ill-fitting clothing does not portray organization or attention to details.
- Scuffed or inappropriate footwear should be avoided (including excessively high heels).
- Do not wear strong aftershaves, perfume, or cologne.
- Plan what you will wear several days in advance of the interview so that there will be time to purchase, launder, or press necessary garments (Akpan & Notar, 2012).

It is recommended that the client attempt to portray a crisp, clean, and professional look. It is intended for the interviewer to listen to what the client has to say during the interview, rather than critiquing what they are wearing. After the interview, a client is advised to send a brief thank you note or message to each person present during the interview process.

Networking and LinkedIn

Networking is generally understood to be one of the primary methods for finding out about potential openings and for having the "inside track" to getting hired in an organization. It is advantageous to have a large professional network, as some openings may never be posted for general public response. Naturally, people build connections the old-fashioned way through personal contact, meeting people at conferences and trade-specific events, and telephone calls. However, technology has blossomed into a new avenue for building professional contacts. Career consultants needs to be well versed in the technology not only for themselves, but to be able to assist their clients with using the technology.

At the beginning of 2013, LinkedIn, a networking and social media site, reached a milestone of 200 million users. Users represented more than 200 countries, and the site has more than 160 million unique monthly users. In other words, the majority of LinkedIn users are regular monthly visitors of the site (LinkedIn, 2013).

LinkedIn, as opposed to other social media sites like Facebook or Twitter, allow a client to focus on professional relationships. The potential breadth of possible contacts provides more exposure to hiring or staffing professionals. Corporate recruiters, or "headhunters," have historically had to research professions in order to locate prospects, sometimes at great cost to their employers. Their job is to seek qualified people to fill existing positions, and they are paid by an employer to do so. They have begun using LinkedIn because of the wide use across the world and the lack of cost involved for using it (Alleyne, 2012). It is logical for both recruiters and clients to use it.

A career consultant can assist the client with making the most of the LinkedIn profile. Sonia Alleyne (2012) reported that 85% of employers indicate that a positive online reputation influences hiring decisions. Clients should be advised to increase their connections and network and keep their profile and content fresh. Their LinkedIn address might even be listed on their résumé. Listed are other recommendations:

- Complete the entire LinkedIn profile. A client is 40 times more likely to be identified through a LinkedIn search when the profile is completed.
- Personalize the profile by writing it in first person.
- Join groups within the system that are related to a client's professional interests or specializations. This is the beginning of networking within the system.
- When sending invitations to connect, an introduction and explanation for a desired connection is recommended.
- Update the page relatively frequently. A client could post links or stories about their work or professional interests. The fresher the content, the more likely the client will appear in searches within the system.
- Use LinkedIn to research a company or organization of interest. This will be particularly helpful if a client is invited for an interview. The client could search for a group or organization's page but could also seek advice and ask questions using the LinkedIn network.

Exercise 10.2: A Linked In Narrative

Exchange your résumé with a classmate (hopefully you have edited it at this point), and receive the classmate's in return. Use your colleague's résumé to draft a narrative for their LinkedIn profile. The narrative is typically a one-to-two paragraph summary of an individual's professional life. You may wish to consult about what types of content to highlight or what type of job your colleague hopes to obtain in the future. Keep in mind that since recruiters use LinkedIn, the use of keywords in the narrative is important. Make an effort to use keywords from the résumé, or keywords that you consider vitally important to the job your classmate hopes to obtain.

Career Training and Education

A career consultant engages in activities and presentations that are intended to educate and train the general public regarding the importance of career counseling, career development, and life-work planning. The consultation activities typically take the form of events, workshops, trainings, or presentations. They require some planning and coordination and can be very time-consuming. However, the information presentations can be distributed to large groups over time. These activities do require some skills in training or public speaking, which may not be everyone's favorite thing to do. Most career consultants in training find that these skills require some practice in order to feel comfortable. In essence, the career consultant is distributing information, recommendations, or general expertise.

Listed are some typical career training and education consultation activities:

- General information sessions regarding a specific topic (e.g., a career consultant in a university setting presenting about what it takes to major in business)
- Interviewing workshops (how-to)
- Internship and job opportunity information distribution
- Networking workshop
- Résumé and curriculum vitae writing workshop
- Meetings with recruiters
- Career fairs
- Mock interviews and interview simulation
- Business etiquette workshop
- Communication skills workshop
- Leadership development workshop
- Marketing or branding (for the client) workshop

Career Consultation Settings

Although we have made an attempt to review some of the current trends in career consultation activities above, it is not an exhaustive list. Career consultants work in a variety of settings, and each setting has its own unique tasks and activities. We will attempt to review other career consultation work settings and offer some additional consultation activities.

Career consultants can be found working in the following settings:

- Schools: Kindergarten through 12th-grade students
- Vocational rehabilitation (rehabilitation counseling): persons with a disability
- Colleges and universities: undergraduate and graduate students
- CareerOneStops: unemployed workers
- Military: veterans transitioning or entering civilian life
- Corrections: ex-offenders
- Private practice
- Corporate business or for-profit agencies
- Nonprofit agencies: specific, target populations (e.g., victims of abuse or intimate partner violence)

Schools: Kindergarten Through 12th-Grade Students

Career consultants can work as school counselors, career development center coordinators, career and technical educators, and career development facilitators.

School counselors can be found in schools that address all ages of children and adolescents. Career development center coordinators, career and technical educators, and career development facilitators are more likely to work in high schools. A career consultant, as opposed to a career or school counselor, may help students to develop skills, such as organization, time management, and effective study habits. They may teach classes on planning for college or careers after graduation, and how to research colleges or secure financial aid and apprenticeships. A career consultant may work with students on finding part-time afternoon employment, résumés, and job interviewing.

Vocational Rehabilitation (Rehabilitation Counseling): Persons With a Disability

Rehabilitation counselors work in a variety of settings. Examples include schools, prisons, independent-living facilities, rehabilitation agencies (state, private, and non-profit), and private practice. One factor of career consultation that is more important in vocational rehabilitation settings, as opposed to other settings, is job development and placement. Career consultants in this setting spend a good amount of time researching resources and funding available in the community for their clients. This requires consultation with potential employers. A career consultant might engage in employer consultation in the following areas:

- Provide consultation to employers regarding accessibility and issues related to compliance with the Americans with Disabilities Act (ADA).
- Give prospective employers appropriate information on a client's work skills and abilities.
- Negotiate with employers to reinstate or rehire a disabled worker.
- Share knowledge of assistive technology in job accommodations.
- Make recommendations for modification of tasks to accommodate limitations of clients (Leahy, Chan, & Saunders, 2003).

Colleges and Universities: Undergraduate and Graduate Students

Career consultation in a college and university setting focuses a lot of efforts on job placement and distributing career information. Job placement has historically relied on networking with organizational contacts, various alumni, and faculty (Niles & Harris-Bowlsbey, 2013). The idea is that the undergraduate or graduate student has an advocate or mentor to help place them within an organization. It relies on the consultative interaction between a career consultant and an organization contact. In some career services offices, it is referred to as employer or corporate relations. Organizational (employer) representatives have continuing relationships with career consultants on campus and are routinely invited to come to campus to recruit, advise, or interview potential employees and students. On a grander scale, career consultants might invite a large number of employer representatives to campus and hold a career fair. Many students are invited to attend the career fair, dressed for an interview, with their résumé in hand.

The provision of career information and career information resources can be a large-scale (large group) or small-scale (one-on-one) effort. The information may contain such items as posted job openings, job search strategies, salary expectations, or financial aid. Many universities and colleges now provide career-planning courses for students where a great deal of information is covered in a formal and structured manner (Niles & Harris-Bowlsbey, 2013). Since it may be logistically impossible to provide individual career counseling to every enrolled student at an institution, it makes sense to offer career consultation services on a large scale. Spencer G. Niles and JoAnn Harris-Bowlsbey (2013) cite some consultative activities in which university and college career centers could target:

- Courses, workshops, and seminars where topics such as career decision making, career planning, and job-search skills are taught.
- Placement programs such as on-campus or online job interviewing.

Case 10.2: Angela, the University Career Services Consultant

Angela works full time as a career counselor in a university career services center at an institution with approximately 30,000 students enrolled. She stays very busy, and the majority of her time is spent in activities that she would refer to as "career consultation," not counseling. In a typical week, Angela can be found in the quad several times, passing out information about what it takes to major in business, social work, communications, or microbiology. She also runs an "interviewing workshop" every three weeks in the classroom adjacent to the career service center. Students can drop in and attend the workshop at their leisure. Every Tuesday, Angela participates in the center's "Résumé Boot Camp." This ongoing program allows students to drop in with a copy of their résumé for a brief review and critique. The students can schedule a follow-up appointment (a longer counseling appointment) after the initial review.

On an ongoing basis, she makes contact with local businesses and organizations to discuss internship opportunities for the university's undergraduate students. At the same time, Angela keeps in contact with industry recruiters, consulting with them regarding various workforce needs. Once she establishes a good relationship with a recruiter or corporate contact, Angela has been known to persuade several of them to serve as mock interviewers. This has been a mutually beneficial relationship for all involved.

Last, but not least, Angela coordinates repeating workshops and career fairs every semester. She hosts workshops on business etiquette, communication skills, leadership development, and marketing or branding self. Her responsibilities typically include arranging space, presenters (if she is not presenting the material herself), materials, and food (if necessary). The career fairs tend to be very large-scale events that draw 500 to 1,000 attendees every semester. She invites the booth participants (most of whom have an ongoing consultative relationship with her), coordinates the logistics for the day, and evaluates the program and event. In Angela's "spare time", she is able to see and counsel students regarding their career development.

CareerOneStop: Unemployed Workers

CareerOneStop centers are sponsored by the United States Department of Labor. They are intended to provide career information and assistance to those looking for work, students, businesses or organizations, and career professionals. Career consultants in CareerOneStops help to connect clients (job seekers) with potential employers and employment training opportunities. They provide occupational information, job search tools, résumé tips, and other resources to laid-off workers and career changers. The consultative relationships that they maintain with the business community allow organizations to relay their workforce needs locally and nationwide. The information they provide might include unemployment benefits, educational opportunities, industry-specific data, and salary data.

Military: Veterans Transitioning or Entering Civilian Life

Career consultants working with military personnel or veterans may find themselves working on military bases, in colleges or universities (two year and four year), government agencies (like CareerOneStops), or organizations specifically targeting transitioning military personnel. Part of the consultation services provided may include networking and communicating with employers in order to advocate for veterans who may be disabled physically (e.g., traumatic brain injury) or psychologically (e.g., posttraumatic stress disorder). Other consultants may provide information, transition tips, and job fairs. Part of the information provided may include the translation of military occupation codes and titles into civilian occupation titles. It can be difficult for some veterans and employers to match equivalent civilian and military job titles, duties, and skills.

Corrections: Ex-Offenders

One of the most challenging populations to work with as a career consultant are ex-offenders. It can be very difficult to assist an ex-offender with finding and securing employment. As a career consultant, more work may need to be done in establishing positive relationships with potential employers. Since there is a known relationship between obtaining a job after release and recidivism, job placement is a key activity of a career consultant. This requires strong relationships between the career consultant and potential employers (Niles & Harris-Bowlsbey, 2013). The importance of obtaining a job after release has been underscored by the increased attention on training career consultants in correctional facilities. This effort has attempted to increase career consultants—labeling them *offender workforce development specialists* (Niles & Harris-Bowlsbey, 2013).

Private Practice

Career consultants working in private practice are, more than likely, career counselors. Their consultation tasks are likely to be very specific. They might work with clients on skills such as interviewing, use of technology, writing résumés, simulated job interviews, and job placement. Some of the consultation work they perform may also be seen as case management, where they will work on behalf of their client in an attempt to find ways to address their needs. Examples of these needs may include proper attire for interviewing, access to transportation to a job site, or access to funding for training (Niles & Harris-Bowlsbey, 2013).

Corporate Business or For-Profit Agencies

There are organizations, typically larger organizations, which will employ career consultants. The career consultants may address and advise regarding issues related to career mobility, keeping a résumé updated, and how to negotiate promotions (Niles & Harris-Bowlsbey, 2013). They may provide consultation to persons in supervisory positions regarding employees and their needs in an effort to increase worker and employer satisfaction. In situations where an organization may be downsizing, a career consultant may help with outplacement of affected workers.

Nonprofit Agencies: Specific, Target Populations (e.g., Victims of Abuse or Intimate Partner Violence)

Nonprofit agencies may target specific populations, but they may also address the general public through faith-based organizations. Niles and Harris-Bowlsbey (2013) have cited that federal funding has increased for faith-based and nonprofit organizations specifically for training, support services, and workforce development. Some of the tasks of a career consultant in a nonprofit agency may include activities that are more supportive in nature (more than other settings). Examples of support include providing assistance with clothing for interviews; housing and food for homeless clients; assistance with child care, transportation, and various elements of vocational training (Niles & Harris-Bowlsbey, 2013). In addition to providing this form of support, career consultants can increase their professional value to an organization by guiding and facilitating the process of program evaluation.

Program Evaluation

Program evaluation is an applied research discipline that includes the collection and analysis of information regarding the efficiency, effectiveness, and impact of programs and services (Astramovich & Coker, 2007). It seeks to provide meaningful information for use in decision making related to proposed or implemented programs (Wheeler & Loesch, 1981). As a career consultation activity, program evaluation helps career consultants to further establish their worth and promote their commitment to quality service (Lusky & Hayes, 2001). It is important in developing and maintaining an organization's programs, with the primary purpose of improving the effectiveness of a program.

Program evaluation refers to the application of procedures for objective and systematic evaluation of "the *P*s": programs, products, personnel, performance, or policies (Hosie, 1994). It includes the consideration of factors, such as costs, needs, ethics, political dimensions, biases, effects, and techniques. Career consultants engaging in program evaluation will need to be proficient in assessment, instrumentation, and experimental and quasi-experimental designs.

Molly H. Duggan and Jill C. Jurgens (2007) indicate that program evaluations in career counseling are used to

- clarify the purpose of an intervention,
- chart the progress of a program,
- assess the effectiveness of a program,
- assist in making strategic decisions,
- help in assessing the direction of a program,
- determine program outcomes,
- facilitate program improvement, and
- provide information that can help decision makers.

Program evaluations use both hard and soft data, but program evaluation is not typically known for rigorous and sophisticated methodology. For hard data, evaluators may use experimental designs or case studies. For soft data, unobtrusive techniques such as satisfaction surveys or questionnaires may be used. An evaluation can be as simple as counting how many people participated in a program and for how long and as complex as observing how participants may have changed as a result of the program (Priest, 2001).

Methodology

There are two types of procedures used to collect, analyze, and report data: quantitative methodology and qualitative methodology. Quantitative methodology (numbers and amounts) typically come from an evaluator's measurement of the responses to surveys or standardized tests. The data, or numbers, can be subjected to statistical analysis in order to describe the information. Questionnaires are probably the most often used quantitative evaluation tool (Duggan & Jurgens, 2007). They can be formal standardized tools or tools created specifically by the program evaluator. Examples include checklists, multiple-choice questions, and rating scales. Qualitative data (descriptions of patterns or characteristics) are collected through notes, interviews, open-ended questionnaires, and observations, including written comments on surveys or in journals (Priest, 2001).

Models of evaluation

There are four common models of program evaluation (Priest, 2001):

- Needs assessment
- Feasibility study
- Process evaluation (or formative evaluation)
- Outcome evaluation (or summative evaluation)

Needs Assessment

The needs assessment is an initial assessment that attempts to determine what gaps a program will address. The assessment attempts to measure the difference between what services or elements currently exist and a desired target state. Measuring the present state of affairs requires the use of surveys, interviews, and observations to assess the context of targeted clients. The same clients are then asked to disclose what they would like to see happen or change. The difference between what exists and what is desired is considered a service or program need (Priest, 2001).

Case 10.3: What Are the Career Needs?

Amy is in her first year as a counselor in a high school (Grades 9–12). She is not sure what types of career development activities have been done with students at the school in the past. There aren't any records of the past counselor's efforts, and no one seems to be able to accurately relate to her what they witnessed the previous counselor doing with the career development program at the school. She's left wondering what should be done and what the needs are of the students at her school.

Amy concludes that she needs to conduct a needs assessment to determine what gaps there are between what has been done in the past versus what is needed. She develops a brief survey to assess the gap. She creates a paper-and-pencil version of an assessment and an online version of the survey. The paper-and-pencil version is provided to all classroom teachers—with a request that they distribute the survey in their home-room classes over the next week. Amy also sits in the lunch area with a computer directed to the online version of the survey. During the week, she persuades several students to complete the survey after finishing their lunch. For these students, she considers them somewhat of a "focus group", and asks them some follow-up interview-like questions. In addition, she posts QR codes all around the school. Anyone who scans the QR code will be taken to the online version of the survey.

She also created a brief online version of a separate survey for the teachers, administrators, and support staff at the school. This survey provided them an opportunity to voice their awareness of past activities and desires for the future for the career development program at the school.

Based on the results that she obtained (the paper-and-pencil responses, the online responses, and the interview responses), she defines some clear direction for her career development program at the school. She was able to obtain some input about what had been done over the last couple of years (from multiple sources and perspectives), and the respondents were very clear about what they would like to see in the way of career development at the school.

Feasibility Study

A feasibility study measures how likely a program is to succeed. An attempt is made to identify all alternatives to the implementation of a proposed program and any barriers and resources that would hinder or help the program. A comparison is made between the alternatives and the proposed program. Other significantly reasonable alternatives may indicate that there are other ways to address client needs and that the proposed program may not be the best or only option. Perhaps other programs need to be considered. The presence of significant barriers (without many resources to help) may also be an indicator that the proposed program may not be the best option (Priest, 2001).

Process or Formative Evaluations

A process, or formative, evaluation attempts to measure how effectively a program was designed or implemented. It assesses the behaviors, decisions, and procedures that are followed while developing the proposed program and compares them with how the services are delivered. The measurements are descriptive and ongoing (Duggan & Jurgens, 2007). The results illustrate a gap between what was planned and how it was executed. The results are used to modify and improve the delivery of the program (Priest, 2001).

Outcome or Summative Evaluations

An outcome, or summative, evaluation identifies the results of a program's effort. They provide descriptions and documentation of changes that took place as a result of the program's implementation (i.e., after implementation). The most common outcome evaluation compares a preprogram assessment with a postprogram assessment. However, an outcome evaluation can also assess such things as whether learning objectives were achieved or if clients are satisfied with outcome of the program. An outcome evaluation compares what was obtained with what was expected. The expectation could be a standard benchmark or earlier baseline assessment (Priest, 2001).

Evaluation Report

It is generally recommended that an evaluation report be written upon completion of a program evaluation. The information collected is presented in written form, and all program stakeholders are provided a report and given time to reflect on the results. Because the intention of a program evaluation is to improve the effectiveness of the program, modifications should be made based on the results obtained and noted in the evaluation report. The program evaluation process should not be used to simply affirm a success or failure of a program. The results should be used to improve upon already successful programs and revise or reconstruct programs that are in need of help.

Multicultural Considerations

There is no doubt that career counselors need to be skilled and proficient in providing culturally competent career counseling interventions (Niles & Harris-Bowlsbey, 2013). The area of focus here is what should be taken into account in consultation in career development settings. Some of the points below have been mentioned previously, but we'll take a look at them now in the context of career consultation.

Exercise 10.3: A Summative Experience

Imagine that you are tasked with conducting an outcome or summative evaluation of the career services office of either your undergraduate institution or your current institution.

1. *What would be the goal of your evaluation?*

2. *What types of programs or services would you evaluate?*

3. *What kind of information would you obtain?*

4. *What type of evaluations, methods, or instrumentation would you use?*

5. *Who are the program stakeholders?*

6. *Draft a sample program evaluation report (based on potential answers to these questions) that you would theoretically share with stakeholders.*

Understand the Cultural Embeddedness of Career Consultation

A career consultant should be able to view the consultation process through a cultural lens (Rogers, 2000). It is important to consider the culturally-embedded organizational forces that may have an impact on the consultee, client, or both. A career consultant working with a consultee on a résumé, cover letter, or interviewing skills (for example) will need to seriously consider elements that have influenced the career development of the consultee and the environment of the potential employer (culture-specific context knowledge).

In order to provide context-relevant services, a career consultant should seek to acquire culture-specific information related to the context. This might also include culture-specific issues in organizations and employers. When appropriate, consultants advocate at individual, group, institutional, and societal levels to examine potential barriers and obstacles that inhibit access or the growth and development of consultees and clients.

Case 10.4: Views of Raymond

James is a career counselor at a local community college. He has a client, Raymond, who has a different cultural background than his own. Raymond self-identified as someone who doesn't interview well and was recently not offered a position at a company nearby. He claims that interviewers told him that he seems rather passive and doesn't make very good eye contact. James and Raymond discuss this characteristic and the reasons for Raymond's behavior. Raymond clearly states that this is something that has never been encouraged in his previous experiences. He realizes that this is a trait that was valued in the organization with which he interviewed. They had expected him to be very assertive and a "go-getter." James and Raymond discuss this expectation within some organizations and how it compares with Raymond's typical behavior. They develop a plan for how Raymond might address this for his next interview.

Understand One's Own and Others' Culture

A career consultant needs to examine his or her own heritage and identity (race, ethnicity, culture) and possess a self-awareness of personal beliefs, prejudices, and assumptions (Rogers, 2000). A career consultant should make attempts to learn about the culture and background of consultees and clients in order to better understand (and possible adopt) others' perspectives and values. An effective career consultant is aware of and addresses the role of multiculturalism and diversity in consulting relationships. The consultant also attempts to communicate information in ways that are both developmentally and culturally appropriate.

Use Qualitative Methodologies When Gathering Data

The validity of some instruments and procedures may not be able to be projected or generalized to diverse groups. Career consultants should be skilled in using naturalistic data-gathering techniques that would account for local culture and context. Career consultants need to be cautious when creating or selecting assessments for culturally diverse populations to avoid the use of instruments that lack appropriate psychometric properties for the consultee and client populations.

Chapter Keystones

- Consultation activities mentioned in this chapter are common to all career-related professions (career counselor, career coach, career development facilitator), and the majority of the activities are perhaps better defined as direct services to a client.
- Career consultants may find themselves working with clients on résumé writing and editing, cover letter writing and editing, how to act in an interview, job search strategies, networking (including the use of technology to do so), or group training or education.
- The primary purpose of a résumé is to allow a client to make it past the first round of applicant reviews and secure an interview.

- Networking is a primary method for finding out about potential openings and for having the "inside track" to getting hired in an organization.
- A career consultant engages in activities and presentations that are intended to educate and train the general public regarding the importance of career counseling, career development, and life-work planning.
- Career consultants can be found working in a variety of settings.
- Career consultants can increase their professional value to an organization by guiding and facilitating the process of program evaluation.
- Career consultants need to be skilled and proficient in providing culturally competent services.

Web-Based and Literature-Based Resources

Websites

CareerOneStop: http://www.careeronestop.org
CCE—Board Certified Coach: http://www.cce-global.org/BCC
CCE—Global Career Development Facilitator: http://www.cce-global.org/GCDF
Council for Accreditation of Counseling & Related Educational Programs (CACREP): http://www.cacrep .org/doc/2009%20Standards%20with%20cover.pdf
International Coach Federation: http://www.coachfederation.org
LinkedIn: http://www.linkedin.com
National Career Development Association (NCDA): http://www.ncda.org
National Career Development Guidelines (NCDG) Framework: http://ncda.org/aws/NCDA/asset_manager/ get_file/3384/ncdguidelines2007.pdf
Professional Association of Résumé Writers and Career Coaches: http://www.parw.com/home.html

Suggested Readings

Toporek, R. L., & Flamer, C. (2009). The résumé's secret identity: A tool for narrative exploration in multicultural career counseling. *Journal of Employment Counseling, 46,* 4–17.

References

Alleyne, S. (2012). Your professional story: Here's how to improve your LinkedIn profile. *Black Enterprise, 43*(5), 44–46.

Akpan, J., & Notar, C. E. (2012). How to write a professional knockout resume to differentiate yourself. *College Student Journal, 46*(4), 880–891.

American Counseling Association. (2013). *What is professional counseling?* Retrieved from http://www .counseling.org/learn-about-counseling/what-is-counseling

Astramovich, R. L., & Coker, J. K. (2007). Program evaluation: The accountability bridge model for counselors. *Journal of Counseling and Development, 85,* 162–172.

Center for American Nurses. (2007, January/February). Career coaching and the professional nurse. *The American Nurse 7.*

Center for Credentialing and Education. (2013). *Board certified coach: About the BCC.* Retrieved from http:// www.cce-global.org/BCC

Center for Credentialing and Education. (2013). *Global career development facilitator.* Retrieved from http:// www.cce-global.org/GCDF

Duggan, M. H., & Jurgens, J. C. (2007). *Career interventions and techniques: A complete guide for human service professionals.* Boston, MA: Pearson.

Egodigwe, L. (2003). Watch out for career scams: How to discern what counselors, coaches, and consultants actually do. *Black Enterprise, 10,* 53.

Gerstner, L. (2012). Kick-start your career. *Kiplinger's Personal Finance, 11,* 64–65.

Hagevik, S. (1998). Choosing a career counseling service. *Journal of Environmental Health, 61,* 31–32.

Hosie, T. W. (1994). Program evaluation: A potential area of expertise for counselors. *Counselor Education and Supervision, 33*(4), 349–355.

Koortzen, P., & Oosthuizen, R. M. (2010). A competence executive coaching model. *South African Journal of Industrial Psychology, 36*(1), 1–11.

Leahy, M., Chan, F., & Saunders, J. (2003). A work behavior analysis of contemporary rehabilitation counseling practices. *Rehabilitation Counseling Bulletin, 46,* 66–81.

LinkedIn. (2013, January 9). LinkedIn reaches 200 million members worldwide. Retrieved from http://press .linkedin.com/News-Releases/165/LinkedIn-reaches-200-million-members-worldwide

Lusky, M. B., & Hayes, R. L. (2001). Collaborative consultation and program evaluation. *Journal of Counseling and Development, 79,* 26–38.

National Career Development Association. (2009, October 2). Career counseling competencies. *Career Convergence.* Retrieved from http://ncda.org/aws/NCDA/pt/sd/news_article/37798/_self/layout_ ccmsearch/true

Niles, S. G., & Harris-Bowlsbey, J. (2013). *Career development interventions in the 21st century* (4th ed.). Upper Saddle River, NJ: Pearson.

Norman, K. (2012). Industry tips to a perfect resume, irresistible cover letter, and stand-out interview. *Applied Clinical Trials, 5,* 10.

Passmore, J., Holloway, M., & Rawle-Cope, M. (2010). Using MBTI type to explore differences and the implications for practice for therapists and coaches: Are executive coaches really like counsellors? *Counselling Psychology Quarterly, 23*(1), 1–16.

Priest, S. (2001). A program evaluation primer. *Journal of Experiential Education, 24*(1), 34–40.

Rogers, M. R. (2000). Examining the cultural context of consultation. *School Psychology Review, 29*(3), 414–418.

Wheeler, P. T., & Loesch, L. (1981). Program evaluation and counseling: Yesterday, today, and tomorrow. *Personnel and Guidance Journal, 51,* 573–578.

Consultation in Organizational Settings

Introduction

In my consultation work with organizations, the most common issue is improving the bottom line. This may mean working on increasing productivity, improving managerial skills, or examining the relationships between management and the employees. Lewis Aron (2012) uses the term *executive coaching* (p. 511) as a role that organizational consultants may play when working with an organization. Consultants may find the term *coach* in use more and more as this style of assistance (and role) continues to increase in the field of consultation (coaching was discussed in Chapter 8). Carolyn Swift and Saul Cooper (1986) also support that in the past, the goal of organizational consultation boils down to increasing productivity and profit. They went on to suggest reducing management issues that lessen productivity could be the main focus of mental health consultation in organizational settings. Alice Mann (2012) states "the *primary* goal of organizational consultants is to help individuals, teams, and organizations perform better" (p. 549). There also continues to be a need for organizations to address diversity issues in both the employee and consumer (Sue, 2008). With the increase in diversity within the workforce changing every year, consultants will need to stay up to date on these changes and how they will affect an organization's dynamics.

J. J. Platt and Robert J. Wicks (1979) discuss how organizational consultation can be traced back to industrial psychologists examining physiological factors (i.e., light, heat, space, fatigue) and their effects on productivity. Psychological underpinnings grew out of the militaries' needs to develop psychological tests during World War I. Intelligence and personality tests were created to assist the military in working with recruits. In the 1920s, many of the tests developed for the military started being used by organizations to evaluate employee's attitudes, motivation, and thoughts about their working conditions (Platt & Wicks, 1979). Organizational consultants were the ones assisting industries in this new and exciting field.

As you read this chapter, you will see how many of the consultation techniques used in other settings are still applicable in organizational settings. The consultant will be challenged in different ways, but the goal will still be helping the consultee (now in an organization or the organization itself) with an issue.

LEARNING OBJECTIVES

After reading this chapter, you will be able to

- Define the components of organizational settings
- Demonstrate and apply how mental health consultants can help an organization
- Explore and be able to discuss the importance of and working with diversity in the role as consultant
- Understand and be able to apply some of the dynamics associated with organization and organizational consultation

What is an Organizational Setting?

If someone asked you to define an organization, what would you say? Did you think about big buildings with everyone in traditional business clothes? What about a small family-owned business in a local community? What about all of the settings discussed in this book? Dale R. Fuqua and DeWayne J. Kurpius (1993) remind us that organizations are very diverse, coming in all shapes and sizes, thus making the consultation process even more challenging. They also mention that organizations are consistently changing and can change in very extreme ways due to internal and external forces. W. Warner Burke (2008) reminds us that organizations combine all of the best (or worst) of the human side and the best (or worst) of the business operations side. One cannot succeed without the other. William A. Kahn (2012) describes behaviors (both group and intergroup) that would be considered maladaptive to exist in organizations. Michael A. Diamond, Howard F. Stein, and Seth Allcorn (2002) discuss an all too frequent maladaptive behavior in organizations of creating working silos within an organization. Many times administrators may think that dividing responsibilities among numerous groups will increase productivity.

This division of labor and workforce creates barriers to collaboration and team cohesiveness. Employees may lose sight of the common goal and only narrowly focus on completing the tasks assigned to them each day. We have all heard the statement "folks are resistant to change." This is also true in organizations. When the new manager comes in with new ideas about productivity, many employees may see this as threatening to their daily routines and resist (either overtly or passively) the requests to make changes.

Kahn (2012) goes on to state "such patterns stubbornly resist change by leaders and consultants" (p. 225). Another example is when administrators refuse to address an issue brought up by employees because they think it will hurt overall profits. Improving unsafe working conditions, reducing long work hours, and examining fair pay for workers are all examples of possible dysfunctional behaviors by organizations.

Did you realize that all of the settings you have read about in this book could be considered to be in an organization? As you have reviewed all of the settings discussed in this book, there have been many common themes for consultation in these settings. A. Michael Dougherty (2009) discusses how organizational consultation deals with helping an organization with issues and dilemmas that affect the entire organization. Case Illustration 11.1 provides a sample of some of the dilemmas faced by organizational consultants. Consultants work with various employees (administrators, managers, workers) to facilitate positive change throughout the entire organization. These organizational settings can include schools, community agencies, higher education, industrial, private and public companies, small business, and large businesses to name a few.

Case 11.1: Possible Scenarios in Organizational Consultation

Conflict Resolution

Shana is a consultant who is called to survey a local coffee shop that is struggling to open its doors on time Saturday mornings. The employees are at odds about who is failing to do their job. After individual discussions with the employees and a survey of the weekly schedule, Shana comes to the conclusion that there is poor communication among the employees and negligence on the part of the manager who has been told to work the first shift every Saturday because of the high demand of the job. Instead, the manager opted to assign the job of first shift to a teenage employee who has to rely on her father to drive her to work. According to this employee, her father is notorious for not getting out of bed on time and making her late. Given this pertinent information, the consultant shares her findings with the owner of the coffee shop, and the manager is met with personally to discuss his failure to abide by instruction. He is given another chance and takes over the opening Saturday shift. The coffee shop now opens on time Saturdays due to the consultant's work and the company's constructive changes.

Employee productivity issues

Gary oversees the blog writers for a local magazine company. He has proposed cutting out one blog a publication to save on printing costs. The blog writers are upset about this proposal and are arguing to keep their blogs. So Gary calls Jordan, a consultant, to help him decide how to save money. Jordan asks for records from the past 5 years that include reader surveys. One of the survey questions concerns the most favored section of the magazine. Jordan points out to Gary that over the past 4 years, readers have consistently indicated that the blogs are their favorite part of the magazine. Jordan then explains why she believes that cutting out one blog a publication may lead to a decrease in readers. Jordan then works with Gary to come up with some ideas of how to save money in other ways.

Consultee and/or Client

Dale R. Fuqua, Jody L. Newman, David B. Simpson, and Namok Choi (2012) remind consultants of one important initial question of consultation: *Who is the actual client?* The size and ever changing landscape of some organizations can make this a difficult question to answer. In large organizations, this seemingly simple question can take on a life of its own. Gathering initial consultation information and finding out who may be your client and who may *not* be your client (Fuqua et al., 2012) can be a big challenge even before consultation formally begins. They go on to discuss that many times, a consultant can begin to answer this question by framing it in a type of ethical responsibility to the consultee. Fuqua et al. (2012, p. 116) list issue such as determine who is paying for the consultation, the relationship involved in the actual intervention, and limits on confidentially.

Exercise 11.1: Who Is the client?

Who is the client?

You are the Employee Assistance Program's mental health professional of a large cell phone case company as well as a private consultant. One day, Gary, the company manager, approaches you, looking distressed. Gary explains that the company has suffered considerable financial losses in the past month and wants to figure out why before beginning a new fiscal year. He asks for your consultation services, and you agree, confident that your minor in business and completed workshops in accounting qualify you to help with financial consultation.

1. *What are some challenges to acting as an internal consultant of a company that you are an employee?*

After establishing a contract with Gary in the role of a consultant, you explain the need to stay objective. You ask for details about how the company is currently organized including a list of all employees. You then ask for financial reports and a written budget, customer services guidelines, and distribution policy. Confident that Gary's managerial position qualifies him for data analyzing, you ask Leo to help you determine what department is accountable for this depletion in profit. After a week of carefully reviewing this information, you and Gary agree that the losses have been localized to the customer service department. You ask to meet individually with the customer services manager, Kay.

2. *Please identify the consultee and the client(s).*

(Continued)

(Continued)

You happen to have been part of the committee to hire Kay 2 years ago. She has always been very compliant and eager to help. You explain your concerns and learn she has implemented a new policy for the customer service department, allowing customers one free cell phone case in the instance their case breaks. You are shocked to hear this, aware of the difficulties in ensuring honest customer complaints.

3. *How can you use your counseling skills to remain calm and graciously work with Kay?*

Kay is very apologetic upon realizing the issues in this new policy and learning how it has resulted in financial losses for the company. She states that she needs you to fix this, and she's afraid of messing anything up.

4. *How do you address Kay's dependence upon you in the role of a consultant?*

Consultant, Consultee, and Client

Figure 11.1 The Possible Relationship Between Consultant, Consultee, and Client

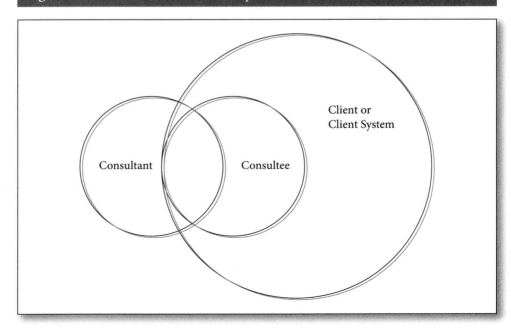

Figure 11.1 provides an example of how the consultant not only works with the consultee, but also has a connection with the client (or client system) that the consultee may be a part of (i.e., working for the organization) at the time. An example would be if an administrator (consultee) asked the consultant to work with a manager (client) on personal communication skills to help reduce the tension between the manager and the employees. Another example could be if a new administrator (consultee and client) asked a consultant to help in the development of leadership skills to effectively oversee the organization. In this example, the consultant only works with the administrator but will impact the entire organization. To summarize, consultants need not assume that they know exactly who the consultee will be until they have explored this question with the parties associated with the initial contact for services. If done properly, this can save time and frustration once the process begins and the consultant is working with the correct consultee.

Trends and Implications for Mental Health Consultants in Organizations

Consultants in Organizations

With the continuous changes in the nation's economic conditions and the most recent economic downturn, organizations continue to try to define themselves and their mission. Many organizations have seen their budgets and workforce constrict and at the same time are trying to maintain the high standards that made them originally successful. Organizations are looking for consultants to help them address the many issues related to these tough economic times. Examples of the various roles for consultants could include the following:

1. Helping organizations with mergers: Working with both organizations to create new cultures of operation and cohesiveness. The consultant may need to work with employees in each organization in dealing with feelings of loss, having to make possibly drastic changes in their daily routines, new supervisors, and other matters.

2. Assisting organizations with the impact of down or right sizing: Consultants can help with the potentially psychological impact of laying off employees in an effort to remain fiscally responsible. Consultants can be brought in to help the released employees understand what may be the next steps in dealing with unemployment. Consultants may also be called in to help the released employees explore other career opportunities and learn about various training opportunities to find new career paths.

3. Assisting an organization with understanding and address needs of diversity within the organization: The consultant could provide workshops and trainings on issues related to diversity in the workplace. Helping administrators and employees understand the need and benefits of a diverse workforce could be a beneficial role of a consultant. A lengthier discussion on diversity is located in the section on diversity in this chapter.

Larry Greiner and Ilse Ennsfellner (2011) report that the consultation industry is a rapidly growing field with over 100 million consultants worldwide. In 2012, Aron reports, "The world of organizational consulting and executive coaching is now more than a billion dollar industry. It has grown rapidly and remains largely unregulated" (p. 511). While these numbers are for *all* types of consultants worldwide, one can quickly see how the demand for mental health consultation services will also continue to increase. One can also see that there is still a gray area in how organizational consultants are formally trained, if at all, for this career opportunity. Mann (2012) states that there is a fundamental difference between providing mental health counseling and mental health consultation. Mann goes on to support the concern that there does not exist an overlapping structure of education, training, and certification that mental health consultants must abide by in providing consultation services. With so many different trends and diverse requests for consultation services, a mental health consultant will need to seek out continuing education opportunities to learn more about the various aspects of organizational consultation and know their limits and expertise!

Guided Practice Exercises
Exercise 11.2: Help With a Hire

Samuel and Leo own a chicken distribution company, serving 500 stores nationwide. They are preparing to open 20 new stores in the southern region of the United States. However, lately, they are in disagreement about who to hire as head director of southern distribution, so they call you for consultation.

1. *What are some ways to ensure you remain objective and do not take sides with either owner?*

Leo believes it's important to hire someone who is from the South in order to better understand the unique needs of the clientele in the region, whereas Samuel doesn't believe there are any qualified candidates living in the South.

2. *What might you want to know about each owner in order to better understand Leo and Samuel's professional relationship and best meet their needs?*

You ask about both owners' preferred candidates at this point and then suggest you administer personality tests to deduce each candidate's strengths and weaknesses.

3. *If the candidates live in different states, how might you conduct a personality assessment long distance?*

4. *How will you handle the results and appropriately relaying the information?*

Will you stay with these consultees until they hire a head director of the southern region?

The Need for Training

Organizational consultation has its roots in organizational development and industrial psychology. Marshall Sashkin and Theodore Kunin (1979) suggested that organizational consultation is not limited to industrial psychologists, but to mental health professionals who have some type of expertise that could potentially benefit an organization. As stated earlier, while many mental health professionals will be contacted by organizations for consultation, it is imperative of the consultant to recognize his or her limits and scope of practice. As a consultant, one of the first questions you need to ask yourself is "Do I understand common business practices and functions well enough to provide effective consultation services?" In 2012, both Kenneth Eisold and Aron encourage consultants to learn as much as possible about the world of business and management before providing consultation services to business organizations. Eisold goes on to discuss a critical aspect of working with organizations that may be overlooked by mental health professionals. Mental health consultants need to ask themselves and explore if they are *OK* with some of the business practices of organizations that may seem detached and not in the best interest of their employees. Oftentimes, the business world is about the bottom line, profits, increased productivity with fewer workers, and shareholder expectations. Consultants may be called in or caught in the middle of a business wanting to do a reduction in force or reduction in employee benefits, and the only reason is to increase overall profits. Eisold (2012) makes a very poignant statement about organizational consultation when he comments in his article that "You don't have to like such practices or policies, but you have to join them where they are—as you have to join patients where they are—if you are to help them improve" (p. 518).

Mann (2012) also encourages mental health consultants to understand the difference between working in traditional counseling venues and trying to translate that into working in more traditional business settings. Gerald Caplan (1995) and Richard D. Parsons and Joel Meyers (1984) remind consultants that, similar to traditional counseling, the consultee (i.e., client) is ultimately responsible for accepting or rejecting the work of the consultant (i.e., professional counselor).

Guided Practice Exercises
Exercise 11.3: Disclosure

Gracie has owned a boutique in a central location of town for 10 years and just recently, her sales have decreased by 45%. Distraught, she decides to seek a consultant and calls you. When you meet with her in person, you ask her to think of any and all things that may be able to account for this change in sales. She reports she cannot think of anything that's currently different from when her sales were strong. You ask permission to do some investigating and speak individually with each employee, careful to assess for anything that could affect sales.

1. *What are some ways you can use your counseling skills to build rapport with the employees you interview?*

2. *How would you handle asking about any personal changes in the employees' lives?*

The head manager, Jenny, informs you she's going through a nasty divorce for the past 6 months and feels very distracted and stressed by this but hasn't wanted to burden her boss, Gracie, with this.

3. *Do you think Jenny's divorce is playing a part in lowered sales? How might you determine if this is the case? Is it important to encourage Jenny to tell Gracie about her divorce? Why or why not? Can you offer counseling for Jenny?*

You decide to continue investigating for factors that may be attributing to changes in sales. You observe employee–customer interactions, conduct a survey of regular customers' satisfaction with their shopping experience at the boutique, read the company's policies for customer service, and survey paperwork covering sales of the past 3 years. After crunching data, you report back to Gracie that a few customers reported a decrease in customer service and a less friendly atmosphere in the past 6 months. In turn, the sales reports show a decrease of sales in this same time period, which happens to also be the timeline of Jenny's divorce fiasco. Without Jenny's permission to disclose her personal struggle, you decide to carefully observe Jenny's interactions with customers for the next week.

4. *What would you do if you notice Jenny treating customers with below-standard service? Does Gracie need to know about Jenny's divorce if it is causing Gracie distress, in turn negatively affecting her interactions with customers?*

Aron (2012) contends that just possessing quality mental health theory and technique will not be enough to become a successful mental health organizational consultant. If organizational consultation is a top career goal, taking classes or attending workshops in the areas of management 101 or business 101 is a proactive and potentially valuable part of consultation training and development. Eisold (2012) encourages beginning organizational consultants to make goals of becoming knowledgeable concerning business vernacular, well-known business and management success stories, and even the current financial issues of the day. The areas of organizational consultation could include, but are not limited to, those listed in Table 11.1 below. The exercise located in the Guided Practice Exercise 11.1 will help in a discussion about the similarities and differences between traditional counseling and business consultation.

Guided Practice Exercises
Exercise 11.4: Traditional
Counseling Versus Business Consultation

Using information that you know about traditional counseling and the new information you have about organizational consultation, complete the questions below about what you think are different and similar roles. Please use information from Table 11.1 to assist in your answers about organizational consultation.

Options for this exercise:

1. Take a couple of minutes to complete the questions below. When complete, get in small groups to discuss your answers with each other. After the small group discussion, share answers with the class and have the instructor fill in with information.

2. Take a couple of minutes to answer the questions. Then share with the class in an open discussion.

1. *List as many roles and settings as you can think of for a traditional mental health professional.*

Roles:

Settings:

2. *List as many roles and settings as you can think of for organizational mental health consultants.*

Roles:

Settings:

3. *List any similarities.*

Emerging Roles in Consultation

Throughout this text, we have provided descriptions of the role a consultant would play in various settings. With an eye on emerging consultant roles, two newer areas of mental health consultation are litigation consulting and applied statistical consultants (Cole & Dang, 2010). Finkelman (2010) describes the difference between the newer litigation consulting and the traditional jury consulting (although litigation consultants do perform many of the tasks of traditional jury consultants). Litigation consultants are involved in trial strategy and analyzing the potential risks or gains from going to trial or settling the claim. Howard M. Fielstein and John Lemanski (2004) report that litigation consulting continues to be a fast growing area in the field of legal consultation. Litigation consultants incorporate aspects from the social and behavioral sciences to support the lawyer in litigation procedures. Finkelman (2010) states that "Litigation consulting is both an art and a science" (p. 19). Case Illustration 11.2 provides an example of a professional working as a litigation consultant.

Jason C. Cole and Jeff Dang (2010) suggest that applied statistical consultants can play a critical role in organizational consultation by providing the organization (consultee) with statistical procedures and analyses of data that would typically require the company to hire a full-time statistician but only need the services infrequently. Companies may find contracting with a statistical consultant is more cost effective

Case 11.2: Litigation Consultation

Litigation Consultation

Max is a lawyer defending a twenty-year-old girl, Anna, who claims to have been sexually assaulted by star-football player John S. at a college party. No witnesses have come forward, and Anna only has her word to back her case. Max is concerned that his client is lacking in proof to convict John without witnesses. When Max first joined the case, he tried to get John placed in detention, but his request was denied. In preparation for Anna's next hearing in a circuit court in front of a grand jury, Max has been coaching Anna on how to react to John's counterclaim and how to remain calm in a court setting. However, Max fears he is not doing enough to prepare, so he contacts a litigation consultant named Tom who has vast knowledge of the court system and psychology and works to prepare lawyers for trial. Tom sits down with Max and reviews the paperwork on the case and then meets personally with Anna so he can hear her story. After talking with the plaintiff, Tom feels he can better predict how Anna will react to various occurrences in court including discussing how juries have responded in the past to similar cases. He works with Max on how he can best coach his client, reminding him that she is a hurting victim. Tom explains how Max needs to use layman's terms and a gentler approach when talking with her because she expressed how she is intimidated and overwhelmed with too much legal jargon. He also communicates to Max that a great deal of Anna's fear revolves around seeing the accused in court and how she will react when she recants the events in question. Then, Tom addresses Max's concerns about the jury and the possibility that they will side with the favored football player. Tom analyzes some data that provides information about the pros and cons of taking the case to trial verses settling. Tom shares strategies Max can use when addressing the jury and key words that repetitively can have a powerful effect on this case. They create a list of the most important pieces of information that need to be shared with the jury, prioritizing the list so the most crucial is stated first. Tom then looks over Max's closing statements and suggests some rewording. With a final vote of confidence in the lawyer's ability to win his case, Tom tells Max and Anna he will attend the hearing. He plans to follow up in any way he can until the final verdict.

than hiring a full-time statistician. Statistical consultants assist organizations by analyzing data and providing results from large-scale surveys, questionnaires and other types of measurement. Cole and Dang (2010) remind readers that most PhDs in psychology (and other fields) had to complete at least one statistics course for understanding research, and this knowledge can be used by a statistical consultant. An example of a statistical consultant could be a consultant hired by a large organization to gather and analyze data on why sales in their restaurants in the north are much lower than other parts of the country. The consultant could utilize large-scale surveys to gather data on participant's views and thoughts about the restaurant in this target area. The consultant could also gather data by interviewing employees at these target restaurants using both

Table 11.1 Consultation Roles in Organizational Settings

These are some of the many roles and tasks for which an organization may seek assistance from a professional consultant:

- Conflict resolution: Help to determine the what, when, and how pertaining to an unresolved conflict within an organization.
- Slowing sales at one location: Assist in determining the reason for unexpected slow sales at a specific location and how to make the necessary changes to improve sales.
- Negative customer feedback: Explore the higher than average negative customer feedback and complaints and steps to address the issues.
- Employee productivity issues: Explore a concern of lowering productivity within the organization or a part of the organization.
- Assessment in a search for potential mangers: Provide psychological assessment of employees interested in becoming mangers or supervisors.
- Provision of professional counseling: Assist organization leaders in developing effective leadership skills.
- Overall data collection: Provide assistance to the organization in collecting and analyzing data pertaining to a certain issue.

quantitative and qualitative measures. Using the consultant's training in statistical analyses, information could be provided to the organization about how to remedy the issue in their target restaurants.

When reviewing the diverse roles of consultation in organizational settings, take some time to reread the case illustrations (Case Illustration 11.1) and also complete the exercises located in Guided Practice Exercises throughout the chapter. These vignettes and exercises will help you understand that there are many different roles a consultant can provide when working in organizational settings.

Know the Organization and Boundaries

As mentioned earlier in the chapter, it will be critical for an organizational consultant to learn as much about the organization as possible. Also, as mentioned in other chapters (Chapters 2, 5, & 6), having logical steps or a model of consultation will improve the chances of a successful organizational consultation endeavor. As for gaining knowledge about the specific organization, the steps below could assist in gathering information about the organization:

1. Ask for a copy of the organization's mission statement. Within this statement, consultants can begin to gather information about the organization's beginning days and philosophy about the goals for the organization. Mission statements can and will change over time. A discussion about why and how the mission statement changed will also be beneficial in understanding the direction of an organization.

2. Ask to review the organization's policies and procedures manual(s). In reviewing these manuals, look for specific policies that may be directly related to the reason the organization reached out for consultation services. Policies on hiring practices, diversity issues, and employees' rights are a good place to start.

3. Have several discussions about the current vision of the organization. Chart if this vision is different among administrators, managers and employees. It is always helpful to discuss past company visions and how (and if) they met these goals. Check to evaluate the commitment from all parties within the organization concerning the current vision.

Another key to working as a consultant for an organization is to quickly learn the power players in the organization. This may not always be the top manager or top executive. Wendell L. French and Cecil Bell (1995) define interpersonal power as "the ability to get one's way in a social situation" (p. 303). Consultants are encouraged to talk with employees and other stakeholders to get a sense of what names constantly pop up as possible leaders. French and Bell describe how power and politics are intertwined in most organizations that consultants work with in the field. Knowing how to navigate these power-and-privilege issues will enable the consultant to increase the chances of a successful consultation. Kahn (2012) reminds consultants to be careful and realize that leaders may not be initially willing or able to make changes in the organization due to their own dysfunctional behaviors.

Guided Practice Exercises
Exercise 11.5: Observation

You are a consultant and receive an e-mail from Dane, the manager of an assisted living home. Dane tells you he is having issues with an elderly resident named Michelle who is continually disruptive at dinner, the only meal all seven residents eat together. The resident's outrage has become so bad that two other residents are threatening to leave, and Dane is unsure how to handle the situation. You e-mail back and agree to meet with Dane at the assisted living home.

When you arrive to the facility, you notice how homey it feels and compliment Dane on the welcoming ambiance of the place. He welcomes you to his office and shuts the door to ensure privacy, stating it's probably not necessary to do so as most of the residents can't hear very well. You ask him more about the situation, first inquiring about the nature of the resident's complaints at dinner. Dane explains that Michelle obnoxiously and repeatedly states how awful the food is, particularly how under-cooked and cold it is. You ask if this is the case, and Dane shrugs saying he's not sure as he's never present at dinnertime. You ask who works the dinner shift, and he says the same lady Debra makes dinner every night, except for holidays. You ask permission to stay for dinner the next two nights to observe, and Dane agrees. In between your next visit, and with Dane's help, you gather data on the home's most recent resident changes, the price of living there, weekly dinner menus, and on Debra's file.

1. *How will you introduce yourself to the residents and to Debra without disrupting the normal routine of the house?*

2. *How will you try to maintain authenticity of the situation for realistic observation?*

Both nights you observe that Michelle is very disruptive and negative concerning the food and that Debra appears immune to this negative feedback and ignores her. However, she is very engaged and caring with the other residents. The other residents seem to retreat into their food and stop engaging in conversation once Michelle begins complaining. You also find the food to be both undercooked and cold both nights.

Next you ask to survey the past five clients who left the home prematurely. All five clients report "poor food" as the main reason for leaving. You ask to speak to the two residents who are threatening to move out to see how they feel about Michelle and how they would evaluate their dinners. Both residents report overall dislike for the meals due to them not being the right temperature and them being undercooked in addition to Michelle's bad behavior. When you ask if they have every complained about the food, they shake their heads no and explain that Michelle does enough of that for everyone. Plus, they report that they love Debra and fear hurting her feelings.

Lastly, you ask Debra if you can observe her in the kitchen. She agrees, and you observe her apparent discomfort in this particular setting, moving anxiously from one dish to the other and never using a timer when boiling things like vegetables and pasta. You also notice she is obviously fearful of the oven, and you when you ask if this is the case, she says she burnt herself badly as a child trying to put a cake in the oven. Therefore, she usually uses a toaster oven, cooking one person's meal at a time. This reveals why the food is often cold because it is baked individually yet delivered all together. You report back to Dane and together come up with some interventions to help achieve your goals.

3. *What do you think are some reasonable goals for this assisted living facility?*

4. *How might you help Dane achieve these goals?*

5. *Are you comfortable with confronting Debra on her lack of cooking skills?*

Throughout this text, we have discussed various models and types of consultation. Selection of consultation models is critical for successful consultation, but one of the most important trends in consultation is establishing boundaries and limits of your consultation services. Kahn (2012) reminds consultants to try to be okay with organizations that exhibit both dysfunctional and functional behaviors at the same time. Defining organizational dysfunction can incorporate decisions, choices, actions, and even policies that are not facilitative of the "mission" of the organization. Examples of dysfunctional organizational behaviors could be

- Administrators actively seeking to hire more women into the organization but neglecting to address their manager's pattern of discouraging female employees from taking all of their leave under the Family and Medical Leave Act (FMLA) after having a child.
- Administrators writing policies that encourage hiring employees with diverse backgrounds (race, gender, culture, physical differences) only to review the hiring of employees over the last 5 years and realize that almost 90% of hires are in the same demographic as the managers that did the hiring.
- Administrators using unfair promotion practices that consistently promote individuals that are racially or gender similar, despite policy discouraging this practice. Employees have even seen cases of subtle nepotism in promotions over the past several years.

Power can also be both positive and negative. Leaders using positive power can facilitate others to reach their goals, while leaders using negative power can lead to oppressive policies that could culminate to mistrust and a poor working environment (French & Bell, 1995). Kahn (2012) emphasized that consultants may need to use their confrontation skills to address administrators about their own maladaptive behaviors that have contributed to the issues of the organization. When the administrators make substantial changes, employees are encouraged and may follow with their own change.

Guided Practice Exercises
Exercise 11.6: Organizational Consultant

Slowing Sales at One Location

Caroline is perplexed at the decrease in sales numbers at her natural foods store. So she calls Adam, a consultant, to help her learn what is contributing to this loss. Adam inspects the locale for a few days and quickly sees the problem: One of the employees recently started bringing her dog because her husband is no longer home during the day.

She doesn't want the dog to be alone all day, so she was given permission to bring the dog to work. Adam noticed, however, that while the dog received positive attention from many customers, others were not as enthusiastic about an animal wandering aimlessly through a building where food is kept. Adam suspects that some customers have concerns about the cleanliness of the food because of the dog. Other customers exhibit fear and anxiety around the dog, causing them to rush their shopping and even keeping some customers from entering. Caroline affirms the need for the dog to stay out of the grocery store but does not want to hurt her employee's feelings since she is one of Caroline's best employees. Caroline informs Adam that she has always struggled with confrontation but also realizes that change (in her and the business) needs to take place in order for the store to remain open. Adam works with Caroline for several sessions on increasing Caroline's communication skills and confidence in talking with employees about tough issues. Adam facilitates a discussion between Caroline and the employee concerning the need to come up with another location for the dog to stay during the day. The employee finds another location for her dog and also states that she really appreciates how Caroline approached her during the discussion. Customers hear that the dog is no longer in the store and sales slowly return to their previous rate.

Discussion Questions

1. *Using Internet access, look to see what the local or state laws are concerning animals in food stores. What did you find for your city or state? Should you provide Caroline with this information about pet laws?*

2. *What types of counseling techniques would Adam use to help Caroline with her communication and confrontation needs?*

Multicultural Considerations

As stated in previous chapters, a consultant needs to view himself or herself as a change agent and be culturally sensitive and competent. This is sometimes easier said than done! Most of us at various times in our life struggle to understand our own identity and how we interact with others. Pat Romney (2008) suggests that even the word *diversity*, can be anxiety provoking—for both the consultee and consultant. The racial and cultural makeup of organizations looks very different now than it did 50 or 100 years ago. Women and people of color are now working alongside White men and are in more executive and managerial roles. The United States Census Bureau (2008) reminds us that by 2050, people of color will be the majority group in the United States.

Respecting, addressing, and working with diversity as a consultant has been in the field for some time now. Caplan (1970) wrote about the need for consultants to work with consultees in a respectful manner and work to address cultural variables so they will not have a negative effect on the process. Consultants will need to utilize the multicultural counseling skills and techniques learned in their graduate programs to work with consultees and to respect their diversity. There are numerous identity development models that can be used to help the consultant understand and work with women and men who have very diverse backgrounds (Belenky, Clinchy, Goldberger & Tarule, 1986; Cass, 1979; Helms, 1990; Kim, 2001; Scott & Robinson, 2001; Sue & Sue, 1990) from the consultant. Derald W. Sue (2008) reminds consultants to not rely on different models and possibly fall into overgeneralization of a group or individual. Consultants will need to use their counseling skills to directly talk with the consultee and others in the organization about diversity and help the consultant understand the individual and others' customs.

Organizations will seek consultation services specifically to help them process and deal with issues related to the change in diversity of their employees and consumers. David A. Scott and Tracy L. Robinson (2001) discuss how the disillusionment of the American dream and the restrictive nature of individualism in the workplace will cause stress in an organization and ultimately hurt productivity and profits. Issues such as oppression, racism, and other "isms" will surface when an administrator decides to address the need to bring in diverse employees. The consultant will have the task of assisting the consultee with addressing these issues of diversity within the organization. The consultant will have to face years of oppressive hiring and firing practices (i.e., hiring employees that are racially and/or culturally similar to the employer) and workplace microaggressions (Sue et al., 2007) that some in the organization are not as eager to dissolve as others. The consultant's goal could include services such as, but not limited to, those listed in Table 11.2.

Table 11.2   Consultation Services to Address Diversity

Possible services that a consultant could provide an organization dealing with diversity issues:

- Gather data on hiring practices in the past
- Gather and analyze data on diversity related complaints to Human Resources
- Survey administrators and employees on their attitudes and thoughts about diversity in the workplace
- Gather data on consumer demographics
- Develop surveys or questionnaires to send to consumers to gather data on any issues related to diversity concerns about the organization
- Provide psychoeducational trainings to administrators and employees about diversity in the workplace
- Provide coaching and/or counseling to administrators and managers to address issues related to diversity in the workplace
- Work with administrators, human resources, and managers to create new policies and procedures that will address diversity issues in the workplace

Guided Practice Exercises
Exercise 11.7: Feedback

Negative Customer Feedback

Brooke owns a gym in town and wants to expand to a new location but has been receiving some neutral and negative comments on surveys she sent out to her members recently. Last week, Brooke was written a strongly worded letter from a member of her gym complaining about the size of the stalls in the bathroom. The writer goes on and on about how small the stalls are and how ridiculous it is to expect people to be able to change into gym clothes inside the stall. Upset at the customer's frustration and lower marks on the survey, Brooke calls Tiana, a consultant, to help her know how to examine and properly handle the situation. Tiana begins by gathering data from the most recent surveys looking for themes. She also reads the letter and decides there must be more to this member's story. Tiana creates a report of the survey data and goes over this with Brooke. She reports to Brooke that one common theme is that many of the members do not feel like they are being heard when it comes to their comments and suggestions to Brooke. Several of the members stated "Brooke always seems too busy to stop and talk with me like she did in the past." Brooke responds that she has been so busy thinking about expanding her business that unfortunately she has not been able to spend much time with the members. She also states that she does not know every member by memory and can't remember exactly who this member is with the specific concern about the bathrooms.

Discussion Questions

1. *What could be Tiana's next steps as a consultant in helping Brooke?*

2. *After Tiana assists Brooke in the next steps, should Tiana suggest a follow-up survey? Why?*

Chapter Keystones

- Organizations are all shapes and sizes, from Fortune 500 to the local bakery.
- Counseling consultants need to understand the dynamics and basic organizational structure and nomenclature.
- It is important to know who will be the consultee and/or client. They can be the same or different.

- Having an advanced mental health degree may not be enough for organizational consulting. Completing training in business courses will help the consultant understand the world of organizations and businesses.
- Consultants who do their homework about an organization and the power players in the organization may increase the chances of a successful consultation endeavor.

Web-Based and Literature-Based Resources

Websites

WorkplaceDiversity.com (dedicated to helping diverse individuals find careers with organizations seeking diverse workers): http:// www.workplacediversity.com
Office of Workplace Diversity (office within the Federal Communications Commission); contains information a consultant may need to learn and understand diversity in the workplace, affirmative action, and equal employment opportunity: http://www.fcc.gov/office-workplace-diversity

Suggested Readings

Gerstein, L. H., Heppner, P., Ægisdóttir, S., Leung, S.-M. A., Norsworthy K. L. (Eds.). (2009). *International handbook of cross-cultural counseling: Cultural assumptions and practices worldwide.* Thousand Oaks, CA: Sage.
Sue, D. W., & Sue, D. (2012). *Counseling the culturally diverse: Theory and practice* (6th ed.). Hoboken, NJ: Wiley.

References

Aron, L. (2012). Psychoanalysis in the workplace: An introduction. *Psychoanalytic Dialogues, 22,* 511–516. doi:10.1080/10481885.2012.717041
Belenky, M. F., Clinchy, B. M., Goldberger, N. R., & Tarule, J. M. (1986). *Women's ways of knowing: The development of self, voice, and mind.* New York, NY: Basic Books.
Burke, W. W. (2008). *Organization change: Theory and practice* (2nd ed.). Thousand Oaks, CA: Sage.
Caplan, G. (1970). *The theory and practice of mental health consultation.* New York, NY: Basic Books.
Caplan, G. (1995). Types of mental health consultation. *Journal of Educational and Psychological Consultation,* 6(1), 7–21.
Cass, V. C. (1979). Homosexual identity formation: A theoretical model. *Journal of Homosexuality, 4,* 219-235.
Cole, J. C., & Dang, J. (2010). Measurement, Monte Carlo, and music: Why doctorates in psychology and other applied fields make desirable consultants in statistics. *Consulting Psychology Journal, 62,* 4–11.
Diamond, M. A., Stein, H. F., & Allcorn, S. (2002). Organizational silos: Horizontal organizational fragmentation. *Journal for the Psychoanalysis of Culture & Society, 7,* 280–296.
Dougherty, A. M. (2009). *Psychological consultation and collaboration in school and community settings* (5th ed.). Belmont, CA: Brooks/Cole.
Eisold, K. (2012). Psychoanalysis at work. *Psychoanalytic Dialogues, 22,* 517–528. doi:10.1080/10481885.2012.717044
Fielstein, H., & Lemanski, J. F. (2004, December 1). Litigation consulting—An overview. *The Metropolitan Corporate Counsel.* Retrieved from http://www.metrocorpcounsel.com/current.php?artType=view&artMonth= December&artYear=2004&EntryNo=2099

Finkelman, J. M. (2010). Litigation consulting: Expanding beyond jury selection to trial strategy and tactics. *Consulting Psychology Journal, 62,* 12–20.

French, W. L., & Bell, C. (1995). *Organization development: Behavioral science interventions for organization improvement* (5th ed.). Englewood Cliffs, NJ: Prentice Hall.

Fuqua, D. R., & Kurpius, D. J. (1993). Conceptual models in organizational consultation. *Journal of Counseling and Development, 71,* 607–618

Fuqua, D. R., Newman, J. L., Simpson, D. B., & Choi, N. (2012). Who is the client in organizational consultation? *Consulting Psychology Journal: Practice and Research, 64*(2), 108–118. doi:10.1037/a0027722

Greiner, L., & Ennsfellner, I. (2011). *Management consultants as professionals, or are they?* (CEO Publication T 08-10 [546]). Los Angeles, CA: Center for Effective Organizations. Retrieved from http://ceo.usc.edu/pdf/t08_10.pdf

Helms, J. E. (1990). *Black and white racial identity: Theory, research and practice.* New York, NY: Greenwood Press.

Kahn, W. A. (2012). The functions of dysfunction: Implications for organizational diagnosis and change. *Consulting Psychology Journal: Practice and Research, 64,* 225–241.

Kim, J. (2001). Asian American identity development theory. In C. L. Wijeyesinghe & B. W. Jackson, III (Eds.), *New perspectives on racial and identity development: A theoretical and practical anthology* (pp. 67–90). New York, NY: New York University Press.

Kurpius, D. J., & Fuqua, D. R. (1993). Fundamental issues in defining consultation. *Journal of Counseling & Development, 71,* 598–600. doi:10.1002/j.1556-6676.1993.tb02248.x

Mann, A. (2012). What organizational consultants do and what it takes to become one: Commentary on papers by Kenneth Eisold and Marc Maltz. *Psychoanalytic Dialogues, 22,* 547–554. doi:10.1080/10481885.2012.719440

Newman, R. (2010). Diversifying consulting psychology for the future. *Consulting Psychology Journal: Practice And Research, 62,* 73–76. doi:10.1037/a0018532

Parsons R. D., & Meyers, J. (1984). *Developing consultation skills: A guide to training, development, and assessment for human services professionals.* San Francisco, CA: Jossey-Bass.

Platt, J. J., & Wicks, R. J. (1979). *The psychological consultant.* New York, NY: Grune & Stratton.

Romney, P. (2008). Consulting for diversity and social justice: Challenges and rewards. *Consulting Psychology Journal: Practice and Research, 60,* 139–156.

Sashkin, M., & Kunin, T. (1979). Psychological consultation in industry. In J.J. Platt & R.J. Wicks, R. J. (Eds.), *The psychological consultant.* (pp. 47-80). New York, NY: Grune & Stratton.

Scott, D. A., & Robinson, T. L. (2001). White male identity development: The Key model. *Journal of Counseling and Development, 79,* 415–421.

Sue, D. W. (2008). Multicultural organizational consultation: A social justice perspective. *Consulting Psychology Journal: Practice and Research, 60,* 157–169. doi:10.1037/0736-9735.60.2.157

Sue, D. W., Capodilupo, C. M., Torino, G. C., Bucceri, J. M., Holder, A. M. B., Nadal, K. L., & Esquilin, M. (2007). Racial microaggressions in everyday life: Implications for clinical practice. *American Psychologist, 62,* 271–286.

Sue, D. W., & Sue, D. (1990). *Counseling the culturally different: Theory and practice.* New York, NY: Wiley.

Swift, C. F., & Cooper, S. (1986). Settings, consultees, and clients. In F. Mannino, E. Trickett, M. Shore, M. Kidder, & G. Levin, *Handbook of mental health consultation* (pp. 247–278). Rockville, MD: National Institute of Mental Health.

United States Census Bureau. (2008). *An older and more diverse nation by midcentury.* Retrieved from http://www.census.gov/newsroom/releases/archives/population/cb08-123.html

12

Epilogue

From the Author's Chair

Writing a text book is part research—part experience—but mostly the articulation of the author's unique perspective on practice and profession. Each author has made personal decisions on how to organize the book and what, from the abundance of information available, should be included. These decisions reflect the author's bias, personal interest, values, and professional identity. We, as editors of the series, have invited each author to respond to the following questions as a way of providing the reader a glimpse into the "person" and not just the product of the author.

It is our hope that these brief reflections will provide a little more insight into our view of our profession—and ourselves—as professionals.

Interview With Richard Parsons PhD and Naijian Zhang PhD

Question: There is certainly an abundance of insightful points found within this text. But if you were asked to identify a single point or theme from all that is presented that you would hope would stand out and stick with the reader, what would that point or theme be?

Dr. Kissinger

I find it difficult to identify a single thread given the dynamics of counseling and consultation. I would argue that a blend of content knowledge, skill competencies, attention to relational and process dynamics (i.e., alliance), and attention to self via the "reflective practitioner" model offers suitable grounding. Within these elements As noted, I also am a strong believer in developing and nurturing a reflective practitioner identity. With attention to these dimensions, I believe you will find consulting to be a dynamic, challenging, and rewarding venture. Finally, I would reiterate my colleagues' imperative about recognizing that consultation, like counseling, is a developmental process and at various points in your career (and certainly as a counselor-in-training) you will almost certainly feel lost or unprepared—and you will not be alone! The knowledge, skills, and experiences of your colleagues and supervisors are enormously helpful (and often comforting). Attending to each of these dimensions will help you to balance your career and personal life and ultimately better serve your clients.

Dr. Scott

My hope is that students will come away with the knowledge that consultation can be a career opportunity for them in the future. I have so many students unsure of what setting they want to work in as a counselor. They know they love counseling but want to utilize all of their skills in ways that are rewarding for them. Counseling students may also have a passion and knowledge about working with organizations . . . consultation could be a way to combine both into a rewarding career. Consultation could take a mental health professional all over the country working with different organizations and different issues at each site.

Dr. Royal

Not all consultation activities are external, for-profit endeavors. Most consultation efforts will likely be internal, individual (1:1) exchanges with a colleague. There will be times, as a counselor, when you will encounter clients with which you struggle. They will present challenging circumstances and situations. You may feel inept, unprepared, inexperienced, or unable to help them. Take heart, you are still in training. It is not expected that you be an "expert" counselor yet. It takes time to develop into a practitioner who displays proficiency in many areas. Even for some practitioners who have been out of school for a while may find that they have deficiencies in some areas or some populations. A good counselor is always developing as a clinician and a person.

When these difficult situations arise (and they will), your task is to seek consultation. You are not alone. Ask for help when you need it, when you are struggling, and when you aren't sure what to do. When in doubt, consult.

Another part of your professional responsibility as a counselor is to provide consultation and a listening ear to colleagues when they need it as well. They may need your insights regarding their clients or themselves. Hopefully, you feel prepared enough to provide a consultative relationship to a fellow mental health professional.

Question: In the text there is a great deal of research cited—theories presented. Could you share from your own experience how the information presented within the text may actually look or take form in practice?

Dr. Royal

When reviewing consultation theories or models (or even considering consultation in specific settings), the content or task can appear very structured, logical, and method driven. I think that this is important—and that you need to have a foundation and basis from which you operate. In practice, however, I've found that consultation tends to be more fluid or dynamic rather than static. You may be in a counseling role and need to quickly shift into "consultation mode." The shift could be as a result of who you are working with or as a result of the needs with which you are presented. Consultation can very well take place in the context of other roles. It can occur between two professionals, between a counselor and parent of a client, or as an individual working with an organization, just to name a few. As a result, I think that you need to have a clear sense of who you are and what you are doing as a consultant.

I routinely assign a consultation field experience for my students. They are tasked with conducting two consultation meetings with individuals who are parents of at least one child. For the purposes of the assignment, I make it very clear that they are to serve as consultants and not counselors. The students are not yet at the point in their counselor education program where they are in a clinical placement. Their task is to consult with the parent or parents on some type of child-rearing problem. The document that they turn in for evaluation is a report and reflection of their experience. At least half of the class usually responds to one of the reflection questions with a statement like this: "It was very hard to stay in the consultant role, rather than move into a counseling role."

I think this reflection is a good indicator of what it feels like in practice. Sometimes, roles will feel similar and feel like there is a "blending" of roles. As a counselor, you need to be clear about what your goals are for the work that you are doing. In consultation, it can sometimes come down to the relationship you have with your consultee and who is responsible for implementing the interventions.

Dr. Kissinger

In boxing, there is a phrase that suggests every strategy is perfect until you get punched in the nose. As a student, I generally assumed that by learning different counseling theories and reading the studies my professors required, I would soon experience (and generate) moments of unmitigated therapeutic brilliance. As a novice consultant, however, I felt the same sense of disorientation and surprise a boxer might who was caught off-guard by a stiff punch to the nose. What I've learned and I hope you will take from this text is that your grounding in evidenced-based theory and research will allow you to withstand that first "blow" by providing a framework for moving forward despite those initial (and expected) moments of hesitancy you will encounter. Still, having experienced firsthand the realities of theory into practice, I humbly admit this sometimes is easier said than done. Remember, though, content expertise will always require engagement in the literature and the willingness to be open to the expertise and feedback of supervisors and your consultees. Thus, continue to seek out additional knowledge and training through supervision and continuing education opportunities, consultation with colleagues, and by engaging in service and leadership activities with professional organizations.

Dr. Scott

I agree with Dr. Royal in that the world of consultation is much more fluid than just reciting theories and stages. I tell students that these theories and stages are the framework, but each situation will call for subtle or drastic changes in how you administer and use the theories and techniques in consulting. I remind students that when the consultant and consultee reach an impasse, going back to the basic theories and stages may help break open the sticking point. By providing the structure of theories and techniques, consultants can keep track of the consulting process and stay aware if things are moving too fast or slow. The theories will also act as a reminder if the consultant feels that something is missing in the process. Questions to ask that are related to consultation theory and stages could be . . . "Remember to talk about issues related to termination before the last day" or "Did I remember to talk with the consultee about boundaries?" I like to have the theories in my consultation toolbox as reminders during the process.

Question: As one of the authors of this text, what might this book reveal about your own professional identity?

Dr. Kissinger

My gut response to this question is, "It's been a process." My journey from undergraduate to counselor educator took years and some fits and starts. It wasn't until I switched from a student affairs track to community mental health that I felt the beginning of a professional identity. Today I proudly identify as a professional counselor and counselor educator. Within these roles my process of developing as a counselor–consultant continues to develop.

Writing this textbook with my colleagues has been a rewarding and challenging experience—and one I wouldn't have undertaken had I not experienced the roles and responsibilities of consultation firsthand. Fortunately, I was the rookie among a team of established and astute consultants. Although I brought content expertise to the table, it was not until I engaged in the consultation process that "theory into practice" made sense to me; the same process that occurred when I graduated and began my clinical practice. So, to repeat a theme, learn and stay abreast of the evidence-based literature, seek out and utilize the knowledge and experience of your professors, supervisors, and other mentors, and consider that the development of one's professional identity is an individual one with no certain path.

Dr. Royal

For me personally, I think the content that I have contributed reveals where my professional passions have been over the last decade. In the past, I have identified myself as a counselor first (primarily conducting family counseling and parent consultation), and as a counselor educator a distant second. The more freedom that I have been given to explore in an academic setting, the more that I have gravitated toward (a) technology; (b) the application of technology in counseling, consultation, and counselor education; and (c) consultation in career counseling settings. I view myself more as a counselor educator now, providing education and consultation to practicing counselors and counselors-in-training. The more "expertise" that I have developed in my interest areas, the more I have served as a consultant in these areas. It is a win–win arrangement. I have simply pursued and followed my interests, passions, and things I enjoy. And as a result, I have become known for these areas.

I think this is a good model for anyone who has an interest in serving in an external, or for-profit, consultation role. Explore areas in which you are passionate about and develop your expertise in these areas. It won't seem like "work" because of your intrinsic interest. Find what you love to do, get good at it, and then share what you have learned.

Dr. Scott

Options. I have always found counseling and consultation to provide so many interesting options for me professionally. I have enjoyed meeting all of the clients and consultees over the past 20 years. And now, as a counselor educator, I can share these journeys with our students as they explore what they want to do with their graduate degrees. Each person has a story and each organization is different. This uniqueness, keeps me interested and passionate about teaching, counseling, and consultation. Counseling and consultation affords professionals in the field the ability to do something "new" each day.

Question: What final prescription—direction—might you offer your readers as they continue in their journey toward becoming professional counselors?

Dr. Royal

You can't be an expert in everything. Even when someone is an expert in one thing, it doesn't happen overnight. Likewise, you can't be an expert in dealing with every type of client or setting. If this were even possible, then it would take time to encounter and gain personal experience with each client or group.

In reality, you're going to repeatedly run into clients and situations that you've never experienced and have no framework from which to work. You'll need the expertise of someone else, someone who has previous experience with that client or situation and can help you develop the tools that you need to continue working. In short, you are going to need to seek consultation whether you like it or not. Your colleagues will as well. Be prepared to function as both a consultee and consultant.

Dr. Scott

Enjoy the ride. I tell my students that they are entering a career field that does not lend itself to discussions or stories around the holiday dinner table. While the family may enjoy the stories told by their aunt concerning some of her experiences at work, mental health professionals do not have the same luxury. Our daily activities working with clients, and the very real issues related to the concerns of mental health in our country has the potential to weigh down professionals in our field. Assisting clients in understanding their life journeys, career changes, diagnoses, and connections to family and community keep me engaged and passionate about my work. One of my goals as a counselor educator is to keep having open dialogue with our students about these real issues for mental health professionals and how they can work to avoid burnout. My hope is that our students, after they graduate, will enjoy getting up to go to work when the alarm clock goes off in the mornings!

Dr. Kissinger

At this point I've been a licensed counselor for 15 years and a counselor educator and supervisor for nearly a decade. Perhaps the best I can offer readers is to honor both the simplicity and complexity of the counseling (and supervisory/consultation) alliance and process. I've found each to be deceptive, enlightening, perplexing, comforting, and at times exhausting. To me it is a humbling and wonderful experience to know that clients/consultees are willing to let me share in their narratives. As a counselor educator I often see students view an "A" grade as the primary indicator of their success as a counselor-in-training. While grades are important, I have never had a client ask me what my grade point average was in graduate school. My challenge to you is to frame success (in graduate training, at least) beyond grades. For example, instead of worrying about your grade on a final, ask yourself a question such as, "what have I learned and what implications does it have for my work with clients". I have also learned that the realities of our profession require us to maintain confidentialities that can, at times, weigh heavily on our lives. During difficult times, seek out and engage with your professors, supervisors, and peers. There is comfort, support, and wisdom in each of these relationships for you and those you engage.

Index

Abuse victims, career consultation and, 242
Academic honors, awards, résumé, 233
Acceptance, 55
Adlerian approach, 206
Adobe Connect, 65
Advertising, 61
Advocate role, consulting, 31
Affective state, addressing client, 165
Allcorn, Seth, 251
Alleyne, Sonia, 237
American Association for Marriage and Family Therapy, 15
American Association of Counseling and Development (AACD), 139
American Counseling Association (ACA), 137, 138, 141, 145–146
American Counseling Association (ACA) Code of Ethics, 48, 157 (table)
American Mental Health Counseling Association (AMHCA), 137
American Psychological Association (APA), 15, 137
American School Counselor Association (ASCA), 137, 139
Americans with Disabilities Act (ADA), 239
Andermann, Lisa, 191
Apple iCloud, 66
Apple Keynote, 65
Apple Pages, 65, 231
Aron, Lewis, 250, 257, 259
Aspirational ethics, 144
Assessment:
    in consultation, 167
    needs, 244
    observation, CBC and, 119
Autonomy, 141

Backup storage, 67
Bandura, A., 98
Becker, Howard S., 79

Behavioral consultation:
    behavioral case consultation, 102–105
    behavioral system consultation, 107–110
    behavioral technology training, 105–107
    behavior change principles, 100
    historical perspective, 98–100
    present-centered orientation, 100
    process of, 100–101, 104
    scientific perspective, 100
Behavioral theory, 28–29
Behavior change principles, 100
Behavior ecology, 107
Bell, Cecil H., 76, 263
Beneficence, 141
Berg, Insoo Kim, 126
Bergan, John R., 87, 99, 102, 110
Berman, William H., 189
Bias, 46, 48, 165
Board Certified Coach (BCC), 227
Bordin, E. S., 20–22. See also Working Alliance entries
Boundaries, knowing organizational, 262–265
Bradt, George, 189
Brand, 61
Branding statement, in résumé, 232
Brief strategic family therapy (BSFT), 131
Bronfenbrenner, U., 110
Brown, Duane, 78–79, 87, 131, 201
Bryan, Julia, 215
Burke, Warner, 251
Buysse, Virginia, 140

CACREP. See Council for the Accreditation of Counseling and Related Educational Programs
Caplan, Gerald, 4, 5, 8–9, 98, 127, 160–166, 171, 187, 188, 190, 257, 267. See also Mental health setting consultation entries
Caplan, Ruth B., 163–166
Caplanian consultation, 162, 171

Career coaches, 226–227
Career consultant:
   defining, 228
   job interviews and, 235–236
Career consultation:
   career coaches, 226–227
   career consultant, 228
   career development facilitators (CDF),
     228–229
   career training, education, 237–238
   college, university, graduate, undergrad
     students, 239–240
   corrections, ex-offenders, 241
   counselors, 226
   cultural embeddedness and, 246
   culture, understanding own, 247
   direct services, 224–225
   for-profit agencies, 242
   military veterans, 241
   networking, LinkedIn, 236–237
   nonprofit agencies, 242
   private practice, 241–242
   program evaluation, 242–245. *See also*
     Program evaluation
   qualitative methodologies,
     data collection, 247
   résumé writing, content and, 228–236
   school counselors (K–12), 238–239
   self-identification, 225–226
   unemployed workers, 241
   vocational rehabilitation, 239
Career counselors, 226
Career development facilitators (CDF),
   228–229
CareerOneStop, 241
Career training, education, 237–238
Carlson, J., 200
Carlson, Jon, 214
Carter, R. T., 215
Cases:
   autonomy, respect for, 141
   Beginning Steps, 7–8
   behavioral case consultation, example, 103
   behavioral system consultation, 108–109
   behavioral system consultation, child
     inattentiveness, 112
   behavioral technology training, 106
   career consultation, 230
   career needs, 244
   CBT behavioral/contingency, 116

child inattentiveness, behavioral case
   consultation and, 103
conjoint behavioral consultation, child
   inattentiveness, 111
consultation stages, 73
consultee with diverse background, example
   of, 47
contract, sample, 57–59
directive role, example of consultant
   assuming, 25–26
documentation problems, CBT strategies, 117
expert role, challenges when assuming, 32
fidelity, 142
interviews, personal characteristics, 247
litigation consultant, 261
negotiation, art of, 63
organizational consultation, 252
process role, example of consultant
   assuming a, 36–37
report writing, 68
trainer-educator role, example of consultant
   assuming, 33
university career services consultant, 240
working alliance, example, 23–24
Case-centered group, 214
Center for Credentialing and Education
   (CCE), 227–229
C groups, 214
Choi, Namok, 253
Chowanex, Gergory D., 86
Chronological résumé, 228–231
Client, defining, 253–255
Client-centered case consultation, 8, 169–170
Client welfare, ethics and, 145–148
Cloud storage, 66
Coaching, 9, 190
Coconut Grove Fire, 4
Codes of ethics. See Consultation, ethical, legal
   codes in
Cognitive-behavioral model, of consultation,
   112–119
   intervention process, 115
   intervention selection, 115–119
   multicultural considerations, 119–120
   observation, assessment and, 119
   problem identification, 114–115
Cognitive states, addressing client, 165
Cohort, develop a, 184
Cole, Jason C., 260, 261
Collaboration, 20, 102, 188

Collaboration for change, 21
Collaborative treatment planning, 146
Collaborator role, 34
College campuses, career consultation on,
    239–240
Combination résumé, 230
Communication, technology consultation and,
    64–65
Communication skills, 44–45
Competency, consultant. *See* Consultant
    competency
Confidence, lack of consultee, 172
Confidentiality, 148–150
Conflict resolution, 252
Conjoint behavior consultation (CBC),
    110–112, 206
Consideration, 55
Constructivism, 126
Consultant, consultee, client relationship, 254
Consultant competency, 145–148
Consultant recommendations, 184–185
Consultant report, 179–180
Consultant response, client-centered case
    consultation and, 170
Consultants, in organizations, 255–257
Consultant skills:
    checklist, cross-cultural competencies, 48
    contract negotiation, 54–55
    cross-cultural competencies, 47–48
    ethical framework, use of technology and, 67
    fee structures, 62–64
    fiscal and organizational responsibilities,
        51–53
    formal contract, 55–56
    foundational, 44–45
    marketing, 60–61
    multicultural considerations, 45–47
    nonprofit *v.* for-profit. *See also* Nonprofit *v.*
        for-profit consultation, 49–51
    proposals, generating, 53–54
    public speaking, pedagogy, research,
        assessment and evaluation, 60
    report writing, 68–70
    skills deficits, 171–172
    technology skills, use of, 64–67
    workshops, 56–60
Consultation:
    advantages of, 9–14
    counseling/therapy and supervision
        alliances *v.* (table), 21

defining, 5–8
educational accreditation, 14–15
effectiveness of, 14
executive, 188–190
historical perspectives, 3–5
multiculturalism and, 15
triage (figure), 10
types of, 8–9, 11–12
Consultation process, steps in (figure), 6
Consultation relationship, working alliance
    and, 18–27. *See also* Working alliance
    entries
Consultation roles, 27–37
    advocate role, 31
    collaborator role, 34
    expert role, 31–32
    fact finder role, 35
    process specialist role, 35–37
    role formulation and structuring, 27–29
    role selection, 29–30
    trainer-educator role, 32–34
Consultation stages:
    data crunching, 83
    exploration, 76–77, 79–80
    file keeping, 80–81
    getting to know you, 78–79
    goal setting, 83–85
    intervention/implementation stage, 84–87
    interviews and observations, 81–83
    multicultural considerations, 94–95
    outcome, 87–89
    preliminary, 75–77
    termination stage, 89–94
Consultation triage, 9
Consultee:
    defining, 253–255
    identification, 181
Consultee-centered administrative
    consultation, 9, 180–182
Consultee-centered case consultation, 8–9,
    171–177
    confidence and, 172
    knowledge and, 172
    skill deficit, 171–172
Consulting alliance (relationship), 166–167
Content capturing, technology and, 65–66
Contextual factors, 114–115
Contract(s):
    behavior contingency, 118
    formal, 55–56

negotiation, 54–55
sample, 57–59
simulated, 64
Cooper, Saul, 9, 13, 250
Coordinate service, 201
Core competence, in résumé, 233–234
Core leadership competencies, 189
Corporate business, career consultation and, 242
Corrections, career consultation with
    ex-offenders and, 241
Corse, Sara J., 79, 83, 84, 90
Cost, of intervention, 86
Cottingham, Harold F., 200
Council for the Accreditation of Counseling
    and Related Educational Programs
    (CACREP), 14–15, 140
Council on Postsecondary Accreditation,
    14–15
Council on Rehabilitation Education (CORE),
    14–15
Counseling/therapy, distinctions between
    consultation, supervisory alliance
    and (table), 21
Counselor education standards, 14–15
Cover letter writing, résumé, 234–235
Credentials section, on résumé, 233
Crisis theory, 4
Cross-cultural consultation competencies,
    47–48
    checklist, 48
    ethical guidelines, 48–49
Cultural embeddedness,
    career consultation, 246
Culture:
    consultation and, 45–47
    understanding one's own, 247

Dang, Jeff, 260, 261
Data:
    collection methods, 35
    crunching, 83
    meetings and, 182–183
    program evaluation and, 243
    qualitative methodologies to gather, 247
Defining statement, résumé, 232
Delivery skills, technology and, 65–66
de Shazer, Steve, 126, 129
Developing Role, 139
Developmental case consultation, 102
Developmental coaching, 189
Diagnostic labels, 118

Diamond, Michael A., 251
Dinkmeyer, Don C., 200, 214
Directive role, in consultation, 25–26
Direct services, 224–225
Diversity:
    consultation services and, 267 (table)
    multicultural considerations and, 266–268
    training in, 46–47
Documentation problems, 117
Document management, collaboration,
    sharing, technology and, 66
Dougherty, A. M., 35, 76, 92, 139, 212, 252
Dropbox, 66
Duggan, Molly H., 243
Dulan, Jeannette, 4–5

Ecological systems theory, 107
Education:
    career training and, 237–238
    résumé section on, 232
Eisold, Kenneth, 257, 259
Electronic submissions (résumé), 231
Elluminate Live!, 65
Employee productivity issues, 252
Encryption, 67
Ennsfellner, Ilse, 13, 256
Erchul, William P., 98, 111
Ethical/legal codes in consultation, 137–139
    ethical guidelines development, 139–140
    ethical principles, 140–156. See also Ethical
        principles
    multicultural considerations, 156
Ethical behavior, 20
Ethical guidelines:
    cross-cultural, 48
    development of, 139–140
Ethical principles, 140–144
    client welfare, 145–148
    confidentiality, 148–150
    professional competencies, 144–145
    professional relationships, 152–156
    public statement parameters, 150–151
    social/moral responsibility, 151–152
Ethics:
    choosing code of, 137
    in consultation. See Ethical/legal codes in
        consultation, 137–139
Evaluation, final, 89–90
Evaluation models, 243–245
    feasibility study, 244–245
    needs assessment, 244

outcome/summative, 245
    process or formative, 245
Evernote, 66
Evidence-based professional interview, 198
Exception question, 131
Executive coaching, 9, 188–190, 250
Ex-offenders, career consultation with, 241
Exosystems, 107
Experience, on résumé, 233
Expert role, consulting, 31–32
External consultation, 50

Facebook, 65, 236
Fact finder role, 35
Family and Medical Leave Act (FMLA), 265
Faust, Verne, 200
Feasibility study, model evaluation, 244–245
Feedback, negative customer, 268
Fee structures, consulting, 62–64, 148
Fernstrom, Pamela, 5
Fidelity, 141, 142
Fielstein, Howard M., 260
Final evaluation, 89–90
Finkelman, J. M., 260
Firewalls, 67
Fiscal responsibilities, 51–52
Formal contract, 55–56
Formal entry, 78–79
Formative evaluation, 87–89, 245
For-profit consultation, 50, 242
Foundational skills, consultant, 44–45
Four Factors, ABC and, 115
French, Wendell L., 76, 263
Fuchs, Douglas, 4–5
Fuchs, Lynn, 4–5
Functional behavioral assessment, 114
Functional résumé, 229–230
Funding, seeking, 184
Fung, Kenneth, 190–191
Fuqua, Dale R., 5, 251, 253

Gallessich, June, 74, 78–79, 87
Glass ceiling, 191
Goal attainment, 102–103
Goal formation, 129–131
Goal setting, 83–85
Google Docs, 231
Google Drive, 66
GoToMeeting, 65
Graduate students, career consultation,
    239–240

Greiner, Larry, 13, 256
Grissom, Priscilla F., 111
Gross, Douglas R., 139
Group consultations, 187–188, 213–214
Group discussion, 135
Group work skills, 45
Gutkin, T. B., 98

Hall, Alex S., 80, 84
Harris-Bowlsbey, JoAnn, 240
Hasbrouck, Jan, 74
Headhunters, 237
Heading section, résumé, 232
Herlihy, Barbara, 141
Historical perspective, behavioral consultation,
    98–100
Holcomb-McCoy, Cheryl, 48, 215
Home-school collaboration, 206–207
Hung Tat Lo, 191
Hybrid résumé, 230

Idol, Lorna, 83
Implementation stage, consultation, 84–87
Independent school-based mental health
    program model (ISBMHP), 208
Individuals with Disabilities Education Act
    (IDEA), 31, 200, 212
Industrial psychologists, 250
Instagram, 65
Instruction-based consultation (IC), 211–212
Intelligence tests, 250–251
Intentional dialogue, 131
Internal consultation, nonprofit consultation
    and, 49–50
Internal dialogue, 116, 118
Interpersonal dynamic, 19–20
Interpersonal skills, 44–45
Interpersonal style, 20
Intervention(s):
    mental health consulting and, 168
    process, CBT and, 115
    response to, 212
    selection, CBT and, 115–119
    stage, consultation, 84–87
Interviews:
    author, 271–276
    job, 235–236
    observations and, 81–83
Intimate partner violence victims, career
    consultation and, 242
Issue groups, 213

Job interviews, 235–236
Johnson, Lawrence J., 214
Joint Committee on The Elementary School
    Counselor, 200
Journal for Counseling and Development, 139
Jurgens, Jill C., 243
Justice, 141

Kahn, Wallace J., 201, 265
Kahn, William A., 251–252
Keywords, 231
Kissinger, Daniel B. (interview with),
    271–274, 276
Kitchener, Karen S., 76
Knowledge, lack of, 172
Koortzen, Pieter, 226–227
Krajl, Mary M., 86
Kratochwill, Thomas R., 87, 102, 110
Kunin, Theodore, 257
Kurpius, DeWayne J., 5, 251

Langer, Susan N., 114
Language, consultation and, 45–47, 120
Learning theories, 99
Lee, C. C., 215
Legal codes in consultation. *See* Ethical/legal
    codes in consultation
Lemanski, John, 260
Licensure credentials, on résumé, 233
Lin, Meei-Ju, 80, 84
Lindemann, Erich, 4
LinkedIn, 65, 236–237
Lippitt, G., 28
Lippitt, R., 28
Litigation consultants, 260–261

MacDonald, Rebecca F., 114
Mandatory ethics, 144
Mann, Alice, 250, 256, 257
Marchand-Martella, Nancy E., 114
Marguiles, N., 28
Marketing, 60–61, 65
Market research, 61
Martella, Ronald C., 114
Martens, B. K., 98
McCarthy, Martha M., 139
Mental health collaboration, 188
Mental health consultation, 3–5, 163. *See also*
    Consultation
*Mental Health Consultation and
    Collaboration,* 163

Mental Health Facilities and Community
    Health Centers Construction Act of 1963,
    161–162
Mental health setting consultations:
    assessments, 167
    client-centered consultation, 169–170
    collaboration, 188
    consultant recommendations, 184–185
    consultant report, 179–180
    consultation process, 166
    consultee-centered administrative
        consultation, 180–182
    consultee-centered case consultation, 171–177
    consulting alliance, relationship, 166–167
    current trends in, 185–186
    data from meetings, 182–183
    evaluation, follow-up, 168
    executive coaching, consultation, 188–190
    group consultation, 187–188
    historical background, 161–163
    interventions, 168
    key points, approaches, 163–166
    multicultural considerations, 190–191
    program-centered administrative
        consultation, 178–179
    school-based counseling, 187
Mesosystems, 107
Messages, 101
Meyers, Joel, 92, 187, 257
Microsoft Office programs, 65, 231
Microsystems, 107
Militar veterans, career consultation and, 241
Minorities, consultation and, 15. *See also*
    Diversity; Multicultural considerations
Miracle question, 129, 131, 134–135
Mission statement, 184, 262
Mobile devices and applications, 65–66
Moral principles, 142–143
Moral/social responsibility, 151–152
Moseley-Howard, Gerri S., 214–215
Multicultural considerations:
    career consultations, 245–247
    CBC and, 119–120
    consultation, in mental health settings,
        190–191
    in consulting stages, 94–95
    ethical and legal considerations, 156
    organizational consultations, 266–268
    school-based consultations and, 214–215
    solution-focused consultee consultation
        (SFCC), 133–135

Multicultural counseling skills, 45–47
Multiculturalism, consultations and, 15
Myers School-Based Consultation Approach,
    187 (table)

National Association of Social Workers
    (NASW), 15, 137, 139
National Board for Certified Counselors
    (NBCC), 139, 227
National Career Development Association
    (NCDA), 226
National Institute of Mental Health
    (NIMH), 161
National Mental Health Act of 1946, 161
Needs assessment, model evaluation, 244
Negotiation, art of, 63
Nelson, J. Ron, 114
Networking, 60–61, 65, 236–237
Neunaber, Donald N., 86
Nevin, Ann, 83
Newman, J. L., 139, 253
Niles, Spencer G., 240
No Child Left Behind Act (NCLB), 200
Nonmaleficence, 76, 141
Nonprofit *v.* for-profit consultation, 49–51
    commonalities between, 50–51
    external consultation, 50
    internal consultation and, 49–50
Norman, Kayda, 231
Novick, Jack, 90

Objectivity, lack of, 172–175
Observation(s):
    assessment, CBC and, 119
    interviews and, consulting, 81–83
Offender workforce development
    specialists, 241
Offer, 55
Oosthuizen, Rudolf M., 226–227
OpenOffice, 65, 231
Operant conditioning, 98
Organizational responsibilities, 52–53
Organizations, consultation in:
    boundaries, knowing organization and,
        262–265
    consultation role in (table), 262
    consultee/client, defining, 253–255
    defining organizational setting,
        251–252
    emerging roles, 260–262
    multicultural considerations, 266–268

training, need for, 257–260
    trends, implications, mental health
        consultants in, 255–257
Outcome evaluations, 245
Outcomes, 103
Outcomes stage, 87–89

Paolucci-Witcomb, Phyllis, 83
Parent effectiveness training, 206
Parents, consultations with, 206–207
Parker, Richard I., 74
Parsons, Richard D., 92, 201, 257, 271
Password protection, 67
Pavlov, I., 98
Pedagogy, 60
Peer consultation, 214
Personality tests, 250–251
Personnel, assess current, 184
Personnel and Guidance Journal, 139
Pinterest, 65
Platt, J.J., 250
Plax, Timothy G., 62, 63
Policy manuals, develop, 184
Portable Document Format (PDF), 231
Postmodern philosophies, 127
Postmodern theory, 214–215
Power, in leadership, 265
Preliminary stage, of consultation, 75–77
Premack's Principle, 116
Presentation, technology and, 65–66
Present-centered orientation, 100
Prezi (software), 65
Principle ethics, 144
Problem analysis, 102
Problem-centered case consultation, 102
Problem identification, 102
Problem-solving skills, 44–45
Process evaluation, 245
Process specialist role, 35–37
Productivity issues, employee, 252
Professional ethics, 138
Professional interview, evidence-based, 198
Professional relationships, ethics and,
    152–156
Program-centered administration consultation,
    9, 178–179
Program evaluation, 242–245
    evaluation report, 245
    methodology, 243
    models of evaluation, 243–245. *See also*
        Evaluation, models of

Proposals, generating, 53–54
Provisional service, 201
Pryzwansky, Walter B., 78–79, 131, 188, 201
Psychological entry, 78–79
Public speaking, 60
Public statement parameters, 150–151
Pugach, Maureen C., 214

Quantitative methodology, 243
Questionnaires, program evaluation and, 243

Raia, A. P., 28
Rehabilitation counseling, 239
Relationship building skills, 45
Remley, Theodore P., 55–56, 64, 141
Report writing, consultant skills, 68–70
Request for Proposals (RFPs), 53–54
Research, assessment, and evaluation, 60
Response to intervention (RTI), 212
Restorative coaching, 189
Restructuring dialogue, 117
Résumé:
    academic honors/awards section, 233
    chronological, 229
    core competence, trade skills and, 233–234
    cover letter writing, 234–235
    defining/branding statement, 232
    education section, 232
    electronic submissions, 231
    experience section, 233
    functional, 229–230
    heading section, 232
    hybrid or combination, 230
    licensure/credentials section, 233
    writing, 228–229
Roberts, Holley, 5
Robinson, Sharon E., 139
Robinson, Sheri L., 105
Robinson, Tracy L., 267
Rogers, Margaret R., 47–48
Role selection, 29–30. *See also* Consultation
    roles
Romney, Patricia, 15, 266
Royal, Chadwick, W. (interview with),
    272–273, 275

Sashkin, Marshall, 257
School-administrators, consultations with,
    203–206
School-based counseling, 187, 201

School-based health clinic (SBHC), 208
School-based mental health consultation,
    206–210
School counselors, 238–239
School settings, consultation in
    group consultations, 213–214
    historical background, 199–200
    instruction-based consultation, 211–212
    multicultural considerations, 214–215
    parents, consultation with, 206–207
    professional interview, evidence-based, 198
    response to intervention, 212
    school-administrators, 203–206
    school-based consultation/collaboration,
        201, 206–210
    system-focused consultation, 213
    teachers, consultation with, 201–203
Schulte, Ann C., 78–79, 131, 201
Scientific perspective, 100
Scileppi, John A., 9, 79, 89
Scott, David A., 267
Scott, David A. (interview with), 272, 274, 276
Seff-reflection, 135
Self-assessment, pretest/posttest, 2–3
Self-identification, career counseling and,
    225–226
Self-instruction, 117
Self-management strategies, 116
Self-punishment, 117
Session note, 115
Setting events, 114
Sexual harassment, 146, 191
Shared effort, 22
Sheridan, Susan M., 111
Simpson, David B., 253
Skills. *See* Consultant skills
Skinner, B. F., 98
SkyDrive, 66
Skype, 65
Smith, Kenwyn K., 79, 83, 84, 90
Social constructivism, 126
Social group efficacy, 146
Social/moral responsibility, ethics and,
    151–152
Social networking, 60–61, 65, 236–237
Solution-focused brief therapy (SFBT), 126
Solution-focused consultee consultation
    (SFCC), 127
    follow-up sessions, 132–133
    goals, forming, scaling and, 129–131

initial phase of, 128–129, 134
initial session, termination of, 131–132
miracle question, 134–135
multicultural considerations, 133–135
solution, finding a, 131
working alliance (relationship), 128
Sommers-Flanagan, John, 126
Sommers-Flanagan, Rita, 126
Sorenson, Gail Paulus, 139
Sperry, Len, 75
Spreadsheets, 65
Srivastava, Rani, 191
Stein, Howard F., 251
Stereotypes, 46
Structural problems, 112
Sue, Derald Wing, 15, 267
Summative evaluations, 245
Supervisor ethical behavior, 20
Supervisory alliance, distinctions between
        counseling/therapy,
        consultation and (figure), 21
Swift, Carolyn F., 9, 13, 250
System consultation, behavioral, 107–110
System definition, 108
System evaluation, 108
System-focused consultation, 213

Targeting markets, 61
Task groups, 214
Teachers, consultations with, 201–203
Tear-repair process, 22
Technology in consultation, 185
    assessing, monitoring, and evaluating, 66–67
    communication, 64–65
    content capturing, presentation, delivery,
        65–66
    document management, sharing,
        collaboration, 66
    ethical framework for, 67
    networking and marketing, 65
Technology, networking and, 60–61
Technology training, in behavioral
        consultation, 105–107
Teed, Elizabeth L., 9, 79, 89

Termination stage, consultation, 89–94
Thayer Conference, 200
*Theory and Practice of Mental Health
        Consultation, The* (Caplan), 4, 162
Time constraints, 213
Tindal, Gerald, 74
Touchette, Paul E., 114
Trade skills, in résumé, 233
Trainer-educator role, 32–34
Training, in organizations, 257–260
Treatment plan, 102
Twitter, 65, 236

Undergraduate students, career consultation
        and, 239–240
Unemployed workers, career consultant, 241
Universities, career consultation on campus,
        239–240
U.S. Census Bureau, 15, 266
U.S. Department of Labor, 241

Veracity, 142–143
Verbal interaction techniques, 101
Virus protection, 67
Vocational rehabilitation, 239

Watson, T. Steuart, 105
Websites (resources), 15–16, 38, 70, 95, 121,
        135, 158, 192, 216, 248, 269
Wesley, Patricia W., 140
Wicks, Robert J., 250
Working alliance:
    bond, 23–27
    early stage example (case), 23–24
    goals of, 22
    model, 20–22
    perspective, 19–20
    solution-focused consultee
        consultation and, 128
    tasks of, 22–23
Workshops, 56–60
World Wide Web, 13

Zhang, Naijian, 271

About the Authors

David A. Scott, PhD, LPC is a Licensed Professional Counselor and an associate professor in the counselor education program at Clemson University. He completed his PhD at North Carolina State University. Dr. Scott has over 18 years working as a professional counselor in clinical and community settings and over seven years as a university faculty member. In the past, he has served as a program coordinator and was the president of the South Carolina Counseling Association. He is also an active member of the American Counseling Association. Dr. Scott has provided consultation services for many years through his private practice that he shares with his wife, Michelle. He has also authored numerous publications dealing with identity development, at-risk youth, and career development.

Chadwick W. Royal, PhD, LPCS, is an associate professor in the counselor education program at North Carolina Central University, where he serves as the coordinator of the school counseling and career counseling programs. He is a Licensed Professional Counselor Supervisor as well as a licensed school counselor in North Carolina. Dr. Royal has over 17 years of experience as a professional counselor and over 10 years of university teaching. His research interests center around the use of technology in counseling, counselor training, and counselor supervision and he has presented internationally on the subject.

Daniel B. Kissinger, PhD, LPCS, is an associate professor of counselor education at the University of Arkansas, Fayetteville, and serves as the clinical coordinator and coordinator of the clinical mental health track. He is a Licensed Professional Counselor with over 15 years of experience and nine years of experience as a counselor educator. Dr. Kissinger remains active in professional counseling organizations and maintains a limited private practice.

⑤SAGE research**methods**

The essential online tool for researchers from the world's
leading methods publisher

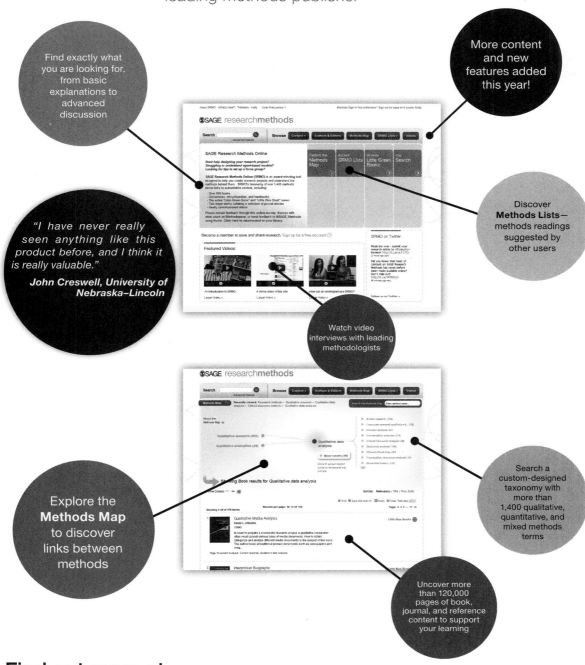

Find exactly what
you are looking for,
from basic
explanations to
advanced
discussion

More content
and new
features added
this year!

Discover
Methods Lists—
methods readings
suggested by
other users

"*I have never really
seen anything like this
product before, and I think it
is really valuable.*"
**John Creswell, University of
Nebraska–Lincoln**

Watch video
interviews with leading
methodologists

Explore the
Methods Map
to discover
links between
methods

Search a
custom-designed
taxonomy with
more than
1,400 qualitative,
quantitative, and
mixed methods
terms

Uncover more
than 120,000
pages of book,
journal, and reference
content to support
your learning

Find out more at
www.sageresearchmethods.com